SINGULAR
VOICES

SINGULAR
VOICES

CONVERSATIONS WITH AMERICANS
WHO MAKE A DIFFERENCE

BY BARBARALEE

DIAMONSTEIN

HARRY N. ABRAMS, INC., PUBLISHERS

For Carl, a true original, a singular voice

EDITOR: ELISA URBANELLI
DESIGNER: RAYMOND P. HOOPER

Library of Congress Cataloging-in-Publication Data
Diamonstein, Barbaralee.
Singular voices : conversations with Americans who make a
difference / by Barbaralee Diamonstein.
p.   cm.
ISBN 0–8109–2698–9 (pbk.)
1. United States—Biography.   2. Celebrities—United States—
Interviews.   I. Title.
CT220.D52   1997
920.073—dc20   96–35204

Published in 1997 by Harry N. Abrams, Incorporated, New York
A Times Mirror Company

 ® Harry N. Abrams, Inc.
100 Fifth Avenue
New York, N.Y. 10011
www.abramsbooks.com

CONTENTS

BARBARALEE DIAMONSTEIN

One of the essential components of a thriving and effective democratic society is its ability to balance and sustain both the vigorous self-assertion of its many outspoken individuals and the dominating powers of the collective voice. For more than two hundred years American democracy has maintained that equilibrium, while in other places and periods the chorus eventually drowned out the expressions of diversity and divergence that once distinguished those societies.

This book serves to document and celebrate some of our nation's remarkable Singular Voices—men and women who have made substantial contributions to the enhancement of American life. Clearly audible as soloists, their voices are unique, and the contributions each has made are integral to the success of the composition.

For the past twenty-five years, I have attempted to chronicle our country's cultural leaders through video and oral histories of distinguished artists, architects, preservationists, designers, writers, musicians, craftsmakers, photographers, museum directors, curators, critics, collectors, and dealers, as well as elected and appointed public officials. A number of these interviews were published in my most recent book, *Inside the Art World* (1994), a work that includes many of the most significant contributors to that field; for that reason artists were not included in this volume.

The conversations presented here are with people from an interesting variety of professions and vocations; the subjects represent an assortment of backgrounds and heritages and differ substantially in race, creed, and temperament. As diverse as their individual careers are, ranging from activist, author, and astronaut, to dancer, diplomat, and diva, one clear consistency is apparent: their valuable work appears to be deeply fulfilling, and it is what they prefer to be engaged in more than any other interest or commitment in their professional or personal lives.

Of those who were invited to participate in this book, a few declined because of a lack of time or interest. The interviews were conducted between the winter of 1995 and the summer of 1996. Some, such as Jessye Norman, Harold Prince, and Isaac Stern, declined because they were preparing their own memoirs. Others did not view themselves as *singular* voices and asked that their partners join the interviews. This was true of Robert Venturi and President Carter, who described the intricately bound collaborative nature of their work and noted that the interviews would be more accurate and meaningful if they were to include their partners and wives, Denise Scott Brown and Rosalynn Carter, respectively. I was pleased to honor that request; however, in the instance of Mrs. Carter, due to a change in the scheduling of the interview, she was not able to join us.

The photographs accompanying each interview were produced by a three-step process, of which it would be fair to say that I might be considered one of the foremost practitioners—*the aim, shoot, and pray* school of photography. Any loss in spontaneity, which may have resulted from taking pictures at various points during the conversations, is unfortunate; however, the photographs are meant to present the participants in a candid manner, and serve to complement and further record the project. The mechanics of the camera and tape recorder were distracting at times, to me and to the interviewees. While most of the subjects were receptive, or tolerant, of the equipment, Twyla Tharp asked that I not take any pictures and provided a photograph. As a result of technical problems, Skip Gates and Gloria Steinem supplied their own photographs.

Most of the interviews were conducted in office settings, allowing me to witness firsthand the individual work styles, schedules, and surroundings. But the intent of this book is to document a larger sphere, the private sides of otherwise public personalities. During the interviews, I learned, by and large, how and where each individual evolved, and tried to respond to the leitmotif that runs through all of their lives—the ability to reach the top of one's chosen, or serendipitous, profession.

To avoid the possibility of misinterpretation, and in order for the interviews to be treated with integrity, I chose to send a copy of the original transcript, with notations identifying the edits, to each of the interviewees, so they could check the edited context of their replies for accuracy. I have used this procedure for more than 500 interviews in the past. Nearly everyone has been especially appreciative of having the opportunity to "set the record straight," without tampering with it, and to correct any errors in transcription. The involvement of each person in this emendation process helped ensure that the interviews remained an accurate, yet still spontaneous, reflection of their thoughts and ideas.

This book would not have been possible if it had not been for these seventeen exceptional men and women who gave generously of their time and thoughts, sharing their work through their words. Our time together, several remarked, offered the interviewees a moment to reflect on, and consider, their own development and beginnings. Of this distinguished group, those born to genuine economic privilege, by coincidence, are nonexistent—rising from genteel poverty would be an accurate description for most.

The importance of education and thrift as necessary to self-improvement is underscored by Elie Wiesel: "I had to choose between taking the bus [to the Sorbonne] and giving up a sandwich for lunch, or walking and having enough money to buy a sandwich. Poor economist that I was, I walked, and ruined my shoes." As a seven-year-old, Sherwin Nuland already knew how to pursue his goal—a way out of his limited environment: ". . . [B]ecoming an American was the key, . . . language was the key, . . . education was the key to the vehicle that was going to carry me out of there."

Many of these Singular Voices have endured emotional poverty as well, and faced adversity at a young age: racial or religious prejudice, a physical handicap, or the loss of a parent during childhood. Through adaptability, a keen sense of the absurd, boundless inner strength, physical stamina, and overriding motivation they managed to became stubborn survivors, as well as purposeful leaders.

While some are widely known (others have yet to achieve wider public recognition), the rise to recognition and prominence of all these individuals can be ascribed in some measure to their focused and efficient recognition and exploitation of their own inner resources and limitations. Although many are now fiercely independent, and have been for many years, most acknowledge the guiding influence of a strong individual—parent, close relative, teacher, or family friend—during their relatively early lives.

The influence of this mentor appeared at some pivotal stage in the individual's emotional or intellectual development. For Beverly Sills and Twyla Tharp, early motivation came from within the family. Sills was guided by her ambitious mother. She says, "I had a career because of my family. Even my father, hating the theater for his daughter, eventually had to admit that my singing gave him great joy." Tharp's motivation came from the belief system instilled in her by her family. "I liked the idea of being very, very good. . . . [B]oth of my parents insisted on excellence . . . [and] the component of religion that was in my life put forth the idea of absolute values and absolute concepts."

The ongoing pursuit of an early talent or interest is clearly illustrated by several Singular Voices. Ruth Simmons explains that she loved the classroom because she "knew that it was a place where tremendous things happened for [her]." William Conway remarks, "I have always liked animals. I became excited about them, and I became increasingly concerned about natural history, ecology, and evolution." And Robert Venturi claims he "cannot ever remember not wanting to be an architect." For others, the chosen career path was discovered a bit later, as in the case of Skip Gates, whose dorm room was typical of a Yale pre-med undergraduate, with the exception that his bookshelf contained no books on science or medicine.

Playwright Edward Albee was taken to see Broadway musicals from the time he was seven years old. His interest in the theater came from its spontaneity: "Unlike film, for example, a play is happening in the present tense. Film is always in the past tense. You go to a film, you know it has happened. Theater is always live, and I guess I was intrigued by that." In sharp contrast, novelist Larry Kramer notes,

You can go inside a person's mind in a novel, which you can't do either in a movie or on the stage. . . . [A] novel is very much an individual relationship between a reader and the writer, whereas in a play or a movie you're inviting a lot more people to share that experience.

Regardless of how—aided by real-life experience, a mentor, or formal education—or when the initial seed was germinated, the genesis of a lifelong work ethic had taken root and was to be nurtured by an intense single-mindedness and by unrelenting ambition and endurance. And, while the forces driving these successful individuals are hardly uniform, the superhuman energies underlying those forces do share some clear characteristics.

First and foremost, they share an almost naïve, but invincible, disbelief in the possibility of failure, combined with a willingness to "hang in there"—to persist and prevail. These individuals have always been at the top of their class, as youthful leaders in athletics and religious groups and as performers. They tasted success early on, which in turn helps to create what I have come to call the "valedictory ego"; early success untrammeled by more mature doubts and concerns permits continuing high-level self-expectations and performance.

From this confidence follows a capacity for determination unmatchable by the less optimistic. A sense of infallibility has allowed these individuals to redefine the limits of their given fields; they are all, in some way, explorers, always driven, as explorers are, toward the new, the challenging, the as-yet-untried. Gloria Steinem advises,

> Listen to your true voice, to what gives you joy and pleasure, to what makes you feel you would want to do it whether you got paid or not. Look at other people for inspiration and ideas, but find the path that is your own.

Because these singular individuals look to themselves to solve whatever complex questions they encounter on their paths, they all seem sharply aware of how their lives affect everyone and everything they touch. Jimmy Carter's perception of the interweaving of one's personal life and national policy echo in his words:

> We must seek the peaceful resolution of conflicts and understand how they relate to us. Secondly, we must be the champion of freedom and democracy. We should champion human rights and work for the alleviation of suffering. These are the principles that are the measure of the greatness of any country.

By never fearing to venture into new worlds in their physical and intellectual explorations, all of the interviewees were able to eliminate walls fabricated by others in order to find the reality, both of the world surrounding them and of who they are. Each of the Singular Voices was able to illuminate elements of life that are in many respects obvious, but also not commonly perceived. For instance, two individuals commented on growing up in a segregated America, a nation sometimes strange, sometimes ugly. Ruth Simmons "worried about . . . the random acts of violence against blacks, the efforts being made at the time to keep blacks in their place." She says, "That is what we lived in fear of more than anything else. I knew that my family couldn't protect me from that, but they could protect me from everything else. So that's what it was like for me growing up." William Styron observes, "The economic situation in Newport News, [Virginia,] compelled an almost total segregation. . . . There was no [daily] awareness in Newport News of the presence of the blacks." Candidly, Skip Gates states,

> You're not born a Jew, you're not born black, you're not born gay, you're not born an Episcopalian. You become these things. . . . [P]eople think that these identities are issued by God or something, that they're like oxygen or like gravity, but they're not. They're socially constructed. . . . That means that we are all in the soup together, which is the bottom line.

Another characteristic shared by the interviewees is the ability to concentrate on a very few selected goals and to pursue those goals with startling intensity, focus, and tenacity. Of her and her husband's practice, Denise Scott Brown says, "Our work is a journey of discovery for us and we've made it a way of life. That's what we wanted. At times the going has been hard, on our staff and us. A few years ago everyone was on a four-day week and Bob and I took no salary." The self-effacing astronaut Ellen Baker notes, "I'm just an ordinary person working an unusual kind of job."

A significant number of these individuals developed long-term self-discipline and focus while participating in sports; two were even Olympian athletes. Bill Bradley notes, "My days in basketball and politics have reaffirmed some age-old truths: only when you pull together can you succeed; it is not important who scores, but who wins; and how you win is most important of all." James Wolfensohn agrees that physical and mental abilities required for athletics are generally carried into one's later career:

> Fencing is a very strategic sport. It is, of course, an individual sport. It's a bit like playing chess and doing exercise at the same time. It's also a sport that has very honorable rules, provided you play by the rules, which both you and your oppo-

nent need to do in order to be safe. It's at once a wonderful exercise and a wonderful intellectual challenge.

Certainly what can be most generously described as fortuitous circumstances have played a considerable part in the intellectual, artistic, and worldly outcomes of the subjects of this book. Yet, the old maxim, "luck is an accident that happens to the competent," has relevance here. Incapable though we all may be of making opportunity knock on demand, we each nonetheless bear the substantial personal responsibility of hearing it when it does. All of the individuals presented here heard the call and responded to it by exploring the furthest corridors of opportunity ever since.

Even in their reflections of their past accomplishments, all of these individuals are unalterably directed forward to what remains to be seen and done in their lives and their world. Jimmy Carter listens to his calling and continues his role as peacekeeper through the Carter Center for Conflict Resolution. Bill Bradley "continue[s] to believe in a strong, intelligent, and caring America—one that sets its compass and pursues a course that can provide leadership by example to the world as well as sustenance and security to citizens." He insists, "Our goal must be a national economy free of the burden of debt, and a country populated by educated citizens who are ready to work and to care for their neighbors." In recalling her experiences in space, Ellen Baker offers this gentle warning: "Every time you look out the window there is a constant reminder that our planet is not all that big, and the atmosphere is not all that high, and we've got to take care of what we have."

The individuals who appear in this book teach constantly, directly or indirectly, by word or example. Their lessons are at one level consistent and straightforward: know yourself, follow your dreams, be true to your vision of your life. At deeper levels, of course, subtleties develop, idiosyncrasies of character and perspective appear, emphases shift. But they are all living demonstrations of how heart-stoppingly wonderful human beings can be, how extraordinary are the things we can achieve.

This book is an appreciation of the interior lives as well as the manifest accomplishments of some extremely gifted men and women who have generously given of themselves to provide vivid evidence of their collective memory. While certainly not a definitive group, I believe it to be a representative collection of some of America's most fascinating people, who bring not just hope, but practical hope, and vision for humanity. They are valuable for what they have accomplished and the messages that they bring—not only for our society, but for our planet.

By hearing these singular voices above the collective drone, we realize that, in reality, we each have a voice—that we can each sing.

The undertaking of a project of this sort is always the result of collaborative efforts. My special thanks go to Paul Gottlieb, publisher; Elisa Urbanelli, editor; Karyn Gerhard, transcriber; research and administrative assistant Ciorsdan Conran; and, especially, Carl Spielvogel for his continuing encouragement and deep devotion.

EDWARD ALBEE

BLDS: What a splendid name: Edward Franklin Albee.

EA: I was named after my adoptive grandfather. You know I was adopted, don't you?

BLDS: Yes, I do.

EA: My grandfather wanted a grandson, apparently, and so I appeared.

BLDS: You were named after the vaudeville theater owner who founded a theater as far back as the early 1880s and who, by adoption, became your grandfather. So, in a sense, early on you belonged to the theater.

EA: Well, very indirectly. That was theater management, basically.

BLDS: But it was the environment of the theater.

EA: I wouldn't say the family was particularly theatrical.

BLDS: From all that I have seen and read I think they were very theatrical!

EA: No, not the way they intended. But they would invite vaudevillians up to the house in Larchmont, New York, quite often. Ed Wynn used to visit there, and Billy Gaxton, Victor Moore, and all those people.

BLDS: Did they engage or amuse you? Did you immediately realize there was something "other" about these people?

EA: I thought they were real nice and weird, too. Except for Billy Gaxton, who I mistook for a businessman.

BLDS: Little wonder that the theater attracted you from childhood on.

EA: Well, my family sent me into New York to see musicals, of course—never straight plays—when I was very young. The first one I ever saw was *Jumbo*, with Jimmy Durante and an elephant, when I was seven years old. It was at the old Hippodrome Theater on Sixth Avenue and 43rd Street.

BLDS: What did Jimmy Durante do in *Jumbo*?

EA: He watched people sing wonderful Rodgers and Hart songs, such as "My Romance" and "The Most Beautiful Girl in the World," and he led an elephant around on stage. The big joke from that show was that he would always say, "What elephant?" when people asked him.

BLDS: What was it about theater that first interested you? I've read that you wrote your first play, a three-act farce, at age twelve.

EA: I think I did, yes. It was a three-act sex farce, called *Aliqueen*. The title character in the play was a British maid. I remember only that fact about it.

BLDS: It sounds more like *Arabian Nights* to me. What does a sex farce mean to a twelve-year-old?

EA: Obviously not anything very accurate, I can tell you that.

BLDS: What was it about "theater" that you can recall?

EA: I guess I remember being entranced by the experience of something live being performed on stage. Unlike film, for example, a play is happening in the present tense. Film is always in the past tense. You go to a film, you know it has happened. Theater is always live, and I guess I was intrigued by that.

BLDS: Did you have any favorite entertainers or favorite plays when you were being taken to all these performances?

EA: No, that was when I was very young. I didn't start going to straight plays, as they call them, until I was in my middle teens. When I was in my later teens I started to see Samuel Beckett and Bertolt Brecht and Eugene Ionesco, all those people.

BLDS: Many place your work in the tradition of Eugene O'Neill, while you maintain it is in another tradition, I assume that of Ibsen/Chekhov.

EA: I prefer Chekhov to Ibsen, but I hate to be pigeonholed in that way. My plays—I've written twenty-four of them now—are so different from one another. Some of them give the illusion of being very naturalistic. There's no such thing as naturalism in the theater. It's all artificial, as we know.

BLDS: For many years, one of the reasons that your work became a lightning rod for criticism was the fact that you felt that artifice—in the French tradition—was an important part of the theater. What does that mean to the body of criticism? What does it mean to you as a playwright?

EA: American criticism in the theater has always been basically more comfortable with what they assume to be almost kitchen-sink naturalism. The avant-garde has always troubled some critics in America who tend to find it very suspicious. And so do audiences who are trained by critics. If a play is not set in a living room and a maid does not come on first and answer the telephone and say, "Madame will not be home for another fifteen minutes, she is off with her lover having an affair," etc.—the old-fashioned play—the audience assumes it can't hear and can't understand. If the set is abstract, if the people are not comfortable to them, if they can't accept what they see as being naturalistic, they believe they won't be able to understand because they have been trained in America away from the avant-garde.

BLDS: Is it your intent to confound audiences? Several weeks ago I reread *Seascape,* the play for which you received a Pulitzer Prize in 1975. In the play there are two couples, but one of them is not in human form.

EA: No, they were great lizards, slightly screwed up on their way up the evolutionary ladder. But that's the most naturalistic play imaginable.

BLDS: Can you explain that?

EA: Those are real human beings and real lizards.

BLDS: But it's also an unusual play, an unusual moment in the theater. It has been described that way because it has a "happy" ending, "one that challenges the status quo." Is that what you had in mind?

EA: Is it exactly a happy ending? At the end of that play, after having discovered brutality and being appalled by their own brutality, the lizards decide they have to go back down and de-evolve, if you

will. The humans beg for one more chance to help and to save them. In the last line of the play, the male lizard stands up there and says—not with any begging, but almost with a threat—"all right, begin." It's not hearts and flowers; it certainly ends up with a challenge. And I tried to make the ending ambiguous, as I try to do in all of my plays.

BLDS: It was ambiguous but optimistic.

EA: It gave the opportunity for change, but almost all of my plays do. At the end of *Who's Afraid of Virginia Woolf?,* for example, are Martha and George going to be able to create a new relationship on the wreckage of their old relationship? I don't know. Some people, some audiences think they can. Some think they can't. At the end of *Three Tall Women,* who is right? The young girl who says that happiness lies ahead always; the middle-aged woman who says don't worry about the past or the future, it's now that matters; or the old woman who says dying is the best part? None of those three is necessarily my point of view. But I try to leave my endings ambiguous enough so that the audience must make a choice.

BLDS: But all of them are nuances of your point of view.

EA: Again, with *Who's Afraid of Virginia Woolf?,* for example, I don't know personally whether or not Martha and George could go on after the events of the play.

BLDS: You must have considered it during the course of your life. On what side do you come down?

EA: I really don't know.

BLDS: Well, I'll tell you how I feel. My opinion has changed. As a very young person, it was stunning to me. I thought nobody ever really acted or behaved that way, and the hyperbole made the point. Now I think the hyperbole of contemporary life is such that there is little room for satire, and that unfortunately one now sees public demonstrations very similar to that of George and Martha. Somehow people manage to stitch together what to one person may appear to be wreckage, and to another catharsis, in order to keep moving on. And it turns out that in some cases, it isn't such hyperbole after all.

EA: No it's not. Not a bit of it.

BLDS: It does come as a bit of a shocking realization. Did you ever expect *Virginia Woolf* to become both a noun and an adjective, as well as a part of the language?

EA: No, of course not.

BLDS: You might, for a moment, speak about how you ever arrived at that title.

EA: Long before I was writing plays—I must have been in my early twenties—I dropped into a saloon in Greenwich Village. I think it was on Tenth Street between Greenwich Avenue and Seventh Avenue. It is now long gone. It was a place where people used to write messages in chalk on the walls and in soap on the back of the bar. One night, I saw that on the mirror behind the bar somebody had written "Who's afraid of Virginia Woolf?," which amused me at the time. Then, years later, I started writing this play called *The Exorcism*.

BLDS: That was its first title, wasn't it?

EA: Yes. Then the subtitle became *Or, Who's Afraid of Virginia Woolf?* Finally, I got smart and called it *Who's Afraid of Virginia Woolf?* In the same way the original title of *A Streetcar Named Desire* was *The Poker Night*. Then Tennessee got wise to himself and thought that *A Streetcar Named Desire* was a much better title.

BLDS: Two of your plays that have become a permanent part of the language are *Virginia* and *Tiny Alice,* one that was, and continues to be, significant to me. It is interesting that I never have to explain those references to people of a certain age. *Virginia Woolf* was your first long play. Before that you were writing one-act plays. Did you feel at that point that you had enough technical mastery to make the leap to the longer form?

EA: No, I always thought that a play should be as long as it should be. I even wrote some ten-minute plays. I've seen Bunraku puppet theater in Japan that goes on for six or seven hours. Everything has its proper duration.

BLDS: So how do you know when a play is finished?

EA: *The Sandbox* wanted to be fourteen minutes long, *The Zoo Story* wanted to be fifty-nine minutes long, *Who's Afraid of Virginia Woolf?* wanted to be almost three hours long. So I let it be.

BLDS: *Virginia Woolf* is meant to be about the exorcism of a fan-

> ... on the mirror behind the bar somebody had written "Who's afraid of Virginia Woolf?," which amused me at the time.

tasy child on the eve of its twenty-first birthday.

EA: George exorcises the child for a variety of reasons, including the fact that in those days you reached your legal majority at twenty-one and really couldn't be controlled after that. And so the fantasy child would become an adult in George's mind.

BLDS: I suspect it was.

EA: That's what *I* had in mind, anyway.

BLDS: Well, that's what happened. In many ways, your plays deal with a loss of real values and the emptiness of false values. What is important in your own life?

EA: Participating in it with as little dishonesty or self-deception as I possibly can. Of course, when you say that you're not really sure if you're kidding yourself.

BLDS: How did you arrive at that enlightened state?

EA: If you do not believe in the afterlife, so to speak, you assume that here you are, and this is it. And you've got to make the most of it.

BLDS: In the most recent period I hope you believe in the Hindu notion of rebirth, because it has certainly happened to you!

EA: But that has less to do with faith than it does with something else. One has to participate in one's own life. I'm so sad when I see so many people who have gone through their lives not really participating, and they come to the end of their lives and they haven't lived them. It's terrible. It's really awful.

BLDS: I suspect more people probably lead their lives that way, caught up in a certain day-to-dayness "without ever living their life, every, every day, realizing their life while they live it, every, every minute." Isn't that a Thornton Wilder line?

EA: That must be from *Our Town*. Of course, Thornton influenced me a lot. I think both *Our Town* and *The Skin of Our Teeth* are extraordinary. There are moments in each one of those plays, whenever I see them or even when I think about them, that I can't avoid crying, I'm moved so much. The moment in *Our Town* when Emily comes back from the dead on the day of her twelfth birthday and she hears her father coming down the stairs saying, "Where is my girl? Where is my birthday girl?" is so moving in the context of the play. Another moment that is breathtakingly moving is in *The Skin of Our Teeth,* when Mrs. Antrobus, in the height of the great hurricane, calls out to her son for the first time, calling him by his real name, "Cain! Cain!" Wilder was a wonderful playwright and a nice man, too. He used to send me, from time to time, a page or

two of this long, long work that he was writing on *Finnegan's Wake*. It was never published.

BLDS: Where is it?

EA: He never finished it, but he kept sending me pages on the assumption that I had read the book, which I had not.

BLDS: Did you save the pages?

EA: Of course, yes.

BLDS: And where are your papers kept?

EA: Most of them are still in my loft.

BLDS: That does not sound like a good idea.

EA: I know, I know. I really should do something about that. I keep everything.

BLDS: Have you always?

EA: No, I didn't keep my first manuscripts, because I didn't know I was supposed to.

BLDS: You must have had a sense of destiny from the very beginning.

EA: No, I don't think I did. I thought it was very interesting, the realization that, oh, I'm a playwright. This is the way it's going to go. I thought that was very nice.

BLDS: That you could identify yourself as a playwright was sufficient. I thought you wanted to be a composer originally.

EA: Oh, I did. I started writing poetry when I was eight, novels in my early teens. When I discovered Bach and Mozart and those types in my early teens, I wanted to be a composer, but I guess I was too lazy or too incompetent. After listening to so much music, I probably know more about classical music than almost any civilian.

BLDS: That is so interesting, because music does not seem to be an integral part of your plays.

EA: Well, yes it is.

BLDS: Then what have I missed?

EA: Writing a play is very much like composing a piece of chamber music. For example, I find relationships, structural ones, between the sonata form and the first act of a play. I find musical references all through my plays. Something else that is very interesting about my plays is that they are written very precisely. The punctuation is enormously precise and careful. After the actors have learned their lines, if you are directing you almost begin to conduct.

BLDS: Is that why you enjoy directing some plays?

EA: Yes. And I only like directing playwrights like Beckett, for example, where I feel that they have worked precisely—that they know what they want, and indicate it.

BLDS: From what I gather, you have since learned to play the harpsichord.

EA: Well, I have a harpsichord. It is now badly out of tune. It goes out of tune every seven minutes, but I improvise occasionally.

BLDS: Where did you learn to play?

EA: We had a piano when I was a kid. Once I started knowing something I would try to improvise in the manner of Bach, for example, or in the manner of Schoenberg. It would sound wonderful to me.

BLDS: Who in your family was so interested and involved in music? Somehow I had the idea that this aesthetic or intellectual component was not a part of your economically privileged background.

EA: It wasn't. I had a dear childhood friend named Noel Farrand who became a composer. Now he's sitting up in Maine as a result of inattention to diabetes, with one leg gone and the other foot gone. He became a composer very, very young, and he was helpful in instructing me.

BLDS: Did he compose anything of note that we know?

EA: He had a couple of recordings. I don't know if they are still available. He began something called the Rachmaninoff Society, too. He almost singlehandedly was responsible for the resurgence of Rachmaninoff's music. He knew the Rachmaninoff family very well, and he arranged for the first performance in America of the *First Symphony,* by the Philadelphia Orchestra with Eugene Ormandy. And he did all of that in his teens.

BLDS: So it is little wonder that by the time you were nineteen and in your early twenties, you were writing poetry and even having some of it published. How did it ever get published in Texas?

EA: There were some little recondite poetry magazines in Texas.

BLDS: *Kaleidoscope?*

EA: That was one of them. Of course, every time I published a poem the magazine went out of business.

BLDS: You don't think it was a question of cause and effect!

EA: I do, I do.

BLDS: Actually, your c.v. should serve as inspiration to any aspiring so-called creative person. I jotted down some of the jobs you

> Writing a play is very much like composing a piece of chamber music. For example, I find relationships, structural ones, between the sonata form and the first act of a play.

have had: radio continuity scriptwriter, advertising agency office boy, Bloomingdale's record salesman, luncheonette counterman, Western Union messenger—that should have been your favorite.

EA: I liked that. It was a good job.

BLDS: You developed the ability to communicate a message tersely.

EA: I met so many people by delivering telegrams. I worked on the Upper West Side of Manhattan between 65th Street and 86th Street, which was then sort of a slum, aside from Central Park West, West End Avenue, and Riverside Drive. It was filled with rooming houses.

BLDS: This was pre–Lincoln Center.

EA: Yes, way back in the fifties. The area was full of poor people and people down on their luck. It was interesting.

BLDS: How much was your first paycheck?

EA: Thirty-eight bucks a week from Western Union.

BLDS: And you managed to live on thirty-eight dollars a week. Did you have an allowance, as well?

EA: I left home when I was nineteen and got disowned and disinherited and all that.

BLDS: Why did that occur?

EA: Because it was either me or them.

BLDS: But why were you disowned?

EA: Because I dared to walk out. How dare I, especially an adopted child. How dare I have the ingratitude to leave. My paternal grandmother, who I think may have had some sense that I wasn't getting along with the family, left me a tiny trust fund. It was a hundred thousand dollars, but I was given twenty-five dollars a week.

BLDS: A hundred thousand dollars in the 1950s was a considerable amount of money.

EA: I know, but I wasn't given it. Only a small portion of the interest.

BLDS: So then you made do on sixty-three dollars a week.

EA: That's right, yes. It wasn't until I was thirty that I got the principal.

BLDS: And what did you do with it when you got it?

EA: I don't remember. Maybe I still have it!

BLDS: Are you that frugal?

EA: No, I'm not. Come to my loft sometime and see all the mistakes I've made in art.

BLDS: In art? But you must have given yourself and someone else pleasure when you acquired it. How did you make the transi-

tion to being a professional writer after this string of jobs?

EA: I guess I was educating myself. Learning, listening. I did a great deal of listening when I moved to New York, to Greenwich Village.

BLDS: How did you end up in Greenwich Village? Was it the place to go then?

EA: I had a lot of friends there. Then it was very much the creative center of New York City and it was very much a real village. You had to go uptown to the Carnegie Hall Tavern to see your composer friends, but painters were downtown at one saloon and writers were at another saloon. Everybody knew everybody. Greenwich Village was a wonderful place. And I had a lot of friends who were older and more experienced than I was, more professional than I was, so I tagged along everywhere, learned and listened, listened and learned.

BLDS: I can imagine that in delivering telegrams you became aware quickly of the range of extreme emotions—either delight, fear, sorrow, or something.

EA: Yes, you do. Especially with death telegrams.

BLDS: Were people informed that way?

EA: It was really terrible. When anybody died in a city hospital a telegram was sent to the survivors saying, "Come and get Aunt Sadie, she died." They sent those telegrams collect. When I delivered these death messages I had to collect a dollar and thirty-five cents from the people. But I learned a trick. Since I had to get a signature for the death messages, if I went to a rooming house and came upon a family that was obviously very poor and very frightened, I would tell the people, "Look, you don't have to accept this telegram. Open it, take down all the information, and give it back to me and say you refused it."

BLDS: You were in collusion with the receiver of the bad news.

EA: Yes, but all good deeds are double-edged, are they not? I would always get a twenty-five-cent tip.

BLDS: So, you are saying that you did good and well at the same time?

EA: Yes. That's right. I still think that was an appalling thing for the city to do.

BLDS: Did you leave home at nineteen because by then you were kicked out of school and you knew it was time for a new life?

EA: I had gotten thrown out of college.

BLDS: What happened? I think of you as very well behaved, and so silent and self-contained. What did you do?

EA: I was very well behaved, very silent, very self-contained. I just would not go to classes. I didn't bomb the chapel or anything; it was Gandhian passive resistance.

BLDS: What did you do when you weren't in classes?

EA: I would read and wander around. I was in Hartford, so I would go to the Wadsworth Athenaeum and see a lot of good art and see plays downtown. I didn't care about classes. And when I was nineteen, I realized that the family environment was a dead end. It was wrong for me, totally. They would not have been happy unless I had become the kind of person that they wanted me to be, and I wanted to be the person I wanted to be.

BLDS: What did they have in mind?

EA: I think they had in mind the conventional life, that I should become a lawyer or a businessman.

BLDS: Did they still have their business?

EA: No.

BLDS: Had it been sold by then?

EA: A long time ago, yes. Joe Kennedy bought them out. It was around 1928, I think. They expected me to get a house in the suburbs, get a wife, have two-and-a-quarter kids, and take the train into New York every day to my nine-to-five job.

BLDS: What did you have in mind?

EA: I wasn't quite sure, but I knew that I was determined to be involved in the arts. That was my nature. I also knew that being gay was not going to be very well received in that particular environment.

BLDS: Did they know?

EA: No.

BLDS: One wouldn't dare tell then.

EA: No. My mother would never discuss it with me after it was common knowledge. Even at nineteen, I think I knew enough to know that, had I tried to play the game, had I tried to adjust and be the person they wanted me to be, something terrible would have happened. I would have always been living a lie. You can't lie. You can't go through your life lying all the time.

BLDS: And you knew that so early on.

EA: I think I knew that much. I'm a fairly intuitive person.

BLDS: What does intuition mean to you?

EA: That I don't think everything through very carefully and reason it out. I just know that something is right for me to do.

BLDS: And I think it has another meaning, that it is a reflexive response to an accretion of detail or an accumulation of experience.

EA: I think it is. Anyway, I knew it was time and I knew something had to be done, so I left my family.

BLDS: But you did reconcile.

EA: Twenty some years after I left I received a phone call from a family friend saying that my mother was all alone, she'd had a heart attack, she was sick, all of her friends were dying, she was unhappy. So I thought about it for a while and made a few overtures, and we started seeing each other occasionally.

BLDS: By then you were fortyish?

EA: Easily. But we never reconciled. We very seldom talked about why I left or anything of that sort. She didn't want to talk about me, who I was, my nature, why I left, who failed, why it happened. She never wanted to talk about anything. I don't think she approved of me or liked me very much.

BLDS: She must have been proud of you.

EA: I didn't approve of or like her, either. I don't know whether she was proud of me, but she would behave very oddly toward the end. Maybe she was getting senile, I don't know. I would be at the Westchester Country Club with her and she would introduce me to close friends as her son, "the playwright, Edward Albee." Is that pride? I don't know. I don't know what it is. I don't think she ever liked my plays.

BLDS: Maybe she never understood them.

EA: I think some of them she understood very well. *The American Dream*, for example.

BLDS: Did she read it?

EA: Oh, I know she went to see my plays. After the so-called reconciliation she would sometimes come to my opening nights.

BLDS: And what was her response to your work?

EA: She always said, "That's very nice."

BLDS: Are you reconciled to her existence in your mind now?

EA: I suppose writing *Three Tall Women* was some help, because I haven't thought about her since unless somebody brings it up. I wasn't obsessed with her, either. Would I have felt very badly had I not seen her in the last twenty-five years of her life? I don't know. I can't tell.

BLDS: Do you believe that a playwright is not only an entertainer but also a social critic?

EA: Sure. All art has to be useful.

BLDS: What does that mean?

EA: Art has got to change our perceptions. That is what consciousness is all about. That is why decorative, more comforting stuff is not as interesting as that which questions our values or teaches us something. So I like to think that maybe, as a playwright, I have been useful so far.

BLDS: Useful—is that how you would describe the contribution you have made?

EA: Yeah, sure.

BLDS: Can you go beyond that?

EA: Well, no, I don't want to go beyond that. Every creative artist has a fairly accurate view of his own value, his own accomplishment, but you don't talk about it much.

BLDS: As a social critic, what do you see as the most urgent contemporary issues?

EA: Getting people to participate in their own lives, rather than sliding through them. Getting people to involve themselves in every way possible, to become knowledgeable politically, to put themselves in other people's places. To not skid their way through life. I think life is wonderful and everybody should live right on the precipice.

BLDS: Do you think you live on the edge?

EA: I think so.

BLDS: Even in this exalted era in your own life?

EA: This stuff comes and goes. Five years from now nobody will have heard of me again. It's possible; you never know. I didn't worry about it when I was being ignored, so why should I worry about it now?

BLDS: Do you think you were being ignored for a period?

EA: In America, yes. Certainly in New York City. During that time people weren't doing my plays in New York City; they were doing them in Europe and in regional theaters in this country.

BLDS: But that happened from the very beginning. You were acknowledged in Europe before you were in this country.

EA: So maybe I'm not an American playwright. But my work couldn't be written by anybody but an American. However, it is a very interesting point to consider. I was involved with the reopening of *Three Tall Women* in London. In London, is it an American play? I don't know. I can't see it from the point of view of anybody who is British.

BLDS: Well, it certainly is a success there.

EA: Yes, I guess we all have aging family of that sort.

BLDS: Do you have any family now?

EA: Of course, I never had a family. I may have a natural family, so to speak. I recently addressed a group of adoptees and mothers who had given up their kids. It is still very, very difficult to get information about your own adoption.

BLDS: Has that pursuit engaged you during the course of your life?

EA: When I was six I was told I was adopted. I thought about it and worried about who my natural parents were, since I didn't like the ones I was living with, but after I figured out who I was I didn't care much anymore. And then doctors would ask me, "Does this run in your family?" I would say, "I don't know, I don't have a family."

BLDS: That is one of the valid reasons for pursuing the information.

EA: It is, I know. I have a kind of interest in it. I would like to know where I got my peculiar mind from, but then, I don't know. A very close friend that I had in the fifties and sixties, a composer named William Flanagan who died, was one of the most intelligent, creative people I have ever met in my life. Then I met his family. Nothing. It is impossible that he could have come from that family. When I was I forget what age, and I started fantasizing about my origins, I decided at one point that I was Italian and Polish. Why I decided that, I have no idea. But then I learned that in the days when I was adopted you had to be adopted into the same background as your adoptive parents.

BLDS: Yes, absolutely.

EA: So, obviously, I am English or Irish or some sort, and my natural parents had to be Episcopalian, for heaven's sake.

BLDS: Do you know the agency that arranged your adoption?

EA: It was Spence Chapin, I think.

BLDS: Aren't they meant to keep excellent records?

EA: Yes. I'll do it someday. When my mother got older, I didn't want to do it because it would have upset her a lot. Everything was upsetting in the last ten years of her life. And she would have had to be involved with the process.

BLDS: How often did you see her?

> Five years from now nobody will have heard of me again. It's possible; you never know. I didn't worry about it when I was being ignored, so why should I worry about it now?

EA: Once every week or two. We used to go to lunch. We would go to the Westchester Country Club, or she would be driven by the chauffeur to New York and we would have lunch at either Caravelle or 21.

BLDS: It sounds like a scene from a play.

EA: It was very much like that, except who would believe it?

BLDS: That is why there is no satire in contemporary life. There is little that one can write that equals the day-to-day nature of things. Some of your works, such as *Tiny Alice,* have been the object of critical scrutiny, in part because of their complexity. What do you expect of your audiences?

EA: Sobriety, intelligence, enthusiasm, and the willingness to suffer an experience and to not come to the theater with so many preconceptions. Whenever I see a play I try to pretend that I am seeing the first play I have ever seen. I try hard.

BLDS: What do you do to prepare yourself?

EA: I say, here I am in the theater, as Walter Kerr said in one of his books, "Astonish me." I want that to happen.

BLDS: I think that is why people go to the theater. The notion of being entertained is really the desire to be astonished.

EA: Most people think that to be entertained is to be relieved of thinking and to be given a good time, so to speak, without any involvement. I happen to find *King Lear* more entertaining than *The Odd Couple.*

BLDS: Your audience obviously has to be open to an absorbing story, even if they are not able to comprehend the complexity or significance of it.

EA: No two people see the same play. No two people approach a play with the same willingness to participate, and no two people bring the same experience, intelligence, and intuition. No two people are alike, so no two people see the same piece.

BLDS: Do you ever worry that you might alienate your audience?

EA: I think I might worry if I didn't alienate somebody. Let's not say alienate—I don't want to drive people away from having to think about what I want them to—but if I offend them, if I make them uncomfortable or unhappy, fine.

BLDS: In the late 1960s you described the focus on the unconscious as the most interesting development in twentieth-century theater. Do you still think that is true?

EA: I think I said the most interesting development was the movement of the catharsis of a play outside of the body of the play and into the mind of the audience after the experience of the play.

BLDS: In the dictionary of occupational titles, a playwright is defined as a person who "writes original plays, such as tragedies or comedies or dramas, or adapts scenes from fictional, historical, or narrative sources for dramatic presentation." What is your definition of a playwright?

EA: Of course, he has to do all that stuff, sure. It would help if, on top of those abilities, he has—what is that awful phrase?—something to say, a question he wishes to pose to people. I am puzzled by playwrights who are filled with answers, since I have many questions; I have very few answers. If I limited the plays that I wrote to subjects for which I had the answers, I don't know how many plays I would have written. One or two, perhaps. But I love to pose interesting questions.

BLDS: I recently heard a speech, during which I almost disrespectfully whispered to the person next to me, "He needs a ghost writer." Several paragraphs later I said, "No, he needs a ghost thinker." So having something to say is not so easy.

EA: Nor is it enough. You can be a terrible writer and have something important to say, or you can be a splendidly accomplished writer and have absolutely nothing of any value or usefulness to say. So you have to put it all together.

BLDS: On what are you working now?

EA: I'm working on a play called *The Play About the Baby.*

BLDS: Which baby?

EA: All I can tell you about it is that it is in two acts and it has four characters—and an offstage baby. That's all I want to tell you about it.

BLDS: Did you ever regret the fact that you have no children?

EA: I have twenty-four.

BLDS: That is the exact number of your plays.

EA: I have never really missed it or regretted it, no. I don't think so.

BLDS: In how many works are you engaged at the moment?

EA: I have two others in the back of my mind that are circling.

BLDS: Have those amorphous creatures reached the page at all yet?

EA: Not yet, no. I keep them up there, circling.

BLDS: When do they emerge?

EA: When they get to the form that they have to be written down. They begin cluttering my mind so much that I can't think about anything else. Then I write the play.

I . . . worried about who my natural parents were, since I didn't like the ones I was living with, but after I figured out who I was I didn't care much anymore.

BLDS: You have been very prolific, writing nearly a play a year for over thirty years. Earlier you made reference to a period in which you were "ignored." How long a period was that? It never permitted you to be fallow, nonetheless.

EA: I guess about fifteen years. Time goes by quickly if you're having fun.

BLDS: Well, you couldn't have been having that much fun then.

EA: Oh, sure! I was having fun, I was writing good plays, I was lecturing a lot. Also, I was having productions around the world, around the country. To a writer, you write. As Thurber said, "If you're a police dog, where's your badge?"

BLDS: Excellent line. How long ago did you hear that one?

EA: I started reading Thurber when I was about sixteen. He is a greatly underrated writer. Nobody reads Thurber anymore.

BLDS: Are there some works of yours that remain unfinished?

EA: I have never abandoned anything in the middle. Once I commit to a piece I finish it. I get as far as I can in it, and then abandon it. We all abandon things, you know. We have to let them take it away from us after a while or we start fussing with it to the point that we destroy it.

BLDS: When do you realize that a play is finished?

EA: When I think for the first time that it is finished.

BLDS: Yes, that inner clock. And then what happens when you see it performed?

EA: It's usually very, very close to what I intended. I don't rewrite much. I cut a little bit. Whenever I write a play, I see it and hear it as a performed piece on stage.

BLDS: Do you cast it as well?

EA: No, I don't know who the people are. I don't know who the actors are, because I don't care. But I see people. Most composers compose, not even at the piano, just on the page. Of course, they hear it perfectly well.

BLDS: Do you still practice the harpsichord or play it?

EA: Not much.

BLDS: Have you ever thought of writing a libretto for an opera?

EA: No. I don't like the collaborative act much.

BLDS: Is that why you try to direct so many of your works?

EA: I like to direct them the first time because I want to be accurate while I still remember what I heard when I wrote the play. Every first production of mine is very close to what I saw and heard. Most libretti are oversimplifications. Compare Shakespeare's *Othello* with Verdi's libretto, for example. It almost becomes a seri-

ous comic strip. So libretto doesn't interest me. And I don't like to collaborate.

> If I limited the plays that I wrote to subjects for which I had the answers, I don't know how many plays I would have written.

BLDS: Are you such a solitary worker? Isn't there some pleasure in having an exchange with another person while you are working?

EA: Only after I finish something. I never show anything to anybody until I've finished it. Then there are a number of people that I like to have read the pieces. Howard Moss was somebody I used to like to have read my work.

BLDS: Which play was the most difficult to write?

EA: I don't know that any one was terribly difficult. I fussed over *Seascape* a lot. It was originally a three-act play, then it became a two-act play. I got myself into a bind and I had to find some way to get myself out of it. However, the act of writing is so exhilarating and so satisfying that I don't think of any of the plays as being a problem or trouble.

BLDS: Do you write every day?

EA: No. I think about writing every day.

BLDS: Well, that's part of the process. What are your favorite plays?

EA: Beckett's *Happy Days* and Chekhov's *Uncle Vanya*.

BLDS: And what is your favorite Edward Albee play?

EA: I don't know. I really can't answer that question.

BLDS: Don't some of them play certain roles in your own life?

EA: I tend to be very protective, for example, over those plays of mine that have been badly received.

BLDS: You are a defensive parent.

EA: Exactly right. And so I feel very enthusiastic about them. But is that any more rational than anything else? I'm not sure.

BLDS: Which do you think was your most underappreciated play?

EA: *The Man Who Had Three Arms*, for example, which was excoriated by its subjects, the critics. My fellow playwrights admired it greatly. They think it's a wonderful play.

BLDS: Do you think any of your plays have been overvalued?

EA: Overvalued? Time will tell. In the end, everybody is known for one or two pieces.

BLDS: Doesn't *Tiny Alice* have a special resonance to you, or even *Virginia Woolf* because it was your first long play?

EA: I enjoyed writing all of them, I enjoy seeing them, I even reread myself occasionally.

BLDS: In 1961, you won the Foreign Press Association award for *The American Dream,* a play in which you examine American home life and values and condemn complacency, among other things. As a playwright, is it your primary role to turn a mirror on American society, to turn the searchlight on your own experiences as a microcosm of American society?

EA: Of course, nothing that I write could be written unless it came out of my own thoughts and my need to share them. Yes, you should hold a mirror up to people and say, "Look, this is who you are, this is how you behave, if you don't like it, why don't you change?" But I don't say to myself that I have a new play in my head that is going to do people good. I start writing a play because it is in my head and I have to write it down.

BLDS: Do you write it down because you think it will provide some new personal insight?

EA: No, I write it down because it's there and I want to get it out of my head. It is that simple.

BLDS: By the way, how has the "American Dream" changed since the 1960s? Or your American dream?

EA: Unfortunately, I am afraid a number of things that the play examined are still valid. For example, the way we treat our old people and the way we destroy our children sometimes are even worse now. Also, the play is concerned with the breakdown of language: the way people don't even listen to each other, or themselves, when they communicate. All of those issues are still valid.

BLDS: As a thirty-year-old, with *Virginia Woolf* you were acclaimed as a great American playwright. You won a lot of awards. Did that change your life?

EA: I hope not. I don't think so. I watch myself. I'm one of those people who can be participating in my situation and also be standing back and observing myself. I don't think I've ever been overwhelmed either by success or critical failure.

BLDS: So you don't feel that you were diminished during a period of less attention?

EA: I don't think I have been diminished by either too much attention or lack of it. I'd like to think that.

BLDS: Perhaps one can conclude that you are your own harshest critic.

EA: I hope I am. But it's important that you not get confused

between what you are doing and what people think, or want to think, you are doing. As long as you don't get confused there, then you're fairly safe.

BLDS: What is the mission and what has been the evolution of the Edward F. Albee Foundation?

EA: Before I started writing plays I would visit friends of mine at various foundations—the McDowell Colony, for example. In those days, there weren't many places for beginning creative artists to improve themselves. After *Who's Afraid of Virginia Woolf?* came out I earned a lot of money and I had to pay high taxes. My accountant suggested that I take some of the money and start a foundation. I said, "What a good idea. Let's start a foundation where younger people can come."

BLDS: The foundation is in Montauk. How long have you been there?

EA: Thirty-three years. I bought a couple of barns not far from my house and renovated them. I invite six creative writers, painters, or sculptors every month for the four summer months.

BLDS: What has been the most public manifestation of your patronage?

EA: Some of them have done very nicely: John Duff, for example, Mia Westerlund, Sean Scully, a whole bunch of them. More and more visual artists come, rather than writers.

BLDS: Do you think that is because of a larger audience and more possibilities for visual artists?

EA: I think it's because I am fairly knowledgeable in the visual arts and I make all of the visual arts choices. I don't have time to read the three hundred manuscripts that come in every year for the few available spots, but I have people that I reasonably trust do it. It may also be that painters and sculptors have greater need of studio space. I'm quite proud of the foundation.

BLDS: So how many people have been given grants through your foundation now?

EA: In twenty-five years, almost six hundred people.

BLDS: That's marvelous. How have the tastes of theater audiences changed?

EA: Audiences' tastes change by three methods: by that which they are willing to participate in, depending upon how they want to view their position and consciousness; by what critics tell them; and by what the commercial people in the arts allow them to participate in. I notice this happening a lot in regional theaters. They

I don't like the collaborative act much.

used to be there to take up the slack and to show people what the best theater possibly could be. Now, more often regional theaters, since they make most of their money if the play transfers to Broadway, are lowering their sights. Many of them are not producing the very best theater they possibly can. They are only doing that which they think will be commercially successful. Unfortunately, those three things determine public taste. It's a shame, isn't it?

BLDS: Yes, it is. You have been a member of the National Endowment of the Arts grant-giving council and the New York State Council for the Arts. What's the proper role for government in the arts?

EA: We are supposed to give people in this country a twelfth-grade education. We are raising a nation of barbarians unless we educate them aesthetically, as well.

BLDS: What about the intense censorship now and the culture wars? It would be fair to describe this period as a time when culture is becoming the symbolic creature of a genuine ideological war.

EA: Yes, and it is a very dangerous period in this country. I have been aware since I started thinking politically, when I was a kid, that danger in this country has never been from the left; it has never been that form of totalitarianism. It has always been from the right. The fascist tendency in America is the religious right, which is neither religious nor right.

BLDS: You better do a play or two about this state of affairs. I don't need to ratchet you up further, because you are already incensed. Which writers have been most influential in shaping your approach to writing?

EA: That is such a tough question to answer. I was quoted once as saying Sophocles and Noel Coward had influenced me. As a writer, every painting I look at, every piece of music I listen to, every political debate, every other play, every novel all goes into the work.

BLDS: In your youth you professed a thoroughly unfashionable admiration for Tennessee Williams. What aspects of his style attracted you to his work?

EA: Quite often his work levitated right off of the floor. It was amazing to me that anyone could write with such poetry and naturalism at the same time.

BLDS: Are there any skills that you feel you have yet to master?

EA: The electric typewriter.

BLDS: Typewriter? How about the twenty-first century? You're not into cyberspace?

EA: I have no plans to participate in computers, virtual reality, or any of that.

BLDS: Do you write by hand?

EA: Yes, I do.

BLDS: And then how do you rewrite?

EA: I look at what I've written, make little corrections, and type it fairly quickly after I've written it.

BLDS: You type it? Yourself?

EA: Yes. Nobody can read my handwriting. I can't read my handwriting if I put it off for too long.

BLDS: So you do it quickly to make certain you retain what the scrawl means.

EA: I make a few little corrections to the typed copy and then I will have my secretary retype it. That's when I go into rehearsal with it.

BLDS: Have you ever wanted to be an actor?

EA: It was fun acting in school, in college. That was great. But no, I have never wanted to act seriously, although I do sometimes when I do a reading or lecture. I'm pretty good.

BLDS: I heard you read last summer, and it was a performance. Actually, there is nothing that I enjoy more than writers reading from their own work. Even the least gifted, in terms of voice or presence, gives a meaning to the work that just doesn't jump off the page.

EA: Actors have told me that when they heard me read from my plays I gave them insights into how to play the role that they never would have gotten otherwise.

BLDS: Do you have elaborate stage directions?

EA: Exits and entrances, sure. I put in a lot of indications as to how a line might be spoken. I underline, I capitalize, I put in "angry," "sarcastically," things like that. I put it down on the page the way I hear it.

BLDS: I have seen "whispers," "shrugs," "woman nods her head" in your plays, but not whole paragraphs that describe the actions as some people do.

> [The] danger in this country has never been from the left; . . . It has always been from the right. The fascist tendency in America is the religious right, which is neither religious nor right.

EA: I find quite often with my students at the University of Houston that if you put down too much about intent or what the character "means," you may leave it out of the play. The character should be revealed through the role.

BLDS: Have you ever thought what you would do if you didn't write?

EA: Oh, I'd probably go on directing or curating museum and gallery shows, as I do from time to time.

BLDS: What's your idea of a perfect day?

EA: I don't have one. Lack of sameness, I suppose, something different happening, something new happening, or a reexamination of something old, as long as it's interesting, stimulating, and fun.

BLDS: What's your idea of a perfect play?

EA: I don't think I would like a perfect play, because I don't think it would be as good as a play with a few imperfections.

BLDS: In your professional life, were there any moments that were particularly memorable? Just winning those three Pulitzer Prizes must have done something for you.

EA: That was okay. The first time I saw a play of mine done professionally in front of a public audience was in West Berlin when I saw The Zoo Story in German. It was the first time I experienced the effect that my work was having on an audience. It is probably still the most profound experience I have had. I noticed while watching that play that I spent more time watching how the audience was reacting to what I had done than what was happening onstage.

BLDS: What do you consider to be the peak of your achievement?

EA: With any luck, I haven't had it yet!

BLDS: Did you ever expect your life to unfold the way it has?

EA: No. I am always surprised and occasionally astonished.

BLDS: If you had your life to live over again, what changes would you make?

EA: I would live even more intensely.

BLDS: Are these the best years of your life?

EA: Always.

BLDS: What haven't you done yet that you would care to do?

EA: Hang glide, parachute jump, write better plays.

BLDS: What is next for you?

EA: The next play.

ELLEN BAKER

BLDS: How did you first become interested in aviation?

EB: My father was an aviation bug, even though he wasn't a pilot. He took us to air shows and read a lot about airplanes and watched airplane movies, and so we all were interested. That was also the early time in the space program and the nation was interested in space flight.

BLDS: Don't you think we are interested in the space program all over again?

EB: I think that's true. I don't think it's in anyone's daily thoughts the way it was during the Apollo program, but I talk to a lot of people and there seems to be a lot of support for the program out there.

BLDS: Do any of your responsibilities include administering medical care if anything occurs while in space?

EB: Usually we have two people on board trained as the crew medical officers and if one of the crew members is a physician, then that's one of the responsibilities. But the way that we ensure that medical problems are unlikely to happen is to medically screen astronauts long before flight. The best way to ensure that you have a healthy crew is to make sure that you send a healthy crew. For the most part, everybody is healthy, no one has chronic diseases, and we are a fairly well motivated population of folks who stay in shape and take good care of ourselves. Nevertheless, things happen. However, we've not had any serious problems medically on board the ship.

BLDS: That's good to hear. So no real health emergencies have occurred?

EB: There have not been any in the American program. I think the Russians have had a couple of emergencies, but I couldn't tell you

> The best way to ensure that you have a healthy crew is to make sure that you send a healthy crew.

what they were. You can imagine that things that happen to people down here on the ground might happen in space and you have to decide how much you're going to be willing to handle. Obviously, you are not going to be able to do a coronary-artery bypass on somebody in space, or if somebody has a heart attack during flight you can't just come right home. There could be quite a delay in getting somebody home if they have a true emergency.

BLDS: I assume you have a rather elaborate first-aid kit.

EB: It's just that; it's a first-aid kit. It doesn't have anything fancy in it. It doesn't have as much as a fully stocked ambulance. Space is very limited on board the shuttle, so we do not have the luxury of carrying all the supplies you might think we would carry.

BLDS: You mentioned that your father was an airplane buff, and he is also a doctor. Where I come from, your mother is not only distinguished, but celebrated. In your official bio from NASA I was interested to read that your parents are referred to as Doctor and Mrs. Melvin Schulman without any mention of your mother's professional role. She is Claire Schulman, the president of the New York City Borough of Queens, the largest Democratic county in the country.

EB: I guess the bios are rather brief. In keeping them brief I guess you don't go into a lot of detail about what your parents do or what your brothers and sisters do.

BLDS: You mentioned that your childhood was during the early days of the space program. Were you affected by that? Did you watch Neil Armstrong walk on the moon?

EB: Oh, sure. I watched all the space shots. At school they would take all the classes into the auditorium so we could watch the little TV up at the front every time there was a space launch. I was in high school when Neil Armstrong went to the moon and, of course, I remember that well.

BLDS: Do you consider yourself more of an explorer or a scientist?

EB: I'm not sure I consider myself either one of those. I'm a little bit of a scientist but I've never done any laboratory research, which would define me as a scientist. Maybe just by virtue of what I do I'm an explorer, but I don't consider myself an explorer. I'm just an ordinary person working an unusual kind of job. I consider somebody like Columbus an explorer. I don't consider myself in that same category.

BLDS: Aren't you charting new territory, too?

EB: In a small way. There have been over two hundred people who have gone into space. My last flight was the one hundredth U.S. manned mission, so there have been a lot of people before me who have done very similar things.

BLDS: Are there ever any reunions of former and current astronauts?

EB: About once a year we have a party, usually in the summer, and we invite all of the retired astronauts and the folks who used to be in the astronaut office. We do get together from time to time, so I know many of the Apollo and Gemini and even the Mercury astronauts.

BLDS: How does one begin to develop the psychological stamina and the kind of tenacity that is necessary to be involved in a program like this?

EB: It's probably not something you think about on a day-to-day basis, but just by virtue of your training you develop some of the social and psychological skills that you need.

BLDS: In retrospect, did you manifest them throughout medical school or even earlier in your life?

EB: I usually stick with something once I start it. I'm not necessarily a risk taker, but in the medical field I frequently worked under great stress in the emergency room or in the intensive-care unit. I think that sort of experience helped me adapt to the astronaut experience.

BLDS: The early astronauts were fighter-pilot daredevils by my standards. Obviously, we now have different kinds of teams, equally courageous but differently trained. How do you think that astronaut candidates' qualifications and final selections have changed over the last thirty-five years?

EB: We're looking for different types of people now, certainly a lot more variety than we did in the previous years. In the mid-sixties they started accepting folks that we called astronaut scientists. These were people who did not come from the military and did not have a test-pilot background. In 1978 they started accepting women into the program and they divided up the astronauts into what they call pilot astronauts and mission-specialist astronauts. The pilots are still the military or ex-military test-pilot folks and the mission specialists come from a whole variety of backgrounds. As far as technical training, they are looking for a lot of different things now. In the mission-specialist category there are physicians, physicists, mathematicians, geologists, and engineers of all types.

BLDS: You are a mission specialist, first accepted in 1984. Am I correct that your first space flight was in 1989 and since then you've had two others at three-year intervals? Is that the usual pace?

EB: After being accepted you undergo a year of training before you're officially called an astronaut.

BLDS: Is there a ceremony?

EB: No. You just go to the bar and drink a beer or something. There's nothing usual about the timing of my flights. It depends on NASA's flight schedule and the type of mission you're assigned to. Between my first and second flights I had a baby and between my second and third flights I got a master's degree in public health, so I probably had a little more space between my flights than most folks do.

BLDS: Why did you think it necessary to get a public-health degree in light of your involvement in this program? Or were you thinking about other careers then?

EB: I was thinking that one day I'll go back to a medical field, and I've always been interested in the public-health field. Having that degree offers a lot of opportunities.

BLDS: Do you still envision that down the road?

EB: Yes. I'd like to go back and do a medical-type job, but maybe not clinical medicine, rather E.R. patient care. I've been out of patient-care medicine for almost fifteen years now.

BLDS: What is the most difficult obstacle for you in completing a mission?

EB: The most difficult thing is not so much the responsibilities of the mission but things such as saying goodbye to the family and leaving behind two little children. It's really hard to say goodbye to them. A week before the flight they quarantine you. Those things are really hard.

> The most difficult thing is not so much the responsibilities of the mission but things such as saying goodbye to the family and leaving behind two little children.

BLDS: How do you prepare your two little girls, six and four, for the absence of their mother?

EB: Well, they're used to me taking trips, so each one is just another trip. My last mission ended up being three weeks long, which is a long time for me to be away from my kids. People ask me if I would like to fly on a space station or travel to Mars, but I couldn't do it with my kids being the age they are. It wouldn't be fair to them. Maybe if they were grown I would consider it, but they're not. By the time they're grown I'm going to be too old for this job. We have some astronauts in their fifties, but I'm not sure I'm going to be doing this when I'm in my fifties.

BLDS: What would make you decide to leave the program, for example?

EB: I'm not sure. I suppose there would be lots of things to consider, as there would be when you change from any job.

BLDS: From what I understand your husband is deeply involved in the space program, too.

EB: He flies the shuttle training aircraft, which is an airplane that we use to train the astronaut pilots to land the shuttle.

BLDS: How do you simulate that? What kind of aircraft is capable of doing that?

EB: Well, it's a Gulf Stream II aircraft, much like a corporate jet. It has a special computer system and a modified cockpit so that it looks like the shuttle on the left side. While flying in the simulation mode, it makes the airplane handle like the space shuttle. It can simulate different shuttle weights, different centers of gravity, different turbulence and crosswinds, and different landing conditions. It gives the student astronaut many, many different environments in which to practice landing the shuttle, so that when it comes time to really land the shuttle he's had a lot of experience. It's a good training tool.

BLDS: His work must be a real asset for you, too, to be able to take your work home and communicate with someone who talks the same language.

EB: We have a lot in common.

BLDS: Did you meet in the space program?

EB: Yes. He understands my job and I understand his job, and that's always a good thing.

BLDS: When did you first become a pilot?

EB: I got my license in 1984, but it's not required that one be a pilot for this program. In fact, I do very little flying. I am not qualified to fly the NASA jets that we have here as trainers for our pilots to stay proficient in flying. I am qualified to sit in the back seat and fly from the back seat, but I always need a real jet pilot.

BLDS: What are your duties on a space mission?

EB: We all have lots of responsibilities. On my last mission, my primary responsibility was to conduct the experiments in the space-lab module that we carried. We have done a number of physiological experiments to study the effects of the three-month space flight on the crew of *Mir 18*, the Russian space station. My primary responsibility in that regard was to organize and conduct the experiments that the investigators on the ground wanted run while we were on board. But I had other responsibilities, from taking pictures and recording video to being prepared to do a space walk to fix something outside, if necessary.

BLDS: Have you ever done a spacewalk?

EB: I've always been the person on board who's trained to do that, but I've never had to do it. We're always glad when things don't break, as much as it would be fun to do a spacewalk. We always prefer for things to go as planned.

BLDS: Do you continue to work with the same team when you return?

EB: We do for a little while, for about a month or two, and then you go off and do your support jobs in the office or you get trained for another flight, if that's what you need to do.

BLDS: It's just about ten years that you've been involved in the space program. What are the most dramatic changes, both technologically and ideologically, that you can detect?

EB: Well, now I think we will build a space station. Ten years ago we weren't so sure.

BLDS: What's changed?

EB: We have better leadership and more support from Congress, though it's been a constant struggle. It's hard to build a long-term project when you have to go and fight a battle for your budget, sometimes three or four times a year, but I think we're pretty well on our way now to getting a station and to having the support to actually get it built. That's been a real advance. As far as the shuttle itself, technically it hasn't changed that much. We made a lot of improvements after the *Challenger* accident. We made some 250 hardware changes and improvements to the nuts and bolts of the thing. We changed how we managed the program and how the chain of command is notified about whatever it needs to hear. The shuttle is pretty much today what it was ten years ago, with some minor changes. We continue to improve the software, for example, but that's transparent to most people.

BLDS: What sort of life-science experiments and data collection did you do on your last mission, STS 71? What does the name stand for, as well?

EB: Well, that's a good question. That's NASA's numbering system. When you create a flight manifest, and you say these are the flights we are going to fly, you number them sequentially. Sometimes the schedule changes so they're not always flown in order. I think we were the sixty-ninth flight, not the seventy-first. As I said earlier, we collected physiological data on the three crew members who had been on board the Russian space station *Mir* for three months. They had launched in March and we docked with them in June. They came aboard the shuttle and we used special medical equipment to conduct experiments that looked at their cardiovascular systems, their exercise abilities, and some metabolic conditions as well.

BLDS: How accurate was the movie *Apollo 13*?

EB: I wasn't here for the Apollo program, but much of what I saw was pretty accurate. I can't comment on a lot of the technical accuracies, but as far as the movement in weightlessness it seemed very real.

BLDS: What are the most significant changes that you have perceived between the *Apollo* and the shuttle vehicle?

EB: Oh, they're totally different. The *Apollo* craft was a small capsule. I'm sure you've seen the *Apollo* capsule in the Visitor's Center or in the Air and Space Museum. It was a one-time-use capsule with very little maneuverability. It would splash down in the ocean and get picked up, whereas the shuttle is a reusable vehicle that acts like an airplane. It can carry a lot of payload into orbit and bring a lot of payload back from orbit.

BLDS: Your first mission involved deploying the *Galileo* probe to Jupiter in 1989. Did it arrive on schedule in December 1995?

EB: It arrived on schedule in December 1995 and is currently in orbit around Jupiter. Its scientific instruments are gathering and transmitting data back to Earth. They had a little trouble with one of the antennae that send the data back to Earth, but we are getting almost all of it now; it is just a little slower. It's going to orbit Jupiter for about two years, collecting information. There are a dozen or so scientific instruments on board to collect data on Jupiter, the atmosphere, the magnetic field, and radiation.

BLDS: As you travel out into space, do you feel any closer to understanding the universe? There must be an enormously liberating perspective in space—among other things, to remind you of how small and fragile the Earth is.

EB: That is something that you can't escape when you travel around the Earth, once every ninety minutes. It makes the planet seem very small. You can see the little, itty-bitty band of atmosphere. It looks just like you're circling a globe like the one you have in your office. I never had a religious experience, but I've always been an environmentalist. Every time you look out the window there is a constant reminder that our planet is not all that big, and the atmosphere is not all that high, and we've got to take care of what we have.

BLDS: What does weightlessness feel like?

EB: If you close your eyes and imagine you're floating, that's what it feels like. It's fun.

BLDS: And what do you see out there?

EB: Looking at the Earth is a magnificent experience. There is really no other way to describe it. If you have seen any of the IMAX movies, that's probably as close as it gets to seeing what the view is out the window. It's breathtaking, no matter what part of the world you're looking at.

BLDS: Any surprises, visually? Or is everything a surprise?

EB: I think everything is really marvelous. You can see things that I didn't think you'd be able to see.

BLDS: Like what?

EB: Things in the ocean, such as ships' wakes. You can see the turbulence in the Gulf Stream as it heads north off the coast of the southeastern United States. The ocean is big. You think water just looks like water, but there are many little things that you can see. The detail is really amazing up there, and not just over water. There's a lot of detail that I wouldn't have thought you would be able to pick out. But you can.

BLDS: Has housekeeping aboard the shuttle improved?

EB: It's not bad. I know we got a lot of bad press about the potty. Every time the potty would break it made the newspaper because, I guess, people can relate to a potty breaking! Certainly you need to put everything in its place. Everything has Velcro on it. You need to be careful about where you put things or you will lose them. We try and keep fairly neat and try and keep things in order.

BLDS: How has being an astronaut impacted your daily life?

EB: Well, I don't know that it has impacted my daily life. It's a great job. I work with wonderful people and I'm happy about that. I could have a job I don't like and work with people I don't care for, but I think I work with the best people in the world. Life is always much nicer when you like what it is you're doing, but I don't know that it's changed me personally. I certainly have had a lot of opportunities that I might not have had otherwise, to go places that I might not have been able to go—not just space, but here on the ground.

BLDS: See, that's an understatement!

EB: I have been able to meet people I might not have been able to meet, and that's been a real treat. But hey, I go home after work and my kids want dinner, and the laundry has to be done, and somebody's got to do the vacuuming.

BLDS: And you do that?

EB: Weed the garden, and yes, I do a lot of that. Somebody's got to do it.

BLDS: How does your husband deal with being married to an astronaut?

EB: He deals with it fine. Other than the times I'm flying, it's just like a normal life.

BLDS: How do your children deal with it? Do they understand what you do?

EB: On my last flight they were aware of the attention. It was fun for them to see a picture in the newspaper or see something on TV, but prior to that they just wanted to know where I was and why I was gone for so long. I don't know if it matters all that much, at least not at my house. Kids just want their parents around. I don't think they care about what their parents do.

BLDS: What reaction does the public have when they become aware that you are an astronaut?

EB: There is a lot of interest and a lot of excitement. People seem to be interested to hear what it's like in space and what we do and why I think it's important. I think there's a good amount of public support out there. I almost always get a warm reception and can feel the enthusiasm of the people that I'm talking to.

BLDS: How would you describe an ideal mission?

EB: An ideal mission is one in which the crew goes and comes back safely and the main objective of the mission is achieved, regardless of what it is you're up there to do. My last mission was a lot of fun. It was somewhat of a novelty because it was the first docking mission. There was a lot of attention paid to it. However, I think every mission is a good mission, and every mission is an ideal mission, as long as you get accomplished what you set out to accomplish and the crew gets back safely.

BLDS: How long does it take for you to get prepared for a specific flight, and how much time is spent in simulators?

EB: It depends on the flight and how complicated it is. For a flight with a space lab you take two years to prepare. We took one year to prepare for my last flight.

BLDS: Why was it accelerated?

EB: I'm not sure. This was our first experience in a long time working with the Russians and there were a lot of details that had to be worked out. In fact, it was one of the more complicated missions we've ever done.

BLDS: In what way?

EB: Just the physical act of doing the docking was a very complicated and precise task. Some flights that have a lot of science experiments on board require a crew for about two years. For my two previous flights I was assigned at eight months and nine months in advance; this one was one year. Some people are assigned two years in advance.

BLDS: Are there any potential losses in having less competition between the U.S. and Russian space programs, now that we are involved in a collaborative space program?

EB: I don't think so. There is much more to be gained by it. The Russians certainly have a lot more experience in manned space flight than we do; they have cosmonauts up there for a year at a time. I think we have technology on our side that they would benefit from, and vice versa. It's only a benefit that we collaborate. Quite frankly, I don't know if we would have had the funding for the space station without this collaboration.

BLDS: Since your first flight in 1989, how has your attitude toward space travel changed?

EB: Well, I hate to disappoint you, but it hasn't changed much. Depending on what your job is, you spend up to two hundred hours in the simulator before your flight. Therefore, there were many things I expected on my first flight. The actual deployment of the *Galileo* was so familiar that we could have been in the simulator throwing the switches and talking to the ground. But then there are some things you can't simulate. You can't simulate the acceleration of ascent. You can't simulate weightlessness, you can't simulate that view out the window.

BLDS: You can't simulate weightlessness in any way?

EB: You can for about twenty seconds at a time in an airplane. If you go through a parabolic flight in an airplane, at the top of the parabola you've got about twenty seconds of zero gravity; at the bottom you're at twice the force of gravity.

BLDS: What's your greatest fear in space travel? Is there anything that causes anxiety?

EB: There are many things that cause anxiety. It's a risky thing to do. There's certainly anxiety associated with the launch; we all remember the *Challenger* blowing up. Of course, the more you know about the spacecraft the more you understand what its weaknesses are and how complex it is. If you're a doctor you worry about diseases that the normal person doesn't even know exist. There's a lot of anxiety associated with knowing what the risks and the limitations are and how likely it is that the machinery will work or not work. We train for a lot of malfunctions. What if this breaks, what if that breaks, how can we work around it, how can we fix it.

BLDS: Are the risks increasing or decreasing?

EB: They're decreasing. We have made things a lot safer after *Challenger*, but just by virtue of what we do it's still risky.

BLDS: You mentioned before that one of the things that you liked about your job is that you get to places that you might not have otherwise. Do you travel extensively on Earth, as well?

EB: I travel some. As part of our job we do public-speaking

> We have made things a lot safer after *Challenger*, but just by virtue of what we do it's still risky.

engagements that might take me to South Dakota, or to New Zealand, depending on circumstances. I do some traveling to a variety of different places. I wouldn't say extensive, but I think more than the average person does.

BLDS: Where do you go on your own holiday?

EB: New Jersey.

BLDS: What made you choose that location?

EB: I go to spend time with our families to make sure the kids know who all their relatives are.

BLDS: Every specialized field has its own technical jargon. Many times I think the phrases are both evocative and descriptive, particularly to outsiders. What are your favorite phrases, or the most commonly used ones, in the technical jargon of astronautville?

EB: We have a lot of acronyms that make no sense to anybody else. In fact, I can't even tell you what half of the things stand for. The abbreviations are so widely used that everybody knows what they are. NASA itself is an acronym. Everything from liftoff to landing has an acronym.

BLDS: Liftoff has an acronym?

EB: We might say we light the SRBs, which are the Solid Rocket Boosters, and eight minutes into flight you hit MECO, which is the Main Engine Cutoff. And then you do an OMS burn, which is the Orbital Maneuvering System burn to raise your orbit a little bit. All the instruments on board have nicknames. The DAP is the Digital Auto Pilot, which is how the computer flies the shuttle. We don't call it a computer, we call it a GPC. This is all NASA-ese. It's like learning a new language.

BLDS: What's the youngest age at which one can be formally recognized as an astronaut?

EB: I think we've had people in their mid-twenties, twenty-six or twenty-seven, but just by virtue of the technical training that you're required to have to be eligible, most people could not be selected much earlier than age thirty. Many of the mission specialists have doctoral degrees, and it would be hard to get through your doctorate much earlier than twenty-six or twenty-seven. The pilots all have test-pilot experience and that requires that you be a line pilot for a number of years first. By the time most of them get out of test-pilot school, they are at least in their early thirties.

BLDS: You're wearing a jumpsuit today, because you're about to fly and this is your flying suit. It certainly is a very natty outfit. Are your spacesuit and equipment custom designed for you?

EB: No. Small, medium, large, and sometimes extra large are the sizes. You can get some alterations done if you need them. I'm a standard size, so I generally wear "off the shelf" items.

BLDS: How do you alter a spacesuit?

EB: The suits can be altered a bit. The gloves and arms can be shortened and lengthened.

BLDS: Are there any conveniences or inconveniences to space travel for women? How do you wash your hair if you're there for two weeks?

EB: We use no-rinse shampoo that is used in hospitals. You can lather it up and just pat off with a towel. I fill up a drink bag with water and use it to get my hair wet very slowly, then I lather it up very slowly, so I don't splatter soap around, and then I pat it out, put a little more water in, and pat it out. I keep doing that until my hair feels clean. It works pretty well.

BLDS: What's the most unpredictable thing that you ever did while in space, or is everything so programmed that there is very little time for that kind of spontaneity?

EB: I don't know that everything is programmed, but I don't know that I've done anything unpredictable either. I try and get all my assigned duties done. I can't think of anything out of the ordinary or unusual that I did personally.

BLDS: How have you managed to stay fit?

EB: I was a competitive swimmer when I was a teenager and I kept that up. I enjoy being in good physical shape.

BLDS: Do you have any lucky charms or talismans or good luck sayings?

EB: No.

BLDS: Nothing superstitious? Is it all based only on skill?

EB: No, I don't have any good luck charms.

BLDS: On your last flight you were able to communicate with schoolchildren on a ham radio. What questions did most of them want answered?

EB: Kids everywhere have the same questions and usually they are not so technical. They want to know what Earth looks like, and they want to know how we eat, what we eat, how we sleep, and how we go to the bathroom.

BLDS: How do you sleep, and for how long?

EB: Just fine. We have sleeping bags that we can tie off or fasten with Velcro around the ship once we find a spot that's comfortable. We're scheduled for about seven to eight hours of sleep.

BLDS: Does everyone sleep at the same time?

EB: Sometimes. We did on the last mission. On the previous mission we had split shifts because we had twenty-four-hour, around-the-clock operations.

BLDS: Who minds what's going on while you're all sleeping?

EB: The computers and the ground. We have the computers set so that we'll get an alarm if something goes wrong. That actually happened once or twice. We had a computer fail on the last flight, so the alarm went off.

BLDS: As you get this signal, who is assigned to the repair? Or is each person assigned to a different part of the ship?

EB: The commander is always in charge and he's the one who decides what to do. He might delegate somebody to take care of the problem.

BLDS: So there has to be a very cohesive unity for those on board. Does it remain after you're earthbound?

EB: Sometimes. We're all people, and you get along with some people better than you get along with others. Certainly while we're up there everyone works together. We are professionals, and this is our job.

BLDS: Do you expect the space program to expand, or retract, in activity in the future?

EB: It's hard to predict. A lot of it depends on funding, of course. We here at NASA would like to see it expand. We would like to go back to the moon, maybe venture out toward Mars, but those are expensive propositions. It's been a struggle to get a budget for a space station and it will probably continue to be a struggle with other expensive programs.

BLDS: Do you see another moon probe?

EB: We'd like to send people back to the moon, but it's not yet funded. It's something we're thinking about and planning. Obviously it would require a lot of money.

BLDS: Americans everywhere are affected, and worried, by the potential of automation. It's odd to realize that even astronauts can be affected. What impact will the use of unmanned vehicles have on the morale, and the existence, of astronaut programs?

EB: I think they complement each other. Certainly there are places I wouldn't want to go. For example, nobody would want to go to Jupiter. That's the ideal place to send an unmanned vehicle.

BLDS: Why would no one want to go to Jupiter? Because of its gaseous nature?

EB: Because it's uninhabitable. The same thing is true with Venus, which is nine hundred degrees in surface temperature. However, nothing replaces having a person there. A person can think on his or her feet, and notice the unusual, and do many things machines can't do. But machines can do a lot, too. I don't believe that you can replace astronauts with machines, nor would you want to send astronauts to places you might want to send machines.

BLDS: Deconditioning of the cardiovascular and pulmonary systems with the occurrence of lightheadedness has been noted as a side effect of long stays in space. Would increasing the length of time in space increase the danger or reduce it? How does that all work?

EB: The danger is primarily there when we return to Earth. There's not much danger while you're in space. It probably levels off so that a three-month stay might not be much different than a six-month stay. It's very variable, depending on the individual. Some people are much less affected than others. The severity of that depends on how much you exercise and how much you rehydrate yourself prior to entry. It's complicated.

BLDS: What happens when you're at the New Jersey shore and a member of the public asks, "And what do you do?"

EB: If you want to know the truth, people rarely ask. I almost never get asked what I do.

BLDS: Are there many other women who are doctors in the space program? Is it especially good training?

EB: We've got a handful. I think it's good training. But we have women from all different backgrounds and their training is good training, too.

BLDS: In speaking to some doctors before this interview, many of them talked about the impact of gravity and other kinds of physiological change. How will your experiments affect our lives in the future?

EB: Right now there's only a theoretical link. What we're doing now primarily is researching how well we adapt to long-term flight, in thinking about going to Mars or going to the Moon. We want to ensure that we can keep people healthy and that we don't do any disservice when we bring them back. Potential medical benefits as a spinoff of the program would be electronic devices and some of the equipment that we develop. One experiment that has flown many times on the shuttle is designed to grow protein crystals and bring them back for study. By growing protein crystals in space you can sometimes yield a very big crystal and then identify its structure. If it happens to be an important biological protein that's involved in a disease process, scientists might be

able to develop a drug for it. Those are the sorts of things that we're looking at. It is a very slow and painful process.

BLDS: What are some of the most important scientific experiments that have taken place on recent missions?

EB: My second flight was called the U.S. Microgravity Lab and it was designed to look at how to manufacture materials in space that are difficult to produce on the ground. For example, we experimented with semiconductor crystals that might be of use in the computer industry. We did some basic research on fluid dynamics and other basic science investigations which could have widespread impact in many, many different areas. Many missions do observation work: anything from looking at the ozone to looking at vegetation on the ground, the progress of droughts, and the effects of deforestation, subsequent erosion, and crop loss. The observations of the planet that we conduct on all missions obviously have a lot of impact on life on Earth.

BLDS: From the vantage point of an environmentalist, what have been the most significant things that have occurred?

EB: There's a lot of evidence of man on Earth. Looking out the window you can see many fires in the Amazon basin and across Africa. Cities are very easy to pick out. You can see smog around big cities, pollution and oil spills on the ocean. Man's effects are very, very noticeable.

BLDS: Is there any motto that guides you through life?

EB: I try to follow some of my own advice. When kids ask me what they should do to be an astronaut, I always tell them to try to do the best job that they can. Be proud of the work you do and do a good job when you set out to do something. I try to be responsible and reliable.

BLDS: Did you have any role models while you were growing up? Any mentors whom you looked to or who really influenced you—teachers, other astronauts, doctors?

EB: Oh, there were lots of heroes. As today,

many of them were sports figures: Mickey Mantle, his teammates on the Yankees. I was a big baseball fan when I was a kid.

BLDS: But living in Queens, which team did you root for?

EB: I lived in Queens before the Mets were there, so I was a Yankees fan. The Mets didn't come along until later. I don't know that I have any heroes. I have a good family, so maybe they were my role models—my parents, my older brother who is a doctor, too. I followed him around like a puppy dog. And I had good teachers.

BLDS: When you first announced to your family that you were going to try for the astronaut program, what was their reaction?

EB: They've always been very supportive, no matter how crazy my ideas are.

BLDS: Do they like what you do?

EB: Well, my mother gets very nervous during my launches, as you can imagine. She's proud of what I do, but she would be just as happy if I didn't do it.

BLDS: What do you consider the peak of your achievement?

EB: Hopefully, I'll raise two good kids.

BLDS: And what do you consider to be your finest professional accomplishment?

EB: I hope that I played a small but significant part in the space program. I can't necessarily point to one thing. Most of what I do, I do because I believe in the program. It wouldn't matter what mission I was on, or what my job was on that mission. I hope I'm playing my part to further the program that I believe in.

BLDS: What sort of mission would you like to be on next, if you had your druthers?

EB: It wouldn't matter.

BLDS: You followed in the footsteps of both of your parents in some measure. What if your daughters wanted to be astronauts?

EB: I suppose I'd support them the same way I was supported by my family.

BLDS: And what if they wanted to be elected public officials?

EB: Well, I suppose I would give them the support for that, too.

BLDS: And which do you think is the more stressful life?

EB: Most of the time, probably my mother's life is more stressful. She certainly works harder than I do. My life is stressful for little chunks of time every couple of years; hers is stressful day to day. Her job is the harder job.

BLDS: If you had your life to live over again, what would you do otherwise?

EB: I'm not unhappy with what I've done. There's not much I'd do differently.

BILL BRADLEY

BLDS: Let's start at the beginning so we have some idea of how your life unfolded, from your childhood, to your professional basketball career, to your political career as a U.S. senator from New Jersey, to the present. In reading *Life on the Run* I realized how much of an influence your family was, not surprisingly, on you. What aspects of your character and your motivation do you attribute to your parents' influence?

BB: I think they are the dominant influence in my life. Usually, parents are the dominant influences in most people's lives. Certainly in my life, everything from hard work, to goal-setting, to spiritual values, to a kind of private sense are all a function of the influence of my parents. My father and mother married late, and had me late.

BLDS: How late?

BB: I think my mother was thirty-five and my father was about forty-two, forty-three.

BLDS: That's not considered late anymore.

BB: No, that's true. But in 1943 it was.

BLDS: Were you their only child?

BB: Yes, I was the only child.

BLDS: What traits do you think you developed independently, or in spite of their influence?

BB: I think my choice to play basketball was a route to independence. My father played baseball, but he didn't know anything about basketball. I took him to his first basketball game when I was in eighth grade. That whole route became mine, and so I worked harder and harder at what was mine, which was a certain

> I think my choice to play basketball was a route to independence.

level of accomplishment and proficiency. And that led to me leaving the small town that I grew up in and coming east.

BLDS: Did you learn to play basketball in the eighth grade?

BB: No, actually, I began when I was nine years old, but I began to play seriously when I was about fourteen—by serious I mean practicing two or three hours a day, nine months a year, and six to seven hours on weekends, each day.

BLDS: Were you a successful competitor in other sports as well?

BB: Yes, I was a pretty good athlete. I played baseball in high school and one year of college baseball in my sophomore year at Princeton. I competed on the track team as well, in the same season. I did the three sports in high school.

BLDS: What was it about basketball that especially appealed to you and made you seek it out?

BB: I was taller than most other kids. At that place and at that time, a tall kid was supposed to be a basketball player. And I took to it. I had good coaches early.

BLDS: Where was that?

BB: In Crystal City, Missouri. I had three coaches: a grade-school coach named Mr. Ryan, Coach Pope in high school, and a former pro named "Easy" Ed Macauley whose basketball camp I went to after my freshman year in high school.

BLDS: With which team did he play?

BB: He played for the St. Louis Hawks and the Boston Celtics. He offered me the aphorism that has guided much of my life since then: "If *you're* not working, remember that somebody, somewhere, *is* working, practicing; and if you two meet, given equal ability, that person will win." I never wanted to lose because I didn't make the effort.

BLDS: So you felt early on that you had to prove that you were more than a rich banker's son.

BB: Yes.

BLDS: Did you succeed, by your standards?

BB: Yes. I think so. You have to keep it in perspective. Crystal City was a little tiny town, and my father's was a little tiny bank; in the world we were not rich, but in that tiny town we were at the upper end of the pecking order. That had an impact on my life—not our place in the pecking order but the income level. I wanted to show that I was like every other kid, and therefore I moved toward an area where money didn't count, where only competence determined success, which was the field of play. The "banker's son" phenomenon really ended by the time I was in fourth or fifth grade. After that it was more the athlete than the banker's son that determined how people viewed me.

BLDS: And you no longer felt you had to prove anything?

BB: No, I felt that I had to prove something every day.

BLDS: Do you still consider that to be an important goal in your life?

BB: I don't—I no longer think of life in terms of proving something, I think of it in terms of understanding what excellence is and wanting to achieve it.

BLDS: What was the effect on your sensibilities, your insights, and your values of being for so long a part of a minority group in a sport that is dominated by persons of color?

BB: It gave me a unique opportunity to be a part of the world that was different from the one I grew up in, and from the one that I lived in while in college, and in England. And it gave me a chance to see firsthand the experiences, histories, rhythms, high points, and low points in the lives of my teammates on a day-to-day basis, as we traveled across America for ten years. I learned a lot more from that experience than I have contributed to it, in terms of friendship or knowledge or information, and I feel fortunate to have had that experience. On a regular basis there

> Crystal City was a little tiny town, and my father's was a little tiny bank; in the world we were not rich, but in that tiny town we were at the upper end of the pecking order.

were moments that were surprising.

BLDS: For example?

BB: In *Life on the Run* I talk about something that happened once while the Knicks were in the playoffs. We had flown all night to get to Los Angeles, following a game in New York the night before, and then we went to sleep. I came into the coffee shop for breakfast the next morning and I took a look at Earl "The Pearl" Monroe. His face was all puffed up. I said, "What happened, Earl?" And he told me the story of how, after the game the night before, he was trying to hail a cab for his girlfriend on Eighth Avenue, which was literally two hundred yards from center court at Madison Square Garden, and it was raining, and he had to get to the airport, and some white guys on the sidewalk started shouting epithets at him. He ignored it for a while, but then one thing led to another and they had words and he was hit. At that point a black guy from the post office, which was right across the street, came over and helped him into a cab and said, "Get out of here, you don't need this." There he was, the next morning, describing a moment of racial violence that occurred two hundred yards from where his virtuosity was cheered by twenty thousand people. That wouldn't have happened if I had been there at that moment.

BLDS: Do I recall that at one point in your own professional career you lived on Seventh or Eighth Avenue?

BB: I lived on Eighth Avenue, yes. In fact, it was two blocks from the old Garden on 49th Street. The only problem was that by the time I actually moved into the apartment the Knicks had moved to the new place.

BLDS: And you were stuck on Eighth Avenue.

BB: Yes, I just stayed there. It was a nice building. And actually, it was a good building. It was where I met my wife.

BLDS: In that building?

BB: Yes.

BLDS: Was she teaching then?

BB: No. She was at that time an independent filmmaker. She was making a film about Marianne Moore. The idea was to have an athlete who was interested in poetry interview a poet who was interested in sports. So, she was instructed to approach me. We set up an appointment to see if I would be interested in making this movie, and that's how we met. It took place in that building, so it was worth it to live there.

BLDS: How far, by the way, is Crystal City from Independence, Missouri?

BB: A long way. Crystal City is right on the Mississippi River, thirty-six miles south of St. Louis, and Independence is over on the other side of the state; I think it's north of Kansas City.

BLDS: You were born just before Harry Truman became president.

BB: Yes, and I wrote my senior thesis about him.

BLDS: And what was the subject?

BB: His run for reelection to the Senate in 1940—his first campaign for reelection after having been elected in '34.

BLDS: What was so intriguing or complicated about that period?

BB: It was interesting that Truman had been elected as a low lieutenant in the Pendergast machine in Kansas City. In Truman's first term, Pendergast was sent to jail for income-tax evasion, which was the hook that the district attorney got him on for a whole set of other corruptions. When Truman ran again nobody thought he had a chance in hell to win. In the primary he ran against the governor of the state, a Democrat, the apple-orchard magnate Lloyd Stark, and the district attorney who sent Pendergast to jail, Maurice Milligan. Truman ended up winning the election. In many ways if you look at that election it was a harbinger of the 1948 election.

BLDS: A harbinger of Truman's role, of what was going to unfold nationally?

BB: It had the same rhythms, it had the same themes. For example, everybody counted Truman out but he managed to win both elections by reminding people of his record and what he stood for.

BLDS: In your book *Life on the Run*, you describe the life of a star athlete as being protected from criticism, often later facing devastating falls from glory. How dangerous was this vulnerability then, and in later life?

BB: I think I described it in the book as a terror that most people can't conceive of—life without the game. When there's no more game, one's life is at best diminished and at worst destroyed. I think that this is pretty typical of the sports culture. Now they make so much money in the game it doesn't matter what their emotional and psycho-logical state is; they're taken care of for the rest of their life. But, if you were a player in my day, and you couldn't adjust to life after the legs went, then your life would be filled with rabid anger. A player never can get beyond that high-school game that he lost. In the case of the pros, he can never get beyond the applause of the crowd when he was a starter on the court, or the sense that people gave him shortcuts along the way, or that he was well known and strong.

BLDS: What made you decide to leave basketball?

BB: Two things. One is that I had always said I would stay in basketball until I felt there were other things I was more interested in. Secondly, I had finished writing *Life on the Run*. Writing the book really put the entire experience into perspective. When I finished writing the book, I closed that chapter in my life and was ready to move on. Physically, I probably could have played another two years, but I felt it was time to go. My interest in public service was increasing, so I decided to leave.

BLDS: You have written another book called *Time Present, Time Past*, and have completed another cycle in your life.

BB: That's right.

BLDS: I assume, since you are a serious thinker and a serious writer, that the experience of writing a book causes you to distill and reflect on many parts of your life. Did that experience accelerate your departure from the U.S. Senate?

BB: Yes. I think that you live life very intensely. And if you are in the public arena, it's very intense and it's very fast. All of your energy has to be put into accomplishing the objective in the arena. Then there's another kind of experience, and that is thinking about what you have just lived, stepping back and developing some perspective. In my view that is what completes the experience. The third level is when you actually find the words to write about the perspective that you attained after standing back and thinking about living it. Once you have found the words to express what you feel about your time, your place, your identity, and your relationships, then that experience is really closed. When you've completed the writing, then there's a closure to the experience. So I knew when I finished *Time Present, Time Past*, as I knew when I finished *Life on the Run*, that it was time to go. Even though I left the Senate, I knew I wasn't going to leave public life. I also felt very comfortable there, and I feel very uncomfortable when I feel comfortable.

> When there's no more game, one's life is at best diminished and at worst destroyed.

BLDS: Has that been a lifelong nagging feeling?

BB: Yes. You know any time you feel you're comfortable it's time to move. It's like growth. It's like your legs—you don't get in shape unless you go through a period of pain, and then you feel good after you're in shape.

BLDS: Spoken like a true athlete—no pain, no gain.

BB: It's the same thing in other aspects of life. You're in a situation in which you're very comfortable, but that means you're not growing and therefore you need to move where there are new challenges. I figure that's what keeps you alive. If you're in the Senate at seventy to eighty, it keeps you alive. If you're in the Senate at thirty to forty you can get maximum growth. But, if you're in the Senate in your fifties and sixties you're in a kind of a never-never land where you have to decide if it is better to stay or go.

BLDS: So, can one conclude then that there is a possibility that you will return to the Senate in your seventh decade?

BB: I've thought about that, but that's several lifetimes away.

BLDS: By the way, how did you ever get the nickname "Dollar Bill"?

BB: There are three theories. The name came from my teammates in the Knicks and different people called me it for different reasons. One theory was that I had kept the first dollar I ever made. I was tight.

BLDS: So I've heard!

BB: The second was because of the amount of my first contract. It was more than most of the players were making at the time, although it's kind of a pittance in today's world. And the third theory was that I was a money player—that when the money was on the line, when the dollars were on the line, I would take the last-second shot. Therefore, I was Dollar Bill.

BLDS: To which theory do you subscribe? All of them?

BB: I don't subscribe to any of the three. I think they called me Dollar Bill in the Senate so I'd go out and buy some new clothes! As you see, I bought this suit during that period.

BLDS: Basketball is a very swift and a very intense game. In contrast, while watching politics one is reminded of how slow and frustrating the process can be, how long it takes to have any point scored, and how, while the Senate is meant to be a team effort—a collaborative effort—it has become decreasingly that. Did you find your role too frustrating, or is it all worth the wait, the bickering, considering the potential results?

BB: I love the Senate. I think that it is a place where you can really make a contribution and improve people's lives. You just have to

understand how the process works. The thing that always interested me was big reform, not marginal change. And I've had some big reforms.

BLDS: Like the tax bill of 1986?

BB: The tax bill is one example, working to resolve the third-world debt crisis is another example, the California Water Act is another example, the way we finance college education is another example.

BLDS: Will those reforms endure in the current climate?

BB: Certainly the experience will. Rarely is there a piece of legislation that remains untouched forever, because people revisit it, change it—particularly if you have taken power away from the powerful. Then they are going to change it because they are more powerful over time. That has occurred a number of times already, in my own experience.

BLDS: In what instances?

BB: Well, tax reform was eroded after 1986. We've ended up with a lot more loopholes, which were put in by lobbyists for particular people and companies and circumstances, and higher rates. I think that is just the way Washington works. Unfortunately, we don't have fundamental campaign-finance reform.

BLDS: Did your experience as an athlete benefit your political life?

BB: I believe that basketball has positively influenced my political career. Perhaps the most profound lesson I learned from athletics was the importance of teamwork. The New York Knicks squad with which I played was made up of men from a wide variety of backgrounds and experiences. We respected one another. Sacrificing individual glory for the benefit of the team aided us in becoming winners. Throughout my life I have always believed that there was a larger purpose—whether it be in school, sports, or politics—than individual achievement. Excellence has been defined for me in terms of the group's success, and this has been the greatest benefit of my experience as an athlete.

In the Senate, a moment of insight came when I realized that the passage of legislation, like teamwork, required getting people with different backgrounds, different interests, and different personal agendas to

> I love the Senate. I think that it is a place where you can really make a contribution and improve people's lives. You just have to understand how the process works.

agree on a shared goal and work toward it. Hard work, discipline, concentration, and integrity are the cornerstones of my success as an individual and as a team member. Slick moves and an enlarged ego can't replace sweat, tears, and hours of hard work when it comes to winning an athletic event or getting a piece of legislation passed. My days in basketball and politics have reaffirmed some age-old truths: only when you pull together can you succeed; it is not important who scores, but who wins; and how you win is most important of all.

BLDS: Are there any particular basketball strategies that you find yourself applying to political life?

BB: What I find is that there is a rhythm. Sports are more similar to a campaign than to the Senate. I think that a campaign has the same ups and downs that a basketball season has. You are encountering the press; you do well one day, poorly the next day; and you have to keep mindful of the season standings. That's really what an election is all about. There are some similarities, though, between sports and the Senate. For example, when I was in the Senate about four or five months, I walked into the cloakroom one night late and saw one person who was angry, one person who was pacing, one person who was reading a newspaper, one person who was on the phone, one person who was telling a joke, and one person who was just sitting quietly. I thought to myself that it wasn't a lot different from a Knicks locker room. And it isn't. It's about people of different backgrounds with different personal agendas coming together and trying to figure out what they can do together, whether that is producing a piece of legislation or playing as a team. In that sense, they're similar.

BLDS: You were present as a page in the Senate in 1964, at the time of the Civil Rights Act debate. I assume that had a powerful influence on you. What impact did the social revolution of the 1960s have on your life?

BB: My exposure to the debate made me realize two things. It made me realize that things that are important for America could be accomplished in the Senate—that's where the idea first occurred that maybe someday I'd like to be a senator—and it also pulled me into the Democratic party. The 1960s were a time of great achievement and tragic sorrow. The passage of the Civil Rights Act in 1964 was one of the most significant events of the decade, marking the start of a new era in race relations in this country. As a young student intern in the Senate, I witnessed the historic vote firsthand. I remember thinking, America is a better and more just place because of this. The establishment of the Great Society programs, such as Head Start and WIC, also got America on the road to a new domestic order. Many of the social programs started under the Johnson administration continue to be some of the most successful elements in our domestic agenda today. However, the sixties brought despair, as well as inspiration, to our nation. Three of America's greatest leaders of the decade, if not the century, were struck down by assassins' bullets. The ability of President John F. Kennedy, Senator Robert F. Kennedy, and the Reverend Martin Luther King, Jr., to inspire Americans of all ages to serve their country and to lead us to a more just society has irreversibly changed the dynamics of American life. Unfortunately, we will never know the full extent of the impact they could have had, and their deaths left the nation with feelings of tragedy and helplessness. Moreover, we are still experiencing the turbulent legacy of the Vietnam War. The divisiveness that the war caused scarred the morale and unity of the nation, and the last [1992] presidential election shows that we still have not fully recovered from that time.

BLDS: You have made a conscious effort to stand for your beliefs, regardless of whether they are critical of your own party or contrary to common public sentiment. How serious is the friction that this has surely caused within your party?

BB: During my time in the Senate I tried to balance the private interests and the public interests, the rights of property owners and the needs of society, the big players and the forgotten players. I haven't always pleased everyone, but I've tried to be consistent on the big issues such as the economy, race, and America's role in the world. I've also tried to take the long view, often passing up a headline to make sure that when I spoke I knew what I was talking about. Questions of structure, whether on

> During my time in the Senate I tried to balance the private interests and the public interests, the rights of property owners and the needs of society, the big players and the forgotten players.

taxes, trade, or the environment, always interested me more than issues of marginal gain or questions of blame or strategies of partisan political advantage. When I made the speech announcing my retirement from the Senate, I said, "We live in a time when, on a basic level, politics is broken." In growing numbers, people have lost faith in the political process and don't see how it can help their threatened economic circumstances. The political debate has settled into two familiar ruts. The Republicans are infatuated with the "magic" of the private sector and reflexively criticize the government as the enemy of freedom, and the Democrats distrust the market, preach government as the answer to our problems, and prefer the bureaucrat they know to the consumer they can't control. Neither speaks to the people where they live their lives. Both have moved away from my own concept of service and my own vision of what America can be. It is possible that some Democrats might resent me saying these kinds of things, but I think that most Democrats understand what I'm saying and many agree. We'll never be able to improve as a party if we do not admit some of our failings and work to become more in touch with the real "kitchen table" economic concerns of working Americans. I continue to believe in a strong, intelligent, and caring America—one that sets its compass and pursues a course that can provide leadership by example to the world as well as sustenance and security to citizens. Our goal must be a national economy free of the burden of debt, and a country populated by educated citizens who are ready to work and to care for their neighbors.

BLDS: Were your parents Republicans?

BB: They were basically apolitical. My father was an apolitical Republican, and my mother was genuinely apolitical. Politics were not part of the discussion at the table.

BLDS: As contrasted to the experience of many of your colleagues.

BB: I guess.

BLDS: What made you political?

BB: I think underlying it all was a drive to try to make things better for people in this country. The quest for racial justice was a big part of that. The history of disenfranchisement and hard knocks that many hardworking people have experienced over the years was another part of that. I also had the belief that going into politics was itself a noble calling. A just calling. I believed that you could

> For the past several years, Washington's feeble efforts to clean up politics have fallen woefully short of the goal of real reform.

not only fulfill your own desire to serve but you could actually make things better for more people by participating in the political arena. Bobby Kennedy has always been the most influential figure in my life, in terms of a relatively contemporary politician.

BLDS: What expectations do you believe the American public deserves to have for its elected officials: governors, congressional representatives, its president?

BB: Honesty, candor, confidence, and, on rare occasions, vision.

BLDS: Do you feel that those expectations are being fulfilled nowadays, on any of those levels?

BB: What's going on in the country is that you find an increasingly larger segment of the middle class feeling economically insecure and threatened by the changes that are sweeping the economy. I think that one would be hard-pressed to say that President Clinton or President Bush or, for that matter, President Reagan was as relevant to the lives of average middle-class families as F. D. R. was to the lives of Americans in his day. People today do not see their economic circumstances, and the chance to have a better life for their children, tied to what a president does. When F. D. R. was president there was a direct connection. When the voice came over the radio, that was a voice of hope.

BLDS: Is that sense of security still possible to accomplish?

BB: Sure. It's still possible.

BLDS: You have said that one of your political goals was to try to get the democratic process to focus on the increasingly precarious position of middle-class America. Can you elaborate on that in some way? If you're not in the Senate, how can you hope to achieve that goal?

BB: There are a lot of places for public service. The Senate is only one of them. Public service also is more broadly definable as something that is not only elected office. I think that there are many places in civil society to make a difference.

BLDS: For example?

BB: Well, there are plenty of people who run community development corporations, some ministers, some priests, and some rabbis who minister to populations that are in need, all of whom have a very significant role.

BLDS: How about university presidents?

BB: A university president today isn't in the same position as he or she was 150, ninety, or fifty years ago, because he or she is under the same kinds of constraints and pressures as modern politicians are in terms of fund-raising and politicking. Therefore, there is not the same possibility of finding that voice that reaches people. Clearly, however, you can reach the middle class out of the Senate. I believe that, or I wouldn't have left the Senate. In some cases you have to be outside government to achieve a certain credibility with people in our current environment. One of the things I've noticed since I said I would not run for reelection is that a big ear has been opened to me by the public. This is because the public believes that politicians only say what they say in order to get reelected, and thinks the only thing a politician wants to do is get reelected. The only way to disprove that is if you decide not to run for reelection.

BLDS: So obviously you agree with that view.

BB: Yes, and it creates an opportunity, since I believe that the key issue is political reform. Political reform must take place prior to economic reform, and that can only be done outside of government.

BLDS: What does political reform mean? It's a very broad concept.

BB: The first thing it means is taking the money out of politics.

BLDS: Campaign-finance reform?

BB: Yes, and I don't mean fringe campaign-finance reform, but real campaign-finance reform.

BLDS: What would you do and how would you do it?

BB: Just take the money out. Say that on your income-tax return you can check off up to five hundred dollars voluntarily above your tax liability and that goes into a pot. Then in September, on Labor Day of an election year, the money is divided among Republican, Democratic, and qualified independent candidates. That's all the money that's available. For the past several years, Washington's feeble efforts to clean up politics have fallen woefully short of the goal of real reform. Legislators have bent over backward to accommodate the Supreme Court's erroneous ruling in the case of *Buckley vs. Valeo* that equated money with speech, and then have further watered down reform by making endless distinctions among sources of money in order to protect their own parties' fund-raising advantages. That's why we need a constitutional amendment to overrule *Buckley vs. Valeo* and allow Congress and the states to put spending limits on campaigns. Until we have a constitutional amendment you will not counter the perception that wealthy candidates buy elections. Now, if that meant that the political campaign in New Jersey, for example—in which Senator Lautenberg spent eight million dollars of his own money and his opponent spent seven—would have to be carried out with one million dollars total, or five hundred thousand each, so be it. The people would be less informed. But that would be their choice, and ultimately the system would adjust, in my opinion. You have to be very radical, otherwise the public will not believe that you're going to make any difference or change at all. The reason campaign-finance reform has never really

> I am going to continue the battle, but it's just going to be on a different ground.

been an election issue, other than in the crudest demagogic way, is because the proposals have never been clear enough.

BLDS: Or extreme enough?

BB: Right. So if you err on the side of simplicity, then you have a chance of shaking some people up. The political process itself should be more accessible, which is also important. That means reforming registration laws so it's easier to vote.

BLDS: How do you do that? Do motor/voter laws appeal to you?

BB: Yes, definitely. And also I think making it easier for ballot access is important. This has been an ongoing concern in my career, because in 1978 I ran in a primary election against the machine candidate—he was a good guy, but a machine candidate.

BLDS: Who was that?

BB: A guy named Dick [Richard C.] Leone, who is presently the head of the Twentieth Century Fund, and was then New Jersey state treasurer under Governor Brendan Byrne. At that time, there were closed primaries in New Jersey. The party machine put their guy at the top of the ballot and they chose the slate—they picked the line—for all the other candidates. Then Democrats came in and just voted the slate as it was, because their jobs were linked to the political machine in power. If you were not on the party's slate, but you managed to get on the ballot, you were way over at the bottom of the ballot and most people didn't even see you. So the reform was to have an open primary—no slates, every Senate candidate on the same line—and that's what I fought for. You've got to do that even more today. It has to be open for more people to participate in both the presidential nominating process and in the legislative nominating process.

BLDS: So many elections are dependent upon raising funds and responding to polls; are those two of the things that you found least attractive?

BB: Actually, I found raising money, when I was doing it, appealing.

BLDS: How so?

BB: It became a kind of a challenge.

BLDS: Were you in a competition with yourself?

BB: Yes—with the polls. However, this pollutes the political dialogue. Basically, you have polls that are dealing with competing focus groups. The habit of catering to polls and developing focus-group phrases won't be broken until somebody decides to talk in complete sentences, and to talk about an overall point of view, and to not simply push the button that they think that day will move a few people to their side. But that means taking a risk. The problem is that very few politicians will take any risk, at any time, for any reason.

BLDS: Before you took this big risk, did polls regarding your future standing in your state have anything to do with your decision to leave the Senate?

BB: Well, I didn't take any polls myself, but the public polls had me as the most popular elected official in the state.

BLDS: What will you miss most about the Senate? There are ideas that you have that may help you move forward.

BB: Yes, they certainly do. But I think that you can still be a part of the world of ideas beyond the world of the Senate office and, in fact, you might have more time for those ideas.

BLDS: A *New York Times* editorial described you as a possible, I'm going to quote, "magnet for the Americans who seek a third-party alternative, not to mention a thinking man's Ross Perot. But the senator's decision begs one very big question. Why did he not choose to stay and fight?" Actually my question to you is the very same. Why did you choose not to do that?

BB: Because for me it was time to go. I think you can be a public servant in the Senate. I tried to be. I think I was, but that's not the only place. I believe that we have to begin to think of the possibilities in public life that go beyond the established institutional channels. It's time for new thinking and for challenging the conventional wisdom. We have never been better able to do that than we are now, given the leaps of technology that we are taking. And so I can appreciate the argument that many made for me staying in the Senate. That is a traditionalist argument. I take it as a vote of confidence in my service of the last eighteen years that people would want me to stay and continue the battle. And I am going to continue the battle, but it's just going to be on a different ground.

BLDS: Where will one find Bill Bradley five years from now?

BB: I am a U.S. senator who is not going to run for reelection, a father, a husband, a washed-up small forward. But I'm not—what do they call them?—a seer. I can't see into the future.

BLDS: Do you want to be president of the United States?

BB: Sometime.

BLDS: Can we assume that in the year 2000 the fulfillment of that aspiration will be part of your plans?

BB: I plan a year at a time.

BLDS: By the way, what are the differences between leaders and heroes, and do we have many of either of them today?

BB: I am dubious about heroes. I don't think there are any living heroes. You can be a hero only over time. I think there are leaders. I think leadership is essential, and governmental leadership is essential. And presidential leadership is the most important governmental leadership in the world. It requires a little different style than a legislator.

BLDS: How so?

BB: In contrast to the presidency, the legislature is not the place for sharp edges and boldness. It is the place for round edges and compromise. However, if the problem is a deteriorating civic culture, then a charismatic leader is not the answer. He or she might make us feel better momentarily, but then if we are only spectators thrilled by the performance, how have we progressed collectively? A character in Bertolt Brecht's *Galileo* says, "Pity the nation that has no heroes," to which Galileo responds, "Pity the nation that needs them." All of us have to go out in the public square and all of us have to assume our citizenship responsibilities. For me, that means trying to tell the truth as I see it to both parties and to the American people without regard for the consequences. In a vibrant civil society, real leadership at the top is made possible by the understanding and evolution of awareness at the bottom and in the middle, that is, citizens engaged in a deliberate discussion about our common future. The more open our public dialogue, and the larger the number of Americans who join our deliberation, the greater chance we have to build a better country and a better world.

JIMMY CARTER

BLDS: Can we talk about your book, *Why Not the Best*, which was published just before you became president?

JC: Yes. I wrote it in 1975, early in the presidential campaign. It sold about a million copies, most of them after I won the Iowa caucus and the New Hampshire primary.

BLDS: In that book you ask two questions. One was: Can our government be honest, decent, open, fair, and compassionate? And the other was: Can our government be competent? Well, I guess you have learned a lot since the time you wrote that book. Your answers then were yes, provided that certain actions were taken. What progress do you feel you were able to make during your presidency that made your statement even more accurate?

JC: I think that when I was president the government was completely honest. There has never been any allegation of lies or fraud or even misconduct on the part of any of my cabinet officers while they were incumbent. We told the truth; we protected human rights. So I think the original idea of a government having as high moral values as its people was realized. As far as competence is concerned—well, that's just a matter of judgment. I know my opinion. We kept the budget deficits low, I instituted zero-based budgeting to make sure we didn't waste any money, and we deregulated a major part of the American industrial complex.

BLDS: Was that a good idea?

JC: I think so. There was a long assessment in *USA Today* recently, a whole page analyzing the deregulation of airlines, and the bottom line was that it was very good for the country—for the fliers, for the consumers, for the airlines. Now it is much cheaper to fly, the planes are safer, and the only downside is that the airline industry doesn't make as much profit as it did. The article said that competition has been increased. We also deregulated the banking industry, the communications industry, the trucking industry, and the railroads. I think in general that was a major, fairly unpublicized step to get the federal government out of a lot of unnecessary regulation and let the private-enterprise system prevail. It cer-

tainly did not result in monopolization.

BLDS: How would you answer those questions now, and what waivers, what qualifications, would you attach to those answers?

JC: There's a much more confrontational atmosphere in Washington now than when I was there, a much more unpleasant interrelationship between leaders, and there is a greatly enhanced influence of powerful and rich lobbyists. I think the interests of the general public are not as well protected. When the environmental laws are being amended, the ones who come in and write the basic paragraphs of the new legislation are the polluters themselves. When there are changes made in national-forest management, the timber companies are the ones who come in with their lobbyists and write the laws. And another difference: When I was president we always had our budget in on time. There was only one budget and that was my budget; the Congress never dreamed of preparing its own budget.

BLDS: How did the contemporary situation evolve so quickly and so poorly?

JC: I think it devolved under President Reagan. When he would send his budgets up to Congress they were obviously just propaganda documents, and they were immediately thrown into the wastebasket. Then the Congress would begin to prepare its own budget and many of the appropriations bills were never actually completed. Between what I proposed and what the Congress finally decided there were some adjustments, but I never had my defense budgets changed more than one-half of one percent. Those times are gone.

> When I was president we always had our budget in on time. There was only one budget and that was my budget; the Congress never dreamed of preparing its own budget.

BLDS: Do you see this more hostile and nonnegotiable environment continuing in the foreseeable future?

JC: I don't have any doubt that in the years ahead there will come a time when the president and Congress can resolve to cooperate and let the American public know that despite partisan differences they are cooperating with each other for the public's best interests. I think that time will come again someday, but I don't know when. I don't see any prospect of it now.

BLDS: You've said that not only did the American public change political horses midstream in 1980, but they chose one galloping in the opposite direction. What horse are the American people riding now, in what direction are we heading, and who is holding the reins?

JC: I think now the American public is simultaneously riding two horses that are going in opposite directions. I can't think of any major piece of legislation now being seriously considered where you see the president and the Congress moving in harmony. When I was in office, my administration and congressional committees worked side by side evolving the paragraphs in the environmental laws, or the transportation laws, or the commerce laws. But that just doesn't happen now. The so-called Contract with America headed by Newt Gingrich—a fellow Georgian—is really not going anywhere. It brought a great flurry of activity in the House, and it was very highly publicized, but none of those bills has gotten anywhere. Either they have gone to the Senate and died, or they have gone to the Senate where they have been dramatically modified and are now in a negotiating

stage, or they have been threatened, if they do pass, with a presidential veto. A lot of those things that concerned me when I read the Contract for America have been aborted, and I'm thankful for it.

BLDS: It seems to me that some of the ardor for radical change has diminished among the Republican freshman class, if they want to be anything more than one-termers.

JC: I think so, too. As a matter of fact, the freshman class, although it's a highly vocal and very conservative group, at least is trying to maintain some commitments to set campaign-finance reform in motion.

BLDS: I thought that famous handshake in Maine was meant to produce a bipartisan campaign-finance-reform agenda, but nothing has happened since then, has it?

JC: Gingrich is blocking campaign reform, but I think about seventy-five of the freshman members of the House are insisting that campaign reform be pursued. And I think that Newt is facing the reality that he's got a very rambunctious and uncontrollable substantial minority among the Republican members of Congress. Mostly these freshmen don't feel they should be subject to domination at all by the Speaker. In some areas they are more conservative perhaps than Newt and others are, though I think they are more inclined toward political reform. I hope the campaign reforms come about. I see the current system of campaign finance as a most serious cancer that is eating away at the vitals of American democracy. As a rapidly increasing form of legal bribery of the members of Congress by powerful interests, it is a detriment to the general public. It is a cancer eating at the public—I really feel that way. Of course, the only ones who speak out are Common Cause and a couple of other groups, but they need some support. Their voices get lost because their positions are so predictable.

BLDS: If you could now enact three legislative reforms in our country, other than campaign-finance reform, what would they be?

JC: I think environmental-protection laws would be one of them. Health care reform would be the second one.

BLDS: What would you do in that area?

JC: President Ford and I have worked with a group that has taken a comprehensive look at the health-care-reform act.

BLDS: What is that group?

JC: The National Leadership Coalition on Health Care is the name of it, and we've been working on it for several years. President Ford has spent a good deal of time on it. Let me give you those two reforms plus campaign financing. I think campaign financing is a big one.

BLDS: If you could change or transform some common attitudes in how our government addresses foreign affairs nowadays, which would you choose?

JC: Well, that's a difficult question to answer. Let me give you a more generic answer. We are now the only superpower in the world. At one time, everything that we attempted to do for the glory of America was affected by the competition with the Soviet Union. Now that time is gone and the question has become what can we do to exalt the principles of our country so that everyone in the world will know that America is the champion of peace. We must seek the peaceful resolution of conflicts and understand how they relate to us. Secondly, we must be the champion of freedom and democracy. We should champion human rights and work for the alleviation of suffering. These are the principles that are the measure of the greatness of any country. Unfortunately, I don't think we have even attempted to achieve those ultimate goals.

BLDS: Well, what deters us from those higher causes?

JC: I'll just take the matter of peace. Every politician knows—in this country and in others—that the most popular thing that our president can do is to go to war. The president instantly assumes the trappings of the commander in chief of our young men and women who go overseas and put their lives in danger. This was the case when President Reagan invaded Grenada, it was the case with the Gulf War, and so forth. It's very difficult to make peace; it's much easier to make war instead of peace. I believe there are now a greater number of conflicts in the world than ever before in history.

BLDS: How many wars are going on at this moment?

JC: There are about 110 conflicts. As far as wars are concerned, the Carter Center defines a major war as one in which more than a thousand people have died on the battlefield. And there are thirty-two of those right now. A number of them are almost ignored. I would say the most vicious conflicts right now are in Burundi and Rwanda and Sudan. I went to Rwanda and Burundi because no one else will go.

BLDS: What do you hope to accomplish in Africa, and how do you have dominion in that part of the world?

JC: The Carter Center has programs in about two dozen African countries. I had been distressed for a long time about the genocidal acts in Rwanda. In 1994 more than five hundred thousand peo-

> . . . in the future I would hope that there would be no need for Camp David because folks could come to the center to negotiate.

ple were killed, and they still have two million refugees in adjacent countries, in Tanzania and Zaire. I wanted to see what was being done about it. But when I got over there and began to ask questions of the representatives of the United Nations and the Organization of African Unity, I realized that little was being achieved. Every time they tried to have a conference it was an aborted effort. So Presidents Museveni of Uganda, Mobutu of Zaire, and Mwinyi of Tanzania decided to have a regional conference, along with Rwanda and Burundi, which are surrounded by those three nations. They asked the Carter Center to coordinate the conference and to mediate. The first objective is to deal with the horrendous problem of Rwanda concerning the refugees.

BLDS: Are they still in camps?

JC: They're still in camps in Tanzania and particularly in Zaire. We want to work out with Mrs. Obata, who is the U.N. high commissioner for refugees, the number of refugees that should be repatriated every day from the camps in Zaire into Rwanda. There are about 1.3 million in Zaire and about six hundred thousand or so in Tanzania. There is not as big a problem in Tanzania as there is in Zaire. My second objective is just to learn more about what is causing the tremendous number of deaths in Burundi every day. The U.S., which has given me the most conservative estimates, says 100 people are killed every day; the Swedes say 300 a day. This is an unconscionable affliction upon the international community and it is almost entirely ignored in this country. You can look in the *New York Times* for three weeks and you might see one reference to Rwanda and none to Burundi. But we will be doing our best to work out some solution to it. The United Nations has given up because the Rwandans and Burundians refuse to meet under the aegis of the United Nations at this time.

BLDS: For what reason?

JC: They don't trust the United Nations because U.N. forces are at least accused of knowing about the genocide and not acting. Some of the Rwandans refuse to meet in a conference that is attended by the European countries like France and Belgium.

BLDS: Because of their history in that area?

JC: Yes. Those countries are blamed for some of Rwanda's problems. And there's a problem in getting the Burundians within the government who don't agree with each other to go to the same conference if there's an international flavor. One of the strengths of the Carter Center is that we are a nongovernmental organization. I go there as a private citizen, as a college professor, whatever. The Carter Center does not represent any government. Quite often countries in conflict consider an official U.S. or European government presence as an interference in their internal affairs. They prefer to turn to us.

BLDS: The Carter Center has evolved to be more than a conventional library museum, but rather a really significant center for conflict resolution, for help in agriculture, for help in medicine. What gave you the idea in 1982?

JC: When we had our first plans for the Carter Center we just had the library on the plans and a little box for some kind of institute. My first dream was that we could provide a place here for folks to come and negotiate differences, similar to what we did at Camp David for Israel and Egypt. In my earliest statements of my vision for the Carter Center, I said that in the future I would hope that there would be no need for Camp David because folks could come to the center to negotiate.

BLDS: You use Camp David as a generic reference to a place where negotiations are carried out by the U.S. government.

JC: Yes.

BLDS: What did you have in mind?

JC: To bring combative parties together, those either at war or on the verge of war, so they can exchange communication between one another to avoid combat or to end a war. A main reason that we've had horrendous wars is that the antagonists are unable to communicate. That's why in 1994 I went to North Korea, because the U.S. government had a policy, even a law, prohibiting any U.S. official from negotiating with any official from that country.

BLDS: But a U.S. "unofficial" could.

JC: Yes, and I was totally unofficial. I was there just to represent the Carter Center, but at the urgent invitation of then-

President Kim Il Sung, who said, "I want to work out our differences with the United States government and they won't talk to us." I got permission from President Clinton to go. The same thing happened in Haiti in September 1994, when the United States was on the verge of an invasion with thirty thousand troops poised off the coast of that country. We got permission from the president to go. At that time the U.S. ambassador in Port-au-Prince was prohibited even from exchanging a note with the officials who were running Haiti. In this case, President Clinton asked me, Senator Sam Nunn, and General Colin Powell to represent him officially.

BLDS: How did you manage to get that permission in the light of all the conversation that appears in the press? There seems to be no secret.

JC: After the Carter Center mission to North Korea there was a lot of discussion in the press. You recall that North Korea was suspected of developing a nuclear arsenal and the U.S. was trying to get the U.N. Security Council to apply sanctions on North Korea for not allowing the International Atomic Energy Agency to carry out inspections. I really thought we were on the verge of war when we went. When we came back, after defusing the crisis, I discovered to my amazement that there was a lot of mostly negative press. I wanted to go to Washington to give a briefing to our government but they asked me not to come.

BLDS: They asked you not to come to Washington?

JC: Yes. I insisted that I needed to go to Washington, because some of the grievances I had worked out with Kim Il Sung were quite significant. But when I got to Washington, nobody met me at the airport and nobody met me at the White House, either. No cabinet officer ever met me. The president wasn't there, the vice-president wasn't there. So I went to National Security Adviser Tony Lake's office and gave him the report. There were doubts that Kim Il Sung could be trusted, so I went back to Plains and sent him a letter, delineating in writing everything that we had committed to do, and I sent a copy to President Clinton and told him that Kim Il Sung would confirm all his commitments in writing to me and to him. Kim Il Sung did send me a letter confirming everything that he indicated to do, and out of that has come a resolution of the crisis.

BLDS: How did the White House react to the role of the Carter Center?

JC: With silence.

43

> Rosalynn and I have an interesting life, we have a lot of callings now. And we see the results.

BLDS: How do you explain that, when this appears to be furthering the goals of this administration?

JC: Well, the *Washington Post* and others reported a furor in the State Department, because Clinton had authorized me to go to North Korea without the department's approval or knowledge. But I don't try to explain their reasons for what their attitude is. When the crisis over Haiti came along, with a probability of the U.S. having to invade, I first called Sam Nunn and then I called Colin Powell and asked them if they would go with me to Haiti and try to resolve the conflict peacefully. They said that they would only go if President Clinton approved their going. So we let President Clinton know that we would like to go, and he ultimately approved.

BLDS: President Clinton does call upon you from time to time.

JC: I have to say yes, he does.

BLDS: Do you wish he would call on you more often?

JC: Yes, I do.

BLDS: What would you like him to be calling on you for now?

JC: To do things that only an unofficial agency can do. For example, there are some things that diplomatic proprieties won't permit and one of those things is communicating freely with someone who is not recognized by us as a legitimate leader. At that time we didn't recognize North Korean President Kim Il Sung as legitimate. We didn't recognize Haitian President Emile Jonassaint as legitimate. I don't need any authority, and I wouldn't accept an appointment as an ambassador who represents the U.S. government. That would limit my flexibility and effectiveness. I do appreciate and need briefings from the government.

BLDS: I've heard you speak about initiatives in the Middle East. You did not sound very enthusiastic about the direction of those negotiations.

JC: The negotiations now between Syria and Israel, if they have ever been very promising, are all about show. As far as trying to negotiate or mediate between Israel and Syria, that would not be a function for me.

BLDS: Are you suggesting then, because of the enormous tragedy with the assassination of Prime Minister Rabin, that the peace process will be interrupted or just deferred?

JC: When you say peace process, it's not much of a process. It's not as though they're on the verge of an agreement and they're down to the last stages. Such a process is not taking place at all. It's just exploratory, with several spasmodic talks back and forth. So nothing really is on the burner right now for an Israel-Syria agreement.

BLDS: But what about an Israel-Palestinian agreement?

JC: Those agreements that have been highly publicized are now the official law of Israel.

BLDS: What do you consider the most difficult negotiations during your tenure as president?

JC: Those regarding the Panama Canal. That was the most difficult assignment I ever had in my life. Certainly it was much more difficult to get the Panama Canal treaties ratified than it was to be elected president.

BLDS: Because of the changes in government?

JC: No, because of the unpopularity in the U.S. of turning over the canal and the Canal Zone to the Republic of Panama and the fact that I had to get two-thirds of the senators to vote for it—which they did, by the way.

BLDS: Did it take the usual arm-twisting?

JC: Every possible means of legitimate influence was used. And I think the ratification was the most courageous act ever taken by members of the Congress. In the next election, twenty senators who voted for the canal treaties were up for reelection. Out of the twenty, only seven came back. And two years later, the attrition rate was almost as great. So it was a devastating adverse political consequence voting for the Panama Canal treaties, but it was the right thing to do. It corrected an old injustice and strengthened our relations with our neighbors in Latin America.

BLDS: In some ways your presidency became the most significant training for what is, arguably, the most significant role in your life.

JC: Well, I wouldn't say that my role today is more significant.

BLDS: The impact that you have around the world is potentially more than a president can have.

JC: In some ways, yes. And the nice thing is that Rosalynn and I have almost an unlimited menu of things that we can choose to do or not do.

BLDS: How do you choose what to do?

JC: I'd say time and financial constraints. I have to raise all the money to support the Carter Center activities, and this puts an enormous burden on me. It obviously restrains what we do, and my own time. You know, it's hard to fit in a trip to Rwanda and a trip to Burundi and Uganda and Zaire and then go to Cairo for a conference and come back and do the other things, of which there are a lot.

BLDS: What do you find to be the most difficult obstacles in conflict resolution, and what would you advise those people who cannot come to the Carter Center? Are there "tricks to the trade" of mediation? You must have certain ground rules.

JC: We do. We study intensely the theory of mediation and negotiation, and we work with some of the finest scholarly experts in the world on how you reach an agreement. We have developed techniques that have been successful in many cases. One is to have what we call a single document. I learn from my daily briefings at the Carter Center the rudiments of a conflict. Much of the work is done by students. I'll have a group of interns who concentrate on one particular dispute. It may involve Haiti, it may involve Liberia, it may involve Sri Lanka, it may involve Rwanda or North Korea or whatever. If I do get an opportunity to go to those countries to help resolve a conflict, by the time I get there I'm thoroughly briefed; I also get briefings from the C.I.A. and from the State Department and sometimes the White House. Then I type up what I think is a fair agreement, all in one document. I go back and forth between the parties and modify the proposal as necessary. And I make sure—I have to make sure—every time either side makes a concession that the benefits are greater than what they concede. Otherwise they won't make the concession. And I have to prove to them that at the end both sides have to win. If they don't, there's no substance, no permanence to the agreement. For instance, in the Egyptian-Israeli treaty that I helped negotiate as president in spring of 1979, both sides won.

BLDS: And they knew it.

JC: They knew it. And they still know it.

BLDS: Is there any part of the world that you would especially like to be called upon to help now?

JC: Yes, I'd like to go back to North Korea. I'd like to do something to help South Korea, but there again the Carter Center doesn't go into any area unless we get a request from both sides.

BLDS: You have always been very clear-voiced about the importance of religion and faith in your life. In fact, I think of you as a truly religious man on a mission, on a life mission. Do you have a sense of calling about the work that you do?

JC: I think so. I taught Sunday school last summer on this same subject, on a calling that we all have. And how do we detect a call, what are the excuses we use not to respond to it, what are the

strengths we need to accept the calling, what are the adverse and beneficial consequences of it, does it restrict our life to assume a difficult challenge, or does it liberate us? What does it mean to have a new task or project that might be challenging and difficult and unpredictable and adventurous—and potentially gratifying?

BLDS: Are these the best years of your life?

JC: I think so. Rosalynn and I have an interesting life, we have a lot of callings now. And we see the results. We go into an area that never has produced more than seven or eight bushels of wheat per acre and now they produce seventy bushels per acre.

BLDS: If you had it to do over again, what would you do otherwise?

JC: I don't think I'd do anything differently. What we're doing right now is a very gratifying culmination of a lot of different careers that I have had. I wanted to be a naval officer, to go to a naval academy, I wanted to be in submarines, to be a successful businessman, to be in the state legislature, the governor's office, and the presidency. All those things led up to this.

BLDS: What next?

JC: This is good. Maybe retirement! I am writing another book.

BLDS: Yes, what about?

JC: Well, it's based on my Sunday school lessons, and one of the topics will be callings. It's called *Living Faith*.

WILLIAM CONWAY

BLDS: In 1966 you became the Bronx Zoo's fourth director and the second general director of the New York Zoological Society (now the Wildlife Conservation Society), carrying on the work of your distinguished predecessors. Let's talk about who they were.

WC: William Hornaday was director of the Zoo from 1896 to 1926, William Reid Blair from 1926 to 1940. Following various temporary arrangements, John Tee-Van became general director of the Society in 1956. In 1962, I became Bronx Zoo director and, in 1966, general director of the Society.

BLDS: And what was the role of that globally minded conservationist Fairfield Osborn?

WC: Fair was president of the New York Zoological Society, the organizational umbrella of an overall effort. He was, especially, the leader of our board of trustees. The function of the presidency has changed over the years.

BLDS: Are you now the president?

WC: I am now president and general director of the Society: its CEO. And I'm also the director of the Zoo. However, this came about in a reorganization. Howard Phipps, Jr., formerly called president of the Society, became chairman of the board. Howdy led the board for twenty-one years—ever since Laurance Rockefeller and then Bobby Goelet stepped down. Laurance followed Fair Osborn. David T. Schiff replaced Howdy last April when he became chairman emeritus.

BLDS: Did you have any doubts about managing such a huge enterprise, such a huge organization?

WC: Well, I remember very well that when Fair Osborn invited me to become the director of the Zoo back in 1962 and described what he wanted me to do, he concluded by saying, "Bill, when I'm not here you are me." And I said, "Dr. Osborn, I can't operate that way. When you're not here, I'm me." We had a wonderful relationship. He was a very inspiring person. Few people realize how important he has been in the international conservation

movement with his books *Our Plundered Planet* and *Our Crowded World*, and his many essays. He, as much as anyone alive, drew world attention to the conflict between the growing world population and its dwindling resources.

BLDS: In the early days, was the field largely restricted to the well-born and well-heeled?

WC: No, Fair was not well-heeled, as a matter of fact. He was a remarkable guy. His father, a most distinguished paleontologist, had been the president of both the Society and the American Museum of Natural History. Fair himself had a long history with wildlife. He used to breed pheasants and I think he was the first person ever to breed the famous Himalayan monal, one of the world's most exquisitely beautiful birds, which he did in New York as a boy. He was an interesting guy, and quite clearly the person that pulled the Society out of the doldrums in the thirties. Fair continued on until 1968 when he retired. At that point Laurance Rockefeller, who had been on the board since 1935, stepped in as president. I'll not forget what he said to Fair about coming in as president. He said, "Well, I've always been a bridesmaid and never a bride." Laurance stepped in for two or three years and made for a very powerful transition period from the Fair Osborn years.

BLDS: What was so powerful about that transition?

WC: Fair Osborn was an extraordinarily well known and talented man with an interesting combination of professional and social connections. He knew the New York scene very well. When a person like that leaves, an organization could lose its rudder. He was a tremendous asset and a tremendous loss. Laurance had the understanding and stature to take us through the transition.

BLDS: After one hundred years, why and when was it necessary to change the name of your organization?

WC: The Society changed. It would be

astonishing, I suppose, if an organization that covered as many areas as ours managed to stay just the same. Our organization has grown, refocused itself, and changed its basic responsibilities. It simply couldn't masquerade under a title that did not indicate either what it did or where it intended to go. So, in 1993, the board changed the name from the New York Zoological Society to the Wildlife Conservation Society.

BLDS: What have been the results of the change in name? Does it now more clearly demonstrate the group's mission throughout the world?

WC: I don't think any name does, but this comes a lot closer. In the past, people would refer to our efforts as that of the New York Zoo, which seemed very peculiar considering we were working in the high Himalayas, or in the lower part of Patagonia, or in the middle of Africa. It's hard to build a national and international base of support for the New York Zoo. We have an American Museum of Natural History whose name dealt with the problem of recognition beyond the city in the first place. There is no other organization that I'm aware of that has made the kind of transition that we have. What we did made eminently good sense, but whether the name was well chosen or not is another question.

BLDS: You have been with the Society for nearly four decades and have obviously witnessed a great deal. How did you come here in the first place?

WC: I came as associate curator of ornithology. A bird man. And I'm still a bird man. I still love birds.

BLDS: And what was your training for that role?

WC: I worked at the St. Louis Zoo as a bird man and also as an assistant to the director.

BLDS: Was that your first job?

WC: My first permanent job, yes. I have been in the zoo field all of my life. I have always liked animals. I became excited about them, and I became increasingly concerned about natural history, ecology, and evolution. And, I just never grew up.

BLDS: After one hundred years, how are the issues different and how have the goals of your field changed?

WC: After the past one hundred years we're lucky to have any wildlife at all, and after the next hundred years I don't know that we will. The world that we live in today is entirely different from the one that existed when the Society was founded back in 1895. It's not simply that species are disappearing, which is the conser-

> After the past one hundred years we're lucky to have any wildlife at all, and after the next hundred years I don't know that we will.

vationist's most common complaint. What we are seeing is an enormous crash, the diminution of biomass, the tremendous decline of every creature that isn't human or of some immediate service to humans. Edward O. Wilson, a Harvard professor I admire enormously, has pointed out that Americans are extremely aware of their material wealth and can't overlook their cultural wealth. They live it, hour by hour. However, they seem oblivious to their biological wealth, upon which we all ultimately depend. We have become increasingly oblivious to the living tissue of the world, which we have to sustain if we wish to survive ourselves.

BLDS: Having a natural curiosity about life and early contact with animals, you say that zoos led you, ultimately, into wildlife conservation. Some of your colleagues, in describing their own personal development, show a direct link between their early years and their chosen career paths. Peter Matthiessen, the snow leopard expert, recounts childhood adventures that include visits to your Bronx Zoo. And George Schaller, your own lion researcher, remembers that as a boy he collected birds' eggs and kept a mini-zoo of salamanders, snakes, opossums, and other creatures at home. Were your childhood experiences similar?

WC: Very. As a matter of fact, George lived only a few blocks away in Webster Groves, Missouri. However, we worked together for the Society more than twenty years before we realized it.

BLDS: What was Webster Groves like?

WC: It was a great place to collect butterflies. I had a superb butterfly collection. I had my own little zoo, primarily of box turtles, snakes, and salamanders, and wonderful big beetles—all sorts of things.

BLDS: And who encouraged you in this pursuit?

WC: I wouldn't say it was a matter of encouragement so much as toleration. Both my father and my mother were very tolerant.

BLDS: Were you an only child? Did you have an assistant zoo keeper?

WC: No, my sister kept her distance.

BLDS: From a mini-menagerie in Webster Groves to this remarkable zoo in the Bronx, it's quite a leap.

WC: It's not such a leap, but going to the Zoo in St. Louis did take three streetcars. I went there very often. When I was fourteen, I was brought to New York for the first time by my father. He was a painter and was having a show at a gallery called Grand Central

Moderns. He dumped me at the Bronx Zoo while he went to Manhattan. It was one of the high points of my life. I just reveled in the Bronx Zoo because there were so many marvelous creatures there—and I knew that lurking behind the scenes were people like Fairfield Osborn, William Beebe, and Raymond Ditmars. William Beebe, of course, was the extraordinary man who explored the ocean's depths in the bathysphere.

BLDS: Was that bathysphere one of his own design, by the way?

WC: No, it was done by a man named Otis Barton.

BLDS: But a fourteen-year-old wouldn't know that, would he?

WC: Oh, yes. I read every book about the Zoo and the Society that I could get my hands on, and I knew of all the people. Lee Crandall, the very famous curator, was still there when I came to work in New York in 1950, as was Beebe. Beebe introduced me to the tropical forest in Trinidad in 1959.

BLDS: Didn't he join the organization at the turn of the century?

WC: Will Beebe came in 1899 and Lee Crandall came about 1908. Beebe was with the Society until he died in 1962; Crandall was with the Society until he died in 1969; and Osborn died very shortly after he retired, in September 1969.

BLDS: These people were with the Society until well into their eighties. In the hundred-year history of the organization there is obviously an enormous amount of continuity among these several persons. Let me jump back for a moment to your father "dumping" you at the Bronx Zoo as he went on to have an exhibition of his work at Grand Central Moderns, which, I believe, was owned by Edith Halpert. It was one of the most distinguished galleries for American painters, and your father numbered among them. Can you tell us a little bit about his life and career?

WC: He was a St. Louisan, born and bred. He won scholarships at Washington University and was sent to France twice to study. He also traveled in North Africa. He became an instructor at Washington University and eventually a professor. He retired from the university in his late sixties and died when he was seventy-three in 1973.

BLDS: Was he a watercolorist?

WC: He was a most distinguished watercolorist, but also was well known for his oils, mostly his semiabstract work. The Pulitzers have a good number of his works. He did a number of distinguished portraits, as well.

BLDS: Any nature studies?

WC: No, he never did any nature studies, but he was very tolerant and occasionally agreed to accompany me on a hike. My mother was much more influential in that regard. She very much liked the outdoors and was not above collecting turtles.

BLDS: Was she an artist, as well?

WC: She met my father as his student, but she would not have considered herself an artist. She was a musician in her earlier days, but she never performed professionally.

BLDS: In your early days managing the zoo, there must have been some difficult transitions. Do you recall any of them?

WC: You must remember that I grew up in the zoo field, so little to do with it seemed a transition to me. Perhaps the major career transition I had to make, and it was a very difficult one, was to decide to become a director, rather than a curator, because my orientation was curatorial. When I became director I received a telegram, which I still have, from Will Beebe, who was at our station in Trinidad. It read, "Hooray for the Zoo, alas for the birds." As far as moving into the field of zoo administration, I am sure that I followed the usual track of being promoted to my level of incompetence. However, I am fortunate in that the Society has never been a one-man institution. We have always had a great many very competent experts in their various areas. This is a key to the Society's success. I have recognized that expertise and have attempted to be guided by it. I also managed to put in a lot of my own ideas. We have had, and continue to have, a marvelous board of trustees. Wonderful people such as Howdy Phipps, Laurance Rockefeller, Frank Larkin, Jack Pierrepont, Lila Acheson Wallace, and Brooke Astor, who became and still is a dear friend. Yesteryear's board had George Baker, whose son George Baker is now on the board. David Schiff's father, John Schiff, as well as his grandfather and great-grandfather, were also on the board. David, the new chairman of the board, is fourth generation.

BLDS: When did the focus of zoos shift from bloodied hunting grounds to battered habitats—the forest, the soil, the water— what you have referred to in your centennial volume, *Saving Wildlife,* as the big tent of human existence?

WC: I'm afraid that the transition is still under way. There are still many institutions that have not yet realized their ultimate mandate. I'm afraid that those zoos and aquariums that do not realize that their basic responsibility is directly related to preserving wildlife in nature, not simply exhibiting it in zoos and aquariums, are bound to become rather baroque and obsolete organizations.

BLDS: You've written that in North America alone there are 822 endangered species and the world may be losing more than a hundred distinct plant and animal species a day. Rainforests, prairies, and savannahs just seem to disappear. Where do you get these numbers from?

WC: They're all really educated guesses. Those who have spent most of the effort in calculating them are people like Ed Wilson. The way it has been done is to extrapolate from the studies of a person such as the Smithsonian's entomologist Terry Erwin, who identified the overwhelming diversity of life in ever smaller parts of tropical forest. Vast numbers of invertebrates may be specific to very small areas. Move away a hundred meters from your site and you find a whole group of other species. Such studies enable us to develop a kind of index of diversity. Thus, when we consider the burning, as we did last year, of thousands of square miles of tropical forest, it is apparent that hundreds, possibly thousands, of species may have been lost. Some biologists believe that the number of species of invertebrates alone exceeds a hundred million. Others believe that the evidence suggests thirty million or ten million. All such guesses are based on area/species estimates but they are no more than crude guesses, as we flop about in our ignorance trying to give people some idea of what habitat modification means to nature.

BLDS: It certainly does dramatize the scope, and the urgency, of the problem. I have also read that by someone's calculation a hundred acres of tropical rainforest is destroyed every minute. We know some of the causes of all the bad news, but what are some of the realistic solutions to the problems?

WC: There seem to be two basic ideas along these lines. One is apocalyptic. It says that we will not be able to get people to focus their attention on the loss of nature until or unless we have an absolutely terrible series of international environmental catastrophes.

BLDS: Haven't we had that already?

WC: No, not one in which millions of people die in a fashion immediately related to an environmental event. The ongoing starvation of millions in less developed countries does not seem to count. Then, this idea goes, people's attention will be focused and they will realize what they are doing to the environment. I don't believe that

> Some biologists believe that the number of species of invertebrates alone exceeds a hundred million.

way of thinking at all. I think this is an utterly useless approach to the problem. Those who make that kind of forecast refer to people as "they." Who is they? There is no one in charge, no focus of accountability. Just because there is an enormous catastrophe in India or Bangladesh or Georgia doesn't mean that national or international leaders elsewhere will be severely concerned or affected. But there need not be a catastrophic stimulus to the generalization of environmentalism as a way of life. It does not take a catastrophe for people to become unpleasantly aware that their options are increasingly restricted. While there will be an increasing division between rich nations and poor ones, there will be more and more vigorous attempts on the part of the rich to preserve a livable environment because the earth is too small to quarantine the majority of its populace. Sustaining a livable environment means preserving biodiversity and, eventually, a lower density of human population. It may be that the problems are not going to be as severe between people *and* the environment as they are going to be between people *over* the environment. I was told by an acquaintance the other day that during the past twelve months the Department of Defense has tallied over sixty-seven wars of various kinds that basically have resulted from fights for natural resources, fights for pieces of the environment.

BLDS: Aren't some of them religious conflicts?

WC: Beyond the surface, I fear many are fights for natural resources—fights for food, essentially. Ultimately, human choices about their society—the number of children people will have, the kind of places they want to live—will determine the future. So, people like me want to provide information that will enable these choices to be well-informed. And we want to save for future generations as much as possible of nature through the difficult decades ahead. Curiously, one of the closest things I would offer as a contribution to a solution is the development of more and more interest in the survival of other species. That is not simply altruistic. If we can sustain a significant representation of the world's biodiversity we can sustain ourselves.

BLDS: Can people and big predatory animals coexist in close proximity?

WC: Sure. Whether they want to or not is another question.

BLDS: What evidence do you have of that?

WC: In some parts of Canada, for example, polar bears walk in and out of town; in India, dense populations sometimes live with tigers; in the western United States we sometimes live with pumas and wolves and bears. In each case, people must make a conscious decision to accept a situation that requires very aware behavior. People say they can't live with lions, they can't live with tigers, they can't live with elephants. What people? What lions? What elephants? What tigers? It's not a simple matter. If you manage the elephants, if you manage the lions, you can do something. However, there will be losses. If you've got some poor fellow out there living on the economic edge and trying to keep all his goats alive, of course not. Under such conditions the "taxes" of predators are being levied against those least able to pay. That is when those who can pay must help.

BLDS: Which predators cause the greatest problems?

WC: Without any question at all—insect predators, on our crops.

BLDS: Any progress in that regard? Any successes?

WC: There have been enormous successes, but it is a constant battle, and we will often lose. Any small, rapidly reproducing animal that has a short generation time is able to move very rapidly in erecting genetic fences against the chemical controls we've chosen to use. Some of the more recent nonchemical, more biological control methods have been fascinating, however; consider the sterilization techniques. One involves releasing sterile male screwworm flies, for example, because flies, unlike humans, only mate once. This technology has virtually eliminated screwworm in cattle.

BLDS: What are some of the more significant developments in conservation today? Have any great strides been made?

WC: In some ways the most significant development has been the rise of "conservation biology," that is, conservation as a science, not simply a philosophy or a feel-good activity. It provides a much better basis for determining what we have to do and for being able to predict what the consequences of our actions will be. The field has been developed through the efforts of many people; I would single out Michael Soulé. There's something else: the rise of the conservation scientist, the field scientist as a hero in our time. It's all very well to consider today's heroes as the people who jump around on the stage and sing wonderful tunes or play roles in movies, or even those who make space voyages. But there is a new kind of hero that is beginning to make a difference in saving the world we live in,

what I'll call the conservation pioneer. These are people such as George Schaller, Alan Rabinowitz, Mike Fay, Charlie Munn, and Claudio Campagna. These people are out there largely by themselves, establishing a level of personal integrity in the minds of all who know them, inspiring young people, bringing them along, inspiring entire nations in ways that we have not seen since the founding of new religions. It's a very interesting phenomenon, and one that I hope will spread. Brilliant young women such as Amy Vedder of our staff are among the outstanding scientists doing this incredibly difficult work out of a sense of personal commitment. Of course, everyone is familiar with the work of Jane Goodall, an icon, but there's also been a rise of effort. As is so often the case, it is the individual that makes the difference. I believe strongly in individuals being able to make a difference.

BLDS: As an eminent conservationist, ornithologist, and wildlife writer, you have not only helped shape and direct this field, but also been involved in all sorts of scholarly pursuits and in shaping the philosophical orientation toward the entire issue. In fact, you say that we are in a period of extinction crisis and that the future of zoos and aquariums in this period is in question. You propose a new approach. Can you describe it?

WC: The conservation park. Perhaps eight hundred million or more visits are recorded in zoos and aquariums around the world every year. And there is virtually no place else in the world of municipal man that attracts people in such numbers. Let's remember, the vast majority of human population is located in the cities. That's where political power is and that's where the intellectual ferment is taking place. Conservation usually is created in the cities, not out in the countryside. It takes place in the countryside, but the creative juices come from those intellectual cities. And that's where the zoos and the aquariums are. So they have tremendous potential. If you were going to try to create an international conservation organization that could really be effective, what would you want to do? Obviously you would like to have its offices in human population centers. Wherever possible you would like the organization to have an independent income. Zoos are in the cities. They do have an

> Conservation usually is created in the cities, not out in the countryside. It takes place in the countryside, but the creative juices come from those intellectual cities.

income independent of conservation actions. My concern then is to get zoos to focus on conservation. It is wonderful to make great, elaborate artificial habitats that inspire people, but we cannot stop there. We've got to preserve the original habitats. We are, after all, not going to exhibit a bunch of dinosaur bones. What is the point? It's too late to save *Tyrannosaurus rex* and the *Stegosaurus*.

BLDS: In a world, and in an era, of diminishing resources, how should the Wildlife Conservation Society and civilization, in general, most effectively expend its time, its energy, its resources, and its goodwill in preserving the universe?

WC: Get out there and act. In the last five years, the Wildlife Conservation Society has successfully worked in eleven nations on park and reserve development, the result being that there are now over 100 million acres of parks and reserves that did not exist before. That's equal to forty Yellowstone National Parks. And we didn't go out and buy this land; that's an illusion. Unless the local people believe in such efforts and are convinced they are going to be a part of them, and conservation is going to be part of their lives, it will not work. You're not going to sustain parkland just by buying it unless you're prepared to put soldiers all the way around the borders. You must work with the land's human communities. You've got to save the land and the wildlife on it for the children of the communities directly concerned.

BLDS: During the 1960s, you were instrumental in creating several coastal reserves in Argentina. Thirty-five years later, are you still involved with that region? And how has your involvement affected the wildlife population there?

WC: Well, every once in a while you do something you feel very good about. Whenever I've been fortunate enough to work with Argentines, I've felt very good about it. The Argentine national and provincial governments have kept every commitment they have made on parks, reserves, and monuments. They're deeply involved in trying to make them better and they're trying to deal with new problems. When I first went to the town of Puerto Madryn, which has been our home base in Patagonia, there were 4,500 people. Last time I went, there were 46,000 people in that town. What could have happened as a result, and what has happened throughout the world, is the loss of wildlife and the desertification of the areas that people move into. But that's not true in Argentina. You can go right into the town on your bicycle and go right to the nearest sea lion colony at Punta Lomas and watch a magnificent wildlife vista right there. It's a wonderful thing.

Throughout the season, buses by the hundreds go out to see elephant seals and Patagonian sea lions. People go out in boats to enjoy marvelous views of whales. It started with a couple of hundred people going each year. Now, we have many thousands of people going out to see the whales. And it is done with great sensitivity.

BLDS: Where was that?

WC: In Chubut, Patagonia, on a magnificent wild shore.

BLDS: Where else in the world has your conservation work taken you?

WC: I've been very fortunate to work a little bit in Africa, primarily at the behest of our other scientists there, especially a very distinguished biologist named David Western who has replaced Richard Leakey as the head of the Kenya Wildlife Service.

BLDS: Now that you have been president and general director of the Society for some time, it may be that Will Beebe's early telegram to you was prophetic. It must be very frustrating not to have the opportunity to do curatorial work if that is one's interest; I wondered if birds were still your favorites?

WC: Oh, yes. I'm still very much interested in birds.

BLDS: How did you first become involved with birds? Is there a particular variety or species that you prefer?

WC: I'm very keen about flamingos and penguins. They're at opposite poles. Whenever I have time I try to devote a little effort to them. I have to say that one of the things that is very special about the Wildlife Conservation Society that is not found in other such organizations is the richness and depth of our staff and the board of trustees. Virtually any sort of support you need, whether it be distinguished veterinary support, artistic support, or a top educator, we have it. There aren't other institutions of our kind with that kind of depth. If I need to get a contact in Timbuktu and one of my staff members doesn't have it I can pretty well be sure I can turn to a trustee and a trustee will have it. I do think that we are in a most unusual position.

BLDS: There are a thousand national parks throughout the world. Where does the United States rank?

WC: In terms of national parks? We don't compare to Tanzania which has given over 15 percent, and is pushing toward 25 percent, of its land to national parks. It's so embarrassing. This is not to say that we don't have wonderful parks in this country. However, the total budget of our national-parks system is less than a billion dollars. Can you imagine that? Think of the United States budget. And this is our treasure house! And what do we do with it? It's just a crime that we're not pushing our national-park system further and that we're not supporting it better. Another problem is that we're confusing the use of our forest lands. Real tragedies. Why should we cut raw timber from our irreplaceable old-growth forests and sell it to Japan at a loss? Why should we put in roads, at national expense, for timber people? It's just preposterous. Why should we run some of our timberlands in ways that will, predictably, put their lumberers out of business, according to independent studies?

BLDS: Let's talk about the Wolong Reserve in Sichuan Province, where you designed a giant panda breeding facility. I always wondered how closely man's efforts can duplicate nature's in that kind of replicated facility.

WC: There was no effort to duplicate nature's efforts in this instance. There was no effort to do a simulated habitat. What was done was to set up a facility where the animals could be managed very much as if they were livestock, meeting their needs in a very simple way. The best one can say about such an effort is that it is a mighty poor second best to letting them breed in nature. However, to do that you have to have nature.

BLDS: What species is the most difficult to breed in captivity?

WC: Oh, goodness, I don't know where the list would begin. There are species that we cannot contemplate breeding in captivity. Let me give you an example: a great blue whale can be ninety feet long and it requires tons of food a day, so no one would contemplate breeding such a thing in captivity, no matter how rare or endangered. At the other end of the spectrum, there are some rare and interesting birds that are quite difficult to breed simply because of their very specialized food habits. So it's hard to say which species are most difficult to breed. In the first place, we don't know how many species of animals there are.

BLDS: What is the numerical reference that is generally used?

WC: We know that we have today named about 1.7 million species of plants and animals. We know that of these about 27,500 are terrestrial vertebrates, animals with backbones like you and me. And then there are another 26–27,000 that are fishes. Everything from sharks to tunas. Those animals that we think of as being in our world, our family, are a very, very small part of the

whole. The vast majority of species are creatures that bear no resemblance to us: the invertebrates. Everything from different forms of beetles to dragonflies and many marvelous species of plants and fungi.

BLDS: With what frequency do you discover or identify new species?

WC: New vertebrates are discovered very rarely. We have had some wonderful surprises in the past few years, for example, in Laos and Cambodia.

BLDS: What was the surprise there?

WC: A marvelous creature called the *Saola* or *Pseudoryx*, a surprisingly large animal and a distant relative of the bovines. There have been two new species of muntjac deer discovered, quite beautiful and interesting—also in that area. Each year now we are discovering one or two species of birds, but I don't think we can expect this to continue much longer. On the other hand, as long as man seeks species of invertebrates he is going to find them because there are so many out there.

BLDS: Have you discovered any?

WC: No, no. It's not an area of my specialty or expertise.

BLDS: You just discover the people that discover them?

WC: I am interested in finding people who are really concerned, dedicated, and prepared to give their careers and their lives to trying to preserve wildlife.

BLDS: Well, it certainly is a calling. It is surely a way of life. How do you go about recruiting?

WC: People are knocking down the door, but it is very difficult to get people who truly have the kinds of talents needed to become a George Schaller (the Society's director for science), an Alan Rabinowitz (a field scientist), or a Jim Doherty (the general curator at the Bronx Zoo Wildlife Conservation Park). These are difficult people to find and you don't know it when you find them because it takes time for such people to prove themselves. There are so many people coming to us now that it is a little sad. I receive, every month or two, a letter from someone who says, "I am forty-four years old and I am a lawyer," or, "I am in the advertising business," or "I am the executive of something or other, and I have decided that what I am really interested in is trying to do something on behalf of wildlife." These people are seeking a position and want to

> It's just a crime that we're not pushing our national-park system further and that we're not supporting it better.

come and help, but it's difficult to find a place for them.

BLDS: Do you attribute this to a heightened awareness, a new consciousness of life and its limitations and the resources and their limitations?

WC: Well, I'm not sure that's what we have. We have an elected federal government that has attacked the nation's efforts to preserve wildlife in an unprecedented fashion. Perhaps these would-be applicants are reacting to negative conditions, but perhaps they represent a more pervasive dissatisfaction with the rewards of conventional careers. I think it's very interesting that during the Reagan years, when James Watt was in office as secretary of the interior, membership in environmental organizations nearly tripled overnight. As a result of his destructive efforts there was a tremendous response and environmentalists became much stronger, efforts to preserve wildlife became ever so much more focused, and I hope the same thing is happening now.

BLDS: It will take a lot of negotiations to get any meaningful legislation passed.

WC: Anything the Congress passes it can rescind. Although a lot of damage can be done by the Congress's current attitude, it's just a matter of time until these people are brought to their knees by the facts that face them. We have absolutely no understandable dominant party environmental policy. That isn't going to continue. We can't afford it to continue.

BLDS: Well, how has it continued so long? For the last twenty years every schoolchild could tell you about conservation. So why don't we have a national policy yet?

WC: If you are right, we seem to have a lot of people that didn't go to school.

BLDS: Public attitudes toward wildlife have always been a contradictory matter. On the one hand, there is sympathetic concern for the plight of animals and the environment. On the other hand, there is a desire for all the conveniences that endangering animals and the environment bring. How do we proceed? Are there any compromises that are possible or desirable?

WC: There are many, but all of them require intelligence. By and large, we

. . . in 1968 and 1969, just those two years, the United States imported the skins of 3,168 cheetahs, 17,490 leopards, 47,348 jaguars, 262,030 ocelots, and 99,002 otters.

have to address the fact that we have too many people and a lifestyle that is not sustainable. So there isn't any hope that what we are doing can be left to chance. We can't sustain our economy. We can't sustain the way we live. We allow immigrants to come in at the rate of five hundred thousand to nine hundred thousand a year, and they adopt our nonsustainable lifestyle, a lifestyle that uses up the environment at a rate from twenty to thirty times higher than the rates that we find in less developed countries. I fear that the compromises we will eventually be forced to make will sadly reduce the opportunities of our children to realize their potentials as human beings. And why will we do this? Just to have more human beings living less fully?

BLDS: How about international cooperation for the conservation of animals around the globe? Have we approached any agreement?

WC: There was a great deal of collaboration. However, if the current Congress has its way we are going to lose a lot of that collaboration.

BLDS: What about the antifur and antivivisection activists? Do they help or harm your cause?

WC: In the broadest sense, they don't affect it much one way or the other. The antivivisection argument, which is an ethical concern, has no relevance to the conservation picture. It does not affect the survival of wild species. As a moral and ethical concern, it is important. The fur industry today is no longer significant in terms of conservation. That didn't used to be the case. For example, in 1968 and 1969, just those two years, the United States imported the skins of 3,168 cheetahs, 17,490 leopards, 47,348 jaguars, 262,030 ocelots, and 99,002 otters. That was serious. It extinguished many populations, but not species. Elephant-ivory importation was serious. All of those things now have been controlled and the fur trade today, for the most part, is focused on either very abundant species or ranch-raised species.

BLDS: Like minks?

WC: Yes. The use of minks is not significant from a conservation point of view, although it may offend individual ethics. Besides, wool coats are not less destructive to the environment than fur ones. And I'm not at all certain that cotton coats are less damaging. These are points few people understand.

BLDS: So what should we be doing, wearing only synthetic fabrics?

WC: I think that if we wish to be truly nondestructive the best thing we can do is stop having children and run around in the nude!

BLDS: Well, they may be mutually exclusive.

WC: You said it, I didn't! Ultimately we have to reduce our numbers or we simply will not resolve these problems. Beyond reducing our numbers we have to reduce the exuberance of our lifestyle. That's what it comes down to.

BLDS: What do you mean when you say exuberance?

WC: I don't think people can have some of the automobiles that they do. I'm afraid they can't eat so much or travel so much. Compare your lifestyle to that of the person living in Suarez, Mexico, or Timbuktu. And then say, what have I got that he or she doesn't have? That's the difference. Now, if we could reduce our numbers from about six billion people, which is where we are, to about a billion and a half, then we could have a lifestyle pretty much comparable to the one we have. It's a question of fewer people living better or more people living worse.

BLDS: If I am correct, nearly 90 percent of human population growth is taking place where the most abundant and fascinating wildlife dwells, in less developed tropical countries. Are there particular countries, other than our own, in which political and economic goals are preventing attempts to save wildlife?

WC: I'd put it a different way. I don't know any nation anywhere in the world that has a serious national program of conservation that is meant to be or is sustainable and that is considering the long-term maintenance of its living resources.

BLDS: We started to talk about the concept of trying to achieve sustainable development. To me, that suggests responsible planning that considers the implication of the actions that have been taken in the past. I think that your views on the matter of planning differ from those that were shared at the 1992 Rio Summit. Nations have either defined this concept or adapted it in a way that is not in accord with your view.

WC: Sustainable development is a marvelously seductive phrase. I dislike its use when it is applied as a technique to preserve nature. In terms of business operations the phrase is probably entirely legitimate, but to take a natural habitat and through sustainable development maintain its biodiversity is quite unrealistic. In fact, it is an oxymoron. You can have sustainable use, but sustainable development of wildlife resources is pretty tough.

> Beyond reducing our numbers we have to reduce the exuberance of our lifestyle.

BLDS: Have nations taken this concept to heart? Have you seen any improvements since the Rio Summit?

WC: No.

BLDS: So what was the purpose of that big meeting?

WC: Well, the purposes were great. Unfortunately, they weren't put in place. The results of the Rio conference were disappointing, in no small part because the United States has been one of the most reluctant signatories. It takes a concrete program of action. I think Rio spoke on such a large and high plane that it became almost useless. It extended beyond our ability to discuss intelligently. After all, nobody is in charge. There is no set of laws or regulations or penalties imposed by some all-powerful authority—except the natural laws that will be imposed upon us by their environmental authority. And I am certainly unequipped, either by my understanding of the history of the situation or my perception of the future, to say what you can do when you are not putting a program in place that has any realistic human regulatory structure.

BLDS: What about the new programs put in place? And what about the major participation of certain people and organizations that dispense enormous funds to those parts of the world?

WC: They're not enormous, are they?

BLDS: Enormous in terms of what is available, not in terms of what has to be done.

WC: And not in terms of human effort. The combined budgets of all of America's major conservation organizations together is rather less than the annual amount of money used to advertise pet food. It's astonishing what environmental organizations have done with very small amounts of money. However, the fact of the matter is that the Society is really not putting significant money into wildlife conservation or any other kind of conservation—no money for maintaining our home.

BLDS: The conservation of wetlands, which has gained significant attention as an ecological issue, comes within your purview as well. I thought everything was well in place with wetlands, and the next thing I see wetlands legislation is being rewritten. If you change the definition of what constitutes a wetland, it can severely alter what is a fragile resource. And government definitions recently appear to be reducing the definition of what wetland acreage is. Is that accurate?

WC: Yes, they are reducing them. This is another problem with the current Congress. There is a complete lack of understanding. It is disgraceful that we let people out of school who do not have a basic understanding of ecology—and then elect them to office. Ecology is our most basic science. It really relates us to our environment.

BLDS: How does interactive management work? How has it been used in the past and how expensive is that kind of project?

WC: Interactive management, in the sense that I have suggested, is a kind of last-ditch method of sustaining populations of wild creatures and wild areas that would otherwise not be viable. I am trying to deal with the reality that the demographic and genetic and ecological problems of certain small areas are overwhelming. We know today that viability requires quite large populations of most of the animals that we wish to retain over the long term. Attempting preservation with only a few dozen animals simply won't work, so we're forced to look at the situation from the standpoint of caring for wildlife populations and even moving animals around. If, for example, we have an area that cannot support any more than a few hundred animals of a particular species in terms of carrying capacity, the only way such a species can be supported is through some interactive effort. This may mean translocating animals, when the demography or the genetic composition of the population warrants it, either back and forth between wild areas or between captive and wild areas, or supplementing their food, or controlling their competitors. I'm afraid it's a technical rearguard action.

BLDS: So what have you done toward that end?

WC: This is a new approach—identifying problems and possibilities is the task now.

BLDS: Where was the first zoo in New York?

WC: The Central Park Zoo did exist as early as 1864. There was a collection of animals immediately to the west of the Arsenal off Fifth Avenue, and we have etchings and early photographs of it. That actually was the first zoo in the United States.

BLDS: Which animals have the most problems with breeding in captivity?

WC: Where shall I start? As I mentioned, there are literally thousands and thousands of species. We don't keep many things that don't breed well in captivity. Where we have a species that does not do well we work on finding ways to resolve the difficulty. For example, birds of paradise were considered very difficult to breed until recently. As a result of four or five years of research we have now learned how to breed some species of birds of paradise. It's mostly a matter of getting down there and really doing your homework.

BLDS: What has changed in your breeding techniques? What did you learn that you didn't know before?

WC: Birds of paradise are polygynous, meaning one male mates with many females and they do not live together. Yet, you have to put males and females together, at least for a little while, if you are going to be successful in propagation. So how to do it? The females are very choosy; they want to pick only certain males. The old hope was that you would put a male and a female in a lovely habitat and they would breed.

BLDS: And that is paradise.

WC: Yes, but that doesn't work with birds of paradise. It proved necessary to create the opportunities to keep males and females next to but not with each other, let the female pick a male and copulate, and then separate them quickly before the males becomes too aggressive. The female builds a nest by herself, incubates the eggs, and rears the young. Not the modern family at all.

BLDS: It sounds very Antarctican. Are there any projects that are among your priorities in the foreseeable future? Are your priorities a real reach for you to be able to accomplish?

WC: For the Society there are several major things coming up, not the least of which is the big Congo Gorilla Forest exhibit. Construction began in October 1995 and we hope to open in 1999. This is a very, very major exhibit that we hope is going to break totally new ground.

BLDS: How so?

WC: We want visitors who go there to be so connected and involved with the animals that they will make small contributions to enter the exhibit and designate those contributions to specific conservation projects. That way, going to the exhibit becomes an act of conservation. The visitors will actually contribute to the welfare of the animals in nature, not simply the zoo. This is a real stretch from the standpoint of operations and design. We also wish to teach science in new ways in this exhibit, which is very challenging. As far as my personal challenges are concerned, I'm very hopeful that we will finish our Patagonian coastal zone management plan for the Argentines and I am hopeful that we will start some new conservation implementation programs that these plans have outlined. And I am hopeful that in some of the exquisitely beautiful, high altiplano areas of Chile, Argentina, and Bolivia, we will be able to get some new programs going to save some of the most bizarre and beautiful environments in the world, which are headed for certain destruction within the next fifty years.

BLDS: Why are they bizarre?

WC: You have to imagine lakes in which the water is blood red next to lakes in which the water is grass green, smoking volcanoes, geysers, purple flamingos, horned coots, herds of vicuñas!

BLDS: Is it minerals that create the red water?

WC: No, it's algae-diatoms. These very strange areas are hardly known outside. This is a fabulous environment, but it is extremely fragile. In order for it to survive, a big enough chunk must be set aside and protected so that the populations of animals that live there can persist in viable numbers, which means not dozens, but thousands.

BLDS: Given the altitude and other climatic conditions, is it impossible to have any of the flamingos in captivity?

WC: No. I brought several here in 1960 and there have been some in several of the world's zoos. They have even been bred, but to breed them on a major basis would require a very expensive commitment that is unlikely to happen.

BLDS: Is it because no one has the resources to do that?

WC: No. No one has the will but Mother Nature. There are so many wonderful creatures, but they are most wonderful in the places they evolved. Altiplano flamingos are fascinating in zoos, but they are surpassingly beautiful beyond description in their volcano-rimmed red lakes—places to which one might aspire to even make a pilgrimage.

BLDS: What do you consider to be the peak of your achievement at the Wildlife Conservation Center, your own contribution? It need not be the most significant to the outsider, but rather something that in your own mind and heart has had special meaning.

WC: Whether or not I can claim an achievement, I am most keen about starting a basic turn—about getting zoos to become proactive conservation organizations, not simply living museums. This must be the role of zoos in the future. As I said earlier, each year eight or nine hundred million people go to zoos, and virtually every major city in the world has a big zoo—or wants one. What a marvelous foundation for conservation efforts. If you were trying to sell anything from toothpaste to Pepsi Cola, being able to say you've got a branch in every single major city in the world is a great place to start. Now, how do we turn this fact into something that is truly powerful and usable, that helps people recognize that wildlife is something worth saving and they have a chance themselves to contribute to the saving? The answer is to teach and train. Inspire. I am constantly encouraged by people who say, "I got interested in animals when I went to the zoo." Eventually, about

the only place we are going to see animals, outside of those on TV or in books, may be in zoos, as well as in parks and reserves, which zoos must help to preserve. I want to see zoos become the ambassadors for nature in municipal population centers.

BLDS: Are you suggesting that eco-tourism is not only viable but is important to your long-term efforts?

WC: No question about it. It's viable, it's essential. It can handle lots of people, which is a problem we've worried about, simply by doing it right. I am terribly discouraged, however, when I see what is happening to some places, such as the endangerment of the Galápagos Islands by uncontrolled fishing and colonization. We could lose one of the finest, most wonderful wildlife spectacles ever.

BLDS: That's what I wondered when you said it was viable. You see so many places that have been eroded and, in fact, are on the edge of destruction.

WC: Yes, but eco-tourism is helping to provide the financial incentive for protecting many more. Where the eco-tourist potential is realized, those places can't afford destruction. Too many people would lose their jobs. The government of Kenya has built a remarkable eco-tourism system, and David Western of the Kenya Wildlife Service is planning a future that I think is enormously exciting.

BLDS: When you wake up in the morning, what ratchets you up to start your day? Is there a motto, is there something that slides across your consciousness?

WC: Oh, I can hardly wait for the day to begin. I'm one of those people who jumps up in the morning. And I can hardly wait to get up and get to a zoo. I saw a wonderful cartoon that showed a nuclear family waiting at a bus stop: the mother, the father, the daughter, the son. The son was very odd-looking. He had a tail like an alligator and a face like a spiny anteater, and he said, "Well, mother, I'm off to the zoo." And his mother replied, "Well, son, all things considered, it's for the best." I'm in that position. I'm the one with a face like an anteater and a tail like a crocodile. I have visions, but I don't have mottoes. And my visions are wonderful wildlife scenes that I have had the chance to see, but not very many people do.

BLDS: And what are the most recurring ones?

WC: Oh, flamingos. Hooray for flamingos! Flamingos and penguins.

HENRY LOUIS "SKIP" GATES

BLDS: You are now head of the department of African-American Studies at Harvard. What was your first experience in Africa, and how did it affect you?

HLG: When I was an undergraduate at Yale I took part in a program funded by the Mellon Foundation called a Five-Year B.A. It sent twelve people to the third world for one of the five years, not to study but to work. My family was Episcopalian and belonged to something called the Anglican Communion. The diocese of central Tanzania is the sister diocese of the diocese in West Virginia where I grew up. And so, from the age of ten I had always wanted to go to Africa. I was nineteen years old when I was selected for this Yale program. The stipulation was that you find your own job. I thought it would be easier for me to find a job through the church, so I wrote to the bishop of West Virginia. I was a good Episcopalian, I was president of the statewide Episcopal youth, and everybody knew who I was. Through the diocese I got a job at a hospital, which was good because I was pre-med at Yale anyway. I recently made a film for the BBC with my family, and we ended up at the village in the center of Tanzania where I lived twenty-five years ago. I had not corresponded with the village one time in twenty-five years, but the whole village turned out and made me, my daughters, and my wife all members of the tribe. We all cried; they had a big church service for us. It was one of the great events of my life.

BLDS: While you were a student in Tanzania you also visited Zanzibar.

HLG: After six months of this village in the bush, where five hundred people lived in mud huts, I got into a big quarrel with the missionaries over politics, over whether they would expand the hospital with some money that had just been given to them, or if they would irrigate the village by plugging into our water supply, which had been sunk by the Germans in 1890—Tanganyika had been a German colony. In fact, the last battle of World War I was

> That year in Tanzania fundamentally affected my life.

fought in eastern Africa, which most people don't remember. Being a good American, I went to the American U.S.I.S. library and asked the librarian if he would hire me to do some work. He asked if I could make a bibliography of African-American literature, and I said yes. He said he had gone to Harvard in John Kennedy's class. He invited me to stay in his big mansion out in Oyster Bay, which is the nicest part of Dar es Salaam, until my money came from the States. I had cashed in my ticket because I was determined to hitchhike across the equator. One day, while I was waiting for my check, I went down to the dock to sail a *dhow*, an Arab fishing vessel, to Zanzibar. Sheik Karoume was in power, and his revolutionary council, which consisted of fourteen dirty old men, had just passed a law saying that they could take any unmarried virgin in the country as a wife if they wanted to. Shortly after, I am pleased to say, Sheik Karoume was assassinated, but for a brief period he managed to violently deflower several Asian-Indian fourteen- to sixteen-year-old girls. These men were seventy plus. It was one of the most disgusting, officially sanctioned things in the twentieth century. Anyway, at the dock I met a guy named Lawrence Biddleweeks who was a senior at Harvard, and he and I and a couple other people sailed with a crew to Zanzibar for a week. The whole island was covered with cloves; I'll never forget it. The whole island smelled like cloves. There were cloves all over the sidewalks drying in the sun.

BLDS: Not any longer, as you know.

HLG: That's what I understand. We drank tea at four o'clock—it was heavily flavored with cloves—and ate fresh lobster. Everything was so cheap. We stayed in these flophouses, really—I mean cheap hotels. And you would say to the guy downstairs, "I'd love fresh lobster for lunch," and he would go out and catch it, come back, and cook it. It was a fantasy. It must be what it is like to just be able to afford anything you want, any time you want. But it was beautiful. That year in Tanzania fundamentally affected my life.

BLDS: In what way?

HLG: I don't think I would have been a writer otherwise. Maybe it's inevitable that people end up doing what they do, but you can't risk it in retrospect. The first thing I burned out on was the medical training. I gave general anesthesia for 227 operations at a 120-bed hospital that serviced a district of fifty thousand people. I saw all kinds of horrible stuff that I would never see in medical school in the United States, and I knew that I didn't really want to be a doctor. For example, one woman came in and said she was pregnant for two years, and so we knew it was a tumor. We took a basketball-sized tumor out of her stomach. It was benign, thank God. You would never see that in the United States.

BLDS: So that was the end of pre-med.

HLG: I just knew that it was not for me. I was sitting in my bedroom at Yale, at Calhoun College, with this girl who I was trying to make, right? We were on my bed, and I was making some grand claim about when I'm a great surgeon and she said, "What bullshit. You will never be a doctor." I said, "Why?" I was deeply offended. And she said, "Look at all of those books. Not one book about science or medicine." I looked—the bookshelves happened to be right there running alongside of the bed—and it was like I had been nailed to the wall. I had been pinned, like a specimen to the page. And I went into deep denial. The next morning I woke up and ran down to the Yale coop, the campus bookstore, and I bought a book about medicine called *Blacks in Medicine*. I came back from Africa as a junior, but because of the five-year B.A. program, all my friends from my class were now seniors. I had lost a year. And they were editing things like the *Yale Daily News*, which was a big deal. It was like the *Harvard Crimson*. People like Henry Luce had worked on the *Daily News*. My friends said, "Look, why don't you do a guest column about your experience in Africa?" I had always written well; I knew that. My teachers had always rewarded me for my writing but it was like an avocation. I had great anxiety about writing these articles but, no matter what

the anxiety was, I wrote them anyway. I managed to overcome that fear and I published several articles in the *Yale Daily News*. One day John Morton Blum, who was my mentor and a great historian, singled me out in a lecture class of two hundred people and said, "Mister Gates, that was an excellent article you published in today's paper." Everybody turned to see who this little colored kid was. I felt great, and I was hooked. It took me a while, it took a lot of gyrations, to get here, but I was essentially hooked on having an idea, shaping it, publishing it, and then seeing the reaction. It's a miracle, actually.

BLDS: By the way, in your memoir, *Colored People*, you use the term *colored*. What is the preferred term now, and why? Is it *colored*? Is it *African American*? Is it *black*? Is it *person of color*?

HLG: It depends on who you're talking to. Nobody prefers *colored*. I prefer *colored* in the sense that it is used when black people are with themselves. When they are most culturally intimate they most often slip effortlessly into the word *colored*. But it's just such a beautiful term—you couldn't use it every day. I would say I am an African American. And among my peers that's the term of preference. But then a lot of people use black. Probably more people use black than anything else.

BLDS: And what about those black persons who are not African American but West Indian?

HLG: Yes, they still call themselves black.

BLDS: I thought there was a status demarcation, too.

HLG: Well, it depends. It's really across the map. Most people use American to describe the New World—South America, Central America, and North America. So a person of African descent in the New World often describes herself or himself as an African American, even if they're not from the continent of the United States. But the other thing about West Indians is that they are Jamaicans or Haitians or Trinidadians; they have nationalities. It's very complicated. There's no simple answer to your question. There have been enormous class tensions between West Indians and African Americans in New York City, which is pretty much the only place the two have been juxtaposed.

BLDS: You have written in very interesting and widely quoted ways about Colin Powell. Among other things, you called Colin Powell the conciliator, and O. J. Simpson the divisor.

HLG: Right. The metaphor of division.

BLDS: If you're using this metaphor, how then would you describe Jesse Jackson?

© Sarah Putnam

HLG: I think that Jesse Jackson has played an enormously important historical role for black people. As I said in the *New Yorker*, he was the first black person to run for the presidency of black America. In the second place, he has been a conscience for corporate America. People are terrified of him. For General Motors, it's like getting a telegram in the middle of the war. You know, Jesse is outside, Mike Wallace is in the waiting room. Just as you do not want Mike Wallace to pay an unscheduled visit, you do not want Jesse Jackson to be boycotting your product, because black people take such measures very seriously. I think that his ability to be that conscience is one of his two most important strengths. The second most important thing is the fact that Jesse dared to imagine that he could be president. That was important. And he won a lot of votes. Colin Powell would not have existed within the context of the American political system, in 1995, had there not been a Jesse Jackson in 1984 and '88 running for president of the United States.

BLDS: So did Colin Powell take away his birthright, so to speak?

HLG: Absolutely. Jesse needs a new job description. And I think Colin Powell's cousin, Bruce Llewellyn, gave the best description of what Jesse is strong at, and what he should do. He should be our shakedown artist. He should make sure that all these companies have their 10 percent, approximately, of black people, and have a good distribution of black people.

BLDS: And what should you do?

HLG: My role is to call it the way I see it, and to write it as long as people keep publishing me. That's what I'm going to keep doing. You go crazy, you become paralyzed if you sit around and think about what your role is. People tend to do what feels good to them and they avoid the things that don't feel good to them. As long as it feels good to teach and write, I'll teach and write. When you think about it, somebody pays me to talk to smart people, some of the smartest people in the country—the students that go to a place like Harvard University. That's a fantasy.

BLDS: Why are you at Harvard rather than Yale, which would seem to have been a natural place for you to be?

HLG: I did teach at Yale. When I was thirty-three Cornell made me an offer. I was an assistant professor at Yale, about to be promoted to associate professor, but without tenure. Cornell was going to make me a full professor. The ritual is that you take the offer back to your home institution. The people at Yale basically said, "Write another book and we'll consider it," but it was said with so much hostility that it was clear they were sending me a message. I left Yale in 1985.

BLDS: Who was then president of Yale?

HLG: Bart Giamatti. It wasn't his decision; it was the decision of my colleagues in the English department. Two years before, I received the MacArthur prize. I was the youngest MacArthur humanist, and it really pissed a lot of people off. Plus, I was outspoken, and very daring in my interpretations. I pushed the limit. I think they made a mistake. And I think that they think they made a mistake. And, if not, they should think that they made a mistake. I was the same person then, but I'm so much more public now. Everybody who cares knows where I stand on just about everything. My first two academic books were already in manuscript when I was at Yale. They had been in the world for years, they had been reviewed, they even won prizes. But people had to read them in typescript and decide what they meant. I can't represent myself as a victim, but my fantasy was just to stay at Yale. I'm a Yalie, as you know. I loved Yale. And I would have built the greatest center for African-American studies that I possibly could have at Yale. But they didn't, and I didn't, and I went, and now I'm here. Now I'm happy as a clam.

BLDS: Is there now a center of African-American studies at Yale?

HLG: Yes.

BLDS: A conspicuous one?

HLG: Yes, it's in the top ten.

BLDS: Who runs it?

HLG: Several good professors. They rotate the chairmanship. My friend Gerald Jaymes is the current chair. The department is quite good. Some people would say it's the best, some people would say it's in the top three, I would say it's in the top ten.

BLDS: You think the Harvard department is the best.

HLG: Yes. I think we're the best because we have the best people. What makes any department good? The quality of the faculty, the number of publications they publish, and their influence. We have all those qualities. As a war we are in spades with each of them.

BLDS: So is it fair to say that that old story about publish or perish really impeded your progress at Yale, or was that an excuse?

HLG: No, I published.

BLDS: Does that proscription still exist?

HLG: Yes, it certainly exists, and will always exist at the research institutions; and it should exist. I had published a lot, I just hadn't

> I think that Jesse Jackson has played an enormously important historical role for black people.

published a book. But I had books accepted in press. It came early, my offer, and it was designed to be a preemptive strike. But I don't even think that if I had published a book it would have mattered, because I was so controversial. Steven Newhouse tells the story about hearing me talk once to Yale's old-guard English department about black literature and multiculturalism—they thought I was like Karl Marx or somebody. Depending on the context, one's political ideology can be misperceived, and mine was. I was just perceived as much more radical than I really am.

BLDS: I don't see you as radical, I only see you as the sensible centrist, in many ways.

HLG: Right, that's what I'd like to be. And that's how I'd like to be remembered. But to advocate teaching W. E. B. Du Bois or Zora Neale Hurston in 1980 is not the same as advocating it in 1995. It was much more daring and threatening then. At the time I got my Cornell offer the Yale English department bounced black applicants over to American Studies, believing they couldn't possibly be interested in the study of English. There was a lot of implicit racism going down that had been institutionalized and nobody knew it.

BLDS: Not so long ago you asked if there was a leadership crisis in black America and I think you said that what was needed is a politics that looks beyond racial unanimity. Is that accurate? And who do you see filling that gap?

HLG: The thirty-five million black Americans.

BLDS: Are there thirty-five million, thirty, or twenty-five? I have a quote from you—a very recent one—where you make reference to thirty.

HLG: Yes, that's because the editor at the publication changed it. But my sources say thirty-five.

BLDS: How did you come up with thirty-five? Nobody else uses that figure.

HLG: It's what the census bureau figured, plus the people I think they missed.

BLDS: What is the "official" census?

HLG: Thirty million people. It's the *New Yorker* fact checker's figure, so you're probably safe with that.

BLDS: And you are saying there are five million that are unaccounted for. Are they illegal immigrants?

> The idea that you would harm someone because they were gay or lesbian or Jewish or black or Armenian or Bosnian should be beyond the realm of possibility for any thinking, rational person.

HLG: There are twenty-seven million Canadians. No one would even think to claim that Canadians would ever speak with one voice. Yet this mythology persists that African Americans should or will somehow miraculously think with one brain and speak with one mouth. It's absurd. What we have to recognize is that we are going to have people on the left, on the right, and in the center; we are going to have people in the upper classes, in the middle classes, and in the lower classes. What we need to fight for is freedom of intellectual and ideological and artistic expression, as well as a shift in what I call the bell curve of class. By that I mean we shouldn't have a higher percentage of our people in the lower classes than any other ethnic group in the United States. In the middle classes we should be as well represented as the best ethnic group in the United States, and the same with the upper classes, but we are not. That's the problem.

BLDS: In May of 1995 you delivered a commencement address at Emory University, in which you talked about the contingent nature of all human identities. What does this mean and how does it underline your own approach?

HLG: You have to learn who you are. You're not born a Jew, you're not born black, you're not born gay, you're not born an Episcopalian. You become these things. And the reason that this small little point is important is because people think that these identities are issued by God or something, that they're like oxygen or like gravity, but they're not. They're socially constructed. And not only are they constructed, but they are constructed in relationship to other identities that are also socially constructed. That means that we are all in the soup together, which is the bottom line. The idea that you would harm someone because they were gay or lesbian or Jewish or black or Armenian or Bosnian should be beyond the realm of possibility for any thinking, rational person. And it's not. In the last four years there has been ethnic violence reported by the U.N. in forty-eight nations. Ethnoviolence, they call it, by which they mean I'll cut your throat or rape you in the name of your religious difference or in the name of your grandfather's ethnic identification. And that's disgusting. I think that all of us who care about human learning and care about the future of humanity have to unite to fight that. Unfortunately, I don't think enough people are alarmed. If we talk about the O. J. Simpson decision,

Mark Fuhrman should have been banished from the police force. That is the bottom line. It should have been intolerable for the police force to keep him on, knowing his attitudes, but it's not. I think that's why black people are deliriously happy with the verdict, and why, despite the fact that many people thought that the scientific evidence pointed overwhelmingly toward O. J.'s guilt, the people took a perverse pleasure out of that verdict. I found it astonishing myself. You could have knocked me over with a feather, because I just presumed that he was going to jail. That was clearly what it was about. In my experience more people—behind closed doors—thought that he really was guilty, but if white people were asking them, who knows what they would say. Of the people I interviewed for the article I wrote for the *New Yorker*, many thought that he was innocent, and these were the upper class, the black elite. The range of response goes from he was guilty as sin to he was innocent, and then that it was drug related. I don't know what the truth is. I think it's fascinating, though.

BLDS: What may be the most significant result of the entire trial is that it has gotten people to talk about racism. It is one of the few times that the issue has been confronted by large numbers of people.

HLG: I think it's great. It makes people confront and talk about their differences. What I don't like are the stories of people refusing to talk about it, because arguing is what America is all about. America was born as an argument. And so I like that.

BLDS: What is your opinion of the Christian right?

HLG: I think that most Americans are disgusted by the Christian right—except them. Do you know the old definition of a zealot? A zealot is a person who knows what God would do if God only had all the facts. Most people do not want that kind of person running their lives, because the zealot is going to climb into their bedrooms and into their heads and into their offices. Nobody really wants that, only a handful of nuts. The average American is a pretty centered, decent kind of person. I fundamentally believe that.

BLDS: What is the recovery movement, and what is your relationship to it?

HLG: The recovery movement is a general term for people who are drugged out and seeking help. I use it as a metaphor. We should all think of ourselves as recovering racists or anti-Semites or sexists—people who are guilty of this affliction but who need to work harder to overcome it.

BLDS: There is so much discussion about multiculturalism and about the black experience as a course of study. One of the most encouraging things you are doing is developing a canon.

HLG: I'm a canon maker. What I chose to do was to be general editor of the *Norton Anthology of African-American Literature.* I asked ten other people to help me. I divided up the responsibility among other leaders in our field. Each expert is responsible for a historical period. In a way, I democratized the decision-making process but, in the end, all selections are somebody's selections. They're arbitrary. They're not given by Plato, they're not vouchsafed by God. They are just someone's selections. You can only do it with as much integrity as you can muster to be able to say, I think this work is more sophisticated than that work, I think this one is more representative in some way. You say, these are my selection principles, take them or leave them, and some will take them and some will leave them. That's true of every anthology, every canon. The same is true of every academic department.

BLDS: From what I understand you are going through the literature and finding a literary tradition.

HLG: The larger literature project is concerned with creating the tradition. The tradition means everything written by people of African descent. The canon contains the jewels. The things that you think are the best, the most representative—whatever meets your criteria. My first project was just to bring everything back that has been lost. So I published forty volumes in what is called the Schomburg Library of African-American women's literature. Then we just published a new series with Macmillan, which is a continuation into the twentieth century of the literature published by black women between 1900 and 1930. Many of these books are out-of-print, too. The main thing is to do it so that subsequent generations never have to do it again. Black people are cursed with having to reinvent the wheel. It's like being cursed with no memory beyond the short-term memory. One of the things that I am determined to do, along with many other people of my generation and our respective subdivisions of African-American studies, is to bring all the tools back, to create the tradition. Hence, my preoccupation in the last fifteen years with something called the black periodical literature project, which is digging up all the stuff that is in the columns of newspapers. Serialized novels, short stories, poems, book reviews, and even

> Do you know the old definition of a zealot? A zealot is a person who knows what God would do if God only had all the facts.

obituaries—it's such a huge repository about actual black people who really lived. Everybody has to die and you die in your local newspaper, right? No one ever thought of going through the newspapers and collecting this information, but that's one of the things that we're doing.

BLDS: Do you have any plans to work on an oral history?

HLG: I think there are CD-ROM possibilities. There are zillions of histories that have been done in bits and pieces with the CD-ROM. I'm trying to raise money for the *Encyclopedia Africana*. It will be like the *Encyclopedia Judaica* or the *Encyclopedia Britannica*, but it would be for black people. It could have a CD-ROM component, like Encarta. The idea is to preserve, in A-to-Z fashion, the lives and times of the great people in our history.

BLDS: Who is the most influential black man in America today?

HLG: Vernon Jordan.

BLDS: You've said that in print, but does that still hold true?

HLG: Yes, because nobody sits on more boards controlling major international capital than Vernon Jordan. He has more say than any other single black person in history. He has more say within the corridors of corporate power. That's real power. Power is not being on the cover of *Ebony* magazine.

BLDS: So who is the most powerful black woman in America?

HLG: There is no female corporate counterpart to Vernon Jordan because of sexism. It could have been Barbara Jordan at one time. Maya Angelou has an enormous amount of one kind of power—she reaches more readers than anybody. But that's not the kind of power you're talking about.

BLDS: Where does Toni Morrison come into this? Or Jessye Norman?

HLG: They are different. Are they great? Are they Nobel laureates? Yes. Is that important? Of course. But they don't have power as Vernon Jordan has power. Toni Morrison might have power over our hearts. Vernon Jordan has power over our lives. And that's a big difference.

BLDS: What is the civil-rights agenda of the Du Bois Institute and how does that philosophy affect your work?

HLG: I believe that the future for the African American is right here. The future of America by and large will be determined by how well it deals with the problems of racism and economic scarcity. What I want the Du Bois Institute to be about is bringing people together—all races, all genders, all sexual preferences, whatever—to study how race and class actually work in America. How can we create a society—not just the cliché of a better society, but an equitable society, a fair society. Every day I walk through Harvard Square, and I climb over a woman who sleeps there. It's absurd. I run the gauntlet from this corner on Church Street over to the Holyoke Center and think, who did I give five bucks to last month? From whom am I going to buy the "homeless person" newspaper this month? I'm not saying this to get something for myself, I'm saying that people should not have to live as these people live. Something is fucked up about this country when that is the way it is. And it's even more disgusting when a Republican majority can be elected on a program of throwing people off the little bit of benefit that they get. I'm not that crazy about the pope, but I'm fascinated by his charisma. I thought it was interesting that he was preaching to America to fulfill its historical obligation to live up to its own ideals. That was a brilliant rhetorical strategy. He said, "Don't look, just be yourselves. Let's let America be America." I thought that was very clever. The point is, in terms of individual opportunity and access to democracy, all things being equal, there's never been anything like this country. In another place and time I would have been a servant. I would have been serving you in most societies. I would have been a flunky.

BLDS: That is not necessarily so.

HLG: It is necessarily so.

BLDS: In fact, to quote you, you're saying that the realities of race do not affect all blacks in the same way.

HLG: No, they don't.

BLDS: So you're making a generalization that certainly someone of your extraordinary gifts would have succeeded no matter where you came from.

HLG: Not under slavery. Not without certain democratic reforms and revelations about personal color. Under slavery I would have been a slave with the same brain. I would have had no choice. Under de jure segregation, how many black people were able to escape and come to Harvard? Two a year. I have a picture of them out there on that wall. Look at it. It's devastating.

BLDS: Not thinking of all blacks in the same way, are there actually different realities of race?

> The future of America by and large will be determined by how well it deals with the problems of racism and economic scarcity.

HLG: There always were.

BLDS: How would you define the realities of race today?

HLG: There always were different realities. I mean, one of the people most eloquent about this was Norman Podhoretz. He talks about what it was like being Jewish at home and speaking Yiddish and being a faux-WASP at Columbia. And it's very moving. Those of us in America who had any kind of hyphenated identity understand that tension. You always were bifurcated. You always were schizophrenic. There always was a vernacular culture at home—mother's milk culture, church culture, underground, sub-rosa, subterranean, whatever word you want to use for it. And then there always was the "around white people." That's the way we would put it. And I'm sure Jewish people would say a similar thing, something like "around the Goyim."

BLDS: What is your vision for this country's future?

HLG: My vision is to have a class division in this society that looks the same by race, so that the bell curve of class looks the same for white people as it does for people of color. That's going to take about a hundred trillion dollars.

BLDS: Is it only money that stands in the way? You didn't say it would take a hundred trillion years.

HLG: No, it's money and programs. It's not just money, it is allocating the money for the right kind of programs. And I don't think that we know what those are.

BLDS: What were your reactions to the Million Man March?

HLG: Well, Colin Powell called me the night before to tell me that it was going to be a major phenomenon, and it was. It was quite moving. I also thought its great success was to have a million black men converging on Washington for no other reason than to say we are here, we have endured, we are. The unfortunate part was Farrakhan's rambling four-hour speech, and the fact that the event was called by Farrakhan, and that probably only Farrakhan could have gotten that many men to come. But his speech was ridiculous. The great tragedy was that in the great speech of atonement, the atoner failed to atone. That was one of the ironies of the march, and one of the reasons that it will not, I predict, have a lasting structural impact on American politics or even on the social development of the African-American community.

BLDS: There have been several attempts to improve the education of minority youths by providing separate schools with programs designed to help them excel academically. Because many of these schools only allow African-American boys, they have been accused of racism and sexism. Are these schools really better for these boys, and is it fair to limit entry based on race or sex?

HLG: Let's address the sex issue first. There are all sorts of single-sex schools, and I believe in them, as long as they are not supported by public funds. The more I read about VMI and the more I understand what it means to be an adolescent girl, I think that some girls need to go to school with only girls, and maybe it would be good for all boys. The state of African-American public education is so bad that I'm willing to let anything be tried to see the results, because it probably can't worsen it. In terms of single-race schools, most black kids go to single-race schools now. Most black people go to segregated schools, but they're not segregated legally; they're segregated by neighborhood. I would be against any form of legal segregation, but de facto segregation can only be resolved, not through busing, but through funding. In fact, that might answer the busing issue. We should bus the money from school districts like Lexington, Massachusetts, where my kids are going to public school, into places like Roxbury, so there's an equal amount per capita for each schoolchild in the whole state. I think it can only be solved by economic integration, so that in the long run you integrate neighborhoods. That is going to take a long time to accomplish. The issue is very complicated.

BLDS: The milestone decision of *Brown vs. Board of Education* occurred just four years after your birth. Now four decades have passed since that decision. Do you think America is still a divided nation, and will America be described as a racist country in the twenty-first century?

HLG: America is still divided, but the division is more subtle than it was before. Within the African-American communities, I've written before, it's the best of times and it's the worst of times. We have the largest black middle class in history, but also the largest black underclass. Forty-five percent of all black children live at or beneath the poverty line. One in three black men between the ages of twenty and twenty-nine are in the care of the prison system. That is a divided society, right there. Before 1954 all blacks lived in the inner city. It wasn't that all blacks were poor, but they all lived in ghettoized, segregated neighborhoods. Now, Vernon Jordan doesn't live in a segregated neighborhood; Harry Belafonte doesn't

> Most black people go to segregated schools, but they're not segregated legally; they're segregated by neighborhood.

live in a segregated neighborhood. More blacks live in New Rochelle and Scarsdale and all those places than have ever lived there before. And being black and poor is not the same as being black and rich, or even being black and economically comfortable. Before desegregation there was much more commonality to the black experience. Now, the black experience has been fissured by class. That's the prime difference. Reverend Benjamin May said eleven o'clock on Sunday morning was the most segregated hour in American society, and it still is. Most black people go to church with black people and most white people with white people, but they do it by choice. So, I would say that there is more fluidity on one level in society, but because of structural poverty there is still a very large segment of the population that is not assimilated into the American economy or the American culture. But if many of us thought the civil-rights movement was about black culture disappearing, about being integrated into a mulatto blend, then most of us now don't really want to see that happen. I don't want to see poor people living together in a segregated community because they are poor. If they live together by choice, fine. You see many buppie communities, like the one in Prince George's County, Maryland, that exist because people want to live in upper-middle-class black neighborhoods, and there's absolutely nothing wrong with it.

BLDS: Did you expect your life to unfold the way it has?

HLG: I was raised to think that I would be successful at something. My mother and my brother always made me feel that I was special. In fact, our whole community reinforced the idea that we were special; even the school system did. Fantasy, like everything else, is relative. For me it was that I would be a successful doctor because the most successful people I could see in Piedmont, West Virginia, were doctors. Eventually, my notions of what success meant and what would make me feel successful changed quite dramatically. It wasn't until after Yale, quite frankly, when I was a graduate student at the University of Cambridge, that I realized deep down what I wanted to be. I'd always loved writing, and always been rewarded and praised for my writing by my school teachers, but I had considered it an avocation, something to do on the way to medical school. Gradually, I realized, with an enormous amount of fear, that deep down I wanted to be the author of a book. I couldn't imagine how I could ever be that.

BLDS: Are these the best years of your life?

HLG: Oh, absolutely. Well, I said that too quickly. I was raised in a warm and nurturing family in Piedmont. That cocoonlike feeling that I often had was irreplaceable. I can't even imagine having it again. It felt good then, it feels good in retrospect. I often wonder if my children, my two daughters, feel that way with me as their father. I don't think of myself as an old man, I think of myself the way I was when my mother and father were around, and then I realize I have these two people dependent upon me—I wonder if I'm doing for them what my parents did for me? My parents did create a very warm environment for me, despite the fact that we argued and things like that. I had a very privileged life within the context of a paper-mill town in West Virginia. And it's because I had a loving, strong, stable mother; and my father always worked two jobs so that we always had more money than everybody else. It sounds ironic to say it now, but I lived like a rich kid, and compared to everybody else I was. I got a new car when I was eighteen, I always had new clothes and got new textbooks, and I was always treated that well. My mother always had cash whenever I needed it. It was a good deal. Professionally, this is certainly the best time of my life. My student years were glorious times, though. I had a great education at Yale and I was very happy there, virtually every day. That was also a very privileged, special time. I've had a good life for a long time. It just becomes good in different ways. I've been a very lucky person. I'm deeply humbled by my good fortune.

BLDS: By the way, how did you ever get the nickname Skip?

HLG: My name at birth was Louis Smith Gates. Smith came from my mother's best friend, an elderly unmarried woman who was Olivia Smith. My mother had promised Olivia, for God knows whatever reason, that her next child would be named after her. Had I been a girl I would have been named Olivia, which I thought was okay, but they hated the name Oliver, so I was Louis Smith Gates. When I was old enough to change my name—I was twenty-five and had come back from England—I changed it to my father's name. My brother, Paul Edwards, is nicknamed Rocky. God only knows where these arbitrary names come from. My family is big on nicknames.

BLDS: You were born in Kaiser, West Virginia, in 1950 and were named West Virginian of the Year in 1995. Do you still go back there, and what changes have you seen in the town and the residents since you left?

HLG: I go back there quite a lot. Now that my father doesn't live there anymore and my mother is dead, I don't go back to Piedmont, but I do go to places nearby. It's very beautiful. It's two hours west of Washington on the Potomac River in the Allegheny Mountains. I like to fish there. It's quite stunningly beautiful. Many young people don't live there anymore. The town of Piedmont has fallen down economically. The schools have been consolidated; therefore, the people who have children all now live in Kaiser because they don't want their kids riding buses on the mountain roads. Without a school, I realize that Piedmont is pretty much on its last legs. A lot of the black people will continue to stay there, but many of the white people have left. It's a poor town, it doesn't have a strong tax base, and it's not as beautiful as it used to be, but I think there will be a movement to tear down the old buildings, to pick up the trash, to do that kind of thing. There are amazingly beautiful houses for sale there. For fifty thousand dollars you can get a mansion. It's a remarkably cheap place to live, and the people there are still very good, but I don't see it being around fifty years from now. On the other hand, it's within smelling distance of the paper mill, and so as long as there is work at that paper mill, and as long as workers choose to live near the factory, some will live in Piedmont, particularly young African Americans.

BLDS: Do you consider the South your home?

IILG. No. West Virginia is really a border state and Piedmont is a suburb of Washington, being two hours to the west of the city. So I consider myself a mountaineer rather than a Southerner.

BLDS: What haven't you done yet that you would care to do?

HLG: I'd care to write a great book about African-American culture and African-American literary history—or a history of African-American literature. I'd like to go the Far East. I've been China, but I'd like to go to Vietnam and Thailand. I'd like to the Galápagos Islands. I'd like to see a lot more of the world I have.

BLDS: What's next for you?

HLG: What's next for me? To edit the *Encyclopedia Afr* Internet, I hope, so that I can help my people to go future!

★ ★ ★ ★ *Conversation with* ★ ★ ★ ★

LARRY KRAMER

BLDS: Let's begin with your adult beginning. Can you describe your world? It is 1958, you are fresh ⸺m Yale and the army, and seeking a career in ⸺heater. When did you decide that theater ⸺your course?

⸺The world is one thing, and what I ⸺do in it was another. In 1958 I was ⸺hopeful. I was working as a mes- ⸺for the William Morris Agency ⸺around for the opportunity that ⸺foot in a door somewhere and take ⸺tep. I think I was always conscious ⸺vement had to be achieved some- ⸺to find how to put each foot ahead of ⸺hing was supposed to stay the same. I had ⸺d William Morris was a very exciting ⸺rk, in the sense that I really thought ⸺g. We got to read everybody's mail ⸺ world out there. I don't think I ⸺e worked very hard at William ⸺ng to cover things—to see ⸺ guys in the mail room. ⸺ut to the ⸺I

> If I knew I was gay, it was something that was put to the side and dealt with only on the odd occasion when I would sneak into a gay bar or meet someone.

and-whisper-low" kind of places. They were just friendly neighborhood bars that guys would go to. But it was a frightening experience for me, because it was a part of my life, a part of myself, that I didn't understand. It was a hunger that was bringing me there, not a desire to stop by for a beer with the boys. One went there for a specific reason, which was to somehow meet a guy and go home and have some intimacy that would then be forgotten about the next day as you went back to work and your job.

BLDS: What first caused you to be intrigued by theater, especially coming from such a nontheater town as Washington was then? Was your family interested in it?

LK: I had loved the theater since I was a little boy and used all my allowance to go sit in the second balcony of the National Theater or the Shubert Theater every other week when the show changed. And Washington did have its share of theaters. First, it was the National. The Shubert came later. And then when I was about ten, maybe younger, the Arena Theater opened. Zelda Fichandler started it. The Arena was right around the corner from the temple where I would go to Hebrew school on Saturday, so I would go to matinees all the time. I don't know where my interest came from. My mother claims to have always loved the theater and was supportive of me, but no one pushed me into it.

BLDS: Did you study theater at Yale?

LK: No, I was a regular undergraduate. The theater school was something separate. My father, a number of uncles on both sides of my family, and my brother had all gone to Yale, so there wasn't any question that I would go to Yale. It wasn't even an option to go anywhere else. My father ripped up my Harvard application, which I actually filled out.

BLDS: You don't regret that, do you?

LK: I didn't. My brother had wanted me to go to Swarthmore because he had been to Yale and he knew that I would have been better off at a small school, which I probably would have been. I was not happy at Yale. It was a white-shoe place, to use an expression that isn't used anymore. It was upper class, trendy, stylish, fraternity-oriented, a far cry from what it is now. An enormous number of the kids had come from private schools, but I had come from a public school, and I didn't get into a fraternity, and I didn't play sports.

BLDS: Did getting into a fraternity interest you?

LK: Yes. It was the thing to do. There was no question that it helped you socially. You were a weenie if you didn't have some kind of a social outlet. I was fortunate that I tried out for, and got into, the glee club in my freshman year; and I got into the Yale varsity glee club in my sophomore year, which was a big deal; and then I got elected into a singing group, which was an even bigger deal. At Yale, then and now, singing is a big deal—you know, the Whiffenpoofs and all that—so that became my social outlet.

BLDS: Were you one of the Whiffenpoofs, too?

LK: No. They didn't let Jews in the group in those days. At all. The glee club and the singing group took me around the country, and it took me to girls' schools, so I had a social life through singing. I really think it saved me and kept me going in a way that the university did not. Yale was not a nice place in those days. I don't think enough has been written about the horrors of trying to conform to some kind of mysterious, almost gentile, norm of what's expected. I have become very attached to Yale in the intervening years for one reason or another, but—oh, let's face it, I tried to kill myself in my freshman year. I went into therapy right after that and was in psychoanalysis for the four years I was there, so it is not a time and place I look back on with great fondness. I was not involved in the theater. I would like to have been, but again the theater then was a very elite crowd. It was composed of people like Dick Cavett and Carrie Nye, people who actually went on to have their own careers.

> To me, there's no question that the play form is the hardest. Screenplays are a piece of cake and actually rather boring to write. . . . A novel is just a great big box or an envelope into which you can throw anything you want to.

The director of it was a man called Leo Lavandero who played favorites with everyone. It was very hard to break into. Austin Pendleton was there; I'm sure I can think of others.

BLDS: You've said that it's ten times harder to write a play that works than a novel, and it's a hundred times harder to write a play than a screenplay. What's the difference? Can you explain it?

LK: Someday I'd like to teach a course on the different kinds of writing because, for one reason or another, I have been successful in maneuvering through them all and in trying to pinpoint the differences between the different forms. They are very different. To me, there's no question that the play form is the hardest. Screenplays are a piece of cake and actually rather boring to write. I'm always amazed that so many people want to do it, because it's the least creative and the least interesting form for a writer. You're basically just writing a jerry-built blueprint for somebody else's building.

BLDS: You write dialogue, so that's why it's an easy form for you.

LK: But dialogue is not something that's very welcome in movies. Screenwriters today basically just outline shots. I think one of the things that's gone wrong with movies is that they've stopped speaking. If you look back at the movies that we all loved so much, there was an awful lot of talking, and there were wonderful actors talking that talk. That isn't there today. The thing that's hardest about a play is that it has only so many pages, so many hours of time, and you have to find a way of making people sit there, surrounded by all the other people in the audience, and lose themselves. That's not as easy as people think, and it's not necessarily narrative that makes them sit there. I think it's much more the tensions and interactions between characters and the things that don't get said rather than what does get said. A novel is just a great big box or an envelope into which you can throw anything you want to. It can be enormously long, you can go off on tangents, skip around in time, tell the story from different points of view. You're not confined so much and you have free range to everything. You can tell the history of the world, you can write *War and Peace,* you can write eight zillion characters; you can't do that on the stage easily. You can go inside a person's mind in a novel, which you can't do either in a movie or on the stage. Also, a novel is very much an individual relationship between a reader and the writer, whereas in a play or a movie you're inviting a lot more people to share that experience.

BLDS: How did you move from operating a teletype machine at Columbia Pictures to producing your first film at age thirty-three, and what was that film?

LK: Do you mean *Women in Love* or *Here We Go Round the Mulberry Bush*? I can't remember.

BLDS: *Mulberry Bush.*

LK: You're talking about ten years in there. They often seem like very, very long years in which I was never going to get anywhere, but, in essence, it was a fairly straightforward progression. I was a messenger boy at William Morris, and I got fired on my birthday. That weekend there was an ad in the *New York Times* for a motion-picture trainee.

BLDS: Why did you get fired, by the way?

LK: Oh, because I was being pushy, being very ambitious, and I frightened several people, especially an agent called Phyllis Rab who was part of the theatrical department where I was assigned. I think they really felt, "Better get rid of this one before he becomes too much of a pain in the ass." Years later, when I went to Hollywood to show *Women in Love,* I was in an office building and there was the name—it said Phyllis Rab. I walked into the office and there was this woman who had been a big agent in New York and was now in Los Angeles working at a little desk under a stairway. I went in and said, "Ms. Rab, you don't remember me, but you had me fired on my twenty-third birthday and I just want to thank you. It was the best thing that ever happened to me."

BLDS: How did she respond to that?

LK: She just looked up at me and I walked out. Anyway, after William Morris I got a job at Columbia Pictures as a teletype operator. It was one of those good breaks, because my office was right across from that of the president, Abe Schneider, and all the vice-presidents were there: Leo Jaffe, Paul Lazarus. I got to know them and they got to like me. Gradually they entrusted me with more and more assignments. Then a wonderful man called Mo Rothman, who was then head of Columbia Pictures International, took me under his wing and made me a member of his family. He used to say things like, "If you don't go to my secretary at least three times a week to get free movie passes to one of the theaters in town, I want to know why."

BLDS: Was he a great influence on your life?

LK: Yes. He got me a job in London as a production executive at Columbia, which changed my life.

BLDS: Who are, and were, the greatest influences on your writing and in your life? Are they the same people?

LK: Certain people have helped me a lot in business by giving me breaks. Mo got me my job at Columbia. In the 1960s London was a much more important film capital than anywhere else in the world, so it was very exciting. A man called David Picker, for whom I worked as an assistant at United Artists, gave me my first opportunity to write a screenplay and put me into production with *Mulberry Bush.* So I have been lucky with people helping me. My brother Arthur, of course, has been my biggest influence in everything—my education, my psychoanalysis, my career, my financial wherewithal. I don't think I'd be alive today if it hadn't been for him. In terms of influences on my writing, I really have to say that I think I made it on my own. I had nothing but discouragement for many years: teachers at Yale saying no, you'll never be a writer; your stuff is no good; why don't you do something else. A lot of that. And the fact that I became a writer had more to do with desperation, I think, than anything else. For instance, when the person who was employed to write the screenplay for *Women in Love* did a terrible job, and I didn't have any more money to pay for another writer, and the movie was about to go down the tubes, I literally holed myself up in an apartment and wrote it.

BLDS: Were you then producing it?

LK: I was producing it only. I had used every bit of money that I made on *Mulberry Bush* to take an option on the book and to pay the screenwriter, David Mercer, who did a terrible job. I saw all my dreams of being a producer rapidly evaporating. After I wrote it myself I went to David Picker and said, "Here's a screenplay by a famous writer, which isn't very good, and here's a screenplay by an unknown I found."

BLDS: Was it signed?

LK: Not right then. He called me and he said, "This screenplay is by David Mercer on an off day, and this one's by you, isn't it? Well, not bad. Let's go."

BLDS: How did he manage to detect it?

LK: I don't know.

BLDS: It may be that from *Women in Love* to your current writing your work has overtly or covertly dealt with the same subject.

LK: I think it has. I don't know that I knew that at the time of *Women in Love,* but I think if you look at what I stand for now and

> I am very much of an instinctive person in that I take each day as it comes with whatever cards are dealt.

the themes in *Women in Love*, certainly there are parallels.

BLDS: For example?

LK: The love between the two men—the Birkin and Gerald Crich characters. And Lawrence's own longing for a male friend, even though he would never have called upon his sexuality. He would have called it a blood brotherhood, but I think we would call it homosexuality. So yes, I think you're quite right.

BLDS: It's been said that you are as famous for your wrath as you are for your writing.

LK: Who said that?

BLDS: I have read it repeatedly. But I am now sitting here with a very gentle, genteel soul. It appears that time has mellowed you.

LK: I don't think so.

BLDS: Here's an article about you in the *New York Times* that says, "The lion is now purring."

LK: Well, that's Alex Witchel, who interviewed me here with my lover, who makes me very happy, but what you're seeing is what I've always been on a private level. In many ways my public persona was made by the media. It served my purpose, or the purpose of my cause, to allow the perception of me to stay that way. "The angriest gay man in the world," blah, blah, blah. AIDS is awful and very much something to get angry about. The intransigence and denial of the system in attending to it, particularly early on, is something to be very angry about. I have been able to develop this anger in a public persona that, of course, I don't bring home with me. I am very much of an instinctive person in that I take each day as it comes with whatever cards are dealt. I don't plan that I'm going to do this, that, and the other thing. The tactics that I used didn't develop overnight. They came as I saw that certain things worked. For instance, I saw back in 1981 that being calm and reasoned about getting Mayor Koch to pay attention to the local problems that initially confronted us here got us nowhere. And eventually the activism just began. I didn't plan to go out there and be angry, but I was financially independent enough to be able to afford to be angry and to not take the shit that was being handed to us. All I was doing was asking for some help in setting up an organization to do work that essentially the city

should have been doing but wasn't.

BLDS: I remember a line in one of your plays in which Mayor Koch's assistant said, "I'll get back to you." And I think you said that you're still waiting for that call.

LK: Yes. By then I was a successful film producer, I had money, I had a place in the world, and I did not like being treated like an outcast. I had a name and a persona and I had been to Yale. Yale taught you that you went out into the world and reaped. Suddenly I began to know what it feels like to be disenfranchised and discriminated against, and it's not a nice feeling. In many ways I had not been discriminated against in my life for who I was. While I was Jewish I had never experienced anti-Semitism.

BLDS: What about the Whiffenpoofs?

LK: I didn't expect to be a Whiffenpoof and that was a social thing. I was not in a fraternity; I didn't move in that crowd. Paul Hall, the leader of our singing group, was Jewish.

BLDS: What was it called?

LK: The Augmented Seven. We sang a lot of calypso songs. We were very popular and considered the best group on campus that year. Our leader fully expected to be elected to the Whiffenpoofs, to break that long-standing rule, because there wasn't any other leader who was as good.

BLDS: But it didn't happen.

LK: It didn't happen. It almost destroyed him.

BLDS: Is he still singing?

LK: Are any of us still singing? No.

BLDS: In the 1980s you founded two of the most visible and vocal AIDS awareness and service organizations: the Gay Men's Health Crisis (GMHC) in 1982, the first and largest AIDS service organization in the world; and the AIDS Coalition to Unleash Power (ACT UP) in 1987, the now international direct-action protest organization. Why was there a need for two organizations and how are their goals different?

LK: As I've written about endlessly in *The Normal Heart* and in many of my essays in *Reports from the Holocaust*, GMHC very quickly became what I didn't want it to become. I wanted GMHC to do essentially what ACT UP eventually did do. I guess the time wasn't right. GMHC was not started to be a service organization, it was started to make the system accountable, to get help from the city, to increase awareness, to spread educational materials. It quickly drew to it a lot of people who were more pastoral than activist-oriented. It was sort of like the church. And they were frightened of being confrontational. They were frightened when I would go on television and say nasty things about Koch.

BLDS: He lives in the very building you live in.

LK: He didn't then. He moved in afterward, yes. The first time I saw him I screamed at him in the lobby, "Nobody wants you in this building!" Mr. Rudin, my landlord, called or had someone call me and say that if I did that again I would be evicted. Fortunately, Koch lives on the other side of the building, on the other elevator bank, so I don't have to see him. He's actually said nice things in print every time anyone in the press asks him about me. But I still think he could have done an enormous amount to contain the epidemic.

BLDS: What could he have done?

LK: It's a public health emergency. How did people overnight stop taking Tylenol when there appeared to be poison in it? How did our officials deal with toxic shock or legionnaires' disease? They worked very quickly to inform the world what was happening and to educate people. But when it comes to AIDS, fifteen years later you're still dealing with a world that doesn't like to say the word *condom*, or to allow the transmissibility of this illness to be taught in schools or talked about in any sort of reasonable way. We've come a long way in that regard but you have to remember that in 1981 things were different. In 1981 we suspected pretty much everything that eventually turned out to be true. It was the tip of the iceberg. We suspected that it was spread sexually, that it was spread through blood and through drugs, and, while the virus wasn't identified for a couple of years, there were still enough reputable scientists who said, "This is a virus and whether we find it or not we know how viruses are spread." We still haven't found certain hepatitis viruses but that doesn't prevent us from dealing with hepatitis in a knowledgeable way.

BLDS: But from what I understand, even now, fifteen years later, the behavior of some young men has not changed conspicuously, in spite of their increased awareness and access to information.

LK: Well, I think you're making more of that than perhaps there is to be made. You're dealing with a population of millions of people. In any population of that size you are not going to have 100 percent compliance to any kind of rules. I think that young people, particularly young people outside of bigger cities, are not exposed to education about this. I don't know if they can be blamed for that. For those who are living in the city and should know better, one can only say it is an enormous sadness, but our lives have been overwhelmed and enveloped in this enormous sadness for so long that one is amazed that perhaps more people are not breaking the diet, so to speak. It is very hard to stay on a diet rigidly for fifteen years without breaking it at some point. And I think we've learned to live with the illness in a way that makes one almost understand how Jews in concentration camps learned to somehow get along. Ten years ago the thought of having sex and sex equaling death was overwhelming. Well, we've absorbed all that into our system now. You find a lot of couples in relationships like mine; I am positive and my lover is not, and it doesn't terrify him to have sex with me.

BLDS: Isn't that a new dimension? As time has gone on, there are more references to zero-dysfunctional couples in which one person is HIV negative and the other is HIV positive, and it seems to be a fact that one faces and moves on.

LK: We've absorbed it into our being and into our lives with an amazing facility. Anyway, I don't have much faith in education as a successful deterrent across the board, which is why I spend most of my effort and energy fighting for the research to be done and the treatments to be accelerated. It just seems to me that the only thing that's going to make it go away is a medicine. It's not going to go away with the Catholic Church or the right wing prohibiting education in any kind of a meaningful way.

BLDS: What caused your rift with GMHC?

LK: I was calling President Reagan names; I was calling Mayor Koch names. I will still do both. We have the third president in a row who is quite frankly out to lunch on this issue.

BLDS: When you talk about the religious right and other factors, have you considered the potential alternatives to the current administration?

LK: I have come to the sad conclusion that I don't believe it makes any difference who is president or which party controls Congress.

BLDS: How will we ever have a breakthrough?

LK: In research or in government or both?

> Ten years ago the thought of having sex and sex equaling death was overwhelming.

BLDS: Both. I think they're intertwined in some ways.

LK: The major breakthroughs have not come from the government, but rather from drug companies, from abroad, from university-funded research, and from private laboratories. Some of it, to be sure, has been funded by the National Institute of Health. However, there is less control over this illness now than there was under George Bush. It's hateful to say, but I think that many Republicans—even Gingrich—see this as a dollars-and-cents expensive illness. Clinton sees it as an illness that doesn't register well on the Richter scale of public opinion. His domestic-policy advisers quite intentionally keep him away from any issues pertaining to AIDS or homosexuality, so it doesn't get attended to at all. Everything that is being done is cosmetic. Yes, there is an AIDS czar, but she is powerless. Yes, there is an office of AIDS research, but it is run by a wimp who is also powerless. Those who were really on the right track and forceful in AIDS research and development have literally been emasculated. Bush wanted the drug companies to flourish. I find myself in an unusual position of being very supportive of the drug companies while at the same time being very critical of what they get away with. However, for the time being, they are all we have and they are the major backbone of what research is being done. And yes, they do charge too much for their product, but we do have a plague on our hands.

BLDS: Are many other founding members of the organizations that you helped found still involved?

LK: Of the other five cofounders of the Gay Men's Health Crisis, three are dead, Ed White lives in Paris, and Larry Mass retired very early from the fray. He is a physician in drug rehabilitation and a writer.

BLDS: How have you managed to sustain yourself and not have AIDS burnout?

LK: I have no idea. I don't know that I haven't had periods of it; maybe it fires my anger and that keeps me going. It's also what I write about. I do seem to be single-minded about it and able to keep it going. The original members of ACT UP have died as well, so there isn't the person power out there anymore.

BLDS: Despite your own impressive inspirational record of achievement, you claim that you are sometimes convinced that everything you've said or written falls on deaf ears. Do you really believe that?

LK: I recently made a speech to a full house of doctors and nurses at grand rounds at Mount Sinai Hospital. I've done a lot of that.

There's usually somebody on staff who knows how awful everything is and wants the staff to be politicized by giving them a shot of anger. At the recent event, the woman who invited me said she always noticed "there's never any follow-through."

BLDS: On whose part did she mean that?

LK: On the audience's. I give them long lists of suggestions of things that they might do and try to bring out of them ideas about things they can do, and everybody feels gung ho when they leave, but nobody follows through. People come to me on the street and say, "Thank you for what you're doing," but I no longer take that as a compliment. My response is, "Fuck you, why aren't you doing it, too?" What I think I've come to represent for a lot of people, which is not uncomplimentary but it's beside the point, is the anger that they're unable to express. And that's not good enough to effect change. All the people who work for GMHC quietly thank me when I criticize GMHC, as I continue to do because it has become another city bureaucracy, but they who are working for the agency won't go out there and help to change it. I don't know what it is about people but there's something that really makes it very difficult for people to fight, whatever the issue, be it women's rights or decent education of our children in a drug-free environment. What do you think it is?

BLDS: I think we are in a period of quiescence in which people are either tired, burned out, or in despair. Some have no historical or institutional memory about all of the subjects that you've just catalogued.

LK: I think it's very sad.

BLDS: Can you explain to me how the word *homosexual* ever came to be synonymous with the word *gay*? Do you know?

LK: There are some writings about it. *Homosexual* is a word that only goes back to 1890 or so. Over the years the word *homosexual* was uncomfortable for most of us because it was used in a medical and somewhat derogatory sense by doctors—oh, he's homosexual, as if to say, oh, he's got TB. I think there have been various attempts at words over the years. Some of them, such as *queer*, are also uncomfortable for many of us. Sometime around the sixties or seventies the term *gay* was chosen. I don't think any of us were particularly happy with it, but it seemed to take root almost as a last desperate attempt, even though it was not eminently satisfactory. It's there, whether we want it or not, until somebody can come up with another word. Lesbians were, and are, and remain comfortable with that word, but gay men didn't have the equivalent of *lesbian*. It's now come to be gay men and lesbians or gay people for all, until somebody comes up with a better term or until *homosexual* gets reclaimed again.

BLDS: One of the things I keep reading is that there is the absence of a power structure in the homosexual community.

LK: I balk at the word *community* because no one refers to the heterosexual community or the white community.

BLDS: It has been suggested that within this so-called community there is an absence of a power structure other than yourself.

LK: I don't even know if I'm included.

BLDS: Where are the leaders?

LK: It's not a group of people that takes very well to being led. In fact, it's a group that rebels very strongly against leadership.

BLDS: How do you explain that?

LK: I don't know, but I suspect it exists in other groups of people as well. I don't know that leaders last very long in the feminist group or in the black population. In the majority communities, leaders usually get paid. There's a potential payoff somewhere. The executive director of a major organization can make a couple of hundred thousand dollars a year, but gay organizations simply have been unable to raise that kind of money, or pay that kind of money, and it's not a stepping-stone to political office or anything. You really must have your heart in it to do it. It's very difficult to maneuver the tricky shoals of any community, so after a few years people just throw up their hands. There have been many good gay leaders who have just disappeared.

BLDS: You've tried every trick from gloom to despair to anger to wrath to inspiration. None seem to have actually worked to your satisfaction. So what next?

LK: I don't know. I take each day as it comes.

BLDS: Is there gridlock now in the gay community?

LK: I don't know that there's ever been anything other than gridlock. Again, I rebel at the word *community*.

BLDS: How should I refer to it?

LK: Population. It encompasses, as every population does, an enormous range of interests and it's hard to draw them all together. You have men and women, for a start. You have black and white, all different races, and people who have different sexual interests.

BLDS: Then there's the religious and economic stratification.

LK: Right. It's hard to see the head of a large corpo-

ration, someone like David Geffen, being comfortable with a person who has had a sex change or who walks around in a dress, so it's hard to register the inclusiveness that we demand be there.

BLDS: Your naming names calls to mind another issue. There are many people, including some gay leaders, who think that it is destructive and coercive to "out" people. One interviewer called it the neofascist front of sexual politics.

LK: This reminds me of men making decisions for women's abortion rights. My calling David Geffen gay is not outing him because he's out himself.

BLDS: But there were other names that not only you but others named, using the notorious activist tactic of naming names. What does it prove? What purpose does that serve? Don't they have the right to decide?

LK: It's a much more complicated issue than you're making it seem. There is an etiquette to outing. It's usually done to people like Roy Cohn or Terry Dolan—people who have been our enemies and who we know to be gay. Aside from that, what we've attempted to do—and I firmly support this—is change the perception of being gay from something that is shameful in the view of many people to something that is just as ordinary as being heterosexual. What we are saying to the person being outed is that if you are going to come into our world and go to all our parties and hang out with all our people, then expect to be identified along with everybody else or be seen along with everybody else. We are no longer here to protect you because we think it's wonderful being gay. If you don't, stay with your wife and keep your life private. The Jann Wenner situation, in which he left his wife to go with a young man, all of which was immediately repeated in the mainstream press, is an indication of what positive—for the gay movement—changes outing has achieved. It's all about equality.

BLDS: Actually it may have done more, between the *Wall Street Journal* and every other paper, to make the general public aware that the divisions are not quite as obvious as they seem.

LK: Right. It is actually very interesting because it shows how far we've come in having the mainstream press agreeing with us.

BLDS: There's a flip side to that. The mainstream press became

Murdochized and used the Wenner situation as a legitimate story because it involved a major business, but I suppose the net result of it is probably very positive.

LK: We want to be treated just like everybody else.

BLDS: That's not too good, though.

LK: In some instances it isn't, but we're prepared to accept all that. You don't have to protect us. We can deal with it.

BLDS: Do you think it's time for a new testament to be propheted in the gay population? Do you see yourself getting beyond your anger, or is that the engine that brought you to speak out? How could you not be angry?

LK: I'm not a biblical person and I'm not a religious person and I don't like the Bible comparisons. I don't do any of this willingly. Or perhaps that's too harsh. I do it more as a sense of responsibility. If I had my druthers I would just stay home and write. I'm fighting to save my life and I'm fighting to save the lives of others. I am motivated more by that than by any desire to be a leader of the gay population. There was a time when I wanted to be that person. It was a brief period and it's long since gone.

BLDS: But within the gay population that I know, you are seen as a leader.

LK: I don't know that they see me as a leader; I think they see me as the only visible person out there who is saying anything. Also, for whatever reason, I have a good relationship with the media, maybe because I come out of the movie business and I know how to *tummel* with the media and enjoy the media.

BLDS: When was the last time you attended a GMHC or ACT UP meeting?

LK: I am persona non grata at GMHC.

BLDS: Persona non grata? Isn't that a little harsh?

LK: No. I had been invited back several times. Last year we had a very good meeting about how they could perform some tasks, but I might just as well not have gone. I went to ACT UP just before David Feinberg died. He made a speech. It was a very painful experience, listening to him, near death, very angry. Anyway, nobody there knew who I was and no one listened to me when I got up to speak. They were very rude and dismissive to David. They aren't the organizations that I helped to start. They're different. Like children, they grow into adults.

BLDS: And often they are not the adults that you had in mind, either.

LK: No question about it.

BLDS: Are those meetings still standing-room-only meetings of committed and angry activists?

LK: No.

BLDS: What are they now?

LK: There's a handful of people who are more like zombies than angry, who just go out of habit and just sit there and don't do anything. For all intents and purposes there is no strong AIDS activist community or organization now. There is no strong gay organization of any type out there. We are in very bad times. I have to laugh when I hear Jesse Helms or the right wing talking about the powerful gay lobby. It's just a joke. And it's a pathetic joke because we have so much money in our community. We have an enormous amount of disposable income. We've got the David Geffens and the Barry Dillers and the Dick Jenrettes and people who are worth zillions of dollars, but we have not gotten the support of those people behind us in order to organize and use our power. Dick Jenrette has been a very disappointing person in my experience. I think he was the first person who ever gave GMHC a big check—a check for a thousand dollars, which in those days of our history was an enormous amount of money. As far as I know that's the last he's done. Of course, with his connections and his visibility, he could have been exactly what we needed. And so could Geffen, in a way. Geffen does give money but he does it in a very removed sort of way. As does Barry. They give safely to the GMHC, nothing controversial. People are not willing to get into what you and I are talking about, the politics of it. Obtaining our rightful power is hard. It's difficult. It's painful, messy, who-needs-it kind of work.

BLDS: Would you rather be known as a writer? A gay activist? How do you think history will treat you?

LK: I don't know. It will forget me like it forgets everybody else. I just really want to be a good writer and I would like to be remembered as that. I don't feel that my work is finished. On the one hand I want to be in your book just so you can have a gay person in your book. I do feel a responsibility for visibility. And it does move me when kids come up to me and say, "I'm out there fighting because of you," or, "You were the first gay author I ever read and now I'm out," or, "I'm now a writer because of you." I think older people, especially minorities, can serve enormously useful purposes as role models for the young. I love going to talk at col-

> I'm fighting to save my life and I'm fighting to save the lives of others. I am motivated more by that than by any desire to be a leader of the gay population.

leges, which I do often. So that's a responsibility thing, but I also really have a responsibility to myself as well, to attempt to be a creative person. Writing is solitary and if you want to be any good you have to stay home alone and shut up. That's harder for me to do, though I am actually happy hidden in my study in front of my computer. I've just got to get myself to do it, now that my health is beginning to show signs of weakening. I've got to go and finish this long novel that I'm working on.

BLDS: Have your latest tests revealed anything?

LK: Well, I have other problems in addition to HIV. I had hepatitis B at one point. I have a cirrhotic liver, and my liver is caving in. So far I feel fine, but you don't know what's going to happen by the next test. I take AZT and I'll be adding another drug shortly. Then the roller coaster starts. While I may be a long-term survivor of HIV, I may not be a long-term survivor of liver disease. I just had a rather troublesome series of liver tests and the doctor said I may require a liver transplant down the road. That's a serious operation and it's one that a lot of people don't survive. I figure I've got five or six years left to work and I want to finish the goddamn book. That's what I want to be remembered for. I don't know if there's anything more I can do in terms of the AIDS research activism. I can get on the phone, and the head of the FDA will take my call, and the head of AIDS research will take my call, and I can yell at them. Recently I went out to Cold Spring Harbor for a conference that I had helped to call into being, which included a number of top immunologists from around the world. It's the kind of thing that should have happened eight years ago, and it certainly should have happened several years ago when the new head of the office of AIDS research took over, but anyway, it's happening now. It's very hard to make people talk to each other. That's the kind of stuff that I keep yelling to try and facilitate. If I can somehow just keep that going, and if I don't have the problems of running an organization to deal with, then I can manage to write.

BLDS: You refer to the AIDS plague as a holocaust. But isn't a biological nightmare—the worst biological nightmare—different from the conscious, premeditated acts of Hitler?

LK: No. I do think a lot of this is premeditated and, as Hannah Arendt went to great pains to describe, a holocaust can occur just as easily by what people don't do as by what they do do. I don't make any distinction between sins of omission and sins of commission. There is no question in my mind that this has been allowed to happen. Even people with whom I disagree on very strong grounds in other areas, such as Mathilde Krim, the head of the American Foundation for AIDS Research, agree with me on this. This is a plague that did not need to happen. It could have been contained from day one. When you have a mayor who doesn't even want to have a meeting, when you have a president like Reagan who literally would not say the word *AIDS* for seven years, these are guilty acts of commission or omission—I don't know which. They are certainly sins and they have certainly allowed the disease to escalate out of control. You don't look at what was done, you look at what has to be done.

BLDS: So how do you mobilize the politicians, the people, the gays?

LK: I do what I do. I write my articles and I make my speeches and I tell the world on television. I can't do any more than that. If I were younger and healthier and richer I'd start an army. ACT UP was almost that.

BLDS: If, tomorrow, the president named you AIDS czar, what would be the first three issues you would address?

LK: One, demand the president give me emergency powers; two, do such a housecleaning at the NIH as you wouldn't believe; and three, start a Manhattan Project for a cure. Of course, this is greatly oversimplified.

BLDS: Is one of your messages that life doesn't make sense, but that change does? Would that be an appropriate motto for you?

LK: I don't know. It's too airy-fairy for me and it's too general. Life doesn't make sense sometimes but some of it makes a lot of sense and some of it is awful sense. Change is not always for the better but a lot of the times it is. I'm not that philosophical about what I do. I know what has to be done logically. If you were running a company you would see the same thing. What makes the company good? What happens when the company becomes less good and how do you get it back to being good? We're not talking about rocket science here. We're talking about a plague, about trying to save a billion lives, about questions that have to be answered before we can save these lives, about identifying those questions, and about finding the best people to research them. If they can't do it, get rid of them and get somebody else.

BLDS: You've said that you spent most of your life wanting very much to be in love and not being successful at it. That doesn't sound very different from most people. But it seems that now you have found a place and a person that are very satisfying to you.

LK: I have had lovers in the past and I had a lover who died and about whom I wrote an awful lot. David Webster is someone that

I have loved for a long time and who has come back into my life now. It's working out in a way that it didn't the first time. Yes, I'm very happy. I want to get back to somethng we started to discuss earlier. If you're facing death, if your own life is at stake, doesn't that make you want to fight to save it? What I say about AIDS exists for breast cancer; it exists for other diseases, other desperate wrongs. When I make a speech now I say, "I'm going to talk to you about AIDS, but every woman in this place can substitute breast cancer for it." I yell at the women, too. I say, how long has breast cancer been around? How much do we know about breast cancer now? Why have you sat there and allowed all this to happen? And women, why have you put up with all of it for so long? It's the same as it is for AIDS. But women do put up with it, as gays put up with AIDS. People do not fight very hard to save their own lives and I'll never, ever understand why not. I will say this: I started out a mess. I was a kid who tried to kill himself. I was very shy and I still am in many respects. I have a terrible self-image, which is something I don't think people ever get over. I hated my parents and I think it was sort of mutual on the part of my father. We didn't have any money. I figure if I can pull myself out of all that shit then it's possible for other people to do the same. It is possible to do these things.

BLDS: How lucky you are to have had your brother, Arthur, who has been a lifelong confidant, a role model in so many ways, a support system. How many people have that?

LK: I agree with you, but I will say that a certain amount of my growing up had to be done despite him. He did not approve of homosexuality. I've had to justify my being to him and maybe he's been almost more useful to me in that way. I had to prove to him that homosexuality was a worthwhile, noble thing because he meant so much to me. So it worked out great.

BLDS: You dedicated *The Destiny of Me* to him.

LK: Well, it's our story.

BLDS: I was amused to read that Lucille Lortel described it as a family play—about a Jewish family. How do you feel about this characterization of your work?

LK: As the producer Lucille thought that a gay AIDS play wouldn't do as well as a family play. It was her money at stake on the play and that's how she wanted to promote it. I don't know whether it helped or hindered the play.

BLDS: What was your response to the play *The Night Larry Kramer Kissed Me*?

LK: I must confess to being slightly embarrassed by it. Not that I don't think it was a good play or that David Drake is a very talented man, it's just hard for me to deal with that kind of attention. That's the shyness in me, I guess.

> If you're facing death, if your own life is at stake, doesn't that make you want to fight to save it?

BLDS: Was your 1978 *New York Times* op-ed piece about gay power born of your need to defend "faggots," or was it solely intended as a publicity vehicle for your novel *Faggots?*

LK: I never thought of writing an op-ed piece until a woman at Random House suggested it to me. Yes, it was used at the time the book came out. Of course, I'm an advocate for gay rights, but my issue has really been AIDS. I am a single-issue person. The gays-in-the-military controversy, for instance, was not something that excited my participation, except to hold a recalcitrant president to his promise. I think it was badly handled. I didn't go out to defend faggots at all.

BLDS: What about the novel?

LK: I don't believe in defending your work on that kind of level. It is what it is. The novel was very controversial. It was also very successful. I made friends and I lost friends because of it. I was surprised it was controversial, but I was naive in that regard. At that time I would not have become a gay-rights advocate to defend it. I was not a political person, really, until 1981 when AIDS came along, and even then my politicization was reluctant. I had lunch recently at NYU with Alvin Friedman-Kien, the doctor who first got me involved in all this. He said then—he could make the same speech today—"Larry, you're well known in the gay community because of *Faggots*. You're going to have to go out there and tell them this is happening because the press is not going to report it. This is just the tip of the iceberg and it's spread by sex." He's one of the first people who said that to me, and it made utter and complete sense.

BLDS: Is that how you evolved from someone who watched the annual gay-pride march on the news to one whom Susan Sontag has described—on the back cover of one of your books—as "one of America's most valuable troublemakers?"

LK: I guess so.

BLDS: Your play *The Normal Heart* has had more than six hundred productions worldwide. Congratulations. Doesn't that really stagger you?

LK: No. I don't think about it.

BLDS: But you have had an impact in South Africa, Poland, Louisiana.

LK: Oh, Barbaralee. Yes, it's nice people have seen it, but why is the president allowed to get away with murder?

BLDS: Don't you think there are some tangible signs of progress? Gay people are winning unparalleled acceptance.

LK: I guess it's whether you see the glass as half empty or half full.

BLDS: I'm from the half-full school, unfortunately or fortunately.

LK: I guess I'm from the three-quarters-empty class. Yes, of course, we've made progress, but again it comes down to right and wrong. That's what fuels my anger. How we're treated is wrong. If I were a woman who'd had a breast removed I would feel the same way, I think, because of my personality. How gay people are treated is wrong and how AIDS has been treated from day one is a holocaust. It's a tragedy of gigantic proportions. With all the acceptance in the world we should still be allowed to die—that's what I see.

BLDS: You've said that being extreme or, as some say, hysterical is the only way to get attention in this country. Do you still think that's the right approach across the board? Is your brand of grass-roots-response activism still the best policy for calling attention to this ongoing plague?

LK: Yes and no. It worked best when we were able to have a multipronged, or certainly a two-pronged, two-level approach, which meant that you had the activists on the outside and the negotiators on the inside. You really need both. You need grass-roots activism, you need the voice of the people heard in the land, and you need people able to go in to make the deal or to present the case in a way that is less threatening. That's the whole good cop/bad cop thing that most corporations use. Indeed, that's what diplomacy is all about. In politics you negotiate around the table but they know you've got an army waiting if you don't agree. Unfortunately we haven't had the two levels of involvement but for those few brief years of ACT UP, from 1987 to about

'91 or '92. Now we have neither. There are all kinds of tactics. I happen to be good at a certain kind. If you don't like my tactics, then you're free to use your tactics and do it yourself. For every person who says, "Oh, shut up, Larry, I hate what you're doing," there's a person who says, "Keep it up." I have learned that it doesn't make any difference what you do. A certain number of people are going to approve and a certain number of people aren't, so you might as well do what you want to do or feel comfortable or capable doing.

BLDS: From *Longtime Companion* to *Philadelphia* and now your film version of *The Normal Heart*, how do you feel about Hollywood's portrayal of the AIDS pandemic?

LK: Plague. Not very good, obviously. I hated *Philadelphia* because it was not about AIDS. It was a courtroom drama. If you hadn't been told that the two men were lovers you would never know. They never touch, they never even seem to relate in any sort of way, and it certainly didn't deal with the political realities of AIDS. It dealt only with a small segment of the discrimination in a law firm. There was nothing about the government or the kind of treatments the guy was not getting. *Longtime Companion* was moving. And I know what an awfully hard time Craig Lucas and Lindsay Law had in getting whatever small amount of money was needed to make that movie. I think Hollywood has been awful and I don't think that's a debatable thing.

BLDS: Is it because they think AIDS films won't make money?

LK: I don't care what they think. There is such a thing as corporate responsibility, which, strangely enough, certainly existed in Hollywood during World War II when F. D. R. would call Jack Warner and say, "I need a movie about the Nazi menace in Hoboken on the docks," and Jack Warner would make the film. In the scheme of things we're not talking about an enormous expenditure here. A ten-million-dollar movie is not going to bankrupt a studio when they're spending 180 million on *Waterworld* or a Stallone movie that flops.

BLDS: How is your collaboration with Barbra Streisand coming along? I've just recently heard that there were some glitches. Is that accurate?

LK: No. She's working on the movie and she'll make it or she won't make it. She works at her own pace. She's not Ms. Speedy Gonzales. I've had a very good relationship with her, I adore her, and I think she's fond of me. It's hard for a writer to turn over anything personal, especially a story of his own life to somebody else. [Ed. note: She withdrew from the project in April 1996.]

BLDS: I read that your goals for *The Normal Heart* were to make people cry, and to see gay men in love, gay men suffering, and gay men dying, just like everyone else. Do you feel that the public, gay and straight, has been inured to this plague?

LK: I think people everywhere are inured to the horrors of what it means to be alive today. That's one of the reasons why it's so hard to get attention for anything. I think everybody today has got at least one awful problem that they don't know how to deal with. They see that the government isn't dealing with it and so they've lost all faith in government. This is evidenced by throwing out one party and putting in another, which I don't think means anything more than a register of this dissatisfaction. People will soon enough realize that it isn't going to change anything and probably throw out this one and bring in the other one again until they realize that the basic system has got to change. But if I were a straight person in a small town in Alabama and I saw my kids coming home from school dumber than when I sent them, I'd be angry about that.

BLDS: You describe images of what is "a normal life," and *normal* is a word that keeps appearing in your increasingly nuanced body of work. In *The Normal Heart,* you talk about the rights to marry and to adopt children, you oppose promiscuous sex, and you talk about this stereotypical family in Alabama. So what's so normal about normal?

LK: Well, that's a good question. The title *The Normal Heart* comes from a W. H. Auden poem. I guess I spent an awful lot of my life being called and thought of as abnormal.

BLDS: And how do you think of yourself?

LK: I certainly think of myself with pride and dignity and I like

my differences. I don't like having to confront hate because I walk down the street holding my boyfriend's hand. I can't even get his name on the lease of our apartment. You could if you were living here with your husband.

BLDS: I might not be able to if I were living here with my lover.

LK: But I'm not allowed to marry, and I would like to get married.

BLDS: When will the courts grant homosexual couples the same rights—shared health and death benefits, property and familial rights—enjoyed by heterosexual couples?

LK: I hope soon.

BLDS: Will the Hawaiian court's decision to sanction single-sex marriages, and the mass wedding ceremony performed recently in San Francisco, bring about national legislation to formally legalizing single-sex relationships?

LK: Let's hope so.

BLDS: You are very romantic in everything that you say and in many things that you write. You have what some might think of as an almost prudish view when you refer to sex as something that must be returned to a more special place. You're often a moralist, too, as you condemn promiscuous sex.

LK: No question. I am a moralist, but I don't think that's so awful. By promiscuous sex I'm not talking about the odd occasional fall from grace, but I was critical of the lives we led in the seventies. That would apply to straight people as well as to gay people who took part in the so-called sexual revolution ushered in by the *Playboy* philosophy. And I don't know where the romantic thing came from. Too many movies when I was a kid, I guess. That's okay. I get teased for it.

BLDS: You often talk about the denial of the rights to marry and to adopt children. In your instance, you have fathered a revolution, plays, books, articles, and the largest AIDS service organization. Is this quest in some way a substitute for progeny?

LK: That's too Freudian. I think I have respect for achievement. If anything, it comes out of Jewish tradition—even though I always say I'm a bad Jew—the sense of achievement, of accomplishment, of wanting to add something to the world. I have certain gifts and I want to express them, use them. I think I have an obligation to use them.

BLDS: How does the novel you are working on about the history

> I certainly think of myself with pride and dignity and I like my differences. I don't like having to confront hate because I walk down the street holding my boyfriend's hand.

of AIDS in America differ from other compelling accounts such as Randy Shilts's *And the Band Played On*?

LK: I think you can often tell more truth through fiction than you can through fact. You can be much more honest about what Nancy Reagan did, for instance, by making a character of her rather than writing a biography, as Kitty Kelley did, as much as I liked that book. There's still a place to which you can't go because of law. But you can in fiction. My novel covers hundreds of years; Randy's book deals with just the specific views of what he thought to be the parameters of AIDS, which, I think, are going to be greatly expanded as we go along.

BLDS: How has your renewed relationship since 1994 with David Webster changed your life? He has described you as loving, giving, gentle, childlike—very different words than some of the people who know you in your activist life might use. Would this always have been an accurate description of the private Larry Kramer?

LK: You have to ask David. The person that you show intimately in the bedroom is not necessarily the person you show to the world. You know what it's like to go from being alone one day to sharing your life the next day. You realize that you could never go back very happily to the former because there's so many satisfactions to being with someone. I get less writing done.

BLDS: It is very time-consuming. You said that Dostoyevsky is your favorite writer, because he dramatized injustices. Do you see that as your role and as the strength of your writing?

LK: I don't know what my strengths in writing are. Now we're getting into a whole other area, which is that of the role of the creative person in the world today. I think that art and literature, in this country anyway, have lost their focus and their usefulness. I agree pretty much with that essay Tom Wolfe wrote a few years ago in which he asked, "Why aren't writers writing about what's happening instead of their belly buttons?" The great thrust of the nineteenth-century novel was issues. George Eliot, Dickens, Dostoyevsky, Tolstoy, Thackeray, Trollope—in addition to writing about the world, they also told wonderful stories. The fiction of today, for the most part, is so insular and self-contemplative. It is not very vital to me. It is the same with theater. Especially now that Joseph Papp is gone, there's very little of interest. It's just real hard to get a play on about an issue.

BLDS: If you had a motto for your life, what would it be?

LK: A day at a time. Even at my most depressed I've always somehow been hopeful. I think that's genetic probably more than

anything else. If you want something badly enough you have to make an attempt at it. What most people don't realize is that it usually requires a lot of hard work and that success just does not come easily. People are easily discouraged. I try to tell people, young writers who expect to be published on the first draft or the first work, how hard really successful people work. It took me a long time to become a reasonably good writer, a proficient writer. I didn't start writing seriously until I was in my early thirties, and then I had to learn to do things that other writers, people who started younger, learned when they were in their teens—the discipline, the skill, the tricks—and it's hard. I remember going through years of "it's never going to be."

BLDS: What moments in your career brought you the most pleasure?

LK: That's a nice question. I remember when I walked into the Random House building for the very first time to have my first meeting with my editor, Bob Loomis. There I was: I had a contract, I walked into Random House and saw that emblem on the wall, and it made me feel very good. I remember the first public screening of *Women in Love* in London. I had been a film executive and a story editor for close to ten years by the time I made the film, and I invited everybody I knew: friends, business associates, people I'd worked with, publishers, other story editors, writers. I said, "Thank you for letting me have one of your great novels to make a movie of. I hope you like it." That was a lovely evening. Another one was the opening night of *The Normal Heart*, the night we invited all the family and friends.

BLDS: How did your family respond to it?

LK: The first production was an incredible experience for everybody. Some of the original cast recently did a reading of it in Los Angeles as a benefit for the Salk Institute, and it was actually reviewed by the leading critic of the *L.A. Times*, who said it was a play for all time, which was lovely. The kids from the original production were interviewed, as well, and said what it was like to get back together all these years later. It was just an incredibly moving experience. Everybody cried. In later productions of the play people said the same thing, that they came together as a family, as a unit, in a way that rarely happens on a play.

BLDS: Do you consider *The Normal Heart* the peak of your achievement?

LK: God, no! I don't know what that means! Life is about climbing mountains. You can't ever be satisfied with the quality of your work. I always try to set different challenges. I've never written the same kind of thing twice. I've written novels, I've written movies, I've written three plays that are all very different in form. The challenges I set for myself technically are never the same; otherwise I find I get bored. I couldn't write a novel like *Faggots* again. People say, why don't you start another organization? And I think secretly, well, I started two and I don't want to do it again. I know all the pitfalls. I want to learn something new. I have set for myself an enormous task with this novel. I wanted to write a really long novel—and I'm talking a *War and Peace* kind of novel.

BLDS: Who helps you research this?

LK: Me! That's what all the boxes are. A lot of it is in the computer. I've already got about a couple thousand pages of text.

BLDS: Do you write every day?

LK: I try to. The technical problems of the novel are really crazy. I really need ten, fifteen years to do it. Different reading and writing skills are needed for long and short novels. And I've had to learn all of these. What's the structure? How do you keep it going? That's been an enormous challenge to me. It's almost too ambitious. I'm trying to do too much.

BLDS: Maybe it's two books.

LK: It's eight books. I don't care. That's irrelevant. It's got to be put together as a whole. And I'm enjoying it. For years I hated it, because it wouldn't do what I wanted it to do. It wasn't yielding in any way.

BLDS: How many years have you been working on it?

LK: I've been working on it off and on for about ten years—since I finished *Faggots* and before AIDS, really. And then AIDS made me want to write another novel, obviously, about AIDS. I've read portions of it in public which have gone down well.

BLDS: Are these the best years of your life?

LK: Oh, Barbaralee, I don't know. They're certainly nice years, but they're also frightening years. I think when you get older and you get scared that you're not going to be around much longer, those thoughts are difficult to live with in a way, but it makes you enjoy life more, so six of one, half dozen of another. I'm happy. Maybe that's a bad condition for a writer, I don't know. I haven't decided.

BLDS: If you had it to do over again, what would you do otherwise?

LK: I don't know. I don't think that way, either. I don't want to be younger, I don't want to go back. Perhaps I would try to have been a not-so-terrified child, youth, and young man—at which, of course, I should not have succeeded. I think I made one great mistake when I left GMHC, when I threw my fit and said, "You do this or I leave," and they were very willing to let me leave. I've often thought that GMHC would have been a much different organization had I stayed. I feel badly about that. Rodger McFarlane, who is my very old friend, has always maintained that I did that subconsciously because I wanted to write about it. I had to clear the decks in order to write *The Normal Heart,* and had I stayed there I wouldn't have written it. No, I have no regrets. I did what I did when I did it. Some of it was the best I could do at the time, some of it wasn't. But I've tried and that pleases me.

BLDS: Did you ever expect your life to unfold the way it has?

LK: Until 1981, yes—I wanted to be a success in the entertainment business, and I was. AIDS changed everything after that, of course.

SHERWIN NULAND

BLDS: You've told me that your childhood was spent in the Bronx and New York City. Your parents, who were Russian Jews, came to the United States in 1903. There were three generations of your family that lived in four rooms in an apartment in the Bronx, a far cry from this pastoral splendor that you live in now. How did you make your way from there to here?

SN: There was my grandmother, who represented the only member of her family, my father, my mother (who died when I was nine), my two aunts, and then the next generation—me, my brother, and my two cousins. My grandmother had seven children in her lifetime. She endured life experiences that were the stuff of a panoramic novel.

BLDS: For example?

SN: Well, she married young and had her first child before she was sixteen. One of the children died in childbirth, but the others came to this country. Her husband came with two boys, the two sons, in about 1896 or '97. As happened so often, their job was to earn enough money to bring the rest of the family over, which they couldn't do until 1903 or 1904. By the time they came a disease had developed that was rampant on the Lower East Side. The population density of the so-called 10B Ward of New York City, on the Lower East Side, was higher than had ever been seen in China, India, or anywhere else. These people lived in small apartments, sometimes sleeping

in shifts. Things were very hard in that situation. My grandfather and the two sons died within a couple of years of my grandmother's arrival with the four girls. One of the daughters died in childbirth, leaving an infant to be brought up by her grandmother.

BLDS: Was this child one of your cousins?

SN: Yes, a male cousin. My grandmother decided to never tell him that he was not their child, because his father disappeared. So he was brought up as the youngest son of the family. He is now in his mid-eighties. Then my mother married. Her first child was stillborn and her second, my brother Martin, died at three. Then the youngest sister married and had a daughter, Arline, who ended up living with us. When Arline was about nine years old her mother died of kidney disease. Then two years later my mother died. So here were all of these children left to be taken care of by their grandmother and their aunt, who never married.

BLDS: Was your aunt in charge, helping to raise these children?

SN: Well, my aunt worked.

BLDS: Where did she work?

SN: She worked where everybody worked, in the garment district on Thirty-seventh Street.

BLDS: Doing what?

SN: She put dresses together. She was what you called a finisher. My father worked in the same industry and he was what was called an operator. He put buttons on dresses and put parts of dresses together.

BLDS: But they didn't work in the same place.

SN: Oh, no, no. They worked in different places.

BLDS: Given your family history it would be fair to say that by the time you were eleven years old you knew more about dying than living.

SN: Well, as I have often put it, and I do have a tendency to put it in exactly these words, death was in the legend and lore of my family. It was the culture of my family. Sickness and disease and death were what our family was steeped in. We were all experts in it. It was almost an assumption that something was going to happen that was not good. We lived in what almost might be called a miasma of illness and death and tragedy. So when you asked me earlier, "How did you make your way?" what struck me was the choice of words, "make your way," because what's implied is a circuitous journey. It's not a straight line. That's exactly what my life was, it was a circuitous journey made by a young man, by a boy, who had gotten it into his head very early on that he was going to get out of this town. There are two words I would use to describe my attitude at that time. One is *determination* and the other is *certainty*. The determination was that I was going to do whatever I had to do to get out of that atmosphere. It wasn't getting away from the family that motivated me, but it was the miasma that enveloped all of us. The certainty is what I needed to have in order to do it. Of course, part of that came from personality and character, but part of it I attribute to the public-school system of the City of New York.

BLDS: Our much-maligned public-school system?

SN: Well, it was a different public-school system in those days. There may be very different reasons for maligning it today than there were in those days, but it was maligned in those days, too.

BLDS: Did it give you your love of learning?

SN: Let me start by talking about the teachers. As you well know, there were few opportunities for women in the 1920s or 1930s or 1940s. What was available to our brainiest women was to become a teacher, a nurse, or a secretary. Those who did work were most likely to be not married. The teachers who brought me up to be an American were a tribe of Irish Catholic spinsters who were determined to teach Jewish, Italian, Polish kids, you name it. Kids who spoke some other language at home were going to inherit from them the America that was theirs. It's such a different attitude than the one found in the whole school system in New York today. Multiculturalism was for the home. School was where you became an American. Citizenship—the sense of responsibility to one's city, to one's country, to the Constitution, to democracy—was drilled into us from a very early age. But more important than that was the language. None of the older members of our family could read or write English.

BLDS: Not even your aunt?

SN: No. The only one who could read or write English was the aunt who died when I was nine. We had all kinds of volumes— Mark Twain, Shakespeare, you name it—in Yiddish, in a huge bookshelf that was in our little living room. But there were no English books at all. Even with those Yiddish books, I would have been nothing without my teachers. I didn't even learn to read Yiddish until I was about nine. I could speak it, obviously, but I couldn't read it. That was not what I was striving for. What I was striving for was given to me by those women in the schools. We had to memorize poetry; the names Wordsworth and Longfellow were known to me when I was seven years old. I understood that knowledge like this was the key, that becoming an American was the key, that language was the key, that education was the key to the vehicle that was going to carry me out of there. Fascination with the English language was a brand new thing. I spoke English somewhat at home, quite a bit actually, but the kind of English that had to do with literature and poetry was not accessible to me until it was given to me by my teachers. The idea that by fifth grade someone would sit down and read *Heidi* to our class had an influence on me that was not conscious—but was profound, nonetheless. The most important thing was that there was a huge world outside of the Bronx, and outside of my neighborhood, and those women had shown me that it was accessible to me. What made it accessible was my willingness to learn about it. It was more than willingness, it was enthusiasm, it was excitement. Books would be handed out the first day of school and I would read right through the history book the first afternoon. I couldn't stop.

BLDS: After discovering your love of language and experiencing firsthand losses, it is little wonder that you became not only a professor of medicine, but one of the foremost writers in articulating that medical knowledge to the lay public. It must have been a great puzzle to you to be immersed in this valley of death.

SN: It was worse, actually, than I described it, because my father had a crippling neurological disease of the spine for almost his entire life. He had very little control over the use of his legs. He had to look down to see where his legs were, for example, and he had to be conscious of his hands when he ate. All of this pervaded the atmosphere.

BLDS: Clearly you had a great intellectual curiosity—a curiosity

> The teachers who brought me up to be an American were a tribe of Irish Catholic spinsters who were determined to teach Jewish, Italian, Polish kids, you name it.

.... it's not an accident that I ended up in abdominal surgery.... Both my mother and my brother died of intestinal cancer ....

about the way things worked. Why your father, and how did it happen?

SN: It wasn't so much curiosity as it was an attempt to get close to the disease so I could understand it. Now remember, I come from a family with no education. My brother was the first person to so much as spend a day in a non-Yiddish school. My father knew nothing about the sciences or mathematics.

BLDS: Was your brother a scientist, as well?

SN: My brother was always going to be the doctor, and I was going to be a biologist. I think the primary motivating force was to get a handle on the disease that could take whatever promise we had and destroy it. On the subconscious level, that was what made me determined that I had to go to medical school. I don't want to downplay the role of the prodding, underlying fear that there was a mystical thing, a specter of death that had all of us somehow in its power and that could take away from me everything I might have achieved. It would be hard for me to believe, especially since I wrote *How We Die*, that one of the reasons I went to medical school was not a need to become closer to, and achieve a greater familiarity with, these terrifying things—death and disease. In fact, it's not an accident that I ended up in abdominal surgery and breast surgery. Both my mother and my brother died of intestinal cancer; I spent thousands of hours of my life operating on intestinal cancer. When I finished medical school, the whole focus of my training was toward heart surgery. That was what everybody expected me to specialize in. I went to England to study heart surgery but, when the chips were down and I had to decide what I was going to do for the rest of my life, I chose abdominal surgery, ignoring everybody's demands. I actually set up an open-heart-surgery program in a hospital in New York and then just abandoned it and went into the practice of abdominal surgery.

BLDS: Was there an element of self-preservation involved in your choice?

SN: Yes, of course there was. In those days, if one did a cardiac procedure in any place other than a big university teaching hospital one would have to spend the next few weeks superintending every single element of that patient's care, because no one else knew enough about it to do it.

BLDS: Is the knowledge now so generally widespread that heart surgery can be performed almost anywhere?

SN: Yes. It was the early days of open-heart surgery and only the surgeon really understood all of the ramifications of what was going on. In that respect it was self-preservation. However, I simply felt that I didn't have the temperament or the personality to be a cardiac surgeon. They are such rigid people. They are so enormously focused on one small part of the human being. I never had the sense with my cardiac-surgery friends that they were involved with sick people in the way other surgeons are. They were involved with sick parts. There's no doubt that self-preservation, as you so well put it, was a major, major factor for all of those reasons. I found abdominal surgery much more attractive. I always enjoyed opening an abdomen more than I did opening a heart. When I was at Guy's Hospital in London working in cardiac surgery, I used to sneak in and watch the abdominal surgeons take out stomachs.

BLDS: It's difficult for a layperson to appreciate the use of the word "enjoyed" in that context. Is it the challenge that you're talking about?

SN: No, it's fun.

BLDS: Since 1991 you are a professor of surgery at Yale–New Haven Hospital and not a practicing surgeon.

SN: Right, I don't practice surgery. Originally, I was never going to be a surgeon. I was always going to be an internist, all through medical school. In the first place, that's what all the smart people did. The smartest kids in the class went into internal medicine, because it was intellectually challenging.

BLDS: Is that still the case?

SN: No.

BLDS: Where do they go now?

SN: It varies. Some of the brightest kids now are choosing surgery, but bright kids are still turning to internal medicine. Physicians like to refer to internal medicine as the cognitive specialty. Anyway, I loved internal medicine—it was interesting, it was enjoyable, I liked the people who practiced internal medicine, although later I found out I liked the surgeons more. One day, the second or third day of my surgery internship, the chief resident stopped me on the surgical floor and said, "Hey, wait, I need you. One of the interns on the private service got sick or his mother got sick and he had to leave for two weeks and we need a sub-intern to take his place. Would you do it?" He said, "I've been watching you and you're very good." Parenthetically, he confessed to me years later that he had never laid eyes on me before.

BLDS: He just needed a "sous-chef," and in a hurry?

SN: He needed a warm body. Now, the resident on the private service was a remarkably charismatic fellow. He was a painter, a sculptor, a great lover of the female sex, and I say this advisedly: he put women on pedestals and gloried in the aesthetic values of the feminine form.

BLDS: Who was this fellow?

SN: His name was José Patino. He is a story in himself. He became the minister of health of Colombia, where he founded his own medical school, and he was honored by the American College of Surgeons. He introduced me to what I call the aesthetic of surgery. The beauty of tissue, the way it looks, the way it feels in your hands, the beauty of holding surgical instruments and doing things with them, of stitching, of tying knots, of dissecting, of how it all feels. By the time he was through with me, in a two-week period, I was determined that I would become a surgeon. So I think surgery is enormous fun. And when I talk to young people, graduates, I always say that no matter what other considerations are involved in your choice of a profession, the first and foremost must always be that it has got to be fun. If it's not fun you shouldn't do it.

BLDS: Well, it is theater, a kind of performance art, as well. Yet it has to be combined with a very high degree of scientific skill.

SN: A very high degree of technical skill. Science, I don't know, but certainly technical skill and use of scientific technology to fulfill what you're after.

BLDS: As a product of the public-school system, when it could fairly be described as first-rate, there is little wonder that you could rise to the level that you did. Can you trace for us your path from your neighborhood school?

SN: One of the things about the New York school system at that time, and I don't know if this is still the case, was that they were very selective in how they formed their classes, so that even if there were only two classes in every grade, they would be divided into the smarter kids and the kids who weren't quite as smart. That immediately brought in a

selectivity of education. The teachers of the smarter kids were more likely to teach in a more sophisticated way. I was always in a class that could take advantage of advancement in the kind of education that we were getting, which was a great break.

BLDS: Did you have that same encouragement at home that you did at school?

SN: Well, it's really funny. Kids talk about the drive of the Jewish family and the pressure of a Jewish mother. I never knew any of that. No one ever pressed me, no one ever pushed me. It was just assumed that we were going to do very well academically. It was an assumption I had; it was an assumption my family had. Then I was lucky enough to go to the Bronx High School of Science.

BLDS: I read recently that the Bronx High School of Science had more Merit Scholars than any other school in the country.

SN: Oh yes, but they've come down from what they were in those days. In those days they were the quintessence of the brightest kids in New York City—outside of Brooklyn, because the kids in Brooklyn went to Brooklyn Tech. Five Nobel Prize winners came out of that school. I was thrown in with the smartest people I have ever known in my life, but they weren't any smarter than the group of people that I had started with in kindergarten. In fact, they were all there. That made a very, very big difference. The general assumption that one could do any intellectual thing that one wanted to was supported by that school.

BLDS: You had no mother, a seriously ill father, an aged grandmother. Who took interest in your intellectual pursuits and your future? It seems to me that they had enough to do trying to stay alive.

SN: Yes, but I was the golden boy. In every family there is a golden one. All the hopes of the family rested on me and I knew it.

BLDS: So you had to deliver for them from then on.

SN: But again, it wasn't pressure, it was the underlying gestalt in the family that I was going to do it. My brother was a very bright guy—any of my relatives will tell you he was a hell of a lot smarter than I am—but he didn't have the drive that I seemed to have. When he was fifteen he got rheumatic fever and was in bed for a very long time. It changed his life and his motivation. This left my motivation and the family's certainty that I was going to achieve something very important in the world of science.

BLDS: And indeed you did. One of the central issues of your life, it seems, is the whole question of death. And, fifty years later, you wrote a seminal work called *How We Die*.

SN: I wrote it by accident, although I don't believe in accidents. I don't believe in coincidences. What happens is that the threads of your life come together in a particular form. The phone rang in the office one Thursday afternoon and a man introduced himself and said that he was a literary agent with an idea for a book, and that the book's title should be *How We Die*.

BLDS: Who was this prescient man?

SN: His name is Glen Hartley. He said he thought that this book should be about what happens when one has heart disease, cancer, or a stroke. I said I had no interest in writing such a book, but, when I went home that night and began talking it over with my wife Sarah, it was as though a huge light went on. How did it happen that this fellow should come to me, someone who had been living with this problem all of his life, whose choice of a career had depended on this problem, who, as a matter of fact, was close to the end of a career that he had devoted to taking care of people? The other thing I began to think about was how I could spend my volunteer time. I volunteered for the American Cancer Society, for hospices, for a couple of old-age homes in the greater New Haven area. Everything I had volunteered for had to do with how we die. And I had never put that together. Without knowing it, this fellow had given to me the opportunity to bring the threads together, to discover what was probably subconscious in my mind by that time: my philosophy of death. It was going to help me make sense of it.

BLDS: What motivated you to spend two years of your life writing a book about dying, a necessary and frank and graphic description of the multiple ways that human life can end?

SN: The woods, the air, are full of lies about what death is like, full of euphemisms, fears, and false hopes. I became acquainted with death by watching people die in that four-room apartment. I knew what it was really like. I then went into a profession where I saw death again and again and again among my patients, many of whom I cared about a great deal. I knew that the things I read in many books and heard on many television programs—and even heard sometimes from a lectern—weren't true.

BLDS: So what did you hope to achieve?

SN: I hoped to provide in one book the education and familiarity with death that I had taken a lifetime to achieve. I wanted the reader to understand that once we face certain kinds of realities that exist, we remarkably find that the difficulties and miseries of death are easier. In other words, it has been my experience that a lot of the problems with death that we have in the late twentieth century have to do with a lack of knowledge of death, which is hidden away and sequestered. We have unrealistic fears, just as we have unrealistic hopes. It's a paradox that on one hand you read about the bliss of going off into the unknown and saying your final good-byes, and on the other hand we are terrified of beeping monitors and tubes down our throats and doctors doing things to us that we don't really want done.

BLDS: One of the myths that you dispel is that there is very little likelihood that most of us will have a death with dignity. That is not the way it really does end.

SN: That's right.

BLDS: Very few of us end our days on a fluffy pillow surrounded by loved ones.

SN: That's right. But one of the reasons for the real misery of modern death is that we go into it expecting these great things to happen

I don't believe in accidents. I don't believe in coincidences. What happens is that the threads of your life come together in a particular form.

and moment by moment they don't happen, so we become terrified that something is going wrong and it is not the way it's supposed to be. In the book I tell a story about a woman whom I had been following for a postoperative mastectomy for about five years. She told me about the misery of her mother's death. She had expected that as her mother came into her last weeks and months it would be wonderful and tranquil, but it never happened. There was too much pain, too much Demerol. And she thought, What did I do wrong? Well, she didn't do anything wrong. She just did not know what death was about. It seemed to me that I could relieve the tremendous unjustified guilt that so many people have if they only knew what death was really like.

BLDS: That sounds like guilt on the part of the survivors. How does one go with grace?

SN: You say "grace," but I found a word that makes a little more sense for me. It's not completely the right word. I call it nobility. I call it rising above the misery. I call it being ourselves in the midst of the kind of pain and other suffering that nothing can relieve, at least in our modern hospitals; remaining true, as far as we can within the limitations of what physically happens in our bodies, to the values that carried us through our lives. One of those values is honesty. For most of us the search for this thing we call dignity is not honest. It's just not in keeping with what has happened to us.

BLDS: What is the best that one can hope for?

SN: Remember that the best that one can hope for may still be granted. I think that's the first rule. If you don't get what you hope for, or more importantly, what the survivors can provide, this is neither a sin nor an omission that you should be punished for. The most important thing to realize is that the circumstances of death are determined by the disease first and foremost—they are not determined by our wish for a dignified death or by the personality or character we bring to death. If we do not achieve nobility or the sense of dignity in death, it says much less about us than it does about the disease that carried us off. How can you expect somebody dying of multiple sclerosis or AIDS to achieve dignity or to die in a way that is a lesson to other people? What kind of bizarre expectation is that? Or a person who has a stroke and is paralyzed through half of his body and drools for the last three months of his life, or someone who has Alzheimer's? There ain't no dignity. The most you can look for is transcending the indignity and achieving a little measure of nobility.

BLDS: What is the title of the book you are currently completing?

SN: I think *The Wisdom of the Body*, but I'm not sure. I wrote a whole book called *How We Die* and I never mentioned my father, and the question is why. There was something obviously severely repressed that I needed to repress.

BLDS: You never mentioned your father once?

SN: My father is not mentioned once in *How We Die*. It's fascinating. And I didn't realize it until it was pointed out to me.

BLDS: Who pointed it out to you?

SN: A friend—who is a psychiatrist. I think it's a very big problem for me. When I write about the central nervous system, which is discussed in the last two chapters of the book I am currently writing, will I write about my father? I have had some discussions with friends about whether I should or whether I should not.

BLDS: Denial is a fact of everyone's life, but I thought that part of the purpose of your books is to remove that veil.

SN: Exactly. I don't know how you did it, but you put your finger right on it. Since I removed some veils about my father for myself many years ago, the question is, how much more a part of my emotional rehabilitation will it be to remove that veil for the rest of the world?

BLDS: And is it necessary? It may be merely an interesting footnote to your own emotional evolution, rather than a critical fact of another book.

SN: Exactly. It turned out that it was very important for me personally to write about my home in *How We Die:* what the home was like, what my grandmother's death was like, and so on. Only the ongoing flow of this book will tell me if I have to write about my father. *How We Die* was written very much like this book is being written, namely, out of a flow of ideas. So I don't know yet if I will write about him.

BLDS: How does the body fight to keep itself alive?

SN: The function of all of those chemical reactions that go on every second is to maintain the stability of each cell in the face of any change that occurs in the cell's atmosphere, to maintain its constancy. I have a friend who has spent his life in protein chem-

> . . . the circumstances of death are determined by the disease first and foremost—they are not determined by our wish for a dignified death or by the personality or character we bring to death.

istry and he introduced me to the term *changing constancy*. There's always change. I was using the term *dynamic stability* to describe it. What really happens is that every cell is being influenced by the immediate environment around it. The whole idea is to maintain what's called homeostasis. *Homeo* as in same, *stasis* as in place. The body's tendency is to stay in the same place while changing just enough to accommodate changed circumstances. For example, if our DNA is changed a little bit chemically, there are enzymes in the cell that cut out that piece of DNA and replace it with a proper piece of DNA. The need to maintain stability is so elemental that it starts at a level that is strictly chemical. It has nothing to do with life per se, it has only to do with the way chemical reactions work to maintain constancy. This grows into what we call life, the automaticity of life, the continuation of life. One can think of life as an extrapolation from each individual cell, but it's more than that because the cells signal to each other. If a given cell is not doing the kind of job it needs to do in order to keep doing its work in the tissue of which it is a part, it gets a signal from other cells about how it must change its performance. In embryological development if there is a group of cells sitting in part of the developing egg that should really be over there instead of over here, it gets a signal from over there saying come over here, fellas; this is where you really belong. A particular order is maintained in which we must evolve, a particular order that is determined by biophysical laws. By natural selection, simple chemical reactions have come together to eventually form a living structure, a cell, which is more efficient if it can live with other cells and become a multicell organism, which is even more efficient if it can become an animal, and bit by bit more complex things grow because they can control their environment better. What allows a single-celled organism to become a multicelled organism is that a multicelled organism has more chemical reactions with which to fight off the insults of its environment. The most complex organisms are the ones that are most independent of their environment. You and I are to a great extent independent of our environment. We may not be able to go downtown because it's snowing, but who cares if it's cold outside? It can't kill us. We're here inside. The complexity of evolution is really nothing more or less than the biological necessity for organisms to resist death. By its very nature a living thing is constantly fighting death. The problem is that the mechanisms only work in each organism for a given period of time: for a dog it's twelve or thirteen years, for you or me it's seven, eight, nine decades—that's

all it is. These biological mechanisms begin to wear out. The ability of enzymes to cut out the wrong piece of DNA and put in the right piece of DNA isn't nearly as good in people of a certain age as it is in a fourteen-year-old. In some countries people die of certain kinds of infectious diseases that are not the result of the breakdown of mechanisms that keep people alive, but the result of outside agents. We are going to die because our ability to fight off the ravages that go on in our cells will be lost when we become too old to fight off certain changes in our blood vessels and in our brains, certain changes in what makes our heart function properly.

BLDS: Those ravages have been imposed in large measure by that which has been transmitted to us genetically—that we have then managed to compound.

SN: Absolutely.

BLDS: So we are what they were. Genes, in the end, are of critical importance.

SN: The basic quality that makes us what we are is our genetic makeup, or what biologists call the ability to express certain genes. We all have the same DNA; the question is which parts of that DNA are expressed and useful. But no matter what our biology is, we can, by the way we live, make the best possible use of that. For example, I carry within me, and I know this, a certain genetic makeup that will inevitably cause me to have intestinal cancer. I know that from my family history and I know that because I have a history of polyps of the colon which become cancerous. Inevitably, if I live long enough, I will develop intestinal cancer. But in order for the so-called intestinal-cancer gene or genes to work, a certain environment is needed within the cell. We know that for many people that environment depends somewhat on the amount of animal fat in their diet, so I eat very carefully. We have recently discovered that for a large group of women, and I have to assume this is true for men too, the simple ingestion of one aspirin every other day markedly decreases the frequency of cancer of the intestine. It has to be because it's a change within the cell; that is the only explanation.

BLDS: So why isn't it more widely prescribed, even mandatory?

SN: It was just published within the past year. Yes, it should be widely prescribed, it should be mandatory; at least people should have a choice. By taking one aspirin every other day, and by eating far fewer animal fats, I am actually changing the environment inside my cells! My God, I can control how my genes express themselves. Actually, by our conscious habits we can decide what the environment within the cell will be and thus determine whether or not the genes will express themselves. It's an amazing concept.

BLDS: So in that environmental self, the question of will is fundamental.

SN: The body builds itself up with the intention to fight off environmental stresses. But that's a biological thing. You can't determine that it will happen, but you can determine the extent to which it will happen. Our body is programmed to stay alive. It's the old Darwinian thing of reproduction and self-preservation, but the self-preservation is built into our cellular structure. It is not just a matter of, oh, my God, I don't want to die; or, I'll jump into the path of that car; or, he's got a knife and how am I going to get out of this room; or, I won't touch him because he's got syphilis. Every organ, every cell, functions in such a way as to maintain homeostasis—stability. If it functions well it is fated by natural selection to survive and be passed to our offspring; if it doesn't function well the species dies out.

BLDS: In some ways even writing *How We Die* helped maintain this stability for you—because it must have been such an enormously cathartic experience, synthesizing so many things in your life.

SN: Absolutely. If our bodies are the product only of our biology, and if our biology works on the basis of homeostasis, then there must be mental homeostasis. We most probably do what we can, consciously or unconsciously, to maintain our emotional balance. Some of the adjustments we make are maladjustments, because we are not very good at it. Some of them are crippled by events that occurred in childhood. We develop ways of looking at things and patterns of thought that are maladjusted and wrong. Some of us go to psychoanalysts, some of us go to faith healers, but wherever we go we try to change our thinking patterns.

BLDS: I'm beginning to think that everyone has his or her own baseline and, when challenged by internal or external circumstances, has the ability to respond.

SN: One of the subtexts of my book is what I call the healing spirit. We have conscious will, which enables us to transcend to a significant degree the basic ground of what we would be. In the book I tell the story of a guy who never finished high school, but he teaches us that we live up to what he calls "a step above." What a wonderful term! He was able to transcend his personality, his biology, a terrible family history (his mother died in her forties),

and habits that he thought were so ingrained he could never break them. That's the kind of thing that I call the human spirit. It's nothing mystical, it has nothing to do with God, or angels, or whatever. It has to do with the human will. A lot of it is unconscious, but I think it is driven by conscious thought—by conscious desire and conscious goals.

BLDS: Speaking of goals, you could have chosen to be a very successful practitioner in a place like Greenwich, Connecticut, instead of a member of the Yale University faculty. And how did you come to apply to the Yale University medical school? Perhaps you could briefly trace the evolution of your mid-twentieth-century professional education.

SN: It was a tough time. It was a very bad time.

BLDS: Where did you do your undergraduate work?

SN: At the time when I finished high school, the New York City system didn't go by years, it went by semesters. Half of the kids graduated in January, half of the kids graduated in June. I graduated from high school in January, so I had two choices. I could either wait until September to start college, or I could go to one of a few colleges that started right away. I was restricted by the fact that I had to go to college in New York City. We couldn't have possibly afforded for me to go to school outside of New York.

BLDS: You had to live at home?

SN: Yes. New York City had City College, New York University, and Columbia University. I would have had to wait six months to go to Columbia. I didn't want to go to City College because the great days of City College were just over. It was not an option for me.

BLDS: It just wasn't good enough?

SN: I didn't think at that time it was good enough. So the best school after Columbia was the New York University campus at University Heights in the Bronx. It was the original college of the university. It was a small men's college in the middle of the Bronx.

BLDS: It was a single-sex school?

SN: Yes. It had a very fine faculty. It had nothing academically to do with so-called NYU Downtown, which was a large, sprawling coed school that was very easy to get into. The school offered a program in which you could start in February and go right through the summer and end up in September a sophomore, which would have put me a whole year ahead of where I would have been had I gone to Columbia. At that time—the late forties and early fifties—getting into medical school was a huge obstacle for certain kinds of people. It was very hard for Jewish boys to get into medical school anywhere except NYU in New York and Downstate.

BLDS: Were they considered good schools?

SN: NYU was considered very good. It was well known that no Jewish boy of Eastern European origin applied to Cornell or Columbia. You just didn't do it. Even though I was first in my class, I never applied to either school because there was no point to it. It's such a ridiculous thing. Today, a large proportion of the faculties at Cornell and Columbia are Jewish, a large proportion of the house staff is Jewish, and a large proportion of the medical-student population is Jewish.

BLDS: Was it restricted then?

SN: The only Jewish kids I ever knew who went to those two schools in the fifties were upper-middle-class German Jewish kids whose families had come in 1848 and opened department stores or something. Kids like me didn't do such a thing. On the applications to medical schools they always asked for your mother's maiden name and your father's occupation. It was well known what that was all about.

BLDS: Was your name always Nuland?

SN: No. That's the other thing, of course. It wasn't changed until near the end of high school. Our name had gone through several evolutions in Europe having to do with the Russian draft. The original family name had been Weinberg. Three generations before me there were five sons. In Russia Jews were drafted for thirty years and did not serve above private level. However, if you were the only son in a family you were not drafted; you were allowed to stay with whatever the family business or occupation was. It was a well-known scam that people would change their names so they could say, "I'm the only son of the Humperdinck family or the Goldberg family." In my family, all five brothers, except one, changed their names. My great-grandfather chose the name Nodelman because he was a tailor—Needle-man. When the family came here someone must have started saying Needleman instead of Nodelman. I had two cousins who hated the name, so they and several other cousins got together in the thirties and

decided they were going to change it. And they changed it three different ways. One branch changed it to Delman. One woman, who was in her twenties at that time, decided to call herself Numan. The others made up this name Nuland. I was three or four years old at the time. When we were in high school my brother and I just did the same thing.

BLDS: Was it ever legally changed?

SN: Yes.

BLDS: How did you know how to do that in high school?

SN: Name changes were very common in those days.

BLDS: In some ways it helped define and prophesy your life. You have just proceeded from one uncharted territory to other uncharted territories.

SN: Yes. I have always felt that the change of name represented an entire transformation of vista. In other words, I had always known that I would get out of the miasma in which I was growing up. I had always known that it would be in some kind of worldly way; to me, at the time, a worldly way was to be a general practitioner in the Bronx. That was worldly enough for me. But I think the name change signified an emotional change. Something in my emotional life must have been ready for a transformation that involved much wider vistas.

BLDS: So where did the new Nuland apply? He couldn't apply to Cornell, he couldn't apply to Columbia, and he didn't have the money to leave home.

SN: He did what everybody else did. He applied to twenty-five medical schools.

BLDS: Even as first in your class you didn't think you would be accepted anywhere?

SN: Yes. In a very short time I was accepted to NYU and to Downstate, where I knew I was just a shoo in, so I didn't have to think about that. But interestingly, the first school that accepted me was Johns Hopkins. That night I heard my sweet aunt on the phone saying to her friend, "Shepsel"—my Yiddish name was Shepsel—"was just accepted to Johnsons Thompsons Medical School." Who had ever heard of Hopkins at that time?

BLDS: Was your given name Sherwin?

SN: No.

BLDS: How did that change occur?

SN: My other aunt, who was quite young when she came here and read more English, gave me the name. She loved jazz and had a collection of phonograph records. One of them was called "Jazz

B Blues" by Sherwin's Broadway Orchestra. Of course, Orthodox Jews named their children with Americanized names that came from their Hebrew names. My Hebrew name was Shabbatai Dov, which means Sabbath Observer and Bear, and my Yiddish name was Shepsel Ber, which means a lamb and a bear. It's customary to choose an American name that has the same first letter as the Yiddish. So Shepsel Ber—Shep and B—became Sherwin's Broadway Orchestra. My first name was Sherwin Broadway.

BLDS: The B stands for Broadway?

SN: Unfortunately, they thought better and changed it to Bernard. So I grew up with this prosaic name and felt cheated over the years. No one has ever called me Sherwin. If I go to a meeting I can tell who knows me and who doesn't. I was always called Shep.

BLDS: So you were accepted to Johns Hopkins, which should have been a welcome surprise.

SN: Yes, it was. The question was how the hell was I going to get to go there? I think they gave me ten days to say yes or no. That was a Friday night. Monday morning I called the Yale admissions office and said, "I just got into Hopkins and they have to know by the end of the week. Can I have my interview this week?" Things were so different then. He said, "Sure. Come tomorrow or Wednesday." So I got on the train and went up to New Haven for two interviews. It was all very pleasant, very nice, like nothing I was accustomed to. Everybody spoke beautifully and looked wonderful. All the men were handsome, all the women were beautiful. I was even taken to afternoon tea. Well, lo and behold, they accepted me.

BLDS: How could you afford to go, though? Did they offer you a scholarship?

SN: It is an interesting story. My grandmother, who lived on the Lower East Side with her girls, took advantage of an opportunity given by Baron de Hirsch, a very wealthy German Jewish businessman who bought up large tracts of land and sold them very, very cheaply to Jewish immigrants so they could work the land and get out of the big cities. She bought one of these tracts of land—it was two hundred acres in Connecticut, north of Colchester.

BLDS: Where did she get the money to do that?

SN: The whole thing was set up so that there was a very minimal down payment.

BLDS: Like a homestead pioneer going out into the countryside?

SN: That was the idea. And if you go now to Colchester there are zillions of Jewish families. Some of them still have little farms. Some of them are still in the egg business. Anyway, the purpose of the farm was to get people out of the city. Relatives and friends would go to her farm, stay with her for two or three weeks at a time, and that was how she supported herself.

BLDS: Did she live there all the time or remain in the Bronx?

SN: She lived there. She moved from the Lower East Side and took my mother and my two aunts. They were teenage girls. They lived there for a very long time. One of the young people who came to the farm was a man named Astrove. He and his brother were the children of janitors in a building on Rivington Street on the Lower East Side, which meant that their father studied the Talmud all day long while their mother cleaned the steps and fixed the plumbing. In his late twenties Astrove established a children's wear company and became a millionaire by the time he was in his thirties. He and his younger brother felt a sense of obligation to the extended family. When my mother was very sick and bills had to be paid, every once in a while a check would come for a hundred dollars, which was a lot of money in 1938.

BLDS: And he was not even related to you.

SN: No. He was remarkable guy. He was self-educated, having left school at fifth grade, and very cultivated. He spoke without an accent and was a very polished man. His brother was the same way. When I started college he came down and said he wanted to pay my way. It turned out I won a state Regents' scholarship. I also had one from the Young Men's Hebrew Association to make up the small deficit between the Regents' scholarship and costs. But when it came time for medical school, there was no way to go except to accept his offer. We finally negotiated that he would pay my way and I would pay him back. I said when I was a doctor and had ten thousand dollars in the bank I would pay him back. In those days, tuition was a thousand dollars a year and rent was a thousand, so it would have been eight thousand dollars for four years.

BLDS: Did you ever pay him back?

SN: No. After I was in practice, a year or two out of school, I called him up and said I wanted to give him back the money, but he refused to take it.

BLDS: Well, you just paid him back, because it's a great story. He must have done it for other people, too.

SN: I don't know how many people he sent to school—I'm sure there were others—but he did a lot of things for a lot of people. His brother did the same. So that is how I got to go to Yale. Of course, Yale opened up a whole new world to me. This was epitomized by something that happened the very first day of school. We were going to anatomy class. You didn't wear your own shirt in anatomy class, you wore a little short coat that you had to change into. There was a little locker room for that purpose. Now, we all had already chosen our cadaver partners—two or three boys to a cadaver. (There were four girls in the class but there were seventy-six boys.) My cadaver partner was a kid named Leo Cardillo who had gone to Fordham. I thought he was in the same economic straits as I was; it wasn't until five years ago that I found out his father was a shipbuilder and he was very wealthy. But Leo was an unreconstructed Italian Catholic Bronx kid even though he had a lot of money. So, when we went to change our clothes in the locker room, I looked around—there were all these young men my age and a lot of them older—and noticed that the vast majority of these young men didn't have hair on their chests. I said to Leo, "What's this?" He said, "Those are the Protestants."

BLDS: You have been on the staff of the Yale–New Haven Medical Center since 1962 and first went there as a student in 1951. In all of the years that you have been at Yale you have witnessed a lot of changes, not only in the world around you but especially in the medical and scientific communities. What have been the most positive changes and what have been the least appealing?

SN: Paradoxically, some of the things that have been the most positive for medicine have been the least appealing for doctors and their patients. For example, one of the most positive was the advent of health insurance, which was almost nonexistent when I was a student.

BLDS: It really didn't happen till 1965.

SN: Blue Cross and Blue Shield started growing in the early sixties, but at that time most people still didn't have it. The advent of the third-party payer was part of the origin of the erosion of the relationship between doctor and patient, to which I attribute a lot of the ills of medicine that have occurred over the years. By the mid-seventies nobody was paying his or her own way. The attitude that had developed among doctors and patients was that anything went, any kind of test could be done, any kind of hospi-

talization could be carried out because it didn't cost anybody anything. That began to affect the judgment of the physicians, as far as their uses of diagnostic and therapeutic skills. It has been a terribly erosive factor in the clinical perfection of American medicine. The average American doctor today is not nearly as skilled with his five senses and his stethoscope and his history taking. A lot of it I attribute to the fact that he gets paid for it and, so what, let's go do another X ray. The other thing that has happened is that those skills, since they are no longer used as much, have gradually been taught less and valued less. We now have young doctors who are simply bad at basic diagnostic skills and rely on sophisticated tests that are astronomically expensive. Diagnoses are no longer being made with the attending physician's hand on the patient's belly, but with the resident's eye on the computer. So whereas, even twenty years ago, physicians were masters of history taking and of the physical exam, now they are what I call masters of the menu. They know what tests to order.

BLDS: But that can be valuable too, can't it?

SN: Yes, but the downside is that it has separated us still further from the patient. By the time you sit with a patient, take his history, maybe put a stethoscope on his chest, look into the back of his eye, and feel his belly, something has transpired between you.

BLDS: So what substitutes for the laying-on of hands? That intimacy, that concern, that reassuring gesture?

SN: What substitutes for it is the patient's image of the doctor as the master of technology that will assure his cure. People today think of doctors as the access to technological innovations that are foolproof.

BLDS: So, the doctor as middleman?

SN: That's a good way to put it, but middleman is not exactly it, because he is actually in control of the situation. It is not as though he is the transitional path to it. When you go to your doctor you have expectations that he can diagnose everything and cure everything. When he doesn't—because, after all, a disease is a disease—you feel the medical establishment has failed. People forty years ago understood that there are diseases that cannot be treated or cured and that there is a phase in each disease where nothing more can be done. Now, because medicine is technologically at a high level, the expectation is that everything should be diagnosable and

> Diagnoses are no longer being made with the attending physician's hand on the patient's belly, but with the resident's eye on the computer.

curable. Technology, on the one hand, has made a lot of things diagnosable and curable; on the other hand, it has provided expectations that can never be met, although even doctors begin to believe they can do these things. Technology has also thrown itself in between the doctor and his patient. It is a paradox that the very things, such as insurance and technology, that are the greatest changes in medicine are also the vehicles by which the all-important relationship between doctor and patient has been eroded.

BLDS: What are the next set of challenges to be addressed by the medical and science communities?

SN: What we have witnessed, especially in the last two decades, is the extraordinary change from what was at its heart a profession characterized by personal relationships between physicians and their patients, to one of increasing distance and technological application to the treatment of disease. On the one hand, this has brought marked increases in efficiency of diagnoses and therapy; on the other hand, it has destroyed the *humanitas* of the art of healing. The direction of research has also changed. At the beginning of my career, when a problem was perceived, those concerned with it would retreat to the laboratory to solve it and emerge after some time with the answer, which they then applied in the care of their patients. These days, the tail wags the dog. Laboratory technology determines what can be done in the treatment of patients. The problems that are addressed are problems that arise not at the bedside but in the laboratory. This is an enormous change in perspective. I never expected that advances in biomedicine would occur so rapidly that we would reach a point in my lifetime where our abilities far exceed the moral and ethical resources of the scientists who have brought them to us. In other words, the consequences of recent biomedicine are so enormous for our community, I am no longer convinced that scientists and physicians themselves are equipped to decide how their own work should be used. Technologies such as genetic engineering and some of the newer reproductive developments are of such striking import for our society, I believe that it is society itself that should be making decisions that have heretofore been left to the scientific community. I even find myself wondering whether

> I have long believed that the only solution to our country's problems of equitable health-care distribution lies in a single-payer system, based on a regionalized division of management, with all doctors on salary.

the old criterion of research should remain, namely that scientists are free to study any phenomenon they find interesting. I know this sounds a bit reactionary and perhaps Luddite, but science is taking us in directions for which we may not be prepared. The scientific endeavor must now be addressed by all of society, including the very studies that are permitted to be done, and certainly their applications.

BLDS: What is your impression of the current health-care situation in America? What do you believe is currently the biggest threat to the health-care system?

SN: In some ways I welcome the turmoil concerning HMOs and certainly look with favor on the dreadful mismanagement and consequences of managed care. I have long believed that the only solution to our country's problems of equitable health-care distribution lies in a single-payer system, based on a regionalized division of management, with all doctors on salary. Those salaries should be equally distributed so that there is a minimal differential between what a specialist and a family physician are paid. The present disgraceful situation that has been brought on by managed care is exactly the explosion we need to make everyone realize the urgent requirement for a total overhaul of our health-care distribution-and-payment system based on what some would call socialized medicine. I have written about this, spoken about this, and will continue to educate for a total overall reform.

BLDS: In one of your articles you talk about the American obsession with megahealth. People want to be in perfect condition, despite the realities of the physical body, age, experience, and circumstance. Knowing what you do about the workings of the human body, have you personally been able to escape that obsession, and do the normal processes ever upset you? You have a very clear and rational understanding of your own health, of the prospects and possibilities, so how do you come to accept the constraints of yourself? And how do you feel about what you have identified as megahealth?

SN: There is an old phrase, from Pascal, that the heart has its reasons. The body has its reasons. Built into the body is the stability we talked about, the maintenance, the ability to change constantly in order to fight off cellular and environmental changes. Also built into it is what you might call planned obsolescence. There is a time when all of the mechanisms that are so efficient to maintain stability slowly begin to break down. Certain genes lose the ability to make certain proteins; certain proteins do not have the effect they should have within the cell anymore. This is an inevitability. We have learned that there are ways for some people to put off the inevitable, to keep the mechanisms in good shape for a little longer. We do this by exercise and a wise diet.

BLDS: Do you do it?

SN: I do maintenance things that everybody should do. But there is a limit beyond which our body cannot function. Our body is made to function at an optimal level for survival. There is no such thing as megahealth or super-vibrant health. There is no such thing as orgasmic health, in which every moment of the day you feel as if you are a Greek god or goddess at the age of sixty-eight or thirty-two or twenty-five. There is only so much our cellular structure allows. Megahealth, which is a term given to me by the publisher of *Elle*, doesn't exist. There is a point beyond which we can't make ourselves super-healthy. All we can do is the best to make normal cellular function continue.

BLDS: You said that in exploring our national obsession with perfect health and the maniacal pursuit of the perfect body, your conclusion was that it is rooted in egotism. Do you still believe that? How do we shake that preoccupation?

SN: I'm going to say something so prosaic that it's a cliché: Live with the constant realization of what your life means to other people. What I mean is that my immortality will consist of the way I have affected the people around me. We must see ourselves with what Percy Shelley wrote about in one of his essays, "moral imagination." Moral imagination is the ability to see ourselves with the eyes of another person, in other words, to live up to the expectations that those who love us the most have of us. Their expectation from us is the expression of love, sanity, and the golden mean. Would my children have expectations of me that I would go jogging ten miles a day every day, constantly look in the mirror to see whether I had lost an ounce, have my face lifted when I reach a particular age, or be obsessed with the idea of my longevity? I don't think so. I think my children's expectations of me are that I will be kind, that I will make sacrifices for them, that I will sometimes give up what I think is in my best interest because it is in the best interest of the group, that I will make the very most I can out of whatever potentialities I have been given by nature. That's what

I mean by moral imagination.

BLDS: What do you mean when you use the word *health* or *healthy*?

SN: Health, to me, is a concept. It is usually defined as simply the absence of disease; I do believe that's as good a definition as any. I have never been a believer in megahealth, in the sense of a certain extraordinary vibrancy that enables us to climb figurative mountains. I believe there is an enormous egotism in such an attitude, which is unworthy of us. I simply want my basic physiology to be working perfectly well, and to be free of disease or of the kind of physiological disturbance that inhibits me from the physical and emotional enjoyment of life. I realize that is not much of an answer, but I am actually describing the sort of health I have at the moment.

BLDS: What does a natural death continue to mean? It seems that the rest of the medical profession doesn't acknowledge the importance of that matter.

SN: To me it means that I recognize the inevitable and give in to it. I think our bodies tell us. I think physicians know far earlier than is generally acknowledged that further fighting is useless. I believe there are inevitabilities of existence. They have to do with the molecular construction of our bodies. I want to have the good sense to know when it's useless to continue fighting and the good sense to remember that the real dignity is the dignity of what will be remembered of me after I am gone.

BLDS: You identify yourself as a formerly Jewish agnostic but somehow you seem resonantly devout.

SN: Do you need to believe in God in a spiritual sense? Do you need to believe in supernatural powers in a spiritual sense? I don't think so. I believe when I go to hear a symphony that I have heard fifty times before, and something in that symphony feels as if it's in my chest and carrying me out of my seat, that is my spiritual sense. I believe that when I go to synagogue, as I do often, and I am moved by the community of Jews with whom I am sitting, their history, how they have reached this place, memories of my father, that is my spiritual sense.

BLDS: Why can't you pray at home?

SN: People who pray at home pray because they want to be sure God hears them. I don't think there's a God, and God's not going to hear me. I love to pray because I love the community of Jews praying together. I love to be in that number. As *When the Saints Go Marching In* says, I long to be in that number.

BLDS: So you have a sense of religious identification.

SN: I have a sense of ethnic identification. To me, religion implies that you believe in God or supernatural things or whatever you believe in.

BLDS: How do you maintain this Jewish identity?

SN: I have known my wife, Sarah, for over twenty years now. She understands this very, very well. She understands that everything that I am, in one way or another—no matter the Irish schoolteachers, no matter the influence of Yale, no matter the influence of Shakespeare or Shelley—is ultimately due to my Jewishness.

BLDS: You never forgot your grandmother.

SN: No, you don't forget your grandmother. Whatever morality I have, whatever self-confidence I have, whatever certainty I have about my ability to overcome adversity, all of it springs from something that I was given in a very strongly Jewish home. To abandon the sense of Judaism or to abandon the personal significance of the rituals of Judaism would be as though I had a face-lift. It's enough to have changed my name; I don't want to change who I am. I have a Jewish outlook on life.

BLDS: As a confirmed skeptic, and I assume this underscores what an honest man you are, you said, "I am bound by the conviction that we must not only question all things, but be willing to believe that all things can be possible."

SN: That's almost my motto.

BLDS: That is a marvelous quote. What have you discovered in your life to have been most wonderfully possible?

SN: The thing that is most wonderfully possible is very easy. It's a four-letter word. It's love. *Amor Vincit Omnia.* I mean love in all of its forms. At the risk of sounding sanctimonious I do believe in the sanctity of home, and I believe the sanctity of family is based ultimately on the love of your two parents. Even if there are no children and it is just the husband and wife, that is what determines the culture of the family and all of the actions vis-à-vis others. Love has saved my life. It's a complicated thing. Initially, it was the love my grandmother, my mother, my aunt, and my father had for me as a child that gave me the certainty that I could do anything I wanted to do and that it could come from within myself. When there is love and understanding, there is a kind of harmony that buffers all of the damn bumps and hits that you get from life. To me, love is a little bit like those enzymes inside the cells that go up and down looking for the busted pieces of DNA to fix them. I'm not talking about statements of love, I'm talking

about an atmosphere that somehow corrects and balances and that somehow creates what might be thought of as a cocoon against the world. No matter how worldly we are, no matter what we must accomplish in the world, we can only do it from a position of very strong roots that come from within us. Those are transmitted very easily to our children. They become matter-of-fact. We learn lessons by doing things for someone we love that we can use in relation to people we don't love. We just want to do things for others and need to do things for others.

BLDS: You once said, "Before there were two digits in my age, I had seen the hope"—and you chose the word deliberately—"that a doctor's presence brings to a worried family."

SN: I have often said that there are three divine professions. For an agnostic to use a word like "divine" sounds pretty awful, but we should trace its roots. The word *divine* comes from the Indo-European word having to do with the natural events from the heavens. To me, the greatest natural splendor is to have a major effect for the good of the lives of others. Therefore, there is something divine about three professions: medicine, the ministry, and teaching. Those are all pastoral professions.

BLDS: And you've managed to combine all three.

SN: I've been lucky. I've been in a situation in my profession in which I've been able to carry out all three, but I've only been able to carry out the ministry part because society has allowed me to do that. Society continues to think of physicians, regardless of how bad things have gotten, in kind of a ministerial capacity.

BLDS: Who has filled that role in your life?

SN: Elizabeth Thompson, Tom Forbes, Bob Massey, Jay Katz, Arthur Chiel, David Clement, and Sam Saltzman.

BLDS: Are these colleagues of yours?

SN: Older colleagues. I seem to have found big-brother figures and a few big sisters, people generally ten to fifteen years older than me. Their good opinion means an enormous amount to me. Their lives have been the engine that drove my work. In other words, I want those people to be proud of me. I don't know where in my childhood that concept comes from, I have not been able to figure that out, but I have the sense that every one of those people is proud of me. I'm their kid brother. Aristotle believed the heart was the center of the brain, the center of the soul, the center of the mind, the center of emotion, the center of everything that is there.

BLDS: Isn't the ability to transform oneself one of the central themes of your current book?

SN: That's right. Even at a cellular level we can transform what seems to be the destiny of our biology. That's what I'm writing about.

BLDS: What do you value most in life?

SN: It's love. What is science? It's just the search for truth. What is love? It's the essence of discovering truth about yourself. You cannot fool yourself about certain things. Find the essence of the thing. All of life is pursuit of that which is true. And again, it's pragmatic. Only what is true works.

BLDS: Did you ever expect your life to unfold the way it has?

SN: Do any of us? Life is, in essence, a series of responses to the cards we are constantly being dealt. We try to evaluate those cards and react to them in ways that seem to make sense, based upon values, goals, and the surroundings in which we make the ultimate decisions. Without question, I have made some wrong decisions, as have all of us. But each time, I have tried to use the mistake as a platform from which to launch the next part of the voyage. Some of my worst mistakes have led to some of my greatest joys.

BLDS: If you had your life to live over again, what would you do otherwise?

SN: I would be kinder, both to myself and to everyone with whom I come in contact. I would be much more forgiving of perceived deficiencies in myself and others. Without question, I would also have spent much more time during my hectic surgical career trying to be more of a scholar and less of a totally focused technological physician.

BLDS: When will you begin writing your memoirs? Or is your current series of books essentially your memoirs?

SN: Actually, several chapters have been written. My current series of books are something of a "batting practice" for actually getting up to the plate to write the memoirs. I plan to give myself all the time I need to become soaked into the atmosphere in which I grew up. We are, as you know, made of memories. I hope to be able to describe for myself and for others the continuity of a life, which is essentially of a single piece.

BLDS: After fifty-five years, have you finally come to grips with your mother's death? How do you handle grief?

SN: Only recently, and partially as a result of writing these last two books, have I been able to understand just how all-encompassing were the effects of my mother's death. I believe that at the age of eleven I was not able to mourn in a way that permitted the necessary psychic repair. I was left damaged by my mother's death in ways that have taken me the rest of my life to understand. I think the autobiographical nature of my recent writings have been a pathway for me to comprehend the turmoil that still, to some large extent, exists in my soul. Grief is best handled by reality. I believe there must be a conscious understanding of the need to integrate every aspect of loss into one overall philosophy, not only of death itself, but of the loss of the specific person we mourn. Each time we suffer a loss, one of the stars by which we steer our lives disappears, and we must reorient the direction of our personal journey.

BLDS: What haven't you done yet that you'd care to?

SN: I would spend several uninterrupted years reading poetry, philosophy, and the great works of Western literature. I don't think of myself as a particularly well educated man, at least in comparison with the kinds of people who trod this earth a generation or two ago, when a truly eclectic education meant a great deal more than it does today. I would love to study the origins of human belief, specifically religious belief. Religious belief, it seems to me, strikes at the very heart of human nature, and is a universal phenomenon that is among the most significant determinants of our culture. I would like to be untrammeled by a need to fulfill the expectations of others, but only to become lost in books and conversations with people I love and people for whose minds I have not only respect but awe.

BLDS: Your involvement in medicine has manifested itself in practice, teaching, and now writing. Which of these three do you prefer?

SN: I loved being a surgeon. Nobody enjoyed the operating room more than I did, nor did anyone feel as much at home in that place as I. I loved patient care, especially at the bedside, and I must admit to you that the self-image of being a physician fulfilled every expectation any human being can have for himself and for his opportunity to be of service to his fellows. There is a certain irony in the fact that I have devoted forty years of my life to trying to be the best doctor I knew how, and yet I will be remembered, except by my medical colleagues and patients, as the person who wrote certain books. Yes, I do love writing, and in many ways the opportunity to write makes me sometimes feel as though everything I have done previously in my life has been preparation for the years in which I am now living. Nevertheless, I am ultimately a man of action. The present years of contemplation would have been impossible without the wonderful years of being in the midst of the hurly-burly of everyday things and the excitement of moment-to-moment challenges.

BLDS: It's no accident that so many of the world's cultures dispensed with ambivalence and made their doctors priests. Is disentangling this ancient link, for yourself and your profession, part of what *How We Die* is all about?

SN: I don't want to disentangle the ancient link between medicine and the priesthood. I believe one of the reasons for the dedication and devotion to improvement of yesteryear's physicians is their willing acceptance of the mantle that society has bestowed on them. With the concept of priesthood goes the concept of the expectation that we will live up to certain standards. Until fairly recently we have done exactly that. Actually, I have tried to instill in students the pride that comes with the principle of priesthood and specialness. I have often said that there are three divine professions: the ministry, teaching, and medicine. All three of those professions are in deep trouble these days, and much of it is because of society's and our own need to diminish the elevated image we have had. I believe that the present egalitarian influence in contemporary culture, which downplays expertness and devotion to duty, is one of the major factors in the destruction of the kinds of loyalty to principle that have made some of our professions accomplish so very much in the past.

> I have often said that there are three divine professions: the ministry, teaching, and medicine. All three of those professions are in deep trouble these days. . . .

BEVERLY SILLS

> I was never just going to be an opera singer, I was going to be an opera star.

BLDS: By the time you were three years old you were named Baby Beautiful—the most beautiful baby—for your performance in the wedding of "Jack and Jill." This is about 1932. How and where did this take place?

BS: In Tompkins Park in Brooklyn. It was the era of the kiddie star—Shirley Temple times. My mother was putting my hair up in sixty jiggly curls to look like Shirley, but she thought we had a different angle—I was going to be a famous kiddie opera star.

BLDS: And she knew what your talents were from the very beginning?

BS: Oh, absolutely.

BLDS: Was there musical ability evident in other members of your family?

BS: None. We can't find a musician in the place, not before and not since. When my mother was saying that I was going to be a famous opera star nobody ever questioned her, or said, oh, by the way, can the child sing? That was incidental, because anything my mother set her mind to do, she was going to do.

BLDS: What gave her such conviction and fortitude?

BS: That was my mother. That's the way she raised us. She said anything we wanted, any dream that we dreamed of, we could have if we were willing to work hard enough for it. So there was never any question in her mind. I was never just going to be an opera singer, I was going to be an opera star. She told that to my father.

BLDS: And obviously you believed it, too.

BS: Oh, sure. I thought it was a lot of fun. Mine was a European family, and if there was any money at all it was going to educate the boys. I remember hearing my dad talking to my uncles

—he had sixteen brothers and sisters and everyone got together on Sunday at Grandma's house—and he would say, "Well, with a little luck she'll grow up to be attractive, and she should be married by the time she's seventeen." My mother hated that whole idea.

BLDS: Did she ever have a career of her own?

BS: No. She lived vicariously through mine.

BLDS: Even during your career's earliest stages?

BS: Oh, yes. She said to my father that the boys will be smart and go to college; this one, she said, will never be smart, she will be an opera star. For him, there was no question about me going on the stage, because only loose women went on the stage. When I was eight or nine I remember asking him, What's a loose woman? He said, It's a hussy. And I said, What's a hussy? And he said, It's a woman who wears too much makeup, changes the color of her hair, and wears low-cut dresses. Well, all of this sounded very appealing to me and absolutely locked me into the idea that I was going to go on the stage. My mom was one of those people who could only answer questions with non sequiturs and this so thoroughly bewildered my father that it never occurred to him to keep the conversation going. He said that he wasn't going to pay for singing lessons or piano lessons because it was ridiculous, a total waste of money. The girl's going to get married, what is she doing with singing and piano lessons?

BLDS: What did he do that provided the wherewithal for these lessons?

BS: He was an assistant manager for the Metropolitan Life Insurance Company.

BLDS: Was that an unusual occupation for someone of European origin?

BS: It might have been.

BLDS: Was he a first-generation person?

BS: He was born in Romania. We are the first generation, my brothers and I. He was so well spoken, he spoke without an accent, and he was a big, tall, and very handsome man. When he said he wouldn't pay for the lessons my mother went out anyhow and found this little piano for me. He came home one night smoking a big cigar and yelled, "Shirley! What is that in the living room?" And she said, "Don't think about it, dear, it's something to put your ashtrays on." He was so bewildered by some of her answers that he never came back with any. She used to say that he never knew what color the kitchen was painted. And he didn't, he never went in.

BLDS: Did he take pride in that?

BS: Absolutely. When we had people coming for dinner he was served first. The chief rabbi could show up, it didn't matter. My father got served first. It was a puritanical house until I was fifteen and went on my first opera tour, over his dead body. I never wore makeup or high heels and my mother cut my hair. He said to my mother, "If this child goes out on this tour she cannot come back home." And without missing a beat my mother said to him, "Morris, half this house is mine, so when she comes home she'll stay in my part of the house." Years later I asked him what he thought about all that. He said, "Well, the way she said it, it made sense, and yes, half the house certainly belonged to her."

BLDS: What did you think about all that?

BS: I knew my mother could always handle my father. I loved my father. He wasn't frightening at all. He said, "Your mother doesn't drink, your mother doesn't smoke, and you're not going to, either," and I never did. It never occurred to me. I think the rigors of an operatic career, by someone who is essentially a loner, force you to be very self-sufficient. I never traveled with an entourage like many singers today. I was so happy for the privacy and the peace and quiet. My husband, Peter, was in his own business, and I had three stepchildren plus two of our own children to raise, so I never wanted people around me when I went on the road. I always liked to travel with my scores. It was a time of great peace for me to just be on my own.

BLDS: Let's back up a moment. I left you at Tompkins Park when you were three, and you said that you went on your first tour at fifteen. Firstly, were you ever an ordinary child, or did you spend all of your time in the presence of adults and, as a result, have an artificial maturity?

BS: No. For years I went to a children's camp run by Larry and

Bobby Tisch's mother—their mother was my Aunt Sadie. I was the most distinguished camper.

BLDS: What was the name of this camp?

BS: Camp Lincoln and Laurel—Laurel for the girls.

BLDS: And where was the camp?

BS: In Blairstown, New Jersey.

BLDS: I thought Larry and Bob Tisch's family owned a hotel.

BS: That's how the hotel business began, but the first thing was the children's camp. My brothers went there, too. Aunt Sadie and my mom were part of a very close-knit group of five women. My uncle Al was in the men's clothing business, I can't remember just where.

BLDS: Was he Larry and Bob's father?

BS: Yes. When the war came he made a good bit of money. He was a dear, fun fellow. We had a lot of fun. And my two brothers were exactly the age of the two Tisch boys.

BLDS: So you were like other ordinary children who went to school and summer camp.

BS: Yes, and when they did the operettas I performed.

BLDS: When did you start to study?

BS: My mother took me to Estelle Liebling when I was about nine years old.

BLDS: She was already a pre-eminent teacher.

BS: Oh, yes. There was a magazine called *Musical Courier* and on the cover was this rather formidable lady. Underneath the picture it said, "Estelle Liebling, teacher of the world's greatest voices." My mother said that nothing was too good for her little girl and off we went, except Miss Liebling thought she was going to hear my mother sing. It was a comedy of errors.

BLDS: And what did you perform for her?

BS: My mom had a collection of opera recordings that she played morning, noon, and night. I memorized them the way kids memorize television commercials because they were playing nonstop. Before she put the coffee on in the morning she turned on the Victrola, which was in the kitchen because that was where she spent

> My mom had a collection of opera recordings that she played morning, noon, and night. I memorized them the way kids memorize television commercials because they were playing nonstop.

97

most of her day. She would crank it up and play these twenty-two huge 78-RPM records. Lily Pons was one of the great coloratura sopranos of her time. By listening to her I began to imitate what I thought, of course, was perfect Italian, never having studied a word of it.

BLDS: By the time you were seven you were singing in Italian?

BS: Yes. I thought it was Italian. And by the time I was seven I had sung in a movie for Twentieth-Century-Fox.

BLDS: How did that occur?

BS: I went on the "Major Bowes Amateur Hour" on the radio and won.

BLDS: "Major Bowes" was the most popular program of the day.

BS: I think he had the largest listening audience of anybody except Jack Benny and Fred Allen. The three of them were certainly kings of the radio.

BLDS: Was the program geared to younger persons or just amateur performers of any kind?

BS: Amateur performers. People like the guy with the dancing teaspoons who played the saw and sang.

BLDS: Did you audition before you got on the show?

BS: Sure. There was a lady there by the name of Bessie Mack who later became a member of the family and my best friend. We used to go to Coney Island and play Bingo by rolling balls into empty holes.

BLDS: How old were you when you were on the program?

BS: I was on the "Major" from about seven until I was ten.

BLDS: Why did I think you were on only one time?

BS: I was. Then he had a program called "Major Bowes Capitol Family Hour," which originated from the stage of the Capitol Theater.

BLDS: An early spin-off?

BS: Yes. There was another youngster on it, a little bit older than me, called Merrill Miller. He later became Robert Merrill. I was a weekly performer with Major Bowes and then the major got ill and was replaced by "Mort Rule and the Cresta Blanca Carnival." Remember? [Singing] C-R-E-S-T-A, B-L-A-N-C-A, Cresta Blanca, Cresta Blanca, boom boom boom.

BLDS: What did you perform for your debut on "Major Bowes"?

BS: I sang "Cara Nome" from *Rigoletto*.

BLDS: At age seven?

> When I took singing lessons, I was ten and using the subway by myself. The subway was a nickel and nobody thought anything about going into Manhattan or Brooklyn.

BS: That's right. Each week I did another aria—I had twenty-two of them. I had an enormous repertoire.

BLDS: There you were, in the middle of a lower-class Jewish neighborhood in Brooklyn, singing Italian operas. What did people think of you?

BS: Well, you must remember that not everybody had a radio. We were not in an affluent neighborhood.

BLDS: Where was this neighborhood?

BS: It was Crown Heights, Empire Boulevard. As a matter of fact, on Sundays when Fred Allen and Jack Benny came on the radio, all the neighbors would come to us. Mom would make the coffee, there would be cakes, and everybody would huddle around the radio and listen. The reason we had a radio was that my grandfather was an inventor, and he invented a radio for us. It had no cover, no nothing, just tubes.

BLDS: Which grandfather?

BS: My mom's father. We were one of the few families in the neighborhood with a radio, and so not many people knew what was going on. This was sixty years ago. The world of communication was totally different. What television? I remember my dad would give me a nickel and I would bring home the *News* and the *Mirror* and have a penny left over for an all-day sucker.

BLDS: It was a safe enough neighborhood for you to go to the store by yourself.

BS: When I took singing lessons, I was ten and using the subway by myself. The subway was a nickel and nobody thought anything about going into Manhattan or Brooklyn.

BLDS: You went by yourself?

BS: Oh, sure.

BLDS: Your mother didn't accompany you?

BS: No.

BLDS: How did you get from "Major Bowes" to the movies?

BS: Well, the movie came first. When I met Bessie Mack she introduced me to Walter Wanger, who listened to me sing and thought it was very funny. He kept looking at me and saying, "Are you sure you're not a midget, kid?" My name was Belle Miriam Silverman. He said I couldn't have a name like that and so he gave me Beverly Sills because he lived in Beverly Hills. He just thought that was funny. Then he introduced me to Jack Skirball, who became like my uncle Jack. He had under contract Willy Howard, the old vaudeville comedian, and started a serial called "Uncle Sol's Problem Court." Each episode featured Willy Howard solving another problem in hilarious half-Yiddish, half-English. One was called "Uncle Sol Solves It" and I sang "Il Baccio" in that one.

BLDS: What was the problem on that show?

BS: The story was that my parents wanted me to study in Europe. They felt that I was a very gifted prodigy. I didn't want to go; I cried and sobbed. Uncle Sol put me on his lap and said, "Where would you like to study, honey?" And I said right here at home. So that was the resolution and everyone lived happily ever after.

BLDS: Did it give you the idea that maybe you should be studying in Europe?

BS: No. I didn't know what Europe was. The moment the entire family landed in Brooklyn my grandmother forbade them ever to speak anything except English, which is why every one of them spoke flawless English. She was finished with Romania, believe me. She was done. In our house, because of our grandparents, we heard Russian and Romanian all the time.

BLDS: Can you speak either language?

BS: Not anymore. I went to Moscow a couple of months ago. It was the first time I had ever been to Russia because my mother was frightened for me to go. She was convinced that they had kept records on my grandfather and that if I went in they would never let me out again. She always said things like, "They'll take one look at you and say, 'You are Meyer Banchikov's granddaughter,' and that'll be the end of you, you'll never get out. I don't even want to discuss it."

BLDS: What did Meyer do that caused your mother to believe they would be after him?

BS: Actually, that is a quite interesting story. My great-grandfather created the sewage system of Odessa. He was an electrical engineer, as they used to call them in those days. The family was very highly thought of. As a thank-you, the government sent my grandfather to Paris to become an engineer. While he was in Paris he read the works of Eugene Debs and when he returned to Odessa he went back as a socialist, which proved to be extremely embarrassing to the family—and to Czar Nicholas. Before there was any further embarrassment, and because he was caught in all kinds of political plots, they deported him.

BLDS: Lucky for you.

BS: He had already married my grandmother. She had three little girls, the oldest being my mother, and was pregnant with what would be the fourth daughter. Debs helped my grandfather, through Catholic charities, to get my grandmother out of Russia and over to the United States. They were real pioneers.

BLDS: Why wouldn't Debs have turned to a Jewish charity?

BS: The Jews were not really looked upon very favorably, even then, and my mother was attending the Catholic school outside of Odessa where the so-called better class, the upper middle class, attended. The Jews had no power whatsoever and not much freedom. Also, they felt that two nuns accompanying a pregnant lady with three little girls in tow would not attract quite as much attention as a lady who was traveling alone.

BLDS: How were you treated as compared to your two older brothers?

BS: From my father's point of view, male children were far more desirable, but he thought I was much cuter than they were. He was always carrying me around, even when I was too big and fat for him to be doing that. Actually, he helped deliver me at birth because there was no plan for my mother to go to a hospital. By the time Dr. Newfeld got there I was already in the bed. My father had bonded with me in a very special way. He was a young man and I'm sure my birth was quite a shocking experience for him. I was a ten-and-three-quarter-pound baby. My father always called me cutie pie, which I could never say. Kewpie dolls were popular then, so for a long time I was called Kewpie doll, which was just my baby way of saying cutie pie. I knew my limitations in terms of education. When I was about ten or eleven I was quite resentful of the fact that I would never be going to college because I knew that I was a rather intelligent girl. I had long talks with my father, trying to convince him that there might be an alternative to the stage if he could promise me that I could be educated. When he asked me what my idea was of an educated woman I said that I'd like to speak languages, I'd like to have a skill, I would teach. He said he just didn't see how that would be very beneficial. There was just no talking to him. In his own family there were primarily brothers, some educated. Of the few sisters none were really educated at all. However, their children were summa cum laude, valedictorians.

BLDS: Were his siblings older than him?

BS: Yes. My dad was second youngest.

BLDS: Of seventeen children?

BS: Yes.

BLDS: So you had an army of relatives.

BS: Every Sunday, Grandma would cook. It was a command performance. We all went and we all loved it. She had this great big house.

BLDS: Where was it?

BS: On Eastern Parkway in Brooklyn. She came over here on her own. She had been widowed three times and always wore black—God knows which husband she was mourning—and smoked little black cigars.

BLDS: Before the age of seven you were memorizing in phonetic Italian the twenty-two arias in your mother's record collection and, obviously, well on the road to being a professional child performer. And then, from the age of twelve to fifteen, you took a hiatus from your career. What happened?

BS: My mother would say that my body was growing and that it was time for me to retire. It's strange. When I call her Mama and I talk about her ambitions, two images come to mind. First, you think of a small Jewish woman called Mama, and then you think of a stage mother. In the first place, she was not a small Jewish woman. She was one of the most beautiful women I've ever seen. She was very theatrical. She went to the Traphagen School of Design and completed four different courses. When my dad died, and things were very tough, she went to work for Lily Daché and designed clothes for the Lillie Rubin label. The "Mama" aspect was the European aspect. When she walked down the street, people turned around. A lot of people I knew in the theatrical world were very interested in my mother. The movie companies were very interested. I remember Walter Wanger asking my mother, in the nicest way, if she had ever thought of going into the theater.

BLDS: And what was her reply?

BS: Absolutely not. It was very difficult to capture her because she was fey, very fey, a little bit off the wall at times, and chaotic. We would sit down to dinner and there would never be a full table setting. She never took offense when my father would say,

"Shirley, just once, could we have the whole set?" And she would say, "Next time," but it never happened. She could do anything with her hands. Embroider, petit point, paint. She made all my clothes till the day I married. She made my trousseau. And she used to say to me that dresses aren't worth a darn unless you can wear them inside out. Every seam had lace and handiwork you can't believe. She was just one of those people. She was forever painting, sewing, fixing.

BLDS: Do you do any of that?

BS: No, I can't do any of it. I can hardly do a button. But that's because she would never let me. I have no gift for needlework at all. I can't paint. Which is why, you know, tchotchkes are my thing. I love funny things.

BLDS: How did she become interested in opera? Did she take you to the first opera you ever saw?

BS: Yes, *Lakme* was the first, with Lily Pons.

BLDS: Was Pons the preeminent star of your mother's day?

BS: Yes. I always tell this story, because it says a lot about my mother. Lily, full grown, probably weighed ninety pounds and was four-foot-eleven. She was a china doll. My mother took me to see her when I was about seven or eight. She told me that someday I was going to grow up and look just like Lily. At that time I was already three inches taller and outweighed Lily by twenty pounds.

BLDS: That didn't stand in your mother's way.

BS: It didn't. Why was that a problem? She would tell me it's very important to have a sense of theater when you go on the stage. The first time I saw Lily in the opera *Lakme* she wore a bikini with a flowing skirt. Nobody had ever seen that in the thirties! This woman came out with a naked midriff. I screamed and said, "Mama, her belly button is showing!" I never saw such a thing on stage. She was so exquisite that she got away with it.

BLDS: When did you first hear the term *coloratura*?

BS: From Pons. First of all, I was so taken with her that I began to write to her. She invited my mom and me to a Carnegie Hall concert and to come backstage to see her.

BLDS: Because of your letters to her?

BS: Yes.

BLDS: These over-the-transom letters from an anonymous person?

BS: Yes. I said that I was however old I was and that I began singing early to Galli-Curci recordings, but then my mom had moved on to Lily Pons recordings and so I had decided that I would rather sing like Lily Pons. Her accompanist Frank La Forge, who at first answered the letters for her, said Ms. Pons is so pleased and wishes you all good things, and is enclosing an autographed picture, which I still have. It's on the wall in my husband's office. I wrote back and, as it worked out, she sent two tickets and a backstage pass for us.

BLDS: How many letters prompted that?

BS: Maybe ten. Of course, by the time she died we were very good friends. She left me an awful lot of her musical scores, which I donated to the City Opera library so that young artists can use them. Most of them are under Kostelanetz orchestrations and are invaluable for young singers. The last time I saw Lily was in San Diego. She still wore her dark hair in a pageboy and she had on a white mink coat. I did the *Daughter of the Regiment* for which she was so well known. Before the performance I said to her, "Lily, don't forget that when you did the *Daughter of the Regiment,* you weighed ninety pounds," and I always called her three-foot-two. "I have to play her differently because I'm so big, so don't expect it to be your Marie, all right?" She came backstage afterward and said, "Is good"—she never lost that French accent, it was part of her trademark—and then she paused and said, "I was very disappointed." I asked why and she said, "When I came in, I came in on a white horse. You should have come in on a white horse." I said, "Lily, they couldn't find one big enough." Then we hugged. I could see that she was very ill.

BLDS: You have had quite a remarkable support system, which served as an extended family and amplified your family's already large investment in furthering your career.

BS: I was very lucky. I had a career because of my family. Even my father, hating the theater for his daughter, eventually had to admit that my singing gave him great joy. Certainly I always had the support of my brothers, even though I used to say to my oldest brother, the doctor, "You know, you never come to hear me sing." He said, "You never come to watch me operate." So we kind of left it at that.

BLDS: Your father, who died when you were about twenty years old, disapproved of you going out in a Gilbert & Sullivan touring company, which marked your return to professional life.

BS: Yes. I came out of retirement. Miss Liebling was so welcoming to me. She knew everybody. And J. J. Shubert was one of her old buddies. She called him and said, "Look, I don't think this girl is ready to do anything. She's never performed an opera on the

> I was very lucky. I had a career because of my family. Even my father, hating the theater for his daughter, eventually had to admit that my singing gave him great joy.

stage or anything. But I just want you to look at her and I want you to hear her." At fifteen I was a very attractive young woman; I was very slim, very tall. I went to Manhattan from Brooklyn on the subway to audition for him.

BLDS: And you were dressed in the clothes your mother made for you.

BS: Yes. It was generally a jumper with a very high neck, a shirt, flat shoes, and one long pigtail. I had nice dirty blonde hair, never enhanced, and wore no makeup. He kept staring at me while my mother did all the talking. Finally, he asked me, "Honey, do you talk at all?" So I loved him. He was like a grandfather to me. On my first tour, the Gilbert & Sullivan tour, he billed me as the youngest prima donna in captivity, which I just adored. Everything was just so exciting.

BLDS: But it wasn't so exciting for your father, who didn't want you to have a singing career in the first place. Then you set out on a national tour and he was further disappointed by the role you selected.

BS: He was disappointed because my mom had always talked about opera and suddenly I was doing operettas and Gilbert & Sullivan, which he thought was perfectly nice entertainment for other people but not for someone who was supposedly serious. My mother would defend it as good experience.

BLDS: How did you learn all the libretti and the scores?

BS: I don't know, I just did. I used to be able to memorize an opera in three days without batting an eye. That isn't to say I was ready to perform it; I mean simply learning the text and the notes. What takes longer is the characterization, the polishing, the phrasing, the elegance and style. That is where the real work comes in. Memorization is nothing. I found that when I got on the stage I was a totally different person. All my inhibitions went away and it was like putting on a mask or a disguise. It was a game with me. I could play that other person, become that other person, but the minute the curtain went down I went back to being Belle Miriam Silverman again. My personality was almost schizophrenic. I was always the first one in the theater for a performance. I would walk the set, pick up every prop I was going to use. I had learned that from Ted Williams.

BLDS: The baseball player?

BS: Yes. Whenever he came to play in Brooklyn, which was not his home stadium, my brothers and I would get there very early and eat our hot dogs and wait for the game to start. Suddenly this very tall, loose-limbed, elegant man—I had such a crush on him, I tell you—would walk the bases, walk to the outfield, walk to the center field, kick the dirt a little bit, walk over to the walls of the stadium, and just familiarize himself with every lump and bump. I followed that example through my entire career. I could never walk onstage without doing what I call my Ted Williams walk beforehand. What happened in that extra hour before anybody came into the theater was that I began to put on the disguise. I would let the scenery swallow me up. That was, for me, the most fun thing.

BLDS: Do you liken the training and discipline of a serious athlete to that of a serious performing artist?

BS: When young people ask me what advice I have for young opera singers, I say forget about the crowned prince who drinks champagne out of your slipper. It's a highly disciplined art form. You cannot fool anybody. You don't sing in front of three critics, you sing in front of three thousand critics and you can't fool them. You don't have to know anything about opera at all. It's instinctive, and the audience knows when something extraordinary is happening.

BLDS: Did you know that when you were general director of the City Opera?

BS: You bet I did, and that was one of the first things I passed on to the kids. Don't underestimate the intelligence of those people in front of you; forget the three critics, it won't matter. If you get a rave review but that audience did not like you, you are a dead duck. And the same thing is true if you get reviews that are not positive. If that audience stood up and cheered you, you did a tremendous performance. It takes discipline. If, the night before a performance, you drink some red wine and inhale somebody else's smoke, you deserve what you get onstage. You just can't live that kind of life. The reason I was a loner when I worked is that I got peace from being alone. I enjoyed the discipline of being able to eat in my room and just close in on what my task was. I loved the preparation for a performance.

BLDS: To say you are confident is an understatement after hearing about your 1958 audition for the title role in *The Ballad of Baby Doe*. The opera's composer, Douglas Moore, thought you would be too tall for the role, so of course you "wore the highest heels you could find and a white mink hat," and said, "Mr. Moore, this is how tall I am before I begin to sing for you, and I'm going to be just as tall when I'm finished." Moore decided you in fact *were* Baby Doe and you sang the part. Has this self-assurance ever gotten you in trou-

ble? Backfired? Is it your sense of humor that keeps you going?

BS: I love to laugh. I think the most beautiful sound the human voice can make is laughter.

BLDS: Incidentally, we now know how Beverly Sills was named. Where did the name Bubbles come from?

BS: I was born with this big spit bubble in my mouth and my father popped it. The doctor came seconds after I was on the bed and my father said, "I just popped this big spit bubble from her mouth, is that okay?" The doctor took me, pointed to my father, and said, "Sure, it's okay. We'll just have to call her Bubbles." And it stuck.

BLDS: And you were called Bubbles until what age?

BS: Now.

BLDS: Who calls you Bubbles?

BS: Everyone. My family, my husband calls me Bubbly. My brothers never called me anything but Bubbles.

BLDS: Who do you think of yourself as?

BS: Bubbles. When I wrote the book called *Bubbles*, there was a great discussion. Actually, everything in my family is decided by committee. When all thirty-two of them came for Thanksgiving there were thirty-two requests for what should be served. It was never quiet or easy. We spoke at such a high decibel level. My mom and her five sisters were like the Gabors. They wanted privacy from their husbands, so they would lock themselves into the bathroom and start speaking in Russian so that nobody understood. They were nuts, these women, and one was more beautiful than the other. We never did anything simple. It was just not in the cards for us.

BLDS: How has your own life evolved?

BS: Same thing. The last time I saw my mother was the day before she died, October 16, 1995. She was in a deep coma.

BLDS: At what age?

BS: She was about to turn ninety-two. I had read that people in comas really can hear, they just can't come out and communicate, so every time I stayed with her I talked and talked and reminisced.

BLDS: Did you ever sing to her?

BS: Yes. It was a song that concluded every recital I ever sang.

BLDS: What is the song?

BLDS: It's just called "The Portuguese Folk Song." The first line is translated, "Tell me why you bid me leave you." And I made

> If, the night before a performance, you drink some red wine and inhale somebody else's smoke, you deserve what you get onstage.

this my farewell to my mom. When she died we disinterred my dad out of Brooklyn and buried them, side by side, in a Jewish cemetery on Martha's Vineyard. She had been alone a long time, since 1949. It was nice to reunite them.

BLDS: In the intervening forty-six years, your mother never remarried. By choice or by circumstance?

BS: She said, "I had perfection, I can't settle for less."

BLDS: Is that true, or is that the myth she perpetuated?

BS: Either one. As long as she believed it, it was true. But he was so handsome. The two of them were extraordinary looking. Dad was six-foot-two, with a shock of black hair, and had the most dominant personality. My God, he spoke with huge periods at the end of every sentence.

BLDS: Your mother sounds like a very dominating woman.

BS: She was.

BLDS: Who did they dominate, since they couldn't dominate each other? Did they dominate their children?

BS: Probably, but they both thought they were dominating each other. If you asked my father, he would have told you that my mother did everything he told her to do, and yet somewhere in the back of his mind he knew the real truth. They used to tease him because he came home every day for lunch. His brothers would say, if they had wives that looked like her, they would go home for lunch, too!

BLDS: Did he work so close by?

BS: His territory was the Bedford-Stuyvesant section of Brooklyn, and that was fifteen minutes from Crown Heights.

BLDS: And he sold insurance to the residents?

BS: Door-to-door. Metropolitan Life Insurance Company was the first company to insure black people.

BLDS: Was Bedford-Stuyvesant then a black neighborhood?

BS: Somewhat, but not the way it is today. My father's office was on Bedford Avenue. Every Sunday he would pack the three of us in the back of the car and we would visit the neighborhood. The black people kept their grocery stores and everything open on Sunday. We would go into the shops and pick up nuts and dried fruits while my dad made his collections. Fifty cents a week was a lot of money for people to pay. My father was so admiring of Met Life for bringing black people into the insurance world that sometimes he would help them with payments.

BLDS: You had the example that, with hard work and nonconventional working hours, if you wanted to succeed at something

you could. And he took you with him because that's the way he could visit with his children.

BS: That's right. And Mom cleaned the house.

BLDS: Your mother spent more of her life alone than she did with your father as her husband. Was it because you, and perhaps your brothers, filled up so much of her life that she didn't have the need, or the room, for a relationship of her own?

BS: Well, I think even the boys would admit it was primarily me. I didn't get married until I was twenty-seven, and I lived with her until the day I got married. She was my best friend. She was so much fun to be with. If you saw her you would know immediately what kind of woman she was. She was fabulous. She had a friendly face and a very, very warm giggle. Nat Leventhal called her up one night when he became president of Lincoln Center and invited her to see *Ariadne* at the Met. He picked her up and took her to the opera; it was really lovely. About four days later during lunch he said to me, "I have to tell you something extraordinary about your mother." She was then in her eighties. "You know, she flirted with me." I said yeah, she's that way. He said it was kind of breathtaking. She was very sexy.

BLDS: Did you ever feel that she was either too focused in directing your life or that she was manipulating you?

BS: She lived through me, but she never manipulated me.

BLDS: As I understand it, your career as a genuine opera singer began in 1947 when you made your debut in *Carmen* with the Philadelphia Civic Opera.

BS: Yes, I was eighteen. And I was Micaela, not Carmen, lest there's any confusion. The United States was a cultural desert. You couldn't make a living here as an opera singer unless you were a famous European artist.

BLDS: Did you expect to make a living as an opera singer?

BS: There was no question in my mind that I was going to be a star. At the time I was singing for tips in nightclubs. My mother may have been ambitious for me, but I knew I was a damn good performer. Something was going to happen. I never could have sustained myself through all of those terrible times had I not believed that I had this talent. Yeah, there was Ma, and yeah, there was Miss Liebling teaching me for nothing, but I had the drive.

BLDS: Teaching you "for nothing?"

> There was no question in my mind that I was going to be a star. At the time I was singing for tips in nightclubs.

BS: For nothing, because she was quite an expensive teacher.

BLDS: So why did she take you on in the first place?

BS: She told me she never taught any little children, and then she said she didn't even know any little children. She was an extraordinary woman and she was very taken with my mother. I remember my mother said to her, "Someday my daughter is going to sit at a dinner table and speak French on the right and Italian on the left, and she's going to be a cultured woman." My mother arranged language lessons for me from two neighbors. She paid each one a quarter an hour; one taught me Italian, the other taught me German. I was already speaking French, because after I was born my mom was very ill and a French girl came to work for us. When later I began to be tutored in French it all came back. I needed about five French lessons and I was back to speaking it.

BLDS: So if an opera singer couldn't make it here without being a famous European artist, it must have been very important for you to sing at La Scala for the first time.

BS: When I finished singing at La Scala I had quite a triumph. I was on the cover of *Time* and *Newsweek*. It was about 1969, I don't exactly remember. Dates have no meaning anymore. In any event, Peter had gone home with the kids already and just Mom and I were left in Milan. On the plane coming home after the last performance, she said, "So what about the Met? After all, if you don't sing at the Met, you really haven't hit the big time." I said, "I can't believe you just said that to me. Do you know what a triumph it is for an American woman to sing in La Scala? You have been with me now for four months. Haven't you seen what has happened?" "Yes," she said. "But I think it would be nice if we sang at the Met." So I said, "If that's what you want, I'll arrange it." Of course, I had made a statement that I would never sing at the Met while Rudolph Bing was the general manager.

BLDS: Was it also possible that Rudolph Bing wasn't going to have you sing at the Met while he was the general manager? What was your problem with Mr. Bing?

BS: Well, it started because *Julius Caesar* opened simultaneously with *Anthony and Cleopatra*, both of our companies having our first season in New York City in 1965.

BLDS: This was Beverly Sills and Julius Rudel at the New York City Opera.

BS: Right. As opposed to Leontyne Pryce in *Anthony and Cleopatra*, the world premiere of Rudolph Bing's Metropolitan Opera. It was the first time anybody was ever allowed inside the new Metropolitan Opera House and there was international press from here to China. Our production cost twenty-five thousand dollars; theirs probably cost a million. Zeffirelli overproduced theirs, so that the scenery broke down; it was one tragedy after another. Sam Barber's opera, which is so beautiful, got lost in the shuffle. Four or five nights later we opened with *Julius Caesar*. And there's no question that it made me into America's darling. When I came back to do the second performance there was a stack of telegrams from every major opera house in the world, inviting me to come and sing. But the Met did not invite me because Mr. Bing somehow associated my triumph with his failure. When one of the board members of the Met asked him why I was not going there to sing, he said, "I would like to spend five minutes of my life without hearing that woman's name." So I went on to La Scala, Covent Garden, you name it, I did it. I did it all. Later, he went on the Dick Cavett show and was asked, "Why isn't Beverly Sills at the Met?" And he said that not all great singers have to sing at the Met. I went on the Cavett show the next day, and that's how the feud began. When Cavett mentioned what Mr. Bing had said, I replied that not all great singers want to sing at the Met. I made a statement on the Cavett show that I would never sing at the Met while Rudolph Bing was there. When he resigned, Gieren Gentele replaced him. He took me to supper and said, "Come on, it's my first season. What could suit me better than to present Beverly Sills?" And I said, "Mister Gentele, I have to think about it. This is almost anticlimactic. I really have done it all. What satisfaction could that bring?" "Well," he said, "by singling you out in your own country it completes a kind of unfinished story for you. You should climax it all with appearances at the Met. I'll let you pick the opera, the conductor, and the time you want to debut, and we'll go to work."

BLDS: Was that something you had to think about?

BS: Yes, because it didn't mean anything to me anymore.

BLDS: It came under the heading of be careful what you wish for in life because you may get it?

BS: I was the highest-paid opera singer in the world and booked six years in advance. I would have had to cancel something to go to the Met. And I kept thinking, What will it do for me? I'm so nearsighted I don't even see what the inside of the opera house looks like. And I had had no contact with anyone at the Met because Bing had kept me so far out of it. He remained angry with me because my biggest triumph was his biggest disaster.

BLDS: But by that time shouldn't he have made amends and invited you?

BS: He didn't. He had Joan Sutherland, he had Renata Tebaldi, he had Montserrat Caballé, he had all kinds of singers. Anyway, Mr. Gentele was tragically killed in an automobile accident before I made my decision, so there was nobody for me to call. Then they appointed Schuyler Chapin and Tony Bliss. After my mother said that to me on the plane, I made a few phone calls and we negotiated. I bought my mother a little gold charm and engraved on the back of it, "So we made it to the Met together." I'm not putting down the evening, it was a memorable evening, but what really made it was the look on her face. The Met people were wonderful to me and I had a wonderful time.

BLDS: What did you give your husband when you made your debut at the Met?

BS: I didn't give him anything, but he gave me something. He didn't come to all of the performances, so we had a little ritual as I was going to work. I'd kiss him goodnight and say, "Wait up for me." He would say, "Of course I will." Before walking out I would say, "I'm so tired I'm going to sing like a pig." Well, on the night of the Metropolitan Opera debut he gave me a gold pig with a great big diamond for a tail.

BLDS: Where did you first meet your husband, Peter Greenough?

BS: In Cleveland when the New York City Opera went on tour. He owned the *Cleveland Plain Dealer* newspaper, and was president of the press club, and he gave a cocktail party for us.

BLDS: Did his family own the paper before him?

BS: His grandfather founded it. Julius Rudel called me and said I had to go to this cocktail party. So I did. Then this beautiful blond man came forward. You know, I used to wear very low-cut dresses when I was young.

BLDS: I thought your father instructed you not to do that.

BS: Well, sure. And I maintain that Peter never saw my face until the third date. He had his eyes down. But he certainly was just a knockout. Wow! He was something. And he flew to New York every weekend after we met.

BLDS: He was unmarried at the time, too?

BS: No. He was in the process of getting a rather messy divorce. He was suing for custody of the children. And he won, which was very unusual in 1956.

BLDS: Did he come from an old-line WASP family from the Midwest?

BS: He is a Bostonian. When he was going to Harvard his grandfather brought him out to Cleveland every summer to work on the paper. He was the only child that seemed to be interested in becoming a journalist, so he worked his way up.

BLDS: And he was eventually the editor and publisher?

BS: Yes.

BLDS: So he was a New Englander, and you were Belle Miriam Silverman from Brooklyn, daughter of immigrant parents. It sounds like worlds apart. How did you ever bridge the gap?

BS: In a very strange way, he had more problems with my family than I had with his.

BLDS: Meaning your family resisted him.

BS: Terribly.

BLDS: Because of the children?

BS: Because of the divorce, the children, and especially because he is a WASP. The only members of my family who came to the wedding were my mother, my brothers, and the wives of my brothers. Nobody else came. My mother's sisters said if my father were alive he would die all over again. No one in my family had married out of the faith, which I found astonishing because we were not a religious family.

BLDS: Did your brothers pursue a more religious life than you have?

BS: No, the second one married out of the faith, too, although the children were raised Jewish and she converted. I don't know what we did. In our case, my daughter Muffy had to go to a Catholic school because she was deaf, and the best teachers of deaf children were the sisters of Saint Joseph. I couldn't have cared less what they wore, I wanted my kid to speak and to be given every opportunity so that she could be a well-educated woman who happened to be hearing impaired. So there was Muffy kneeling and crossing herself. My mother kept asking me how I could allow that to happen. I said, How else do you want me to teach her about God? It's we human beings who have to divide it up into religions. I really do think there was only one God, it's those lunatics who divided everything up in pieces. I couldn't care less. Rituals don't mean a thing to me. When anybody asks me, "In what faith did you raise Muffy?" I always say Catholic. There's never going to be any doubt, because the truth of the matter is these nuns taught her about a God, taught her some rules she had to obey, gave her a code of ethics, a moral code to live by. That was all I cared about. And, you know, she's a terrific human being. She graduated from hearing colleges, made the dean's list. She's an oral deaf person. I gave her the choice.

BLDS: What does that mean?

BS: That means she can speak. As one woman said to me, What's the point of talk, talk, talk if they can't hear, hear, hear? The point is choice, choice, choice. There are people who are opposed to giving a deaf person opportunities to speak. I said, if she wants to make a stab at it, fine. If she can't cut it, she can learn sign language in six weeks. Actually, when she went to college, she took a crash course in sign language and we got her an interpreter because the lecture rooms were so large she couldn't lip-read the professor.

BLDS: When did you become aware of her hearing loss?

BS: When she was twenty-two months old. She was so smart, and I'm not saying this as a doting mother. I mean, here was a child who was not speaking and yet she was doing jigsaw puzzles at a four- and five-year level. The delivery man would come with the groceries and she would put things away. She knew where everything was, and she was a real little busybody. She was very independent.

BLDS: So you had no realization at first of a hearing problem. Did you just think that she was a late talker?

BS: When I brought her to the pediatrician, he told me the story about the kid that never spoke for four years and finally said, "Please pass me the salt and pepper." His mother said, "You haven't spoken in four years and the first thing you say is please pass the salt and pepper?" And the kid said, "Yeah, up to now everything tasted fine." While the doctor was telling me this story, he took out his keys and said, "See? She made a grab for them." I said, "But she made a grab for them because she saw them." I kept saying, Here's a kid as bright as this, why can't she speak? She went near the stove one day and I grabbed her hand and said, "Hot, hot, hot!" And she looked at me and said, "Hot, hot, hot!" That was the first clue that she was deaf. I realized she was lip-reading. So I finally got her to the children's hospital, where the doctor told me she was aphasic. And I said, "She's not aphasic. I am convinced this child cannot hear." And he said, "There's a nun out at the Boston School for the Deaf. If she tells you your kid is deaf, then your kid is deaf." So I went out to see Sister Dionysius. She took Muffy by the hand and led her into a room. She came out not five minutes later and said, "You've got the smartest little kid I have met in thirty years. The kid can't hear." So she called Doctor Paine and said there's no aphasia, the kid is deaf. We've got to get some hearing aids, we've got to get some tutoring, and we're going to try to teach her to speak. I credit her with what Muffy is today.

BLDS: And how would you describe what Muffy is today?

BS: Independent, fiercely independent. Very smart, humorous, pretty as a picture, with big green eyes like her father.

BLDS: She has a satisfying career as well.

BS: Oh, yes. Very successful. She is a personnel manager at NYNEX and secretary of a national organization for disabled people. She is on the board of the National Theater of the Deaf.

BLDS: The irony of you having a child who cannot hear—how have you dealt with that?

BS: I'll tell you. I have a daughter who genuinely loves me. It has nothing to do with who I was as an opera singer. Performances were of no concern. At my opening at the Met, when everybody was standing up and screaming, she turned to Danny Kaye, who was seated beside her, pulled his sleeve, and asked, "Was she good?" Just like that. And Danny said, "Yeah, she was terrific."

BLDS: How did you deal with it earlier in your life, some thirty-five years ago?

BS: I became paralyzed. Not physically, but mentally. I simply sat and stared at this child.

BLDS: What was your mother's reaction?

BS: When I told my mother the diagnosis, she said, "In my eyes she'll always be perfect." She would call every day and ask, "Have you got the hearing aids yet?" No, no, I haven't done that. "Have you got the tutor yet?" I said, "Mom, I can't move. Don't pick on me now." So she came up to Boston, where we were living by then, and said, "Honey, I know this is a very difficult time for you, so I'll tell you what I'm going to do. I'm going to take Muffy to New York with me and I'm going to get her fitted with hearing aids. I have found a very nice audiologist who is going to help me find a school for her. And then, when you snap out of this, you can come and get her and bring her back. But we are not going to stare at this child and lose precious time." And I told her she was not going to take my daughter anyplace. "Well," she said, "If we're both looking out only for the welfare of your child, you're certainly not helping her. I'm not going to let this gorgeous baby sit here in a world of silence." I couldn't move. I could not accept this.

BLDS: So what happened?

BS: I told her, "You're not taking my baby out of this house," and she said, "Good. Put your coat on. We're going to go get some hearing aids." So that's what we did. Muffy's favorite lady in the whole world was her grandmother. She loved my mother beyond belief.

BLDS: Were you performing then?

BS: No.

BLDS: What did you plan to do with your career?

BS: Well, I really had no plans at all. When this happened I just was immobilized. Anyhow, we got the hearing aids. I saw her little face light up when she heard the first sounds she had ever heard. It was the dog barking. She had never known that the dog barked. And she was beside herself. No language, this kid. It was a remarkable time. I got her a tutor, a wonderful girl who crawled on the floor with her, and I had to go to the Sarah Fuller school with her and do the same thing. Everyone had to continue the process of teaching her when we were home. Her stepsisters had to learn, too. They went right to work with her. Then I got her into the Boston School for the Deaf.

BLDS: You describe yourself as someone not having a central organizing religion, but you do not deny faith. Not only did this extraordinary thing happen with Muffy, but an extraordinary thing happened with your next child, as well.

BS: My son Peter was born with multiple handicaps.

BLDS: Do you think of yourself as a religious person?

BS: Yes. I just don't have a name to my religion.

BLDS: Unless it's eclectic.

BS: Unless it's eclectic, yes.

BLDS: How and where did you develop the philosophy and the inner resources, not only to deal with all of this, but also to go on with your life?

BS: I think that happiness is a decision. Once you make the decision that there will be some joy in your life, you don't cry. You have to go on. I once said that I'm not a happy woman but I am a cheerful woman. The difference is that a happy woman is someone who has no cares at all. A cheerful woman is somebody who has cares but is determined nevertheless to have a good, cheerful life. So I went on with it.

BLDS: You were immobilized from the difficulties with your first child, then you faced the trauma and disappointment of your second child. How did you pick up the pieces of your life?

BS: I had already had my lesson and realized by that time what could be done for children. The boy was certainly a much more hopeless case. I don't know how I got through the early stages.

BLDS: How did Peter deal with it?

BS: Well, Muffy has always been his golden girl. From the moment he saw her, they were inseparable. She also had a special relationship with her grandfather, Peter's dad. Peter would be in the family room and she would walk in, crawl up on his lap, and they would watch football together. It was not so important that she was watching football, but that she was in her father's lap. It never occurred to her that there was any other place in the room for her to sit. If I had had my way I would have wrapped her in cotton, protected her, taken her to school, picked her up, never left her alone for two minutes. It was Peter who turned her into a very competitive woman. She's very competitive.

BLDS: Maybe it's the combination of his Yankee independence and your urban competitiveness.

BS: Maybe. When she was about three Pete insisted that she be taught by a professional how to swim. If this child was going to swim, she was going to be a damn good swimmer. Tennis? She was a crackerjack tennis player. He had her professionally taught. His child was going to compete. And she did. When she went off on her first trip riding the rapids of the Colorado River I didn't speak to Peter for five days. I had said it was out of the question. What if she goes overboard? She did go over and got right back in the raft because she was such a strong swimmer. He told me I was going to rob her of any decent chance for a normal life. He said that she was not going to have any joy in life unless we just throw her out there and let her fend for herself. People with bigger handicaps have made rich, full lives and I was going to deprive her of all that. So he won. Some of us are caretakers.

BLDS: Do you think that's a role assigned to you in life?

BS: I think we're part of a grand design.

BLDS: Are you ever tired of always putting a good face on everything? When do you express emotion when you can't do it in an operatic role?

BS: I simply think the alternative to a good face is a complaining one. Complainers are bores—and bores are the pits as far as I'm concerned.

BLDS: Did you ever have a negative reception from an audience?

BS: No. Never. There were times when I had off nights, but I never really had to suffer through a uninterested audience.

BLDS: How important is approval for you, then and now?

BS: In terms of which part of my life?

BLDS: Professional and personal.

BS: I had a new attitude when the children had all these problems. Singing was an escape. I couldn't wait to get to the theater, put on somebody else's skin, pick up somebody else for four hours, and escape. Certainly I would have been very unhappy if the audience's response was negative; it was such a joyful time for me and I couldn't wait to come here and do it.

BLDS: When did you come back to it?

BS: 1965.

BLDS: And what brought you back to New York?

BS: My son, Peter. He had to be put into a special school for autistic children. The three older girls—Peter's children, whom I adopted at ages nine, six, and three—were out of the house. Muffy was in high school. Peter senior was retired and sold the paper. He had been a financial editor for the *Boston Globe* for a while and did some financial writing for Baird's newsletters. He had the idea to move. All the commuting was ridiculous. We had a twenty-five-room house, and it was just Muffy, Peter, me, and my housekeeper. It seemed silly. We have been here in New York ever since.

BLDS: Did you resume your singing career when you returned to New York?

BS: Actually, before that, I began to sing with Sarah Caldwell in Boston. Peter said to me, maybe it's time we think about going back to singing. Julius Rudel, who was the manager of the New York City Opera, kept writing to me, and every time I would ask for another leave of absence until the next season. Finally he wrote me a funny letter and said that I owed him all these performances. He said that a contract is a contract, and that there was nothing wrong with me physically, so I simply had to do these performances. He made it a very funny, official letter.

BLDS: By then you had already been at La Scala.

BS: In 1969 I went back to La Scala for *Lucia*, then I went to Venice, Covent Garden, Berlin, and Buenos Aires. I can't even remember all I did.

BLDS: What was your favorite role?

BS: Usually the one I was doing. I was very fickle. Obviously, it must have been *La Traviata* because I sang it at least four or five hundred times, I think.

BLDS: How many performances did you do as a professional opera singer?

BS: I don't know! The Library of Congress has all my memorabilia and they were supposed to add it all up. My God, it was a long career; it has to be in the thousands. If *La Traviata* alone was over five hundred, think what the rest would be.

> I had a new attitude when the children had all these problems. Singing was an escape. I couldn't wait to get to the theater, put on somebody else's skin, pick up somebody else for four hours, and escape.

BLDS: You had the categories of powder-puff and meat-and-potato roles. Which roles do you assign to which category, and how did they evolve?

BS: Well, as I got closer and closer to retirement, my voice was fine; it was my stamina that was giving out. So with roles such as Rosina in the *Barber of Seville*, Norina in *Don Pasquale*, and *Fledermaus*, I began to bore myself. Queen Elizabeth in *Roberto Devereux* was without question the biggest challenge, and I think it was my finest accomplishment. I will probably be remembered for *Manon, Lucia*, and *La Traviata*, but from my personal point of view, I don't think I ever gave performances in my entire career on the caliber I gave Queen Elizabeth.

BLDS: And that was just twenty-five years ago. How did you develop the kind of professional judgment that you have?

BS: When you become a superstar, and find yourself on magazine covers, there's always somebody to come backstage and tell you how wonderful you were. I realized that in order to keep myself stabilized, so that my feet were still on the ground, I had to be my own critic. I decided that if I thought the performance was good, it was good. And if I thought it was bad, nobody could change my opinion, no matter what the reviews said. I'm not going to say I was not affected by reviews, because of course I was. The only time I became depressed about an unfavorable review was when I agreed. If I knew the performance was good I was annoyed, sometimes I was sad, sometimes I was a little bit embarrassed because I came with such ballyhoo and the critics didn't respond properly.

BLDS: But I assume you have always been your own harshest critic.

BS: It never really bothered me if I knew the performance was at a level that I had set for myself. When I went into a real blue funk is when nothing worked. The opening night of *Roberto Devereux* was without question the finest performance I sang in my entire career.

BLDS: That was about a year after you returned to New York. And Queen Elizabeth I was a really difficult role.

BS: No question about it. It was the only time I walked into the theater and did everything I set out to do. I used to mark my scores with a little funny yellow marker where I had made a mistake in timing or things had not worked. Then I would work on those things. When it was fixed I would put a red mark over it, which always alerted me that there had been a problem there at some time but that I had solved it. That way, if it kept repeating itself, I knew it was a hurdle that I should look out for. By the opening night of *Devereux* I didn't have a mark in the score. I walked out with Peter to a party afterward and I said to him, "Show me somebody who would do better." And that was the only time I ever said that. It was a memorable night for me, and although fortunately all the press agreed with me, it wouldn't have mattered. But I would have been damn angry if they hadn't had the brains to realize what a performance I had just given.

BLDS: What made you decide to retire?

BS: I wanted to get out while people were saying, "It's too soon," rather than, "When is she ever going to quit?" I don't believe in singing until death. And I made a pact with Peter. He said to me that I didn't seem desperate about staying on after fifty. And I said, Why is fifty a magic number? He pointed out that the ladies I played, except for the old queen, were all such young women. And he was right. I didn't want people to remember me as an older woman playing young roles. When I look at the cover of the *Manon* record, I look at myself and I say, Yes, that's what I looked like and that's what *Manon* should look like. And I'm very proud of that. If the character is Louise, who is a young girl, you shouldn't have to look at a sixty-six-year-old face, no matter how nice the face. You should have in your mind the young, radiant Louise.

BLDS: How did you get the idea to move from performer to opera impresario?

BS: I didn't. Julius wanted to leave the City Opera to become a conductor for the Buffalo Philharmonic and John Samuels, who was then chairman of the board of the New York City Opera, invited me to take over—but Julius himself talked about it before Samuels. It was Rudel's idea.

BLDS: One of your innovations at the New York City Opera was adding the supertitles. How did you get the idea?

BS: I saw it done in China.

BLDS: How did Muffy respond to the supertitles?

BS: She thought she was at a play. It's the first time she understood everything.

BLDS: And then after ten years, by the 1989–90 season, you were through with the New York City Opera; you had done that. In the meantime you became a member of corporate boards: Macy's in 1983, Warner Communications/TWI in 1983, and American Express in 1989, among others. You are the managerially minded

aesthetician. I must say, it has always amused me to see the delight you take at being a managerially minded corporate person.

BS: I love it! Do you know how I got into this?

BLDS: How?

BS: When I married Peter, of course, I was very poor. However, Peter was a very well-to-do man. There were enormous legal problems concerning the three stepchildren in the event of his death, and he was appalled at how little I knew about such matters. My father-in-law said to me, "You don't have an income? You don't have any inherited income?" I said no, I don't. He said he had never met a woman who didn't have an inherited income. And I told him he traveled in rarefied circles. Peter told me I was going to have to learn a little bit about portfolios because if something happened to him there would be enormous decisions to make on behalf of the children. So my husband began to teach me. *The Plain Dealer* would come and he would open it to the financial section. He began to buy me books.

BLDS: He was a financial writer, too.

BS: His whole life has been finance and economics. His degrees were in business and finance and journalism. He went to the Columbia School of Journalism and he won a Pulitzer Prize.

BLDS: I understand why everyone calls you Bubbles. The Bubbles dimension is a very significant one in the very complex package that we know as a cheerful woman. I have often thought that when you were performing a role, you took on another coloration. I guess long ago you realized that the world really was a stage, and learned to deal with it in that way.

BS: I guess. There's one other thing, and that is Rose Kennedy's influence. I got to know her very well. We worked together at the Mater Dei School for the Blind up in Boston. It was also open to deaf children, which is how I became affiliated with it. One time I went down to Palm Beach to sing and I met her for a walk on the beach. It was after both boys had been murdered. I said, "Rose, I don't know how you withstood all the things that have happened to you." I expected her to say it was the church or the support of the priests. She looked at me and said, "Every day I get out of bed and I shake my fist at the heavens and say, 'I won't be licked.'" I told her that was the

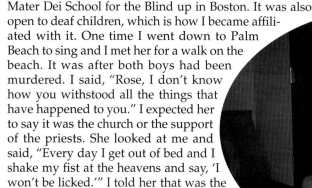

last answer I expected from her and that I thought she was going to say something like, "God never gives us things that we can't handle."

BLDS: For the last two years you have been chairman of Lincoln Center of the Performing Arts, the most significant arts institution of its kind in the country. Thirty years after the federal government has intervened in the arts, and just as you become a major arts administrator, the federal, local, and state governments are removing themselves from the arts. Clearly, you must have some elaborate new arts initiatives, programs, and marketing devices. What do you plan to do?

BS: There is such a thing as American know-how. We do know how to get things done. I think we have to just arrive at the conclusion that if we want a little beauty in our lives we're going to have to pay for it.

BLDS: Did your transformation from prima donna to director hold any unexpected surprises for you? What was the most memorable aspect of the "learning experience?"

BS: I was surprised at how many people did not want me to succeed. And I was delighted with how many more wanted me to.

BLDS: First as a child star and then as adult performer your travel and rehearsal schedule must have been very demanding. Do you feel you missed out on anything? Is it possible to "have it all?"

BS: I enjoyed everything about my professional career. I was ecstatic every time I was onstage. To have it all means different things to different people. I had an awful lot.

BLDS: Did you ever expect your life to unfold the way it has?

BS: No. Each day has been a surprise. Some were wonderful ones.

BLDS: If you had your life to live over again, what would you do otherwise?

BS: Nothing. I believe man plans and God laughs. So I'm not a planner or a changer. I'm grateful for what I have.

I was surprised at how many people did not want me to succeed. And I was delighted with how many more wanted me to.

110

RUTH SIMMONS

BLDS: Why don't we begin with a recent event in your distinguished career. On July 1, 1995, you were named the ninth president of Smith College, and the first African-American president of what has been described as one of the country's most elite women's colleges. Your friend and mentor, Skip Gates, calls you the Jackie Robinson of college presidents, which you can or cannot dispute. Actually, there are twenty-eight African-American college presidents in the United States, so why was so much made of your appointment? You have the burden of being a "first" although you weren't a first, even though you are referred to that way. Perhaps you can describe the journey from the corn and cotton fields of East Texas to Northampton, Massachusetts.

RS: I appreciate the opportunity to comment on this business of being the first, because it's been puzzling to me why people think of it as such a dramatic occurrence. I am very much aware that there are many distinguished African Americans who are leading important institutions in this country, and it does seem a bit odd to me when people say that I'm the first to lead an elite institution. So I think it's not correct and I think that it points to the fact that so many people view the Seven Sister colleges and the Ivy League as the real prize—whatever other colleges in this country achieve, and whatever the level of excellence is in those colleges. The people who cite my appointment as being particularly important are really those people whose standards are perhaps dominated and defined by Northeastern institutions, and that's irritating to people in the rest of the country. Secondly, some element of it, to be certain, is the fact that institutions like Smith represent, for a lot of people, forbidden terrain. People never expect to see, in this era, an African-American president of any of these institutions, precisely because they are in that realm of elitism that seems to suggest that no African American could dare hope to lead one of these institutions. Please remember that when Harvard appointed Neil Rudenstine as president, people couldn't believe that Harvard had appointed a Jewish president who came from a different social class. His father was a prison guard. There was a lot of attention at the time of his appointment around that issue. These are institutions that are thought of as belonging to the wealthy of this nation. They are not supposed to belong to the rest of the people.

BLDS: Are those atavistic views held by the fifty- and sixty-year-old alumni who sometimes perpetuate the values that prevailed when they went to school there? I wonder if it is not the younger persons, but older alumni, who help to perpetuate the myth.

RS: To some extent, but the strong reaction to my appointment has come from people of all ages, in a sense. I think that the students at Smith were just as flabbergasted as the sixty-year-olds because they too tend to see these institutions as being in a separate category. They are the highest prize the educational system in this country affords. And they are the highest prize in terms of getting into the highest social and economic stratum. It's the combination of the educational elite and the social elite that's rather shocking. Add to that the fact that I am someone with my background. That was the part that made it somewhat more interesting. Had I been someone who had middle-class parents and who had looked very similar to many other people who might aspire to that position, I don't think the notoriety would have been the same. It's the combination of my background and the fact that it is Smith.

BLDS: Regarding your background, you come from a large family; your parents were sharecroppers. Can you tell me what it means to be a sharecropper—and just where is Grapeland, Texas?

RS: The sharecropper system was developed to help the owners of large farms harvest crops. Big crops. Farmers offered homes and land on their farms to families in exchange for their working the

> . . . institutions like Smith represent, for a lot of people, forbidden terrain.

farm. It was really a plantation system that was the successor to slavery. The system of sharecropping was intended to create a kind of indentured status for the tenants or sharecroppers. All kinds of services were available on the farm, which were obviously to be paid for by the sharecroppers themselves. For example, if there was a commissary on the farm, the sharecroppers would build up huge debts at the commissary during the season that had to be repaid at the time the harvest was brought in. The accumulated debt was such that, in fact, they never could get out of debt. They were locked into a system in which they were seen as tenant farmers but in essence they were slaves; they could not get out of the system on account of the debt structure that was built into it. I think Nick Lemann's book *Journey to the Promised Land* is a very good description of what went on in the sharecropper days. I've confirmed this with my older sisters and brothers.

BLDS: You are the youngest of twelve. What's the age span?

RS: The oldest is about twenty-one years older than I am. I have talked to them about the experience my parents had trying to keep up with that kind of system, and it was a deadly system, because one had to have a certain number of people in the family in order to try to break even. One had to bring children in to work the fields and bring in the crops.

BLDS: That helps explain, in part, the very large families. They were part of the work force.

RS: They were absolutely part of the work force. It also explains why the children couldn't go to school, because what came first was the crops. My older sisters and brothers tell stories of how they were kept out of school for very long periods of time because of the system of sharecropping. They could not go to school when there was field work to be done.

BLDS: Was this in the thirties and forties?

RS: This was as late as the late forties. The sharecropping system started to disappear around 1950, because they had found another means of picking cotton. Mechanization essentially changed that.

BLDS: What did your parents' parents do?

RS: My parents' parents similarly were farmers. My mother's father and mother owned land, which was very unusual in East Texas, and I believe that my grandfather was one of the people who had gotten land as the result of the end of slavery. It had come into his family. He worked that land as a farmer. When he died, my grandmother inherited the land and passed it on to her chil-

> My older sisters and brothers tell stories of how they were kept out of school for very long periods of time because of the system of sharecropping. They could not go to school when there was field work to be done.

dren. I own some of that land today. That's on my mother's side. On my father's side, my grandparents were farmers who worked for some of the large landowners in East Texas, in Grapeland. Most of the blacks in the region at that time were employed by farmers.

BLDS: And their parents—your great-grandparents—were slaves?

RS: Yes.

BLDS: Where? In the same area?

RS: Actually, we have not been able to trace where they came from, but I suspect it was in the same area of East Texas. There was not a lot of movement possible for them in those days. Typically, they would move from town to town, but they didn't come from great distances.

BLDS: In the early fifties, when you were about seven, your family moved to Houston, which must have had a very radical effect on your own life. Your father became a factory worker and a pastor and your mother became a housecleaner.

RS: Yes. Well, my mother was primarily a housewife. She stayed in the home most of the time and did different kinds of work to supplement our family income. She took in ironing. I'll never forget those mountains of ironing that came in. She spent a good deal of time at home doing that. On occasion she would take jobs outside of the home, cleaning houses. When we were older and she was able to be out of the house she would do that. When I was small she would take me with her on her jobs if it was a Saturday and she was cleaning house.

BLDS: You were the very youngest so she had to take you along. What did you then envision as your future?

RS: I think I envisioned doing the same kind of thing. I envisioned perhaps cleaning houses or, if I finished school, I thought I might do something more ambitious than that, something on the order of working in a store. In that era, anything that did not involve manual labor, or housecleaning, or construction work, or hard labor was considered a very fancy job. That's hard for people to understand. We looked up to people in the community who were train porters or store clerks. Anybody who did not have to do backbreaking work was considered a very privileged person.

BLDS: Growing up in a large family must be a very special experience.

RS: It's wonderful.

BLDS: What was it like being the youngest of twelve children? And what lessons from childhood, including survival tactics, do you still use today?

RS: First of all, I had this huge, protective network surrounding me. I had not only my parents, who I knew were there for me, but I had all these other people who I knew would look out for me. I knew that because over the course of time one learns of all of the things that the children of the family have had to do in order to protect each other. I heard stories growing up of how my sisters were protecting each other in school, or how my brothers heard about something that had been done to a brother or sister and stepped in to protect them, and so on. I grew up knowing that there were essentially eleven sisters and brothers and my parents who would protect me. There was only one thing they couldn't protect me from, and that was the hideous racist machine that operated at the time. Nobody could protect you from that.

BLDS: Were you going to a segregated school?

RS: Oh, sure. Always. At the time, that seemed entirely appropriate and normal. What one worried about was the random acts of violence against blacks, the efforts being made at the time to keep blacks in their place. That is what we lived in fear of more than anything else. I knew that my family couldn't protect me from that, but they could protect me from everything else. So that's what it was like for me growing up. I felt both that bond and that sense of protection. How did it help me? In some ways it was good and in some ways it was bad. In a way it made me a very independent person. I really didn't need other people because I had that security. I think it probably made it harder for me to develop friendships because I had sisters close in age to me who were my friends.

BLDS: Are they still close to you?

RS: Yes. My family is still close to me. Absolutely.

BLDS: Is anybody in the Northeast with you?

RS: No, but my sister is going to move to Northampton to be near me.

BLDS: Does she have a family of her own?

RS: Her children are now grown and she's divorced, so she's going to relocate.

BLDS: And what is her career?

RS: She worked for IBM for many years in computer programming. She took one of the IBM buyouts and has wanted to go back to school to become a teacher, so now she is going to finish her undergraduate degree.

BLDS: At Smith?

RS: No, heaven forbid. I wouldn't want her to be at Smith. At one of the many colleges in the area.

BLDS: Your father was a part-time pastor, a position of status and responsibility in a community. How did he evolve from farmer to factory worker to pastor?

RS: If you look at the African-American community in this country you will see that there are a good many who came to the ministry through this particular route. That is to say, they are called to the ministry, which means that somewhere in their spiritual development they take responsibility for spreading and preaching the word. They seek the assistance of a mentor in the church to help them with their education and with their progress in training for the ministry. It's not the kind of program that many are aware of, in which you go to seminary and you study for long years and you come out a theologian and a minister. That wasn't the case. Those opportunities were not available to people in the African-American community, especially not in the Baptist tradition. More typically, ministers were formed through this alternate route. There was some study, but it's nothing like what you imagine in divinity schools. My family was one of the founding families of a church in Grapeland called the Greater New Hope Baptist Church, and so from the time of their early years in Grapeland members of my family had been deacons in the church. For African Americans in the rural South, at the time, the church was a focal point of all activity, not just religious activity, but social activity as well.

BLDS: It was the organizing principle of life.

RS: Absolutely. On Sunday, families came from all around the area, from great distances, to attend church. And because they had come from great distances it was an all-day affair. One began early in the morning with Sunday school and followed with eleven o'clock church service. Often there was a picnic on the lawn after church service and then another service after that. Church was a part of one's life in a way that people today find very hard to understand. After we moved to Houston my father began studying for the ministry in this informal way that I described. Eventually he was invited to be the minister of a church in Houston.

BLDS: So it would be fair to say that your family always had visibility, identity, and a status within the social structure of your group.

RS: Oh, no, I don't think that's fair to say at all. For a long time my father was not the minister. He was studying for that responsibility and he was a religious person in the church, but he was not a pastor. This kind of thing happens quite routinely in the black community and there is no particular status attached to it. Many people come to the ministry this way. He wasn't a pastor until much later in his life, in fact, not until after the death of my mother. As I was growing up he was more an assistant in the church and still studying to become someone who could pastor a church.

BLDS: Was he the greatest influence on your young life?

RS: Oh, no. Not by a long shot. I think my father was a typical Southern father, that is to say, very traditional, very dominant in the family. Our family always understood that he was in charge and that we followed a course set by him. It was totally driven by his wishes and his vision. It wasn't very participatory. My father spoiled me outrageously as the youngest child and so I was aware of his protection and of the fact that I was a favorite child, but it was really my mother who influenced me more than he did. This was in part because I was a girl and she was more of a role model for me, and in part because of the kind of person she was.

BLDS: How would you describe her?

RS: She was a very dignified and elegant person who was kind beyond words. She was kind in a way that's deeper than the show that people make of kindness to strangers. She had a generosity of spirit. When nobody was around to know what she thought, that's

> Church was a part of one's life in a way that people today find very hard to understand.

when she was saying to us never think of yourself as being better than another human being. She was deeply and genuinely kind. I was very impressed with her personal qualities and her ability, always, to look for and to seek out the higher road. Those kinds of attributes really stuck with me over time. I didn't know it when I was young, but over time that's what made a big impact on me.

BLDS: You were fifteen when your mother died. Obviously, your household must have gone through enormous changes after her death. Were you raised with the help of older siblings, or did you become independent from that time on?

RS: I don't think of myself as having been independent when I was a teenager. I underestimated my father horribly because he seemed such a distant kind of parent. He was a ruler, more than a father, when I was growing up. Yet, when my mother died, he was the parent who became responsible for us. I was fifteen and just going into my junior year in high school. My twin sisters were already seniors at that point. There were really only the three of us left. My brother was about to go off to college. We were old enough to be able to prepare meals and we really didn't need people to be around constantly. Even so, my brothers and sisters stepped in to try to help out with various things, because my father was old-fashioned and knew nothing about the lives of young people. He simply couldn't have understood what it was like for us to be girls in high school in that era. My oldest sister tells the story of the time when she got married—we were still living in Grapeland—and she and her husband wanted to move to Houston. It was during harvest time and so my father refused to let her go, even though she was married and wanted to leave to start her new life. He thought the most important thing was to bring back the cotton harvest. It was my mother who said no, she has to go. That was the balance we had in my family. My father really didn't understand why this girl, once she was married, wanted to just take off and go to the city and forget about the family that had to bring in the crops. So imagine that person who then has the responsibility of completing the rearing of these three girls. He simply didn't have any idea what to do with us. Nevertheless, he was there for us as a father, and we finished our high-school years mostly with the help of sisters and brothers who really did understand.

BLDS: You moved to Houston in 1952, two years before the

Brown vs. Board of Education decision. There must have been vast changes, some of them incomprehensible, particularly in your part of the South. There you were, in the segregated South, Ruth Stubblefield, a bright, capable, and eager student. Where did you get the idea to go on to college? How did you think you would pay for it?

RS: I didn't have any idea. What I knew was that there was something about it that I loved. It was just that simple. Every day I would get up and go to school and I knew that it was a place where tremendous things happened for me. There's nothing like it. I had unlimited access to books. There were libraries that otherwise I didn't have access to. In those days I couldn't have simply gone to the public library in downtown Houston.

BLDS: The library was segregated, too?

RS: Everything was segregated. And if it wasn't segregated there was a certain understanding that there were some places where you simply did not go, where you were not welcome. School was a place where I felt comfortable. There were teachers, there was order, things were clean. It was a different world, a fantasy land, that I stepped into every day. Almost. For the time that I was there I could focus entirely on my mind, with no distractions.

BLDS: You must be powerfully self-motivated, considering that as recently as 1992 Texas still had the lowest rate of public-high-school graduates in the nation. According to the *World Almanac*, 56 percent of Texas high-school students graduate. What about the influence of your siblings?

RS: My siblings were not driven in the same way that I was, in terms of education. In that regard, my older sisters and brothers had difficulty finishing school because of this plantation system in which they had to be taken out of school for large portions of the year. Their education was brutally interrupted by this pernicious system. In a sense they could not grasp the full effect of having the kind of complete education that I had.

BLDS: Was it teachers that made the possibility of college a reality for you?

RS: Unquestionably, it was the teachers. I don't know when the idea was first planted in my mind, probably not until junior high and the beginning of high school. Someone must have said to me, "Perhaps you should think about going to college one day." I

remember going home and asking my mother what she thought of that idea. And she answered "Yes, if the money can be found then you can go to college one day." Well, I know now that she must have known there was absolutely no way in the world that my family could find the money to send me to college, none whatsoever. So I'm not sure what she was thinking in terms of what would actually be possible for me. It most certainly must have been teachers who began to talk about the possibility of college.

BLDS: So what were your thoughts when you started packing to go off to Dillard College in New Orleans?

RS: I don't know what prompted me to do that. I'm amazed now that I did.

BLDS: I often think innocence is what propels many people along.

RS: Ignorance. Complete ignorance.

BLDS: Where did you find the money, by the way?

RS: When I graduated from high school there was a wonderful award called the Worthing Scholarship. It was an endowment that had been set up by a wealthy white man in Houston to fund scholarships for top students graduating from the inner-city high schools in Houston. And I won one of those scholarships. It was a thousand dollars a year. Imagine that. It's amazing.

BLDS: And that was the passport to your new life.

RS: Oh, unquestionably. In the main, that funded my college education. My teacher, who went to Dillard, wrote to the college and asked them to give me a scholarship to supplement the Worthing award, so my education was fully paid for. I don't think I could have come up with fifty dollars.

BLDS: Did you work during the summers?

RS: Nope. There was nothing I could have done really to earn the money. At that time, people did not think of summer jobs in the way that we think of them today. There were no opportunities for me to work like that in that era. So my sisters and brothers got together and provided money for me to get off to college. I'll never forget that train ride from Houston to New Orleans. It was long. It was wonderful and frightening at the same time. It was the first time I had been on a train, the first time I had ever left home, the first time I had ever been without my family. It was an amazing trip. I'm surprised that I did it, but I think I must have been

> I underestimated my father horribly because he seemed such a distant kind of parent.

an adventurous person. A couple of summers later I was off to Mexico, alone again, to learn about that strange country.

BLDS: By then you were a seasoned college person. Even then, what caused you to think of foreign languages as a course of study?

RS: I thought of it because, frankly, I was totally inexperienced with other cultures. I didn't really even know white American culture because I lived in a completely segregated world. I left that segregated world and I got on the train, and that train took me to a segregated school, which was Dillard. It was always clear to me that whatever the life I lived on a day-to-day basis there was always a different world available to me, and that was the world of books. Books brought another world to me in the way that today television brings it to some people. Of course, I didn't have television and I didn't go to films, but I had books.

BLDS: How did you grow up in America without going to the movies?

RS: Well, where would I have gone? Remember, it was a segregated world. There were some theaters for blacks but we didn't have that kind of money. It was not until much later, toward the end of high school, that I really got to see films. The opportunity to learn about what there was in the rest of the world came to me through books. When I went to college I knew that it was important for me to study languages, because it was a window to other worlds. Initially I had no intention whatsoever of majoring in language, it was something that I just wanted to learn. My first intention was to major in the arts, but I later thought better of that and decided to focus on languages, mainly to learn about other cultures. I knew fundamentally that there was something wrong with the way this country had projected me and my capabilities. Everywhere in my life I had been taught that I could not expect to be anything, that I couldn't expect to use my mind, because it wasn't worth much.

> Everywhere in my life I had been taught that I could not expect to be anything, that I couldn't expect to use my mind, because it wasn't worth much.

BLDS: Didn't you have resentment, frustration, and anger as a result of that awareness?

RS: I must have had some, but it did not overwhelm me because my studies must have told me a lot about why this country was like it was. That's why it's so important for young people to read history and to study other cultures. A lot of the young people in this country grow up believing that there is something aberrant about this country when there really isn't. One of the things I learned when I started studying other cultures was that the kind of racism that existed during my time has been prevalent throughout history in other areas of the world, and people have had to deal with it in exactly the same way I was having to deal with it.

BLDS: It doesn't make it any better, though, when you're living through it.

RS: But it made me understand that it was simply a fact of history that I was in the situation I was in and it relieved me of the burden of being angry about it. Then I was free to go about my work and study without carrying that burden.

BLDS: Do other members of your family have the same attitude that you do? You seem almost free of any kind of rancor or anger or frustration.

RS: I wouldn't say that. I get angry like anybody else about things that are unjust. What I'm trying to say is that I did not internalize all of that anger, which can prevent you from doing anything. I've known people in my life who have been immobilized by rage. The reason that didn't happen to me was simply because through my studies I learned about the struggles of peoples around the world and I saw myself in a much broader context.

BLDS: In rapid succession you were bombarded by remarkable new experiences. In your second year of college you went to the International University in Mexico, and in the very next year you went to Wellesley as an exchange student, which might as well have been a foreign country to you. How did that come about?

RS: I'll never forget how it happened. The Dillard campus looks very much like a plantation, some people say. All the buildings are white, there is a lot of greenery, it's a lovely campus, but it's a small campus. There were only nine hundred students enrolled when I was there and so the president of the college knew everyone. I was a student that people noticed for reasons that probably had to do with my activism on campus. One day I received a call from the president asking if I would come to his house. He said, "We have a junior-year exchange program with Wellesley College in Massachusetts, and we would like to send you as Dillard's representative." Well, I was quite flabbergasted. I didn't know anything about Wellesley, but I did know that Dillard had an opportunity to send one student, one woman, and they chose me. It seemed to me that I had an obligation to go, if the president of the college thought it would be good for me. And so I said yes.

BLDS: Did the experience validate your efforts as a student, or by then did you know that you were on some kind of worthwhile career path?

RS: I'll tell you one of the things that happened to me when I got to Dillard that may surprise some people. For the first time I had white teachers. I had never had much interaction with whites before, except as a housekeeper or something like that. I had never had any jobs. I had never been evaluated by whites. However, I knew that in the culture in which I grew up everybody thought I was inferior. Not just whites but blacks, too, thought that blacks were substantially inferior. No one had ever been able to tell me that my abilities were comparable to that of any students, black or white, in the country. That had never been tested for me. At the time when I went to Dillard a lot of people were beginning to have an intense interest in the civil-rights struggle. A number of whites came to the South to do what they could to help. Wonderful people from Northern universities ended up teaching at places like Dillard. When I was a freshman I had an English teacher from New York, a rhetorician named Lou LaBrant. At the same time I had a faculty member from South America named Saucedo who taught me Spanish and a white instructor from New Orleans named Yvonne Ryan. I had black instructors, too, but it was probably an equal mix of black and white. By my sophomore year I had come to feel that the grades that I got were based on more than people just trying to support me because they liked me; rather, they were based on what they thought my real abilities were. When I got feedback from the faculty about essays I had written, I learned that I could express myself well.

BLDS: What did you write about?

RS: Anything outrageous. When I was a first-year student I wrote about the rights of homosexuals. At that time, I guess, that must have been a bit unusual. I was a crusader in every sense. I would write about Adam Clayton Powell and how scandalized I was by his behavior. I would write about anything that engaged me, anything that provoked thought, political or moral. I loved philosophy classes and existentialism. By that point I knew that they thought I was a pretty good student.

BLDS: What did you learn from being in New England in the mid-sixties? Was that a really catalytic time in your life?

RS: It was. It was a difficult time. It was a lonely experience for me in many ways, because I was very far from home. I had never really been in that part of the country before. It was quite cold; it was beautiful. I was alone with my mind in a real sense when I was at Wellesley, and I was having a tough time. I had studied French at Dillard, but clearly not the kind of French that was taught at Wellesley.

BLDS: How did the instruction differ?

RS: At Dillard the emphasis was on acquiring an understanding of the structure of the language and the grammar, whereas at Wellesley the emphasis was on both speaking and writing; it was a much less passive method of learning. So I was thrown into classes where only French was spoken and I didn't understand a word. I hadn't yet been to France; I had only been studying French in textbooks without any understanding of the language itself. That transition was so painful for me. I literally sat in classes at Wellesley for two months not understanding anything that was going on, feeling stupid and unable to function.

BLDS: What gave you the courage to go on? Or the stamina?

RS: Well, I didn't have a choice. I wasn't someone who had the personal means to simply pick up the phone and call my parents and say, I'm miserable, I want to come home, and they would send me a ticket. I didn't have that option. I had to stick it out because I was there on a scholarship. I had been sent there. I had no choice.

BLDS: Rather than having a sense of privilege, it must have been a very painful experience for you.

RS: It was very, very painful. One day I went to see one of my instructors and I confided in him that I did not understand anything that was taking place in class. I was missing assignments because the assignments were being given in French. He said to me, very simply, "Oh, don't worry. You'll understand it eventually. And don't worry about the assignments that you miss."

That's all he said. I thought that was really odd, but he was so persuaded that this condition was temporary that I decided to just let it go. So I just continued to do the work and go to class. And he was absolutely right. One day it happened that I started understanding French, and that was the end of it. At first Wellesley was very awful, but I grew to love it. More than anything I loved the fact that women were challenged in just that way and the fact that this instructor absolutely refused to say, "Oh, if you can't do it, we'll find an easier course for you." It was the first time I began to understand what it was like to be in an environment of high expectations, where people said to you, "Yes, you can do that, in fact, I insist that you do it." They were not prepared to make an accommodation for me at all. They thought I should stick with it and they were confident that I would be able to do it. It was an important moment for me.

BLDS: I assume that same value—that attitude of high expectations—has permeated your professional career as well, when the roles were reversed and you were the one who was making the determination.

RS: Yes, I would say that is very true. I have always tried to remember that lesson for students I teach and others I supervise. It's so seductive to let people off the hook and to say, "It's okay, you really can't do that." It's much harder to say, "I think that you can work to that level," and to set higher expectations. Inevitably people do better with those expectations. I feel very strongly that in the inner cities there's not enough of that going on. We have to expect students to achieve a higher level and not allow them to settle for much less. I think that's what my teachers did for me. When I came along in this segregated environment it would have been fine for me to do a minimal amount, but my teachers wouldn't have it for a minute. And they continued to insist that I keep pushing ahead. I would just go through books. I mean, I would just eat them up. And as soon as I would get through a book the teachers would say, "Okay, on to the next level." They kept me going that way throughout my years in school.

BLDS: After you were graduated from Dillard, you then spent time at a university in Lyons. How did you make the leap from here to there, especially when you didn't even have the plane fare? How did you manage that one?

RS: Again, I can't say enough about the programs that help people make transitions to very different experiences. The Fulbright program at the time had an orientation program, but I have to say

that I had already been to France by that point. I had spent a summer in France with the Experiment in International Living. After the Mexico experience I think I was hooked. I just tried to find every opportunity for a foreign experience. In any event, the Lyons experience, notwithstanding all the preparation, was somewhat difficult because Lyons is not a very open and friendly city. That's its reputation.

BLDS: To Americans it's not!

RS: Even to the French it's not. The French call it a very cold place. But I actually loved it. I met lots of friends during that year. I lived in the Cité Universitaire, which meant that I had an opportunity to meet students from all over the world. Then I had the great luxury of focusing my efforts at an advanced level. No more required courses. I got to do what I wanted to do, I got to study as I wanted to study, and so it was an opportunity for me to develop the kind of personal discipline for independent research and scholarship. That was the value of that year. I must say, I loved it. It was wonderful.

BLDS: As I read the story of your life and realized that you started out with something, frankly, as elite as the Romance languages, I wondered on what would the plot turn and how you would move those studies to a relevant contemporary pursuit. How did you do that?

RS: I believe that language is a relevant contemporary pursuit. It may seem esoteric, but I actually think it's not as esoteric as people think. I did have some difficulty, both in graduate school and as a beginning faculty member, with one aspect of this, and that is that French is a language that certain people chose to study. When I started my teaching career at the University of New Orleans I discovered there were no black students in my classes. They weren't interested in French.

BLDS: For good reason. Where would they apply it, or how would they earn a living by mastering it?

RS: Yes, exactly. I realized that, as a faculty member, if I stayed in French and in French literature, I would have an influence on very few minority students in the course of my career. And I thought it was important for me to do that, frankly. So Cooper Mackin, the dean of the College of Arts and Letters at UNO, asked me if I would come into the dean's office to help him on a part-time basis. I decided to go into administration as a way of interacting with more minority students and to help me get a better feel for the impact that I might have on them. That probably saved me because I'm not sure how long I would have stayed in the profession otherwise.

BLDS: Did you have a doctorate at the time?

RS: Yes.

BLDS: On what subject was your doctoral thesis?

RS: It was on the poetic language of Aimé Césaire, a Martinique poet.

BLDS: Obviously, your interest in the Caribbean had some relevance. As I read about your thesis, I kept thinking, why weren't these same teachers guiding you to the larger issues where you could really have made a wider contribution? I came to the unhappy conclusion that maybe they didn't realize what you were capable of doing, either.

RS: Well, I'm not sure. First of all, I think it's to my good fortune that I persisted with French. I think being in that field helped me enormously in terms of both becoming the person that I am and leading a place like Smith, for example. People might have said to me at some point, "Why don't you switch and do education or sociology?" But French and literature are the most elite of the elite. In a sense, it helped me to be in French, because it gave me the credibility that I needed in order to be an academic leader. I'm glad I stayed in it for that reason.

BLDS: You went from the University of New Orleans to California because your husband got a job offer and you were a dutiful wife. Were you married when you were a graduate student? And where did you meet your then husband?

RS: I was married after I returned from the Fulbright year. He had been a student at Tulane University when I was at Dillard. I was introduced to him by my roommate's boyfriend. We started dating when I was still at Dillard, and then I went off to France for a year, a year in which he happened also to be in England on an exchange at Warwick University. We were married when we got back. He decided to start a master's program at George Washington University and so we ended up moving north. In any case, after New Orleans we went to Los Angeles. He was by that time an attorney and he got an offer to head up a company, a subsidiary of MCA. He was in his late twenties and being made president of a company of MCA; well, that was pretty heady. It's not the kind of thing that you would pass up, particularly if you were black. The opportunity was extraordinary.

BLDS: For anyone. Which division of MCA?

RS: It was called MCA New Ventures and it was a venture-capital company that MCA created.

BLDS: And what were you meant to do with your career?

RS: Well, it didn't matter. Once I got there, I was meant to see if I could possibly find something to do. Not a lot of thought was given to it, to be perfectly honest with you. Frankly, at that time if you were in a marriage and one of you got an opportunity to do something really extraordinary, you didn't ask. I think couples today try to work things out so that both of their careers can be satisfied. I also had one child, my son, at that time. Once I got there I started looking for jobs at the universities, but it was the greatest unemployment period for people in my field in California and it was impossible to get a job. I couldn't find a job for over a year. It was very tough. Eventually I got an opportunity to go to Northridge. Once I got back into the system I was able to do okay. Then I became assistant dean and associate dean of the graduate schools at the University of Southern California. It was fine eventually, but at first it was tough.

BLDS: But you didn't give up.

RS: No, I didn't give up. When so many people worked so hard to make it possible for me to be educated it would have seemed unworthy for me to ignore that and not put my education to good use. I would have continued to look as long as it took to get a position because I thought I owed that to all of the people who helped me.

BLDS: By then you had earned a master's degree and a doctorate in Romance languages from Harvard University, which was, and continues to be, an outstanding achievement. When did you leave California?

RS: In 1983. I left California and went to be director of studies at Princeton University. By then I had two children and I had become very worried about the quality of life in California. It was not a place that I enjoyed, I must say. I think I was an Easterner by taste. I didn't like the culture and the social scene, and being in the entertainment industry was a different thing altogether. By the time my second child came along I was worried about drugs and about how difficult it would be to raise my children in California. At that juncture, my husband and I

> When so many people worked so hard to make it possible for me to be educated it would have seemed unworthy for me to ignore that and not put my education to good use.

were having serious problems. We agreed that it would be good for me to bring the children back east to Princeton and that he would relocate later to the area. At that point, we were not sure what we would ultimately do, but later we were divorced.

BLDS: You were willing to go to any part of the country, particularly the Northeast, for the right job and also to leave California.

RS: To leave California and to be in a good place for the children. I was persuaded that a college town, and certainly a smaller town, would be a better place to raise children.

BLDS: Do you still cherish that idea?

RS: Yes. It's the best decision I made, actually. I instinctively thought it would be right. Shortly before I left California, I went to pick up my son, who was eight or nine at the time, from a friend's house and when I got there the parent of his friend was completely stoned. That was not an unusual occurrence. Drugs were everywhere in California. I was terrified of drugs. In my family, smoking and drinking were thought of as being serious problems. It was very hard for me to ever feel comfortable in that domain because virtually everywhere you went there were drugs. I was just terrified of the easy way that people accepted drugs in California and I never, ever adjusted to it. Moreover, I was fearful for my children growing up in that environment.

BLDS: So you moved to one of the most conservative environments, Princeton.

RS: It was pretty conservative, yes. It turned out to be a good decision for me, and for the kids it was a good wholesome environment. It was not good in a racial sense; it was limited in terms of what my children experienced from an ethnic point of view. Still, it was safe.

BLDS: What surprises lay in store for you as a faculty member at an Ivy League school?

RS: I started at Princeton in the French department as a director of studies and an instructor. Then I was promoted into the position of associate dean of the faculty. What was it like? It was wonderful. Princeton was a terrific experience for me. Very tough.

BLDS: How did it differ from other schools where you had studied or worked?

RS: First of all, I fit in more at Princeton than I had in other schools, which surprises people now. I fit in because of my intellectual disposition more than anything else. That is, I had a very strong liberal-arts background. I was committed to the kind of education that I had had and I wanted to be in a place that valued

language and literature and traditional education. I am a staunch traditionalist in terms of educational content, though in some other ways I am quite unconventional. I believe in the classics and in certain elements of a required curriculum. And Princeton education, in the way it was designed, was very appealing to me. It fit my own values. At the same time, I have to admit that I thought there was something lacking in that environment. It was not sufficiently diverse, racially and ethnically, and I thought that the curriculum needed the addition of first-class courses on African-American studies, for example, and other areas.

BLDS: So did you prompt the president of the university to ask you to prepare a report that reviewed the state of race relations on campus? How did that come about? The Simmons Report has become a model for schools in the rest of the country.

RS: Well, I started at Princeton by building the Afro-American studies program. That was the work I was happiest with and proudest of. I wanted to be able to demonstrate that it was possible at a place like Princeton to have an Afro-American studies program of equal quality to those for classics or French, for example. I began by trying to recruit people like Nell Painter, Toni Morrison, and Cornel West.

BLDS: You transformed what was a marginal program into one of the strongest in the country. One of the ways you did it, I assume, was by bringing high-profile scholars there.

RS: Some were not high profile at the time; they became so subsequently. I'd like to believe they did because Princeton supported them. Toni Morrison had been a faculty member at SUNY Albany. She had not yet won the Pulitzer Prize, and certainly she hadn't won the Nobel Prize. When Cornel West was recruited he was a faculty member at Union Theological Seminary. I felt very strongly that there were many high-quality African-American scholars who didn't have access to the same resources that other faculty had at places like Harvard and at Princeton. What I wanted to do, in a very powerful way, was to say to the world that there were scholars of that quality in other communities and they deserved a place at Princeton and Harvard, and so on. That was the point I was trying to make. So coming to Princeton gave them the resources they needed in order to make that next step.

BLDS: The report you wrote resulted in a number of initiatives that received widespread attention. What were some of your findings and proposals that Princeton and other universities ultimately adopted?

RS: There were nineteen recommendations and I just want to cite the ones that I thought were the most important. First of all, the most important thing was that we were talking about diversity in the wrong way; that is, diversity should not be icing on the cake, it should be a fundamental element of providing a sound or even an excellent education. Therefore, I asked that the university write a mission statement that explained what we were trying to do. In that mission statement I tried to articulate the reasons that it is educationally important to have a diverse student body. Secondly, I argued that our way of doing affirmative action was not effective in creating the kinds of programs that fostered understanding across races and ethnic groups. That is to say, taking affirmative action and enforcing diversity efforts was not a good way to have people accept them. One had to designate some effort within the university to really work on bringing people together, building community, and helping people understand diverse groups. That effort had to be a separate function in and of itself and it ought not to be a policing function, which naturally caused people to resist such efforts. Thirdly, I said I thought that we had not really understood that diversity requires a good deal of attention and that the fractiousness arising out of the presence of many different ethnic groups was here to stay. What we needed to do was adopt a way of dealing with all of that fractiousness. That was an important goal for us. So I recommended the creation of an ombudsman position within the university that would be able to address those kinds of issues and reduce conflict within the community. Those are some of the things that I did in that report.

BLDS: Have you tried to implement those same things at Smith?

RS: At Smith I'm now looking at the way we manage the area of affirmative action with the intention of revising it. Someone is now doing a study and, I expect, will recommend to me a different approach in that area.

BLDS: To my surprise, only 19 percent of the students at Smith are minority students, and those are largely Asian. There are only 15 black faculty members out of 346 persons. How has this managed to be the case as late as 1996?

RS: First of all, those figures are not unusual in the nation's professoriat. The numbers still are small wherever you look. They're small at the best universities in the country, as well as in some of the worst colleges and universities in the country. Part of it is the fact that we have not had the kind of success that we wanted in recruiting faculty. Mary Maples Dunn, my predecessor, worked very hard to recruit additional minority faculty. She had some success but nowhere near what she had hoped. It's just a very tough thing to do. I have some considerable experience in this area and I hope that it is going to benefit Smith in the end. I think we will make some advances. One of the most exciting things for me is to be able to bring this kind of knowledge and expertise to the college.

BLDS: How do you attract a mix of students from different backgrounds, with different goals and expectations, to a school like Smith? And very frankly, how do you expect to attract more black students?

RS: One of the ways I hope to attract more black students is by being a better place for black students. As I've said frequently, Smith has got to be the right place for students from different backgrounds. It simply has to be. If it's not a good place for black students it's not a good place for me, either. That involves supporting the interest of those families and those students, being welcoming to black students, being of an intellectual disposition that responds to the interests of those students. When those students come forward to say that they are very interested in studying the works of Toni Morrison, for example, we have to acknowledge that as a valid academic pursuit in the same way that studying Saul Bellow is a valid academic pursuit. There is work that we have to do, there's no question about that. And I hope always that black students will see my presence as an indication that even when Smith doesn't get it right at least it is trying very hard. And I think that's a lot. What we forget often in this country is that we won't always get it right, but we ought to show every evidence of trying.

BLDS: From what I understand it was a long courtship between you and Smith. Why did you resist initially?

RS: Because I was very skeptical about whether or not they were serious. I had a very bad experience with a search committee at another university the year before. From time to time I had been sought out by search committees of different colleges and I knew that they were not serious.

BLDS: Was it window dressing versus a real offer?

I'm now looking at the way we manage the area of affirmative action with the intention of revising it.

RS: Yes. These search committees want to give every indication to the campus, and particularly to minority students and faculty, that they are making a good-faith effort to identify minority candidates. It's very important for them to have a minority candidate in the pool. However, it's also true that often they haven't the vaguest intention of taking that candidate seriously. It's so hard for a candidate to know when it's fake and when it's not. It was a bad experience for me because in the very end I made it far enough in the process that some people were really very concerned about the fact that I was a finalist and started doing things that were quite unethical. They called people to ask what my taste was in music, for example. They asked questions that in no way had anything to do with what I offered intellectually or as a manager, but rather had only to do with a means of trying to disqualify me from the search. When I learned of some of the things that individual members of the search committee were doing in an effort to disqualify me, I began to question whether or not I should ever get involved in that kind of search again. At the same time we had a situation at Princeton that was very difficult and I didn't want to leave at that time. Princeton had been a wonderful place for me and I felt very reluctant to subject them to any kind of difficulty. Those were the reasons that I really didn't respond when Smith first approached me.

BLDS: Minorities are not the only ones who benefit from emphasizing equal opportunities. Anyone not born into "the loop" would be given the opportunities traditionally available only to those who could be fairly described as well-connected individuals. Why has this aspect of the issue been so frequently ignored?

RS: I have no idea and it is another thing that is perplexing. I always point out that affirmative action benefited white males probably more than any other group because, frankly, it opened things up and forced people to advertise positions that ordinarily would not have been advertised. It's very frustrating that people rarely acknowledge the positive effect that equal-opportunity programs have had for the general population.

BLDS: It seems to me that the race issue is not raised as much anymore at a place like Smith, but that another issue seems to be of concern to alumni and applicants, and that is the lesbian issue.

RS: The issue of sexual preference is the new frontier, and I think that's true on every campus in the country.

BLDS: And Smith is among the leaders along that frontier. Northampton has been known for quite some time as a particularly hospitable place for homosexuals. It doesn't take concerns of sexual preference as a limiting factor. Does that limit other applicants? Does that limit the participation of more conservative alumni, and so on?

RS: Well, yes. Certainly it must to some extent if people perceive that not just are there lesbians at Smith, because there are lesbians at every college and university in the country, but that lesbians feel comfortable there. Some people won't like that. Some people did not like the fact that blacks were admitted to certain colleges. There were holdouts who wouldn't even consider going to those places when they found out that blacks had been admitted. I remember my ex-husband telling me the story of the way that he was hazed constantly at Tulane because he was in the first class that admitted African-American students. I think the parallels are striking there. So when I say that equal opportunity for homosexuals is the next frontier, I think it really is. There are particular times on all campuses when homosexual students try to place before the campus issues of equal opportunity and there are always some very strong reactions when it's done. In this country we know very little about this area. We still feel very uncomfortable with the boundaries of gender and sexuality, yet it is one of the things that we are going to have to increasingly face, just because we haven't confronted it yet. The reason that race is not such an issue in admission is because we have been through a period of time in which, as a nation, we have confronted it and dealt with it. I think sexual preference is something that we have not confronted. As a society we are going to have to deal with the issue of sexual preference and how we feel about it, how we relate to it, and what our public policies are going to be. I see that as one of the things that I have to deal with as president of Smith.

BLDS: And how are you dealing with it?

RS: One of the ways that I'm trying to deal with it is to reduce the hysteria about it. I regard many of the students that I see on campus as being very much the way I was as an undergraduate. They are on campus because they are students. Some people want to say to them, "You look different and you have a different sexual preference," and they want to focus on that. It's like discrimination in housing. If a black couple is trying to get decent housing, they want to focus on housing, but everybody else wants to focus on the fact that they happen to be black. I feel so strongly about this, precisely because I lived through a time when my opportunities were severely curtailed because people thought that if my skin were black it meant that I couldn't think, I couldn't articulate ideas, I couldn't go to a theater, I couldn't drink out of a glass that was going to be used by somebody else later. It was simply too hideous to imagine sitting next to me or that I could be standing in front of a class teaching white students. That's how passionate people were about this hideous thing called blackness. So the issue becomes not one's qualifications or one's goals but one's personal attributes. Similarly, when people ask about the sexual preference of students, they appear to me to be missing the point. My feeling is that other countries succeed much better in dealing with this than we do as a nation.

BLDS: The same way that they deal with the issue of choice.

RS: Yes.

BLDS: Can we talk about single-sex education? Is it a relic of the past or, as current research reveals, is it really a better idea for many persons?

RS: On this question I am really a pragmatist. I acknowledge that not every person learns the same, not every person benefits from exactly the same environment, not every person has to follow the same path. I believe in options in education. At the time when I went off to college I knew that I was a victim of this country's segregated school systems, but I didn't know that going to a little black college in New Orleans was going to benefit me as much as it did. It was segregated but it gave me an opportunity, as a young person with no experience whatsoever, to begin to experience life in a way that helped me build confidence. It was a good experience for me. I believe that single-sex institutions can be a good experience and the best experience for many, many students. They should not be deprived of that.

BLDS: What do you want graduates of Smith to be most prepared to face?

RS: I want them to be prepared to face a world in which the terms of achievement and survival will be shifting for the rest of their lives. I want them to be prepared to be creative, to find solutions as their lives change constantly. I would say to students that you cannot predict what life will hold for you. The best that we can do for you at Smith is to prepare you in a broad-based way so that whatever you encounter you will have the equanimity and the intellectual capabilities to be able to do well. That's why I believe so passionately in a liberal-arts education. People say to me all the time, Why French? What does that have to do with anything? Well, what it has to do with is life. I was broadly educated in a liberal-arts education. I learned how to think, I learned how to analyze, I learned argumentation, I learned not to be bowled over by every idea that I was confronted with, I learned how to see through things presented to me. That's what I hope we do for every student who comes to Smith. We should encourage them to be independent thinkers and truth seekers in every dimension of their lives, to always be prepared, and to look for every important dimension of a question or a problem. If you have that intellectual disposition, you'll find yourself on the right path whatever you end up doing.

BLDS: You touched peripherally on that age-old question: Should the role of undergraduate education be focused on specific career goals or should it be broadened to encourage a well-rounded outlook? And is it possible to really provide both? Should students be obliged to complete core requirements or should they be allowed to focus on their own interests? Is the undergraduate level the place to give the broadest possible education, and is graduate school a place to determine a specific career discipline?

RS: As I say, I'm a pragmatist. I believe that what the nation needs is variety, a citizenship trained in a variety of ways. There's no question in my mind that a group of people trained broadly in a liberal-arts approach is of great importance for the future leadership of this country. At the same time, there's no doubt that we need some people who are trained technically and even narrowly. There's no way to reduce education in this country to one formula. However, I hope for Smith to remain a place that values more than anything that broad approach. I believe that our students end up going out to be leaders and, when it comes to leadership, the things that are most valuable and that sustain you throughout your life are the things you learn in that kind of broad-based education.

BLDS: While you have this broad agenda you are also faced with the problems of most other university presidents: how to attract and retain a distinguished and, in your instance, renowned faculty; and how to deal with an aging physical plant, financial assistance, competition for students, higher tuition fees, parents who demand more vocational and technical skills, and all the realities of day-to-day life, compounded by running one of the most significant educational institutions in the country. How do you balance all of this? With difficulty, I assume.

RS: With difficulty—but with tremendous hope, frankly. Smith has been around for a very long time. It is an institution that will survive for a very long time. It survives because it is good. It is good because its graduates go off and do spectacular things. If we were a place that graduated students who have no success we would dry up overnight, but the fact is that something we are doing makes us a spectacular success. My job as president is to make sure that nobody tampers with that and diminishes the impact that we are having on our students. That is to say, we are doing for them what Wellesley did for me. It taught me a very important thing, that one day I can find myself in a situation where I understand nothing but through my intelligence and my perseverance I can find my way to knowledge and to clarity. That's what Smith teaches a lot of students—to be self-sustaining. They learn to have confidence in their ability and to rely on it in the tough times.

BLDS: It's a funny question to ask someone at the beginning of their tenure, but for someone as young and as promising as you are, what can you envision as your next career?

RS: What could be better than this? I can't envision anything as a next career.

BLDS: What could you be faced with in your current situation that fills you with surprise? It's hard to imagine what it could be, but you haven't been an ambassador yet. With your knowledge of the Caribbean Islands, and the works of Césaire and David Diop, and your Francophone background, your experience has been multicultural—I hate to use the term, because it has become so abused.

RS: Oh, don't be afraid to use it. My life as an undergraduate studying French was multiculturalism at work. People associate the term with particular racial categories today, but it really shouldn't be. The only thing that I can imagine doing one day is to take advantage of every opportunity to be involved in international outreach.

BLDS: Do you have a lot of international students?

RS: Yes, we do.

BLDS: How do you recruit them?

RS: We travel abroad to recruit students and we also have affiliations with various schools overseas that send us students. Smith has done this for a long time because it was involved in years past in relief efforts overseas. There's a long international tradition at Smith. Quite apart from that, once I finish my term as president of Smith and when I retire I would love to do volunteer work that gets me into communities around this country to work with children and into organizations that bring relief to areas of the world in need of it. There are wonderful things that I can do after retire-ment, but I can't imagine that I would ever do anything of this import again in my life. I don't think it's possible.

BLDS: I suspect that's what you thought with each of your jobs. What's the best part of your job now?

RS: The students. Bill Cosby called me and said, "You know, what you're doing is so important, not because of all the reasons you think, and not because of what Smith thinks, but because you will have a chance to influence thousands of young women who are going out into the world to make a life for themselves and to do something for this country."

BLDS: Practically 100 percent of whom will be in the work force.

RS: Yes. Thousands of women who will be leaders of this country. Every day when I walk across the campus I encounter young women who say to themselves when they pass me, there's Ruth, I know what her life was all about, I know what she was able to do, and consequently I know what I can do. That's the most important and exciting thing about what I do. It's the impact that I have on the individual students who come to Smith. There's not a question about it. That's the greatest fun for me.

BLDS: Do you still have the chance to take Friday afternoon teas with students?

RS: Yes. Absolutely. And dinners with them too.

BLDS: On a more personal note, you have two college-age children of your own. You have such high expectations for everything and everyone. What do you expect from them, and how do they react to your dreams for them?

RS: My expectations for them are all in the personal area only. It's very much the way my mother taught me. My expectations have to do with how they treat people. My expectations have to do with what responsibility they take for helping this country and for helping the world. I've never imposed my expectations in terms of careers or education.

BLDS: Are they still in college?

RS: My son is graduating this year from college.

BLDS: And what does he plan to do?

RS: He is a composer and he plans to devote his life to music.

BLDS: And what is your daughter's interest?

RS: She thinks she would like to be a vet. She loves animals. She's now working in a vet's office to get some understanding and experience and then she'll decide.

BLDS: Smith was founded in the 1870s by Sophia Smith because she believed women deserved a chance at education, unimpeded by the notion they couldn't do academic work. You must be able to identify with her very strongly. Do you find that there is a change in the attitude of men, younger men, toward women?

RS: Yes.

BLDS: How would you describe that?

RS: I love it. It's very different from when I was a girl, and my efforts were always minimized or considered superfluous by friends and others of my peer group. What really mattered was what the boys were going to do, what the men were going to do. That was true when I was in high school and throughout undergraduate school. It was always clear that what women were up to was completely superfluous. I think men today have a tendency to place a much greater value on women's aspirations. I see it all the time with young men who are supporting our students: their boyfriends and their brothers and their fathers. I love talking to the fathers who bring their daughters to college because it's clear that they believe that these young women should have any opportunity that life offers them. That's very different from when I was a girl.

BLDS: Are women's perceptions of themselves changing?

RS: In some ways yes, in some ways no. When I was working in coed colleges I was still surprised to see the low self-esteem of so many women in those settings. I think our expectations are that women's self-esteem is much stronger than it was in yesteryear, but sometimes that's in fact not the case. It's something that we have to continue to be attentive to in order to make sure that the girls who come along through those schools really are getting the kind of support they need to develop into whole human beings. A lot of women of my age had to do that in later years because they didn't get that support when they were young. What we want to accomplish in schools, as well as colleges, is to make sure that the environment supports the idea that women can achieve in an unlimited array of areas.

BLDS: Calvin Coolidge once said, "He who chops wood is twice warmed." What do you feel you are doing that has an effect on yourself, as much as on your long-term aspirations for the college?

> When I was working in coed colleges I was still surprised to see the low self-esteem of so many women in those settings.

RS: My interaction with young people. One thing that I will say about my position is that it has put my life in the path of young people who have aspirations and don't know how to fulfill them. For example, I hear from young people in the inner cities who want to know how it is possible for them to change their lives in a significant way. When I'm able to reach young people who are like I was, that's when I feel that I'm doing what I should be doing.

BLDS: If you had your life to live over, what would you do otherwise?

RS: I wouldn't be smart enough to design anything as good as what I have. I'm grateful that life has taken me through some very difficult times and, as a result, that my values are in the right place. I would not have chosen to have my mother die when I was fifteen under any circumstances. I probably wouldn't change anything else if I could change that. At the same time, her death then changed the way that I saw everything in my life. The fact that I was poor as a child is not something that I would recommend to people because hunger is real, you know. It's painful psychologically and physically. At the same time, growing up in those circumstances taught me a lot about life that I'm sure I wouldn't have learned if I had been wealthy. It's very dangerous for people to second-guess their lives and to try to sort out how to put them together in a different mix. I'm grateful for every day that I've had because each day has brought something beneficial into my life. You have to reflect on and appreciate the different dimensions of what circumstance provides to you. If you are fortunate to live long enough you know that the ebb and flow of fortune brings many different things. There are incredible highs, like being inaugurated president of one of the best institutions in the country. No amount of imagination could have helped me dream that. The one regret for all of us in my family is that our parents couldn't live to see it. That's been tough for us. Otherwise, my sisters and brothers are just flabbergasted. They really cannot believe how my life has unfolded.

BLDS: Can you?

RS: No, not yet. Maybe one day I will.

GLORIA STEINEM

BLDS: The term *unconventional* has often been used to describe your childhood education, which included no full year of schooling until you were twelve. How, and where, and under what circumstances did you, the 1956 Phi Beta Kappa Smith graduate, receive your early childhood education?

GS: Well, I read all the time. I don't quite remember learning how to read. I think I learned from labels on cans and things, but somehow I learned how to read. And I loved books. I was mainly not in the company of children my own age.

BLDS: Why not?

GS: Well, I wasn't in school, and we moved around a lot.

BLDS: And why weren't you in school?

GS: My father had a summer resort in Michigan, southern Michigan, which was what we did in the summer. As soon as it got cold in the winter, he would put us in this house trailer and we would go to Florida, or California, buying or selling little antiques along the way. I might have gone to school until around Halloween, but then we would get in the house trailer and leave.

BLDS: Did you realize then that yours was a different lifestyle than other people followed? Other young women?

GS: Oh, yes. I certainly knew it was different. Actually, I kind of wanted to go to school like everybody else. But looking back on it, I'm not sorry that I didn't, because I also missed a lot of brainwashing. So, in some ways I'm grateful for my parents' conviction that it was okay to live in a different way.

BLDS: Did you go to school in any of the places where you stopped along the way?

GS: No, not really, because we didn't stop that long. My sister, who was nine years older, was more likely to do that because my parents felt she needed high school so she could get into college.

> In the summertime I wore my bathing suit almost twenty-four hours a day, I caught turtles in the lake and put them in tubs and turned them loose again at the end of the summer . . .

But at my age, nobody thought it mattered that much, and my mother had a teaching certificate that warded off truant officers—even though it was for calculus.

BLDS: Did your mother and father have sisters and brothers?

GS: My mother had a younger sister; my father had three older brothers.

BLDS: And their children were schooled in conventional ways?

GS: Yes. Well, my mother's sister had no children, and my father's brothers, who basically I never saw, were much more conventional about their kids. My father was the rebel, or the misfit, in a way, in that family.

BLDS: What did you do all day long?

GS: In the summertime I wore my bathing suit almost twenty-four hours a day, I caught turtles in the lake and put them in tubs and turned them loose again at the end of the summer, and I spent my time in sneakers with a flashlight going around underneath the pier at my father's summer resort to look for pennies that people had dropped through the slats.

BLDS: What happened to the summer resort? Was it a hotel?

GS: No, it was a dance pavilion built out into the lake, the slogan of which was "Dancing Over the Water and Under the Stars."

BLDS: Is that the source of your early interest in dance?

GS: In a way, yes, but I think it was more going to movies and seeing Shirley Temple and others in all those Hollywood musicals. If you were a little girl in those days, pretty much the only place you saw women who were nonconforming was in the movies. And they were in show business; therefore, they were often singing and dancing.

BLDS: Were they your early role models?

GS: Yes. In the same way that a boy from a racial minority might

126

only have seen people who looked like him in sports, so he wanted to be in sports. It isn't very realistic, but it's just the only thing you see.

BLDS: So where did you get your sense of identity? With whom did you play?

GS: When I was young and living in Michigan, I had first one and then another girlfriend who were a year or two older than me.

BLDS: In what part of Michigan were you living?

GS: Southern Michigan, Clark Lake, a little south of Jackson. There are tons of little lakes around there. My first girlfriend's parents had a little farm nearby, so we used to play together a lot—paper dolls, making up stories, and things like that.

BLDS: Whatever happened to her?

GS: She came to see me after a lecture, with her mother, a few years ago. She's married, has kids, still lives in the same place, and seems happy. It was great to see her. The second girlfriend was in junior high, and I used to stay with her and envy her life—but now I've lost track of her. I wasn't with children in the way that children usually are because we would be gone for most of the school year. When I started school I was a little bit of an outcast because I had the wrong vocabulary. Kids who are around grown-ups all the time talk funny, you know.

BLDS: I have heard that a beauty contest was your ticket out of Toledo. So the first question is, how did you *get* to Toledo?

GS: Well, after my parents separated when I was about ten—they later divorced—my mother and I lived mainly in Toledo, which had been the home of both my parents. She had a house there that

> . . . in those days, pretty much the only place you saw women who were nonconforming was in the movies. And they were in show business; therefore, they were often singing and dancing.

had been her parents' house, an old farmhouse that was by then in the middle of what for Toledo was a poor neighborhood, where most of the men were dependent on the ups and downs of the local factories. I lived there from the age of eleven to seventeen.

BLDS: At that point, how did you adjust to the day-to-dayness of school? Or was it something that you were longing to do?

GS: Well, I wanted to be like other kids. I guess I didn't ever adjust too well, though, because I never was on time, I never got my homework done, things like that. But I managed. What got me through it, I think, was my vocabulary, because from reading and being with grown-ups I had a big vocabulary for somebody that age, even though I didn't know my multiplication tables, geography, or all those things.

BLDS: By the way, did you also learn a great deal about antiques?

GS: I absorbed a fair amount of knowledge, yes. I wasn't conscious that I was learning it, but, of course, you do learn just by hearing things. I once tried to get out of Toledo via a beauty contest—that was the Miss Capehart television contest—do you remember Capehart television sets?

BLDS: Was that an early manufacturer of televisions?

GS: Right. Exactly.

BLDS: Who gave you the idea to enter the beauty contest?

GS: I was working at a radio

station cuing in records after school when I was in high school; I was sixteen. I think it was through the radio station that I knew the contest was happening. Or maybe it was through my dancing school, because I was also taking dance lessons and making a little extra money by dancing.

BLDS: Where did you dance?

GS: Supermarket openings, nightclubs, Elks Club meetings. It wasn't usually even the Elks Club, it was the Eagles. The Eagles were the guys who worked on the assembly line, and the Elks were the foremen. Of course, I was two years underage to enter the contest, so I had to lie and make myself eighteen, as I did for many dancing jobs, too. I was as tall as I am now—5'7"—when I was twelve or thirteen, so in costume and makeup I could pass.

BLDS: Was there a bathing-suit competition?

GS: Yes. It was on television, a little local station. There was also a talent contest, for which I danced.

BLDS: And what kind of dancing was that?

GS: You know, show-business dancing. I did a little of several things. I did a little bit of a Spanish number with castanets, a little of a Russian number, an Arabian part with finger cymbals, and a little tap dance.

BLDS: Your act sounds like an early U.N.

GS: Right. That's a great way to put it. But I didn't win.

BLDS: But it is of interest that you chose to represent yourself with such diversity in your act—you didn't choose Ginger Rogers or even Shirley Temple.

GS: Yes, that's true. I never thought of that. Maybe you're right. I had an international doll collection when I was little, so maybe that was an influence.

BLDS: So you didn't win the contest. It must have been a great disappointment.

GS: Not only did I not win, I came in third, I think, and once they found out that I'd lied about my age they even took my third prize away!

BLDS: What was the prize?

GS: An awful set of rhinestone jewelry with fake rubies.

BLDS: Now, isn't it all for the best! Moving ahead, do you think your education in a women's college in the 1950s helped shape your feminist politics?

GS: Probably, but not because the fifties were feminist.

I had been taught . . . that marriage was women's only life-changing mechanism. You decided which man to marry, then you lived his life.

BLDS: No, but being educated in a single-sex institution, it does focus the mind, doesn't it?

GS: Well, I think it helped, even though the degree of consciousness in those days was quite low. When I was at Smith, the administration was still bragging about having four times more male than female faculty, because that made the college seem more serious. They'd never had a woman president and they assumed they were training the wives of executives. Their main reason for educating women was that, if we were ever going to have educated children, we had to have educated mothers. The feminist books were locked up someplace in a rare-book room; I never even knew they existed. It was definitely not a feminist atmosphere in the 1950s.

BLDS: Including people coming around to the campus to sell china and silver to the potential brides.

GS: I didn't see that, but I bet you're right. Everybody got engaged, including me in my senior year. I remember everybody having diamond rings.

BLDS: Did you do it because that's what everybody did?

GS: I did it because that's what everybody did, and also I had discovered sex, which was a major event, and I didn't know what to do about it. I was hooked on this very nice, very attractive man. I didn't want to get married, but I didn't want to leave him either, so I got engaged.

BLDS: And did you realize at the time that your engagement would never culminate in marriage?

GS: Yes, but not very consciously. Mainly because the idea of marriage just made me feel very, very depressed.

BLDS: Why?

GS: Because I had been taught, as a fifties person, that marriage was women's only life-changing mechanism. You decided which man to marry, then you lived his life. Now, if you really believed that you had to take on your husband's identity, then marriage became like a little death. It was your last decision. In fact, your only decision. You left your own home, interests, and separate identity behind. It wasn't that I said to myself, I'm never going to get married. It's just that I thought my life was over once I made that decision, so I kept putting it off into the future. I was engaged, but when my friends on campus would congratulate me, I would turn around to see whom they were talking to. It was extremely depressing, through no fault of the man, who was a very nice person.

BLDS: Do you still have contact with him?

GS: Yes, absolutely. We still see each other. We have a relationship that he calls "same time next decade."

BLDS: What does he do now?

GS: He does a variety of things. He writes and has a kind of cultural television show. He lives in Denver.

BLDS: He sounds like a likely person for you to have been interested in.

GS: No, we didn't share his major interests, because the truth is that if he were left to himself, what he would love to do most is hunting and sports.

BLDS: Did he come from Colorado?

GS: No, he came from New York. His family was in the music world. His mother was the sister of Jascha Heifetz, and his father had been Heifetz's accompanist, and later founded the NBC Orchestra with Toscanini. They were all very talented and sophisticated. So here am I, from the wrong side of Toledo, and here's this creative, wonderful family. And I thought I could never do anything myself, so I should not pass up this opportunity to be a supporter in this talented and interesting group. It was very difficult not to do it. In part that's why I went to India. I knew that unless I got

very far away, I would be tempted to stay with him—and that would have been very wrong for both of us.

BLDS: So India was also a way of phasing out the relationship as well as declaring your own interests.

GS: Well, I had already gotten un-engaged, because practically everybody around me, including his family, made me feel even more at sea. I think some part of me realized that I had to get very far away or else I would make the wrong choice.

BLDS: After you were graduated from college you went to India on a two-year Chester Bowles Asian Scholarship program. Why did you select India? Obviously, you were the kind of student and person who could have made a wide range of choices. Why India, and at that time?

GS: I don't know if I could have made a wide range of choices because there weren't very many. There still aren't choices for people who don't have any graduate study, and at that point, Rhodes Scholarships and such were only for men. It happened that I knew about this one because Chester Bowles had come to Smith to speak, and the proceeds from his lecture had been used to start this scholarship for India, where he was ambassador. The whole scholarship was one thousand dollars. That was it. I was attracted to India for two reasons, I think. One was a historic reason, that is, historic in my own life, because my mother and

© Sigrid Estrada

129

both my grandmothers had been Theosophists. As a very little girl, I used to go with them to the Theosophical Lodge meetings with my coloring book—*Lotus Leaves for the Young,* whatever. So early on I had that sense of affection for and attraction to India. The second reason was that, in the fifties, people with a sense of idealism or hope of social change were not directed into activism within this country, where there was no activism that was very visible. The civil-rights movement hadn't started, there was not much consciousness of poverty in this country, and Michael Harrington had not yet written his book about hunger in America.

BLDS: It was just two years after *Brown vs. Board of Education,* so the most significant changes in American life had not even begun to form or take shape, nor was there a high moral authority supporting those legal decisions at that point.

GS: I'm sure that there were many committed people, but there wasn't yet a visible movement. Therefore, many of the idealistic activists of my generation tended to be drawn to what were then called Third World countries. I had taken a course on India from Vera Michaelsdean, who was teaching part-time at Smith and was active in the United Nations. I went to India for all of those reasons, plus trying not to get married.

BLDS: Trying not to get married to your fiancé, or trying not to get married in general?

GS: Trying not to get married to him—not because of him, but because of marriage as an institution. I didn't say to myself, it's because of marriage as an institution, what I said to myself was, I'm going to conform and I'm going to do everything everybody wants me to do, get married and have children—but not right now. I thought that once I did that I couldn't make any other choices. I had to then follow my husband's life.

BLDS: You may have been accurate. If you had children, what sort of education would you favor for them? Would it be the same sort of education that you had, knowing that there have been so many turns of the screw?

GS: I would definitely want my daughter—or, if I married a man of color, I would want my daughter or son—to have the experience of being in their own group, so they could see people who looked like them who were honored in authority. But that should not be their only experience. I just think that if you live in a society in which you don't see your own group honored in authority very much, that experience is very important. Therefore, if my daughter went to a big public high school as I did, then I think

going to a women's college would be good; or, if I'd married somebody who was black, going someplace like Howard would be an important experience for my son or daughter. If they went to a small preparatory school, then going to a big university might be a good experience.

BLDS: So you would want a diversity of experience.

GS: Right, I would urge them toward it—but the decision would be theirs.

BLDS: Looking back, do you think your time in India significantly shaped the later course of your life and your work?

GS: Yes. Absolutely. Ironically, I don't think I quite understood how much until recently. Only when I was writing an essay called "Doing Sixty" for my last book, *Moving Beyond Words,* did I look back and discover that, as a feminist organizer, I'd spent more than twenty-five years traveling from place to place in pretty much the same way I had traveled with Gandhian organizers in India. But when I came back from India in 1958, I couldn't figure out how to integrate those two years in India into the rest of my life. People were not interested in India yet. If I started to talk about it they fell asleep. After a while, it felt emotionally as if those years were kind of an absence, not a presence, in my life, and only later did I realize how much they had influenced me. One of the major ways was that I realized most of the world did not live like this country. And I realized that there was a terrible monochromatic quality to the people I had known in my life, that white people were a small minority in the world, and that I was being kept from knowing the true diversity of people, even in this country. I got accustomed to, and began to value, racial diversity in India because that's part of one's life there.

BLDS: Did you travel throughout the country?

GS: Yes.

BLDS: Southern India, as well?

GS: Yes, I loved southern India. In a sense, it's the most truly Indian region, because the waves of invasion, whether it was the Moghuls or the British, never quite made it to the tip of India. So it's more its own self. And the culture of southern India is also very different, being more Hindu and less Muslim, not to mention that it still has some legacies of an ancient female-run culture that used to exist in Kerala—such as the highest literacy rate and most of the egalitarian traditions.

BLDS: How influenced were you by Gandhi's philosophy and activism?

> I believe that Gandhi was right—the means you choose determines the end you get. You can't have a violent means and get a peaceful end.

GS: Very, very influenced.

BLDS: What connection did that have with your daily life?

GS: When I was there the people I met who were social activists were almost all Gandhians. Not altogether, but mostly. This was not long after the Independence Movement. I worked with them, I went to classes with some of them, I walked through the villages, as I wrote about in "Doing Sixty," and I was very, very, very drawn to them as human beings, because they were kind and open and nonviolent and not narrowly nationalistic at all. They were very open to world culture, and to including non-Indians in their culture. And, I think, women are drawn to nonviolence anyway because we are the major victims of violence. We are always the huge majority of peace movers. Twenty years later I went back to India and saw many friends there, including one of my still closest women friends, a Gandhian economist whom I had known in the fifties. We had both become feminists, both of us, and we talked about how we should take Gandhi's teachings—he didn't really write books, he wrote letters, basically—and we should go through his letters and take out those precepts that would be especially helpful to women's movements all over the world. This would be useful not only because women are drawn to nonviolent methods, but also because I believe that Gandhi was right—the means you choose determines the end you get. You can't have a violent means and get a peaceful end. And so we got all excited about this and we were going to make a book of Gandhian tactical wisdom for women's movements all over the world. Then we went to see a very distinguished woman who had worked with Gandhi. She listened to us with great patience and at the end she said something like, "Of course, we taught him everything he knew." It turned out that he had adopted the nonviolent

> It matters less what we choose than that we have the power to make the choice. And women around the world are supporting each other in acquiring the power to make a choice. . . . A woman has the right to decide what happens to her own physical being.

tactics of the women's movement that had been very active in India from the late 1800s into the 1900s, before it contributed to, and then was subsumed by, the Independence Movement.

BLDS: How recently were you there?

GS: The last time was in the mid-seventies. I've been trying to go back and I believe I will go back in '96 or early '97.

BLDS: Because it remains a place of interest and concern to you?

GS: Right. I'm very drawn to it. The political impact, too, for me was important. I was in college during the Joseph McCarthy era, and there's nothing more likely to make you a Marxist than any vision of Joseph McCarthy. But two things happened. First, while waiting for my visa to India, I worked in England as a waitress in an espresso bar that was right around the corner from the place where Hungarian refugees were being welcomed and sheltered as they came out after the revolution in 1956. So this little espresso bar was full of Hungarian refugees. I began to realize that maybe Communism—authoritarian Communism—was really a problem. Then, when I got to India, all my Indian friends impressed on me—the Gandhians and everyone else—that the Communist party in India had betrayed the Independence Movement by supporting the British.

BLDS: Consider what happened in South Africa, too.

GS: Yes, right. Well, India was a little less dramatic, but it was my own version of the Hitler-Stalin pact. I began to realize that hey, wait a minute, just because Communism seemed to be the only Western movement addressing parity didn't mean it had all the answers.

BLDS: That was an interesting sequence of events. I've often thought about the significance of internationalism in the women's movement. The positive things seem self-evident. Is there a great deal in common among the concerns, the issues, the problems of a woman in New York and a woman in Calcutta?

GS: The most important shared concern is the absence of self-determination or self-authority. In other words, the issues may or may not be the same, but what we're all trying to do is to give women the power to make our own decisions. It matters less what we choose than that we have the power to make the choice. And women around the world are supporting each other in acquiring the power to make a choice. I think that's fundamental. There are also shared issues that flow from the fact that we're all living in some form of patriarchy. The primary one has to do with reproduction, because the definition of patriarchy is controlling our bodies as the means of reproduction. So, in Ireland, it may be trying to get contraception, and in parts of Africa or the Middle East, it's trying to combat female genital mutilation, and here it's trying to maintain legal abortion and get contraception, and so on. In parts of this country and of the world, it's the right to have children in safety, because that's part of reproductive freedom—it's not just the right *not* to have, it's also the right *to* have. In the Soviet Union, where abortion was the major form of birth control, it was trying to get contraception so you didn't have to have unnecessary abortions. It takes different forms in different countries, in different cultures, but the shared goal is reproductive freedom. A woman has the right to decide what happens to her own physical being.

BLDS: Why has feminism become such a "bad" word?

GS: Well, it's better than it used to be.

BLDS: Do you really think so?

GS: Oh, yes. I mean, if you look at the public-opinion polls, it's much better than it used to be. There was a Harris poll done a couple of months ago that showed that, given the dictionary definition of feminism—which is what it is, "the belief in the economic, political, and social equality of women and men"—60 percent of men and 70 percent of women said they were feminists. However, there has certainly been an effort on the part of the right wing to distort words, so that *affirmative action*, *liberal*, and *feminism* have become distorted words. But I think it's fair to say, if you look at the polls, that there are more women who call themselves feminists than those who call themselves Republicans. When they talk about feminism, they rarely say, compared to what?

BLDS: There's a good article for you to do. Especially now, because it would give support and encouragement to those people who in their heart of hearts know they believe in certain issues, but fear or are reluctant to identify themselves as feminists, because they don't think they have the sanction to do so, either by the larger society or by their particular group.

GS: They're not wrong, because the difference is that even though the same number of people, or perhaps even more people, identify themselves as feminists, the Republicans are much more in power. So they punish the ones who do identify themselves that way. It's not wrong to think that if you stand up there and say, "Hello there, I'm a feminist," you're going to get punished; but if you don't say, "Hello there, I'm a feminist," the personal punishment in the long term is worse, because then you lose your sense of self-respect.

BLDS: When I was living in the South in the 1950s and 1960s I referred to myself, and was referred to by white persons and persons of color, as Miz Diamonstein. I was, of course, Mrs. Diamonstein. I still often refer to myself as Miz Diamonstein in the Southern colloquial sense rather than the feminist sense. How did the term *Ms.* become widespread in usage, and even in non-English-speaking countries? What was its origin? What is its genesis?

GS: When we were starting *Ms.* magazine I thought it had come from secretarial handbooks of the 1930s, forties, and fifties to refer to a woman whose marital status you don't know. Therefore, it was very useful because it was the exact equivalent of *Mr.* Obviously, if men don't have to identify themselves by their marital status, women shouldn't have to, either. Later, I discovered that the term had started as *Mis*, an abbreviation of *Mistress*, which indicated respect, not marital status, in the sixteenth or seventeenth century.

BLDS: Did you create the title of the magazine?

GS: Well, no. I thought *Ms.* was short and symbolic, but as you can see, *Ms.* had been around as a term for a very long time.

BLDS: But certainly your magazine, and that period, are what gave it currency and widespread usage.

GS: Yes, I think so.

BLDS: To this day I find people both hostile and aggressive about that reference. Do you?

GS: Yes. Sometimes I notice that when it's used in television scripts, people will say, "Oh, I'm Ms. so-and-so." "Oh, you're one of those." But the fact is, about a third of American women use it with their own names and more accept it in others as a form of address. The *New York Times* was the last to give in, but now it

> Obviously, if men don't have to identify themselves by their marital status, women shouldn't have to, either.

is accepted by the media, in government usage, and in business usage.

BLDS: All these years you have had an extraordinary kind of staying power, to use your words, particularly for someone who has laid it on the line every day, in every way, of your life. One of the greatest testimonials, I think, is your ability to endure when you have taken such strong positions as writer, editor, lecturer, activist. What do you think are some of the most important unresolved issues of our time?

GS: There are so many. I'm very honored to hear you say that, but I would like to say that there's been more joy and more reward in doing what I do than punishment. Also, not to do it would be harder than to do it.

BLDS: What does that mean?

GS: To swallow your anger, to laugh at women-hating jokes; to feel isolated in a group because only the men are talking to each other, the women don't feel right about taking over the conversation and talking; to get angry because the culture tries to dictate what race your friends should be, or what class, or whatever—all that is worse. It's hard to make change, but I think in the long run it's harder not to. What happens to women especially is that, if we don't speak and we swallow the anger, we turn it into depression or collect grievances until finally one day we burst forth inappropriately because we've been holding it in for too long. There are so many ways in which, in the long run, it's harder not to try to make change.

BLDS: What were some of the most significant issues that *Ms.* magazine dealt with?

GS: In a fundamental way, they're the ones we're still dealing with, they just take different forms. For instance, there are the economic issues, there are health issues, there are reproductive issues, there is safety, physical safety. They've changed form but their umbrella is a familiar umbrella. When *Ms.* started in 1972 it was common for women who went to get jobs to be told, "We don't hire women," or they were just paid less as a matter of course, because women were thought to not need the money. That doesn't happen much anymore. At the entry level, for the most part, you can get the job and you can be paid equally. However, it happens ten years out, in a different way, when you hit the economic ceiling. Then you don't get the promotion or you don't get whatever because the barrier has moved up, but it's still there. It happens similarly with marriage. When we started the magazine, we were doing pieces about how to keep your own name and not give

up most of your civil rights when you got married. That doesn't happen anymore, mostly, although there are still some remaining inequities there. But when children are born, the inequalities start, because men don't take care of children or change their job patterns as much as women do.

BLDS: Even younger men? I am often so encouraged by the attitudes of younger men. They appear to be generally more aware of the privileges and responsibilities of parenting, and at least publicly seem to do a better job of it.

GS: Some do; it's better. But it's still difficult, even for the man who wants to be an equal parent, because the company where he works, the campus, the factory, whatever it is, probably does not have parental leave. It probably won't let him stay home when the new baby arrives, much less allow both parents of young children to work a shorter day or week. It probably would look askance at a father if he said, I need to be home when the kids come home from school, therefore I'd like to work slightly different hours. Can you imagine a guy who wants to be partner of a law firm saying, Well, I want to be with my kids? Most men are not brought up with the idea that they are going to be taking care of babies and little children as much as their wives, but even the man who has that idea still is penalized by the system. So there's a very, very long way to go. At this juncture, we've convinced the majority of the country that women can do what men can do, but we have not convinced the country that men can do what women can do.

BLDS: That's a good point.

GS: So right now most women have two jobs, one outside the home and one inside it.

BLDS: But you have spoken out regularly and eloquently against what you've called the myth of the superwoman, and the fact that no one can really have two jobs.

GS: No one can do two jobs, yes. Superwoman was invented by antifeminists, not by feminists. What society did was to first say, No, you can't be a lawyer or a mechanic or whatever it is you want to be. Then when we became lawyers or mechanics or whatever anyway, society's next form of resistance was to say, Okay, you

> At this juncture, we've convinced the majority of the country that women can do what men can do, but we have not convinced the country that men can do what women can do.

can do that, but only if you keep on doing everything you did before—so you don't disrupt male privilege. In addition to being a lawyer or a mechanic, you have to raise two or three perfect children, dress for success, cook gourmet meals. It is a setup for failure. You cannot do two full-time jobs.

BLDS: So what do you advocate for those women?

GS: Revolution—from changed job patterns and equal parenthood to a national system of child care, which every other industrial democracy has more than we do. You also have to feel okay about saying that you are not going to have children unless the man is going to be an equal parent. There are very few women who even feel they can say that, or that we have a right to a changed job pattern. We all do. Men and women. So, instead of wondering how I can spend eight hours in the office, I am going to wonder how I can make a group within this company that changes the way we work, which we can change. You know, we used to have a seven-day work week, then we had a six-day work week; we had a ten-hour day. It has changed before, it can change again.

BLDS: I was struck by what you said about women in 1972 going to a workplace and being told, No, we don't hire women here. It sounded like the recent dark ages. And then I was reminded of the *Ms.* project that we were both involved in, published in the first issue of *Ms.*, which related to decriminalizing abortion. That was a dark age, too. Yet the changes have been remarkable in the past twenty-five years. Do you agree?

GS: Oh, yes. Whenever we get discouraged we have only to look backward and see the enormous distance we've come. But we must understand that this is not a little integration we're carrying on here. This is a major transformation of five to ten thousand years of patriarchy and racism. So we are going to get opposition. On the abortion issue, it is because the desire to control reproduction is the basis of a patriarchal and racist system, so it's the whole ball game. Once we seize the control of the means of reproduction—that is, our own bodies—the whole system starts to unravel. Certainly the right wing is very clear about that.

BLDS: They do know it very well, better than we know the converse.

GS: Yes. That's why the major right-wing issues are antiequality ones—whether it's women's reproductive rights, or maintaining the male-dominant family. They know that's the basis of a male-dominant state but, unfortunately, our liberal friends are less clear that a democratic family is also the basis of a democratic state.

BLDS: What was the public reaction to the article called "We Have Had Abortions" in the first issue of *Ms.*?

GS: Many well-known women said publicly that they had done what was then an illegal act. It was patterned after a similar statement that women had made in France. It was the beginning of an organization that was then, or later became, known as Choisir. It was composed of well-known French women who were stating publicly that they had had an abortion, and that they supported the repeal of laws against abortion.

BLDS: Interestingly enough, as the author of the article, the most calls I received were from sportswriters. It was the heyday of Billie Jean King.

GS: Oh, that's right. She was on the list.

BLDS: She was then married and her marriage was coming apart. And that's all they wanted to know.

GS: I think they were also using it to accuse her of having been so selfish as to have an abortion so she could play tennis. The main response that the magazine got was women sending in their names saying, I, too, have had an abortion and I want to be part of this list. People made similar lists in each state and gave them to their state legislators. It was quite contagious. So the main response was the relief that someone had finally said this out loud.

BLDS: Well, that was our intent, wasn't it?

GS: Yes, absolutely. But there was also opposition. I'm sure it was difficult within some of the families of people on the list. Coming from the repressive fifties, I also had not discussed sex with my mother or sister, nor had they discussed it with me. We had never discussed the fact that I had had affairs with men, yet I couldn't ask people to be on that list without putting my own name there. So I had to tell my mother and sister before it came out.

BLDS: I think that a number of people may not themselves have had abortions, but in the sense of "Ich bin ein Berliner," they signed out of solidarity.

GS: I remember people asking us that question. And we essentially said, "It's up to you."

BLDS: Exactly. It was left ambiguous. But I thought it was very important to do that, largely to protect those people who did not feel comfortable in identifying themselves personally. It was the demand for safe and legal abortion rather than personal involvement that was important.

GS: Also, we were discussing whether or not we should include men who had caused women to have abortions. It was important for women to have a voice.

BLDS: You are the president of Voters for Choice and a founder of the Women's Action Alliance, of the National Women's Political Caucus, and of the Ms. Foundation. Can you tell what, in fact, those four organizations are for, on which issues they focus, and how much of your time you spend with each of them?

GS: The Ms. Foundation is my major charitable commitment and Voters for Choice is my major political one. Voters for Choice is a bipartisan political action committee that supports candidates of both parties and both sexes who support reproductive freedom. That means raising money for them, campaigning for them, helping to research and produce literature, doing seminars, doing ads, all kinds of ways of supporting candidates who are pro-choice, as the huge majority of the American public is.

BLDS: How can you substantiate the claim that the huge majority of the American public is pro-choice?

GS: You just look at public-opinion polls.

BLDS: Then why aren't the elected officials reflecting those numbers in their votes?

GS: Well, they often are. The reason that the ultraright wing has turned to terrorism against clinics is because they haven't won what they wanted to win at the ballot booth. Only 40 percent of eligible voters in the country vote, while the Right-to-Life groups vote 90 percent of their membership. As we know, that is the fundamental problem. But if you look at the public-opinion polls, and if the question is asked properly—Who should make the decision about an abortion, a woman and her physician or the government?—90 percent of Americans say it should be the woman and her physician, not the government. Even if you phrase it in a stupid way—Do you support abortion? Are you pro-abortion? (nobody wants to have an abortion, it's not a pleasurable experience)—there is still a 60 percent majority of Americans who support it. The problem is that the antis are better organized, better financed; for instance, they have nine thousand fundamentalist Baptist churches with a voter operation in the basement of every one, plus the power of the Catholic Church. Anyway, I was talking about organizations.

BLDS: Yes, the Ms. Foundation.

GS: The Ms. Foundation for Women is dear to my heart. I'm very proud of it, because we started it at the same time, though separate from, the magazine, and it was, and still is, the only multi-issue, multiracial women's fund at the national level. There are now a lot of regional funds, which is great, but ours also had the job of being a catalyst within the national foundation community. It takes up issues first and educates about them in the world of philanthropy, whether it was battered women twenty years ago or women's economic empowerment and microenterprise now. It also has a National Girl's Initiative, the most visible part of which is the Take Our Daughters to Work Day—but there are many other programs.

BLDS: Isn't it incredible how significant that has become, how things take on a life of their own.

GS: We had no idea that that was going to happen; we were going to try it in New York City first—but it got in the national press and spread like wildfire.

BLDS: While I do not agree with the practices of some elected officials, mostly male, I did notice that many of them took their daughters to work, too. Did you observe that?

GS: Yes. And kids were on television with their parents doing something. The largest part of this program is not individual parents taking their kids, it's whole classes full of public-school kids being taken into the workplace by all kinds of public and private employers. That's why we call it Take *Our* Daughters. Not everybody has a parent who can do this, so it's important that it be done by the society, by the community. You can take a friend's child or you can call up your local public school and ask what you can do to get involved.

BLDS: Are you childless by choice?

GS: Yes. I was saying to a friend of mine that together we ought to write one of those books that you can read in two directions; half of it would be "how to have a child" and the other would be "how not to have one."

BLDS: I think you would make a remarkable parent.

GS: I don't think I would have at the time when I would have had to do it. I wasn't ready until much later.

BLDS: There are lots of ways to have children. We are surrounded by men considerably older than you who are having children now. Some biological parents, some elective parents.

GS: Well, it's complicated why I didn't want to have a child. I didn't ever say to myself that I was not going to have children, I just kept putting it off. Part of it was because I took the role of my mother's mother, because she was frequently ill or incapacitated, and part of it was the conditions of motherhood. I didn't see anybody who was a mother who looked free. I didn't realize how much those conditions were part of my thinking or assumptions until the same woman we talked about before, my best friend from India, tried to persuade me to come to India to have a baby on my own. I was then in my late thirties or early forties. She had two wonderful sons. She was telling me all the wonderful customs and rituals in India. They have extended households; you get lots of support—ideally. Obviously, there are many poor women who don't have this. But culturally, there are traditions of support. Motherhood began to sound pretty good. When I heard her talk about the Indian traditions of motherhood, I felt much more like having a baby than I ever had when some man was telling me why I should have one, so I realized it had a lot more to do with the conditions of motherhood than I had thought. There were unfair political pressures against having children—yet at the same time, I don't regret not having children. Somebody has to not get married and not have children to make clear that people who do so have made a choice. If all of us do one thing, it can't have been a choice. And I feel I made the best choice for me, given the alternatives I had. I've never regretted it for a minute.

Somebody has to not get married and not have children to make clear that people who do so have made a choice.

BLDS: There are by my observations few parents who haven't endured some very great disappointments. It certainly takes a lot of courage and commitment to persist in that role, or even to take on that role, if one is aware of the truths, the risk, and the world around them.

GS: Yes, that's true. Also, we can become parents in different ways. I have acquired a fair number of daughters while traveling through life. There's a young one living with me here now.

BLDS: Now back to the Women's Action Alliance. What is it?

GS: The Women's Action Alliance is off there on its own now. We started it so that women who did not belong to organizations could find a specific kind of information—how do I start a child-care center, how do I get computer literacy into my daughter's school, that sort of thing.

BLDS: Germaine Greer said that the role of First Lady actively disempowers women politically and should therefore be abolished. Do you agree with that view?

GS: I don't think anything should be abolished; it should be there

as a choice. But if we are going to ask the wife of a president to play a ceremonial or other role, she should have a salary. It should be a job. And if we are going to ask the husband of a president to do the same thing, it should also have a salary, be a job.

BLDS: That's optimistic.

GS: Yes.

BLDS: Do you see that possibility in the foreseeable future?

GS: Yes, I think so. The husbands of women in political life have already been more accepted in your and my lifetime. I remember when Martin Abzug was thought to be some bizarre, unnatural man, because otherwise how could he be married to Bella?

BLDS: Dennis Thatcher was thought of, in some ways, as an irrelevant accessory, a good golfing companion.

GS: I think somebody like Patricia Schroeder's husband would be interesting to interview about this because he's been through it all. She was first elected to Congress in the early seventies.

BLDS: So how do you think the role of First Lady should be redefined?

GS: It should be a job that you can choose to do or not. If your husband or wife gets elected into a political office, there is an available job as a hostess, a ceremonial position, and you could take the job or you could hire someone else to do it—a son or daughter, or a friend and colleague. If you, the spouse, are a lawyer or an astronaut or something and you don't have time to do it, then it's a job that could be taken by someone else, if there's a need for it.

BLDS: Do you think that's politically feasible?

GS: Eventually it will be. Not at the moment.

BLDS: *Self-esteem* is a term that has been overused and is sometimes the object of ridicule as a therapeutic cliché, but it's central to the issues of our concern. How do you give the term back an appropriate meaning and status?

GS: You just keep talking about it, because it's the root of everything. Like feminism or any other term, it's ridiculed because it is subversive. In fact, democracy doesn't work without self-esteem. Unless you believe that you have the right to decide your own life, even if you technically have the vote, you can be led around like a sheep. I tried to make that point in the title of *Revolution from Within*, by combining a political word with self-esteem. But I think you can see in its adversaries exactly what the problem is. It was the right wing in California, for instance, that was against the Council on Self-Esteem there, and similarly in Congress, when there was legislation on the subject, it was the right wing who blocked it. It's the idea of self-authority that is seen as subversive—and it is. It's important to point out that there are two origins of self-esteem. The first is core self-esteem, the concept that you are fundamentally a good, worthwhile, unique, valuable person. Not more valuable than anyone else, but not less valuable, either. That really should come very early in life. For instance, when you listen to a child, you let the child know that she or he is worth listening to. When you love a child, you let a child know he or she is lovable. That's core self-esteem. Situational self-esteem comes a little later, and is comparative. It comes from knowing you can do X or Y. That's important, too, but it's less important. Because if you don't have a core feeling of being worthwhile, you can get hooked or addicted to achievement, money, possessions—whatever. We all see men who are very powerful, very rich men, and nothing is ever enough for them. No amount of power, no amount of recognition, because inside is this empty pit.

BLDS: Do you see that in some women, too? Women of genuine achievement?

GS: Oh, of course. I'm only citing men as an example because I think they make it very obvious by having so much power and it's still not enough. But it's more true of women because thousands of years of patriarchy have been devoted to keeping us from trusting our judgment, from feeling that we can stand on our own, and from feeling that we are as worthwhile without men as men are without women.

BLDS: Helen Gurley Brown, in a recent conversation, told me that even the *Cosmo* girl has changed her focus, that even she does not have to be defined by a man alone. I think that magazine, thanks to Helen, has a vast readership in thirty-one countries. If the *Cosmo* girl is refocused, that is a good sign, don't you think?

GS: I agree. In its day, *Cosmo* was quite a step forward because it admitted that women were sexual

> ...democracy doesn't work without self-esteem.

> *Cosmo* was quite a step forward because it admitted that women were sexual beings. When Helen took over *Cosmo* the other women's magazines still had a formula: If you had sex before marriage or outside of marriage you had to come to a bad end.

beings. When Helen took over *Cosmo* the other women's magazines still had a formula: If you had sex before marriage or outside of marriage you had to come to a bad end. I think *Cosmo* is not as far forward as it would be if it were not dependent on advertising, because it is still devoted to telling you that you need to push up your breasts and put on your blusher. It's still very hooked on externals.

BLDS: In the information age, when more and more new technologies will aid in the dissemination of information, some of them, I believe, will not necessarily be advertiser supported.

GS: And that will be a relief. I learned the influence of advertisers the hard way.

BLDS: As a publisher and editor?

GS: We were trying to get advertising for *Ms.* and were never able to get quite enough to break even because we wouldn't write articles in praise of products in order to get those products to advertise—which is what women's magazines do. We wouldn't have recipes in order to get food ads, for example, or fashion spreads in order to get clothing ads. When Kissinger is photographed, they don't credit his suit. But when a woman on the board of a Fortune 500 company appears in a women's magazine, they credit her clothes, makeup, even her fragrance—which always strikes me as most surrealistic.

BLDS: You have encouraged women in recent years to value intuition more highly. I've always thought of intuition as a reflexive response to considered information. So what is generally thought of as intuition is this very quick response to a lifetime of information and experience that goes through your circuitry very quickly, particularly for those who are philosophical. How do you define intuition?

GS: I agree with you. Intuition is not mystical or magical. It is a combination of information and sensitivity.

BLDS: What's the difference between intuition and spirituality?

GS: I would say that intuition is a sense of what the people around you are feeling, what is likely to happen, what the possibilities are. It is as if the greatest computer ever imagined, which is what our brains are, helps you sort out reality and prepare and anticipate what's going to happen. Therefore, surprise is the measure of the lack of intuition—and intelligence. For instance, you will notice men will say things like, "We've been married for ten years and she just left and I didn't know she was unhappy." Okay, this is a lack of intuition.

BLDS: I think that's a lack of awareness.

GS: Well, it's the same thing.

BLDS: I mean, they are totally oblivious to the reality of their life.

GS: It's not different. Women have too much intuition and men have too little. Women are forced to have intuition because we are dependent to a larger degree than men are. We have to be very tuned in to every flicker of need and of thought. And men have unearned power. Obviously, it's not true of everybody but, in general, they don't have to be so tuned in.

BLDS: Do you share my view that we are each of us more obvious than we prefer to think we are? If people only took the time to look and to listen. And the antennae of women are out there all the time.

GS: Yes. Too much. Because we are empathy-sick. We know what other people are feeling more than we know what we are feeling. Men are the other way around. They have an empathy deficit.

BLDS: Do you think they know what they are feeling?

GS: Well, perhaps not, but they know what they're thinking and what they want. They don't know what's going on inside someone else's heart and head as often as women do. So depression is women's cultural disease, because it's an absence of feeling your own self as real, an inability to express your own wants or anger, and so on. Narcissism is men's cultural disease—being cut off, trapped in one's own head, not knowing what others are feeling.

BLDS: How about aggression?

GS: Well, narcissism is a necessity of aggression. If you know what other people are feeling, you can't be so cruel to them. You can't hit them, or dominate them, or shoot them if you empathize with them. But you asked about spirituality. I think that's a little different. Intuition is sensitivity to the microcosm and spirituality is sensitivity to the macrocosm. It's the sense or understanding that we're each part of something larger.

BLDS: And then how do you contrast spirituality to religion?

GS: Spirituality is to religion what self-empowerment is to domination. They may be antithetical. They shouldn't be, but they may be, because religion has for the most part been a way of making the ruling class sacred. God looks like the ruling class, God is white, God is a man.

BLDS: But not to you. I noticed that you pray to "Dear Goddess."

GS: Well, yes, but we shouldn't only pray to a goddess. God is present in women, men, and every living thing. If you look historically at 95 percent of human history, it was what we would call pagan, which just means country. It means nature. God was recognized to be in everything—in us and animals—and God was represented as everything. But as patriarchy was arriving on the scene—that is, as the process of conception was understood and therefore the freedom of women began to be limited in order to establish the ownership of children—women and nature began to be conquered. In order to justify or allow the conquering of women and nature, God was withdrawn from the women and nature. And you can see it, actually, if you travel on the Nile. You can absolutely see God being first represented as everything: women, nature, flowers. Then the woman is smaller, she has a son, not a daughter, then the son is the consort, and then by the time you get to Cairo both have disappeared from the mosques. The gods are all male. Religion is politics made sacred—not always, but usually. What we are trying to do now is to depoliticize religion, to get back to spirituality. It's a revolution of anthropological depth—but it's happening.

BLDS: The fastest-growing age group in the United States is one hundred plus. Isn't that amazing?

GS: That's great. I hope I make it into that group.

BLDS: When you turned sixty, it seemed that it was just another birthday on the one hand, and a special milestone on the other. A time to reflect on your life and your career and to plan the next sixty years. You said it was like approaching, I think, another country?

GS: Yes, because the country in which I had been living from the age of about eleven or twelve up to somewhere after fifty was a "feminine" terrain. Now, you may fight it or you may conform to it, but you're enmeshed with the role. After fifty, the feminine role is over because you've raised kids or you're past being a sex object in the popular view.

BLDS: But not in your view.

> Religion is politics made sacred. . . .What we are trying to do now is to depoliticize religion, to get back to spirituality.

GS: No, but I'm talking about the culture, which really doesn't have a role for women over fifty. And actually, that's progress, because it used to be over forty. At first it feels like dropping off a cliff. It feels unfamiliar. But after a while you realize that there's a whole other, freer country out there because you no longer have to engage with the feminine role, either to rebel or to conform. The map is gone and suddenly you're free. That's very exciting.

BLDS: So what replaces it?

GS: Hopefully, your unique self. But if somebody had told me this when I was twenty or forty I would have not believed it for a minute.

BLDS: Didn't you think of a sixty-year-old as some archaic creature formerly referred to as a senior citizen, having little relationship to your status?

GS: Yes, it was totally out of the question. It was someone else. The best way I can explain this for women who aren't sixty yet is to ask them to remember when we were eight or nine or ten, and we were this independent, autonomous, tree-climbing person who said things like, "It's not fair." And then at twelve or thirteen, the female role descended upon us so we became a female impersonator. Suddenly we were saying, "How clever of you to know what time it is," all that stuff. We continue to struggle with that role until we're fifty or so. But after that we go back to being the free creatures we used to be at eight or nine or ten. Only now you have your own apartment and a little money. Unfortunately, most older women have economic problems. But, at least potentially, you have more autonomy than you used to as a child, and all the experience and freedom besides. So, after sixty, there is a wonderful country.

BLDS: But now that you've been an occupant of this new country for a while, any new perceptions? Any new insights?

GS: One is that you acquire a kind of benevolence toward younger obsessions and turmoil—and the people who are still in them. Remember in *The King and I*, there was a song called "Hello, Young Lovers." Well, now I see people locked in obsessive romance, all the exhilaration, despair, and so on. I think, Oh yes, I remember that, but it doesn't engage me anymore. Of course, one day you won't have to wait to find that true center and become yourself. However, at the moment Carolyn Heilbrun's insight is right: Women become themselves after fifty when the artificial role is over. I think it is true for a lot of us.

BLDS: Do you think our country has made any significant strides during your adulthood on the way to achieving equality among all of its people?

GS: I think individuals and groups within the country have made significant strides in treating each other equally. I don't like to generalize about "the country" because then it sounds as if the government did it, or as if there is not tremendous diversity of feeling within the country. Change does not happen from the top down. A revolution is like a house, change is like a house—it gets built from the bottom up. We've had a first wave of the abolitionist and suffragist movements that finally achieved a legal identity—as citizens and human beings—for men of color and women of all races. Before that century of struggle and the Civil War, we had all been chattel, legal possessions of white males. Now we're in the second wave, which concerns striving for legal and social equality. By all precedent, we have at least seventy-five or so years to go, but in these past decades we've at least achieved a massive majority support for equality and begun to integrate the system in a way that should eventually transform it. Of course, that's only counting this country's history from when the first European arrived. The 500 very advanced nations that were displaced and slaughtered by the Europeans often had a much better balance of power between women and men—and with nature. A Native-American scholar like Rayna Green says that feminism on this continent is actually memory. Even in European history, the fate and status of women were usually ignored. For instance, medieval times were much better for women than the Renaissance, which I think is why medieval times are spurned and the Renaissance, which rediscovered the misogynist texts of the classics, is supposed to be good. Part of our progress has been this rediscovering of history, this looking at history as if women mattered.

BLDS: By the way, do you ever think of yourself as a senior citizen? Even asking you the question makes me laugh, but it suddenly struck me.

GS: I'm looking forward to discounts at the movies.

BLDS: They won't believe you. How about the air fare?

GS: And the air fare. I'm really looking forward to the air fare.

BLDS: So there are some advantages. Lots of them, actually, and most of them are liberating. I was looking at your beautiful hands, and I was reminded of something that you wrote, a very long time ago, about why you like long fingernails. Why do you?

GS: I'm accustomed to long fingernails. They have become a kind of aid in picking up papers, parting my hair, whatever. If I were a sculptor or musician, I would have short fingernails. There's got to be a choice, like everything else.

BLDS: I want to go back to the question I asked before, about entering a new country. Now that you've had time to look around, how would you describe that territory?

GS: Well, it is free. There are many adventures and very few maps. But there are explorers out there ahead of you whose lights are dancing along various paths. It may not be the path you want to take, but it does tell you that there is a world out there. It's a lot more adventurous than the country that went before.

BLDS: Are you comfortable with being referred to as an icon?

GS: No. Absolutely not.

BLDS: Because icons are not allowed to be outrageous?

GS: No, because a movement that's about empowering each individual shouldn't have icons. It doesn't make sense. Icons sound like the Catholic Church.

BLDS: Russian Orthodox.

GS: Russian Orthodox, right!

BLDS: If you had it to do over again, what would you do otherwise?

GS: I think I would have done the same things, only faster, because I think I've wasted a lot of time. That may be too simple an answer, but that's what I feel. I don't regret what I've done, but I do recognize that I sometimes continue to do over again things I already knew how to do, rather than facing the fear and the uncertainty and pushing forward more quickly.

BLDS: Would you have married?

GS: No. Maybe in the future, a time when marriage and raising children is a truly equal partnership. Even now, marriage is a different institution, though still not equal. If I were twenty now it would be different. But I am not twenty now. So I'm happy with my choice. I think what we need to realize is that there is not one way of living, there are many ways of living, and all the more so because we live much longer now. Margaret Mead said this very smart thing, which was that marriage worked well in the nineteenth century because people only lived to be fifty years old. We live thirty-five years longer than we did in 1900, we're almost a different species, so no wonder we're all going to live differently. Some people are going to get married young, have their children, raise them together, and go off amicably—more amicably because there will be more equal power—to other parts of life. Some people are not going to get married at all, some people are going to love members of the same gender, some people are going to get

married, or lead bisexual lives—you know we're probably all bisexual anyway. There are just going to be all different ways—and some people will live them all, serially.

BLDS: Are these the best years of your life?

GS: I don't know the answer, except that looking back I feel happier now. So, in the relative sense, yes. And perhaps the happiest will be in the future. I almost always feel that the time I'm in is the best of my life. Perhaps that's the result of a childhood that was difficult enough to make me an optimist—nothing could ever be that bad again—or perhaps I've been able to say no to what I don't want, thus gradually finding more and more of what I do want and what I can uniquely do.

BLDS: There must be some great, inner self that tells you that you have managed to achieve something quite remarkable, even if you can't give yourself that much latitude. There are so many goals that you had that you are very far along with.

GS: I do acknowledge that. Because I happen to work in the media and I am recognizable as part of this movement, I get a kind of reward that is infinitely moving. Women and men come up to me and tell me how their lives have changed for the better and what's happened. That's incredibly rewarding. I, like a lot of women, am sufficiently nonconfident so I tend to think that I'm just lucky. I notice that in women; we all say that we're lucky, not that we worked hard and accomplished something.

BLDS: You've devoted a good part of your life to some of the most compelling issues of the day. And fortunately, you have received personal satisfaction while working for the public good.

GS: We all want to know we are alive in the world, to know that we have made some kind of impact. If people aren't allowed to make a positive impact, they make a negative one to prove they're alive. I feel grateful and happy that I've been able to be part of social changes that I'm very proud of.

BLDS: What advice would you give to younger women today?

GS: Don't listen to advice! Listen to your true voice, to what gives you joy and pleasure, to what makes you feel you would want to do it whether you got paid or not. Look at other people for inspiration and ideas, but find the path that is your own.

BLDS: Do you have any role models?

GS: Lots.

BLDS: Still?

GS: Oh, yes. My two main role models are Bella Abzug and Alice Walker. Bella, because she has a sense of history, a vision of the world, and a bravery in taking on conflict, which is something I'm trying to learn. Alice, because she is always true to her inner self and also empathizes with everything: friends and adversaries, people, animals, even trees and the earth. One teaches me about the outside world, the other about the internal one. But it's up to me to keep those worlds in balance on my own path.

BLDS: Did you ever expect your life to unfold the way it has?

GS: No, never. I've traveled such a long distance in my life that at any given moment I was probably imagining a long and diverse series of lives—from dancing so I could get out of Toledo, to marrying a professor when I fell in love in college, to marrying a diplomat so I could see other countries, to being a journalist on my own so I could observe but stay invisible.

BLDS: What haven't you done yet that you'd care to?

GS: Many things, from learning to be less vulnerable to criticism, misunderstanding, and conflict, to learning to trust my voice more and agonize less about writing. I'd also like to learn to skateboard, to spend time living with wild elephants, and to travel to every part of the world where there are remnants of the more gender-balanced, nature-balanced way that humans lived for 95 percent of human history; that is, until the last five to ten thousand years of patriarchy, racism, monotheism, and nationalism. We can't go backward, but we can learn from the past to create a different future.

> We all want to know we are alive in the world, to know that we have made some kind of impact. If people aren't allowed to make a positive impact, they make a negative one to prove they're alive.

WILLIAM STYRON

BLDS: You grew up in Newport News, Virginia, often referred to as Tidewater, during the 1930s and 1940s when the population was nearly 40 percent black. How would you describe this environment and its impact on you?

WS: I have been pondering this question for some time. It's something that's very important to me in terms of my own feeling about race. One of the most interesting things about the town, with its large racial composition of blacks, was that it demonstrated how little intimacy there was between blacks and whites in a place of that size, as opposed to a smaller town, rural towns.

BLDS: What was the population of Newport News then?

WS: It was about thirty thousand in the thirties and it was originally segregated. Fascinatingly enough, you could go across the river to Southampton County or Princess Anne County, or any of the rural and semirural coun ties throughout the rest of the South, and find that there was an intimate connection with blacks. That is not to say that there wasn't stiff racial consciousness and segregation too, but in rural areas and in small towns in the South during periods of segregation there was far more interplay between people than there was in a place like Newport News. The downtown part of Newport News at night, and, largely, in the day, was as lily white as Stockholm or Salt Lake City because black people had their own area. The economics allowed this kind of segregation in a bigger town like mine, which was fairly prosperous, even during the Depression.

BLDS: Because of the shipyard?

WS: Yes. The economic situation in Newport News compelled an almost total segregation. In a small town you would have a little store that blacks and whites would equally patronize; you would have a theater in which blacks would sit in the balcony but you would nonetheless be aware of their presence. There was no awareness in Newport News of the presence of the blacks. They were profoundly segregated in what was called, generically, the Jefferson Avenue area, which was their avenue. Washington Avenue was our avenue. So, to answer your question more directly, Newport News was somewhat dissimilar from the rest of the South because of its size and relative prosperity. People in my generation who grew up in small towns had an infinitely larger understanding of blacks. It is very important to understand about the white/black relationships in the South that there was an intimacy, an interplay, a friendliness—and hostility too, but I'm speaking of the bright side. One could get an understanding of black people in a rural town. However, Newport News was more like New York with its Harlem, or Philadelphia with its black section. It was a Southern town that had Northern guidelines, in a sense. No one in the white power structure wanted intimate or even casual relations with blacks if they could get away with it. So you saw very few blacks in the stores in the white part of town. They patronized the stores, owned largely by Jewish merchants, in their own section near Jefferson Avenue.

BLDS: In that period, too, Newport News became the home of the military. Therefore, there was a very stable middle-class population, as well as the officer class in all of those bases that ringed Newport News and Hampton Roads. The Air Force and Army were there and the Navy was across the way in Norfolk.

WS: That's right. The presence of the military altered the character of the place radically. So did the shipyard, which was a huge industry that had many, many Yankees working at the professional managerial level. The influx of Northerners altered the character of the town. It was not a typical Southern city. It was not like, say, Augusta, Georgia, or Raleigh, North Carolina, where in those days you would not have had nearly the same infusion of an outside population.

BLDS: Your father was a marine engineer who worked at the Newport News Shipbuilding and Drydock Company. Was he from Virginia?

WS: No, he was from eastern North Carolina, a town called Washington in Beaufort County, halfway down the state to South Carolina.

BLDS: And your mother was a Northerner.

WS: She was from Pennsylvania, yes.

BLDS: Unfortunately, she died when you were in your early teens, and your father remarried by the time you were fifteen. Apparently, you had a period in which you were what you refer to as a hell-raiser, sufficiently so that you were sent off to an Episcopal boarding school, the Christ Church School, and then after that you attended Davidson College, also a church-related school.

WS: That's right.

BLDS: How important have religion and faith been in your life? And what was the impact of the loss of your mother and of your father's remarriage on your early life and your continuing life?

WS: Certainly, I suspect the heavy dose of religion I had as a kid caused me to be, at least theoretically, religious. I think I had a tenuous belief in the deity and a proper, God-fearing attitude in general, until probably through my middle teens. I remember at Christ Church I felt myself being an observant young Christian in the sense that I enjoyed the ritual. I think one of the hooks used to get people into religion at that age is the music. Some of the hymns are glorious. And that's part of the seduction of religion. When I went to Davidson, I got a little bit more perspective on it because

I was forced to take compulsory Bible courses, which began to diminish my enthusiasm. I didn't see any relevance in learning Hebrew history as a functional component of my life, and I think I began to lose my interest, and perhaps my faith, along about then.

BLDS: What did you plan to study when you went to Davidson?

WS: I didn't know. I was drawn to the written word, certainly, but I didn't think I would be a writer at that time.

BLDS: Did your father go to Davidson?

WS: No, he went to North Carolina State.

BLDS: What lured you there?

WS: Well, he wanted me to go. He tried out various places. He could have sent me to the University of Virginia, and he would have almost gotten a free ride because he was a Virginia taxpayer. He also thought of sending me to Washington & Lee, but a lot of drinking went on there. He was not an intolerant person, but he was fearful of my becoming a drunk.

BLDS: At UVA?

WS: Yes, and he had good reason to worry, because shortly before I went off to college a Hilton Village neighbor kid was delivered back home from UVA in an ambulance suffering from delirium tremens. That evidence of heavy-duty alcohol consumption shocked my father into the belief that he wanted me to be free from such debauchery. Davidson had a fine academic reputation—it still does—but it also had very harsh restrictions about alcohol. In those days you didn't just make up your own mind in regard to colleges. Your input was helpful, but your parents called the tune. If your parents wanted you to go somewhere, you went there. So I went to Davidson and I understood that his intentions were good, meant for my benefit.

BLDS: Can we talk about the influence of your mother, father, and stepmother?

WS: Well, my mother was an invalid from the time I was six until I was thirteen. She was suffering from a very slow and debilitating form of cancer. Her presence in my life was that of an invalid. It was baffling and perplexing because she did suffer badly, especially toward the end. Therefore, it was a strange situation. My father was not making a lot of money. He was a middle-range engineer and his pay was what you might imagine. It was not a lot, but it was better than blue collar by far. Then, as now, if you had high medical bills such as she had, so much of it was drained off. They were horrendous, I remember that. Endless bills.

BLDS: Were you the only child?

WS: Yes. There were reasons I felt I was shortchanged. For example, I wanted a sailboat like everyone else had but I didn't get it. Therefore, although I was never deprived I always felt that the kind of money that would make people really happy was beyond our reach.

BLDS: And now that you have that money and beyond, you realize that's not what makes people happy.

WS: It certainly is not what makes people happy! But at that time, I felt differently. I can give you an example of how precious the idea of money was. I remember once when I was about eleven—we were living in Hilton Village—my father wanted me to go to the grocer and pay the weekly bill for the first time. It was fifteen dollars, so he put a ten-dollar bill and a five-dollar bill in my hand. I remember it almost burned my hand. I had never seen that kind of money. I mean, I had seen it, but I had never experienced its sheer tactile quality.

BLDS: In what year did this occur?

WS: It was in the mid-thirties. The Depression was not as bad in Newport News as it was elsewhere, because of the shipyard. Still, people were strapped. I remember that fifteen dollars. I remember how magical coins were: fifty-cent pieces, nickels, and dimes. A kid could buy a whole ice-cream soda with three scoops of ice cream for a dime. A dime was important.

BLDS: With your mother so debilitated for so much of your early life, your father must have played a singular role.

WS: He did. He was so devoted to her, but it was exhausting. I loved him very much, he was a great man, but I felt that there was a certain kind of benign neglect that I was experiencing from him. It was an unconscious neglect, but I never felt that he was a father in the way that fathers are supposed to be.

BLDS: Does anyone? Or is it just that your expectations were probably for more?

WS: That's right.

BLDS: And then soon after your father remarried you went away to boarding school.

WS: It coincided with my going to boarding school. That was important because my stepmother was a true prototype of the wicked stepmother. She was a weird one. Very resentful of me, very hostile.

BLDS: And how about you toward her?

WS: The same, I think. However, there is somewhat more responsibility for the older person to be outgoing, generous, and responsive to a fifteen-year-old kid. So I'll take part of the blame, but not all of it.

BLDS: Was she devoutly religious, too?

WS: She was Episcopalian and very pious. And she didn't like my behavior at all.

BLDS: Soon after your eighteenth birthday you decided to join the Marines. You were born in 1925, so that would have been 1943, in the worst part of World War II. What caused you to leave school, where you had a safe and comfortable life, to join what continues to be thought of as the fiercest of all the military services?

WS: Well, the Marines had an enormous appeal for me. It was a glamorous organization, as it is even today. I just wanted to be a Marine. I certainly didn't want to be drafted into the Army as a private. That was much too drab for my own romantic tastes. So I enlisted in the Marines. By chance, I did want to be an officer and I started my training in college. After I joined the Marines they put me into what was called the V-12 program, which took young seventeen- and eighteen-year-olds and gave them an education so that by the time they were conditioned enough to be officers they had a little bit more poise and maturity. They sent me to Duke in the V-12 program.

BLDS: That was quite fortuitous.

WS: It was. I certainly wanted to be there and, in fact, I did become an officer.

> I just wanted to be a Marine. I certainly didn't want to be drafted into the Army as a private. That was much too drab for my own romantic tastes.

BLDS: What rank did you attain?

WS: I eventually became a first lieutenant. I went to the Parris Island boot camp, then to Camp Lejeune for further training, and finally to Quantico for Officers Candidate School.

BLDS: So how many years in total?

WS: I was in from 1943 until '45, and then the war ended. I was headed out for the Pacific to be in the invasion of Japan, and there was prepared to die for my country on the shores of Kyushu, when the bomb was dropped, which has always allowed me to be somewhat less censorious about the bomb.

BLDS: So you were heading for Okinawa just as the war was ending. Okinawa had very heavy casualties.

WS: Well, that had all been secured. The fighting was over by the time I was headed that way.

BLDS: How has seeing war changed your person?

WS: Radically and forever. I escaped seeing most of the war, but I saw almost enough to have the kind of mortal fear and fatalistic horror that we all have. I must say, as a footnote, that part of me very much regretted not having the experience. I missed the baptism of fire that a lot of guys who are slightly older than I had seen.

BLDS: Did you feel deprived of something, at once terrible and magnificent, as was thought? Or were you spared an experience that ultimately might have been traumatizing to you and your talents?

WS: Yes, it might have had a destructive role, although I don't think there is any ground rule about this. I think just getting as close as I did to the fighting could be as potentially traumatic and destructive. Be that as it may, there was a dichotomy. I was incredibly relieved that my life was spared and, though part of me regretted not seeing combat, I felt a kind of ecstasy.

BLDS: You said that you were not as harsh about the bomb because of the timing in your own life. How do you think the atomic bomb altered the course of your life, the lives of your generation, and America's role in the war?

WS: Well, I think it was crucial. We have mercifully been spared the nuclear holocaust that we all thought was going to happen. I think it's been argued persuasively that the dropping of the bomb on Hiroshima and Nagasaki might have prevented a later holocaust. I think the bomb was thoroughly justified.

BLDS: So you have a view different from John Hersey's.

WS: I knew John Hersey very well, and I'm fairly sure that, despite his graphic description of the bomb's horrors, he felt it was a necessary evil. I do think the bomb was inevitable and justified. I have been vigorously opposed to the revisionists' claim that the bomb was an evil mistake on the part of Harry Truman. I don't believe it for a minute. If it were true that the Japanese had been ready to surrender it would be another matter, because then you could say the bomb was not justified, but every bit of evidence that I have seen indicates to me that the Japanese had no intention of

surrendering. This was the only way of stopping the war.

BLDS: Have you ever been, by the way, to the Hypocenter in Hiroshima?

WS: Yes.

BLDS: However primitive that little museum is, just reading the material and seeing the photographs, the timetable, and all the attempts that were made before the bomb was dropped leads one to think that we did try to exhaust the possibilities.

WS: I have no doubt that it was essential that we dropped the bomb. God knows it was tragic. No one wants to think that it should have happened. But let me give you a short anecdote. About eight or nine years ago, I was invited to Tokyo by one of the Japanese broadcasting systems. I happened to be interviewed on television by a very intelligent interrogator and the inevitable question came up: "What was your feeling about the bomb?" I said that I had deep regret, but that I was convinced that the bomb saved both Japanese and American lives. Then he asked me what my feeling was when I heard about the bomb dropping and the cessation of hostilities. I recalled one word. "I have to be quite honest," I said. "I felt ecstasy."

About three days later I was at a cocktail party at the embassy and a Japanese gentleman about my age who spoke very fluent English told me that he was very impressed by what I said. "I'll tell you something," he said, "at the time you were heading for Okinawa and the bomb dropped I was on the northern part of Kyushu with my own military unit. You know what I felt when I heard the bomb had dropped? Ecstasy."

BLDS: Because he knew that the war was over?

WS: The war was over for him, too. So that has to be understood.

BLDS: You had a rather diverse and complicated series of experiences while you were in the military, which you ended up writing about. One work was called *In the Clap Shack*, which was published in 1973, thirty years later. This play tells about your experiences in Parris Island when you were misdiagnosed with what was then considered the ultimate venereal disease, syphilis.

WS: Right. I want to add that I wrote a long piece in a September 1995 issue of *The New Yorker* about the same thing. It was called "A

> I have no doubt that it was essential that we dropped the bomb. God knows it was tragic. No one wants to think that it should have happened.

Case of the Great Pox," and was about being at Parris Island and being misdiagnosed.

BLDS: Perhaps you would like to talk about that incident. How did you get misdiagnosed with syphilis?

WS: Well, it turned out that I had a false-positive blood test, but instead of being told, in a sympathetic way, that this was a possibility, as one with HIV might be told now, I was kept totally in the dark. I was made to believe that, in fact, I had this disease swarming within me and that I was possibly beyond any kind of hope. There was also at that time a terrible stigma about acquiring a sexually transmitted illness, especially if you were an officer candidate. So I thought that both my career and my life were doomed.

BLDS: Did you genuinely believe your life was in danger?

WS: Yes, I thought I had a very good chance of having the illness—although penicillin had just begun to be used. For some reason they waited around endlessly taking my blood.

BLDS: For how long did this misdiagnosis endure?

WS: About three weeks. I was in the hospital all that time.

BLDS: Did you protest?

WS: When you're a kid, you try to protest, but you don't have a way of protesting to authority figures.

BLDS: And then, in the strangest way, it came to light that it wasn't syphilis.

WS: It came to light that it had been a case of trench mouth, of all things.

BLDS: A dentist discovered it?

WS: A dentist discovered it and instantly treated it with a topical solution, which killed all the nasty spirochetes. The blood test went down to zero. It was terribly traumatic. It was as if I'd been told that I'd had AIDS.

BLDS: Did that experience provide you with more empathy than most of the rest of us?

WS: Of course it did. I must say it was that experience that led to my first bout of depression. I was deeply depressed. I'll never forget what that did to me. I don't think it is stretching the analogy; it really was as if I had been told I had AIDS. The treatment was not offered to me and I was just given the sense that this disease was making its terrible course through my body and anything could happen. So it was very, very harrowing.

BLDS: When you found out otherwise, did you again feel ecstasy?

WS: Of course I felt ecstasy. As I tried to demonstrate in *The New Yorker* piece, there was a comic overtone to it, too.

BLDS: You also wrote a novella in 1952 called *The Long March*, which related to a forced march that you had endured at Camp Lejeune in 1951. Why would you have a forced march? Or is that typical procedure in a Marine camp?

WS: It was not typical. It was very unusual.

BLDS: What is a forced march?

WS: A forced march is where you are made to march a certain number of miles in a certain number of hours. In this case it was to march thirty-six miles in something like fourteen hours.

BLDS: Did you endure it?

WS: I did. And it was one of the great ordeals of my life. Thirty-six miles is an enormous distance for inexperienced troops. It would be nothing if you were a tough Marine raider that had been training for such a hike, but we were all untrained reservists. We had just been called back in the reserves for the Korean War. The colonel who ordered the march was one of these hard-nosed, tough Marines who was going to show us just what a tough Marine can do. So he did it. We started out at about six or eight, and marched straight on until nine that night. Only a few of us made it. I was determined to make it. Lots of people dropped out. Out of the whole regiment of about five thousand men, I think only about a thousand made it.

BLDS: The British author Alan Massey wrote, "Do you know what a soldier is, young man? He is the chap who makes it possible for civilized folk to despise war." What is William Styron's definition of a soldier, or of a war?

WS: My career has spanned a period in which I have been able to observe many wars, including what I am convinced was a just war—World War II. I'm not talking about its politics, which may have been weirdly unjust, I'm talking about our involvement as a nation in a war that was essential. I never felt anything but a kind of pride in having participated in the struggle against fascism. On the other hand, my lifespan has allowed me to observe totally disgusting conflicts. I'm talking about the Vietnam War, not to mention other little excursions, imperialistic skirmishes like Grenada, Panama, and our involvement in Nicaragua.

BLDS: You also served in the Korean War.

WS: Yes. I didn't like that in the slightest and I felt that it was unnecessary for me to join. I had nonchalantly stayed in the reserves, and I was very resentful at having to go back five years after I had served. But I did it because I had made the dumb choice and had to live with it. Fortunately, an eye defect got me a discharge after six or seven months' training in the North Carolina swamps.

BLDS: After World War II and your discharge from the Marines you had a brief adventure in the merchant marine, delivering cattle to postwar Trieste. Was this your view of a Hemingwayesque experience, a way of seeing the world?

WS: It was the summer of 1946, I was out of the service, footloose and fancy-free, as they say, and I was bored in Newport News. The ship itself was tied up at dock in the port.

BLDS: Is that where you found it?

WS: Yes. I was told about it and they said they wanted recruits to help feed the cattle on the way over. So I signed aboard and went over with the cattle boat.

BLDS: Had you had any experience with farming or cows before that?

WS: No, none at all. But I became the assistant to the young guy who was the veterinarian by virtue of having gone to college like he had. Most of the other young guys hadn't gone to college. I had slightly privileged conditions in the situation.

BLDS: For how long did you do that?

WS: It was a long haul, ten days from Hampton Roads to Trieste, by way of the Adriatic. But it had its enticements. I had never been to Europe. The idea of driving to a bombed-out port such as Trieste, going to Venice, and seeing paintings and murals was a big

draw. It was a romantic situation.

BLDS: For how long did you stay?

WS: I didn't stay very long, but the stevedores in Trieste were on strike so the ship had to stay in the harbor a longer time. I think I was in Trieste for a week, which was three days longer than we had originally planned. So I had a nice little sojourn.

BLDS: Then you returned to the university and received a B.A. in literature by 1947. How did you move from inchoate ambition to literature?

WS: When I was first at Duke in the war, I had encountered a wonderful professor named William Blackburn. I was totally devoted to him. He was a man of great charisma, passion. He was teaching writing and he just made me become a writer. And he's now a legend because he taught various others, such as Anne Tyler.

BLDS: What did he do that so motivated you?

WS: Well, he was just extraordinary. Without being in any sense flamboyant he had some quality of passion that made him a great teacher. He pretty much convinced me that I could be a writer and from then on I was hooked.

BLDS: After completing your studies at Duke you said you headed for New York with the seed of a novel in your head. What prompted your move to New York City?

WS: Well, I think I had always wanted to go to New York City. It was a great magnet, a great draw, as it is for so many. I was not one of those Southern-born kids who felt that my destiny as a writer lay in staying in the South. I felt that was a dead end for me. In the first place, I had trouble at home and there was no place else for me. I didn't feel any roots in Virginia. I wanted to get the hell out of there. I didn't want to teach. I played with that idea for a while, but not very long. So I went to New York and got a job at McGraw-Hill as a manuscript reader.

BLDS: For how long did that last?

WS: That lasted about six or seven months.

BLDS: Were you fired from that job?

WS: Yes. I did not fit in. I was bored by these awful manuscripts I had to read. It was just a drag. There was a dreadful little man who was editor in chief. His name was Edward C. Aswell, and he had been Thomas Wolfe's editor. He had a huge reputation. It turned out later that he presented a lot of his work as Wolfe's own when Aswell had actually written it. He was a complete fraud, an awful little man. We just didn't see eye-to-eye, so he got rid of me, which was fine.

BLDS: Then you turned to the New School, which had a burgeoning intellectual life at that time because of the World War II emigrés that went to teach there. You took a course with the then editor in chief at Crown, Hiram Haydn. He obviously was taken with your gifts because he gave you an advance for a novel. In what year?

WS: This would have been around 1949. He was a man of great charm and appeal and had great enthusiasm for young people, young writers. I took his course in creative writing and he liked my work very much. It was experimental.

BLDS: What were you writing? Just papers for the class?

WS: Yes, short stories. He liked the quality of what I wrote so he offered me an option on my first novel. I'll never forget it. He took me out to a bar and said, "I wish it could be more, but we do want to give you an option and so we are prepared—Crown—to pay you one hundred dollars." Well, one hundred dollars wasn't much even then, but it was considerably more than it is now. I said, Terrific!

BLDS: Because it validated you as a professional writer?

WS: Yes, of course. The money wasn't nearly as important as the recognition.

BLDS: How did you get by?

WS: Oh, I was doing all right. My father was really helping to support me. That was why, among other reasons, I was always devoted to him. He had faith in me. He sent me a small check each month. Also, my maternal grandmother had died and left me just a small amount, just a couple of thousand dollars, which was enough to help you along in those days. I put it in a book.

BLDS: Where did you live?

WS: This time I lived at 94th and Lexington Avenue, way uptown. I lived with a roommate from North Carolina, a very nice guy. In those days you wouldn't dare shack up with a girl, although I wanted to, because of the mores. It just wasn't done. I didn't have a girl anyway.

BLDS: Who was the man?

WS: His name was Edgar Hatcher. He later became a career advertising man. Anyway, I was taking this class, and Hiram gave me this munificent one-hundred-dollar option, which compelled me to sit down and write the first pages of *Lie Down in Darkness*—my first novel.

BLDS: With this advance of one hundred dollars, the small stipend from your father, and a small inheritance from your grandmother, you were free to devote yourself to writing this first novel. What if you had to have a nine-to-five job? Do you think it ever would have been written?

WS: That's a hard question because if I had had a nine-to-five job I probably would not have been able to focus on it. But I was determined to never again have a nine-to-five job. I made that perfectly clear to myself and I never did have another one.

BLDS: You never had to have those stopgap-measure jobs that most struggling people in the so-called creative community need to have?

WS: No, as I say I was lucky. My father was not a rich man but he had enough to help fund me. It was his investment. He was unusual. Not every father has that kind of faith in his son. But he was adorable. So I struggled away there on Lexington Avenue and I finally realized I needed something else. I went down to North Carolina, back to Durham where Duke is located and where I had some friends, and I lived there for a year, trying to get my act together and struggling away at this first novel. It was not very successful; I had a very nice time there, but I wasn't getting any work done. So, like a Ping-Pong ball, after a year I moved back to New York and briefly went out to Brooklyn. For several weeks I stayed in a rooming house in Brooklyn, which I wrote about in *Sophie's Choice*. At that point I was rescued by a young woman, a friend of mine named Sigrid de Lima. She and her mother had a lovely house up the Hudson River in a little town called Valley Cottage near Nyack. They took me in, and I lived up in their house for another year while I really got rolling on *Lie Down in Darkness*.

BLDS: Was she a lady friend of yours, or just a chum?

WS: She was a chum.

BLDS: That was a very generous thing for her to do.

WS: Yes. We were great friends and so I stayed up there and worked hard on the book. I dedicated *Lie Down in Darkness* to her. I finally moved back to New York and shared an apartment on West 88th Street with a young sculptor.

BLDS: Who was the sculptor?

WS: His name was Howard Hoffman. He never made it as a sculptor, but he later became a psychology professor down at Swarthmore. At any rate, I finished *Lie Down in Darkness* on West 88th Street.

BLDS: You were twenty-six years old, an important young novelist, a recipient of the Prix de Rome, and you had really not lived through terrible professional adversity to get there. How was your life altered by public recognition at such an early age? Did you view it as just the beginning? Did it inhibit you? Did you think you had arrived?

WS: In those days, if you were a young novelist, a novel had an incredible cachet—far more than it does now.

BLDS: Because there appears to be so many more of them.

WS: Maybe so. But anyway, the novel was an act of glory in those days. Being a young novelist was like being a rock star. Norman Mailer had published his *Naked and the Dead* and he was having fame and fortune. James Jones, who was a very good friend of mine, wrote *From Here to Eternity,* J. D. Salinger wrote *Catcher in the Rye,* and Truman Capote wrote *In Cold Blood. Lie Down in Darkness* was quite successful. It was not a runaway bestseller, but it lodged itself very respectably on the bestseller list. It got, generally speaking, very good reviews. It had some clinkers, but that's to be expected, too.

BLDS: Was that story in your mind for a long while, since it relates so heavily to your life in Newport News?

WS: Yes. I had always wanted to write it. Anyway, I felt very, very happy about this thing. For a first novel in those days it sold very well. I got twenty thousand dollars for it, which was a lot of money for a young bachelor in 1951. You could really go a long way on twenty thousand dollars.

BLDS: Well, you went all the way to Europe. Is that what liberated you, freed you, and made it possible?

WS: Yes, it certainly did. It certainly helped.

BLDS: Do you think of yourself as a Southern novelist living in the North, or as a novelist who is influenced by Southern traditions that were a part of your life?

WS: I have always defined myself as an American writer with strong Southern roots. I have never defined myself as a specifically Southern writer, although I certainly have to emphasize that my Southern upbringing was essential to my development.

BLDS: How would you describe your working habits? Are you still the night owl, as you've talked about yourself?

WS: I still tend to gravitate toward the evening. I am not a night owl in the sense that I stay up until four in the morning. That's long past. On the other hand, I don't turn in at 9:30. I usually stay up until about one o'clock reading and get up at eight or nine.

BLDS: You describe writing as a slow and painstaking process. How many pages do you produce in a day? Do you still write in longhand?

WS: Yes.

BLDS: Then how do you have your notes transcribed?

WS: I write very clearly, and I have a very good typist who lives not far from here. She takes it and puts it into a word processor.

BLDS: And then you edit from there?

WS: Yes.

BLDS: You've spoken often of the relationship between the reality of a novel and the reality of the street, arguing for a peaceful and a symbiotic coexistence between the two. Your own novels are often premised on the reader's knowledge, or at least awareness, of the underlying facts behind the novel and the novel's artistic, shall we say, rendering of events. Nowadays, when the idea of almost any real historical awareness on the part of American students is beginning to seem presumptuous, do you think that a new attitude toward the quasi-historical novel is needed? I'm suggesting that the novel's presentation of history may be the reader's only awareness of history.

WS: For whatever reason, I have seized upon several major themes in history that I can make sense out of and I've done my best to render them in a dramatic way, if that helps answer your question; I'm not so sure it does.

BLDS: Well, let me pursue it a little further. You have chosen two of the central and most horrific themes of modern history, America's slave era and the Holocaust. I am awed by the scale of your themes, but I am also mindful of some of the criticism that you have suffered as the result of it. For example, the question arises as to how you get beyond the obstacle of really seeing an event of this magnitude through someone else's eyes. How does a white Southerner delve into the soul of a black slave? How does an Anglo-Saxon Protestant male reflect the Holocaust experiences of a Polish Catholic woman? And then, as a New Deal liberal in the Reagan era and the post-Reagan era, how do you even take on the question of the anticommunist paranoia in this country? You set themes, and obstacles, that are overwhelming as subject matter. What gives you the idea and the courage to do that?

> I have always defined myself as an American writer with strong Southern roots. I have never defined myself as a specifically Southern writer . . .

WS: There's an underlying psychological need in me to deal with a certain perpetual theme—and that theme, to be quite simple, is domination, human domination. We are the only species that deliberately sets out to dominate ourselves—our fellow human beings. And human domination at its most extreme is almost a definition for absolute evil. The existence of this absolute evil in the form of domination has created more human suffering than anything else in the history of our species. I might add that human domination in my own work extends to the family. I think *Lie Down in Darkness* is a description of the power struggle.

BLDS: There is, in many ways, a crimson thread that ties these works all together. Based on your work, and your life, what have you concluded about the evil of human domination?

WS: Well, I don't think I have ever come up with an answer. To me, there was a link between American chattel slavery and the experience of the Holocaust. It is very important to recall, and remember, that although the Holocaust was at its worst a form of extermination, it was also a form of slavery. It was the first real manifestation of human slavery since the American experience in the nineteenth century. So there is a connection. I don't mean to say that I deliberately set out to do one theme and then another. I didn't intend to have these two books involved in that way. But there was the linking.

BLDS: What was the genesis for the ideas of both books?

WS: My interest in the Holocaust emerged in my mind intellectually about the same time as my interest in slavery, but I wrote the slavery book first. It was right after World War II, when I went back to Duke. I was fascinated by the Holocaust. There was only rudimentary stuff being written at that time, in 1946, but the facts were emerging.

BLDS: When were the Nuremberg Trials? During that period?

WS: They were about a year or so later. But there had already been written, for instance, a very powerful book called *Five Chimneys* by Olga Lengyel, a Jewish woman. She doesn't identify herself as Jewish, but it's plain that she is. She was a medical assistant, the wife of a Hungarian doctor, and was taken to Auschwitz, where she had to make a determination about her children. It was not a distinct choice, like the one Sophie had to make, but she had lost her two children and her mother at the camps. At the selection she describes the infamous Doctor Mengele. It was almost the first mention in any literature after the war of Doctor Mengele and I read that in 1946 at Duke University. I will never forget it. The

book is still in print. I was utterly fascinated by that book and it haunted me all through my writing life up until the point when I began to write *Sophie's Choice*. It was a very important book to me. However, chronologically, before I dealt with the Holocaust there was the question of slavery. I had to get that off my chest before I could deal with Auschwitz.

BLDS: You have been celebrated for dealing with these things, but you have also been criticized. Many of your critics have said, How can a white Southerner write honestly about a black slave? How do you respond to that? What is the role of the novelist who works within historical confines? Is there a need for fiction, as you see it, set in historical climates?

WS: Oh, yes. To answer the last part of your question, I think that whatever viability and vitality my works have, the fact that they are still widely read is due to some essential link between this literary art, if you want to call it that, and the historical grounding of those books.

BLDS: A widely respected commentator and writer, Elie Wiesel, criticized you for writing about the Holocaust and writing about the unimaginable. Do you think that when one cannot identify with an experience, one's writing should be restricted to only autobiographical subject matter?

WS: I think that Elie Wiesel is full of balderdash, to be polite. I think this is just garbage. Among other things, Elie Wiesel is profoundly offended if anyone dares to try to step on his turf. I think he has a ludicrous proprietary view about the Holocaust and wanted to hog the scene himself. I say that with as much conviction as I can muster. I am not the only person who does. I believe that any subject is fair game to a writer. The only question ultimately is whether he is successful in dealing with the theme and the subjects in a way that makes people feel that he succeeded.

BLDS: Is there anything in life or experience that you think others should not, shall we say, intrude upon?

WS: Absolutely nothing. And I think the touchstone to all this is Shakespeare. Here was a man who ranged through all times, all places, all sexes, all genders, and did it magnificently. There is nothing off-color or off-place about Shakespeare. It doesn't mean that everyone is going to be a Shakespeare dealing with these subjects. It does mean that a writer has the right to become a woman—as Shakespeare did with Cleopatra, or a black like Othello, or an ancient king like Richard III. He can become anything if he is convincing. The autonomy of art, to my mind, allows for anything, and to suggest that any subject is off-limits to a writer or a poet is preposterous.

BLDS: How can our approach to presenting history influence future generations' perceptions of the past?

WS: Just by the virtue of a book being written at the top of a writer's form and creating a moving and compelling experience. I've never maintained a work like *Sophie's Choice* is the definitive work on the Holocaust. However, it seems to have had a lasting effect and has made people view what went on at a place like Auschwitz with a certain appalled wonder. The readers' reaction that I still get is an indication that the book has served a catalytic and educative function. It has illuminated a great deal about what transpired at Auschwitz.

BLDS: In an interview about twenty years ago you said that men in revolutions destroy so much of the thing they love, namely, they destroy their own notion of humanity by committing acts of violence against humanity. Does your character Nat Turner find himself in a similar quandary, grappling with a paradox of both humanity and ideals?

WS: The history of revolutions is one of horror and violence. Our own famous revolution, the one that gave us our independence, which, of course, was still a bloody war, is the only major revolution that did not have a terroristic sequel. There was no equivalent, either, of the slaughter of the czar and his family. I am rereading Robert Massie's book about the Russian Revolution. That was one of the most horrendous acts of senseless barbarism in modern history. Taking these harmless people—a rather bumbling, well-intentioned, not-too-bright man, his wife, their beautiful daughters, and their son—and murdering them. To me, that epitomizes the evil of the Russian Revolution, not to speak of what happened afterward. I'm just trying to extrapolate from that in Nat Turner. His tragedy was that he committed these acts of violence in the name of freedom and he realizes at the end that, as the saying goes, it was all for naught. Nothing. I don't condemn him, because a true revolutionary may be like Martin Luther: When asked why he did what he did, he said, "I can do no other." All revolutionaries have the same psychic motivation of absolute necessity.

BLDS: And all of them need not express it the same way. We have our contemporary example of Daw Aung San Suu Kyi, the Burmese heroine who has unflappable courage. She uses the exact opposite approach and baffles her adversaries by calling for reconciliation and dialogue. She refuses to fight, and only wants to talk.

WS: Precisely. And this is why the principle of nonviolence has taken hold so imaginatively in modern times, beginning with Gandhi.

BLDS: She is Gandhiesque.

WS: Yes, of course. And also, of course, Martin Luther King.

BLDS: Have you found that your writings are well received by historians and academicians?

WS: I would say, in general, yes. *The Confessions of Nat Turner* is now lodged in the canon of historical novels, and has in general been accepted as a responsible fictional representation. It was never severely panned, except by the black critics who had axes to grind. The book is taught widely in courses on Southern history.

BLDS: How do you manage to get beyond seeing the world from your point of view to seeing it through these historical characters' eyes? Does it come from your own experience?

WS: Well, I think that's what an artist's job is: to make the leap into the void, so to speak, and to use the imagination. Returning to the idea of what I should, or should not, be able to do, I think one of the most defective views now prevalent is that men cannot deal with issues concerning women, that a woman's mind is off-limits to a male writer. This is part of at least some feminist propaganda. In reality, it is so restricting. Women should be allowed as writers to deal with men, and vice versa. Some of the greatest female characters have been created by men.

BLDS: For example?

WS: Emma Bovary, Anna Karenina.

BLDS: Two novelists—Flaubert and Tolstoy—whose works are very influential on yours, and two characters who have markedly influenced your characters.

WS: I don't know how successful I was in some people's view, but I feel that I created a full-fleshed woman in Sophie of *Sophie's Choice*.

BLDS: In all of your works the characters seem to be yearning to be whole. Is this something that you have dealt with on a personal level for a good part of your life?

WS: Yes, I think it tends to reconcile things in one form. One of the goals in my work, although subconscious, I think, is always completion.

BLDS: Then it is to be hoped that there is no resolution to this search.

WS: Probably not. It is the search itself that's important.

BLDS: You have described yourself as being descended from a long line of American storytellers. Who were these storytellers, and how does this tradition make you a more descriptive author?

WS: People like me who write non-postmodern novels—relatively speaking, conventional novels—are in a story-telling tradition. I am not the slightest bit ashamed of it. I think it is a noble tradition and all my predecessors—Faulkner, Hemingway, Fitzgerald, etc.—would agree with me.

BLDS: We talked before about the Southern tradition. While you don't identify yourself as a Southern writer as such, you have often been referred to as being an heir to the Southern tradition, yet you moved to the North more than forty years ago. Why did you choose a New England home, and why and how did you find this New England environment receptive to someone with a Southern background?

WS: Well, I had no roots left in the South. After my first years in New York I had a lot of friends up here and so I decided that somewhere in the New York area would be an ideal place to put my roots. I don't like the city as a permanent abode. I just decided to be rural, and moved to this tiny little town. To this day, I think, there are 167 towns in Connecticut, and this is the third or fourth smallest. After all these years, it's an ideal place to live.

BLDS: Do you ever feel like someone in exile, or like an expatriate?

WS: Never. I am not cut off entirely by any means. I have many, many friends in the South. I go back to Mississippi regularly, where I have lots of friends. I have lots of friends in North Carolina, Tennessee, Georgia.

BLDS: How about your original Virginia?

WS: Some in Virginia. Oddly enough, I don't have as many friends in Virginia.

BLDS: And you don't have family there either?

WS: No.

BLDS: Let's talk about how direct your link to slavery was. I reflected for some time on the fact that your grandmother owned

> . . . here we are approaching the end of the twentieth century and as a little boy I had physical contact with an old lady who in her childhood had owned slaves.

slaves. And you say that your own mother, when she was able, was active in working for human rights. How did both of these realities manifest themselves; how did this heritage manifest itself in your life?

WS: It is astonishing to reflect on the fact that here we are approaching the end of the twentieth century and as a little boy I had physical contact with an old lady who in her childhood had owned slaves. It still astonishes me. In 1863, at the age of twelve, my grandmother Marianna Clark was on her father's plantation in eastern North Carolina when it was attacked and pillaged by Union troops led by General Burnside of Ohio. She had in her possession two little slave girls her own age whom she adored. These soldiers ran off with all the blacks and left her and her family to starve on the plantation. As a result, she harbored a deep enmity against Yankees. One of the odd things was that she could barely stand my mother, who was a very decent woman. The very fact that my father would go to Virginia and, about the time of World War I, marry a young lady from Pennsylvania was almost more than my grandmother could bear. So they had a frosty relationship. Oddly enough, my father's two brothers married women from the North. This was a cross that she had to bear. But it still is astounding to recall sitting in her presence in her big house in North Carolina and hearing her tell about that terrible time when she literally starved to the extent that she was forced to eat rats.

BLDS: In what way was your mother active in working for human rights?

WS: She was a member of the board of the YWCA, which was dedicated to good works. One of these was to establish a hospitality center in Newport News, because it was a port of embarkation from which the troops went to France in World War I. She became the supervisor, the director. The place was on West Avenue, down from the shipyard. There was a public dining room there, which is where my father discovered my mother. He was working in the shipyard and took lunch and dinner there.

BLDS: Is that how he met her?

WS: That's how he met her.

BLDS: And the Clark of your middle name is the family name of this grandmother?

WS: It was taken from her maiden name.

BLDS: How do you explain the fact that Virginia, the mother of presidents, the home of Jeffersonian ideals, maintained this agrarian economy with slave labor for so long, and that these attitudes persisted beyond the landmark 1954 Supreme Court decision? It was Virginia that proposed a doctrine of interpositionism, I believe it was called. And the state currently is home to some of the most conservative elements in the country, such as the Christian Coalition. Pat Robertson is there, and so are Jerry Falwell and Oliver North. How do you explain this phenomenon in the most northerly of Southern states, with its extraordinarily rich historical tradition?

WS: That's a paradox. But I think it's no greater paradox than the fact that North Carolina, which is a far more liberal state in the eyes of most people than other Southern states, should have someone like Jesse Helms as one of its senators. But he's on his way out. Virginia, with its hegemony of patrician landowners, never developed the populist tradition that has caused somewhat more liberalization in a state like North Carolina. Certainly there is immense conservatism and traditionalism still, which to my mind tends to mediocritize the state both culturally and politically. It is almost a form of Shintoism. Not that a sense of the past is unimportant. But to live in the past, as so often Virginians do, to live with a phony and artificial sense of traditional values, has cost Virginia both in the cultural and political sense.

BLDS: In a 1994 American Heritage survey, in which you were asked how America has changed since 1954, your response focused on the rise of alcohol- and drug-related crime, the development of gangs, and the availability of high-powered assault weapons. In fact, I recall you saying the worst institution ever created in the United States was the National Rifle Association, and that politicians essentially are powerless against the NRA. Can you give us an update on those views?

WS: Despite temporary setbacks that the NRA has from time to time suffered, the organization remains the most evil group of its kind ever to exist in this country. It has the politicians in its pocket. I think that almost single-handedly the NRA has done enormous damage to our society. Our subculture of guns and drugs is nurtured by the NRA. Without the NRA someday we might satisfactorily envision some decent gun control, but we don't do anything to stop it. As a result, we are dying as a culture.

BLDS: Are you saying that at the end of the American century we have a weakened America?

WS: I think the single most dangerous and harmful social development of our time has been the rise of the gun culture in tandem with the drug culture. This has done more than anything to turn this country into a desperate and, in many ways, lawless nation.

BLDS: You have been active on behalf of writers, between your wife Rose Styron's involvement in Freedom to Write, your lobbying on behalf of writers and the copyrights of their works, and your involvement with the PEN American Center's response to the scheduled execution of a death-row journalist. Do you think that there is more of a network, and a sense of community, among writers today than when you started writing? And are their voices paid more, or less, attention to?

WS: I do think there has been an increased awareness of writers as being effective forces for social change, as opposed to the way it was many years ago. One of the factors is the organization of PEN, which has done an amazing job in recent years. Most Americans don't give a damn about writers, and writers and books don't have much importance in the scheme of things, but it has been kind of exhilarating to see how PEN and the other writers' organizations have been effective forces.

BLDS: Let's come back to your characters for a moment. How well do you know them when you begin your story, and how well at the end? Do the characters evolve before and/or during the writing process?

WS: Well, for me, they become who they are as the writing goes on. I found incredible transformations when I was doing Sophie. She took on a life of her own and began to say things. The best example is early in the book when she has a long monologue in which she describes to the narrator Stingo growing up in Poland and that her father was a professor who had risked his life to save Jews during the war; what amazed me was, as she spoke, I realized she was lying. Unbeknown to me, this character had taken on such reality that I realized her lying to the narrator was an integral part of her personality. It caused me to see the whole book in new light.

BLDS: And how did that reveal itself to you?

WS: It was instinctual. It was a subconscious revelation in which I began to see the key to the whole book: when she said that her

> I think the single most dangerous and harmful social development of our time has been the rise of the gun culture in tandem with the drug culture.

father was a noble figure saving Jews it was important for me to understand that it was quite the opposite and, in fact, that he was a vicious anti-Semite. Therefore, from then on I was able to explore one of the essential themes of the book, which is Polish anti-Semitism.

BLDS: You have said that you daydream as part of your writing process. What character does William Clark Styron play in the stories in your head? Are you the hero, the villain, the observer, or the entire cast?

WS: All of the above.

BLDS: How about the critic?

WS: The critic is somewhere else. I don't pay much attention to criticism.

BLDS: Except that you don't like it that much.

WS: I don't know many writers who do. I don't know why I say that, because I have had my share of very favorable criticism over the years. I have also had vicious and unworthy assaults. I guess, on balance, I'm like every other writer. I have had my brickbats and I have had my bouquets.

BLDS: Music is a recurring theme in several of your books. How did your interest in it come about? Are you a musician? What special qualities does it offer for your writing?

WS: I have no professional understanding of music and I can't read a note, but I have loved music ever since I was a child. My mother studied music in Vienna. Her father was a prosperous coke-oven operator in western Pennsylvania during the heyday of the great steel industry. He sold coke to Andrew Carnegie. He made quite a bit of money. He wasn't a millionaire but he was very well off. He had enough money to send my mother and her sister to Vienna to study music. My mother studied voice and her sister studied piano. As a result, music has always been a very important part of my life. My father loved music, too. He listened to all the classical-music radio stations, the few that were existing.

BLDS: How different are you in real life from the characters that you write about?

WS: I don't know. I think that you should look at it the other way around and ask, to what extent are your characters a projection of yourself? And I would probably have to say that in all my characters there is a large part of me. I was especially aware of this when I recovered from depression. I began to see how intentionally the depressive mode in my life infiltrated the personas of the various characters.

BLDS: You are referring to a very important part of your life, at least one that was identified in a more tangible way ten years ago when you were diagnosed with clinical depression. While you seem to live in a very stable and serene environment, obviously your private life—or at least your internal life—was not so serene. You have made reference to problems with drinking and depression. Has this illness plagued you off and on all your life?

WS: Yes.

BLDS: You mentioned that during the syphilis incident in Parris Island you realized you were depressed.

WS: I didn't understand what it was; I had no name for it, but I recognize it now.

BLDS: Was that the first manifestation of your depression?

WS: I believe so. I realized that a dark shroud of horror loomed and overtook me with a sense of death. It might have inflicted anyone, anywhere.

BLDS: If we turn a little farther back than that, it was a great trauma and a great tragedy to have an invalid mother from the time you were six to thirteen, followed—by your own description—by the wicked stepmother. That doesn't make for a buoyant childhood. It's a triumph to survive at all.

WS: Yes, it was not a happy childhood. It had moments of happiness. My father was a wonderful man. I wasn't abused or anything like that, and there were moments of serenity, but it was a terrible childhood that I remember. My father also suffered from depression and was hospitalized. He went to Buxton Hospital. In those days, before they understood what to do, he was just confined to a room. It wasn't a proper mental institution. I realized many years later that when I was fourteen I had notations in my diaries about going to see Pop at the hospital. I thought he was suffering from some sort of physical complaint, but he was suffering from severe clinical depression.

BLDS: Was this right after your mother died?

WS: Yes, it was. In other words, there was a hereditary strain, too. The episode at Parris Island was rather a terrible blow added only a few years later.

BLDS: As a man with your insights, when did you first come to grapple with this? Not until ten years ago?

WS: The general understanding of what depression is has only been recently a matter of discussion. What is astounding to me, though, is that I always prided myself on being a little bit more knowledgeable and understanding of illness, and yet I went through life as I had until ten years ago, not realizing that for most of my life I was under the grip of a low-grade depression. It was a depression of a certain intensity that never became clinical, but was always hovering around me and was treatable, in my view, only by taking copious amounts of alcohol.

BLDS: To make you feel better?

WS: Yes, to make me feel better. I had what I called my daily mood bath. It was essential to my being.

BLDS: Didn't it make you feel worse?

WS: No, no, no. I was never a problem drinker, and I never drank more than I could handle. Never. I never drank during the day. But it was essential to me that whenever I was in my leisure hours I was pretty high most of the time. This was a way to defeat the depression that was stalking me twenty-four hours a day. It reached its apogee ten years ago with this catastrophic depression.

BLDS: And how did that reveal itself?

WS: It just came. Oddly enough, it came because I suddenly realized I could not drink. I had a distinct physiological reaction rather suddenly. I began to see that alcohol was making me physically ill. Even though I had a hard time rejecting it, I had to reject it because I couldn't stand the nausea. It still causes me nausea when I drink more than a small amount. After getting this strange reaction to alcohol, I suddenly decided I couldn't drink. For that particular summer, in 1985, I had to stop, but in stopping I was allowing these demons, which alcohol had fended off for so many years, to enter my soul. And it caused a cataclysmic depression.

BLDS: How did you deal with this crisis and how did you emerge from the depression?

WS: Well, I dealt with it as many people do, by letting it overwhelm me until the point that I had to go to a hospital, where I stayed for seven weeks. And I recovered.

BLDS: Did you go voluntarily?

WS: Oh, yes. Finally, the agony was so great that I couldn't exist in this world, and so I just ended up in the hospital. For some reason, I mysteriously recovered, and it was fairly rapid. I got out of the hospital, became well, and have had only one or two dips since then. Still, I have to confess, I'm not ever free of it. I still have a certain amount of depression all the time.

BLDS: I read something that you wrote that said while you were in the hospital a doctor handed you a newspaper and asked you to read a paragraph of 150 words and to tell him what you had read. You realized you could not respond to that and, among other

things, you seriously contemplated ending your career during your recovery.

WS: That is partly accurate. Certainly the part about being unable to read a paragraph was true. By that time my brain cells were scrambled in the depths of some form of depression that can only be described as stupidity. My brain was no longer functioning. But the impulse to end my career, i.e., my life, came before that. It was that suicidal impulse that led me to go to a hospital.

BLDS: Didn't you call a friend and ask him for a bullet?

WS: I did. I called a very close friend of mine, an ex-convict, a very gifted writer who lives in California. I called him and said, I have got to find a way out. He was humoring me, I later realized, but in my delusion I thought he could take care of me. I really did not want to die, but this was in the first week or so of my hospitalization. Fairly soon after that I began to climb out and the suicidal fantasy world disappeared.

BLDS: What helped you to conquer this battle?

WS: Hospitalization, support and patience from my wife Rose, support from friends, not much from the psychiatric profession. Not that I am anti-psychiatry; I'm not. But I think that it's an iffy situation. The shrink I had was not very good.

BLDS: Suicide, let alone depression, is still a taboo subject, but in your 1990 work *Darkness Visible* you discuss both of them. What was your motivation, not to write the book, but to publish the book?

WS: I think my earliest motivation was to correct what I realized was a general impression that there was something indecent about having depression, that it was a character defect, and that people were personally responsible for the illness. That got me so enraged that I wrote an op-ed piece in the *New York Times*. It was connected with the suicide of Primo Levi. I read about a group of scholars convening in New York unable to comprehend why he killed himself, without any awareness, presumably, of the fact that he was clinically, profoundly depressed. He couldn't climb out of it and therefore jumped down the stairwell. After I wrote this op-ed piece, which received an enormous amount of attention, a professor of psychiatry at Johns Hopkins University wrote a letter asking me to give a talk on depression. I accepted the invitation. Part of the lecture was delivered in New York and Tina Brown was in the audience. She came up afterward and asked me if I would expand it into a long article for *Vanity Fair*. I said, certainly. Then there was such a clamor—I was deluged by mail—that I turned it into a little book. The rest is history. It became a number one bestseller. I must say that surprised me.

BLDS: So both the literary and the medical communities embraced it.

WS: Yes. I've been gratified that it was really embraced by both laypeople like myself, who have either suffered from depression or have family and friends who suffer from it, and also by the medical people.

BLDS: When you mentioned that you spoke at Johns Hopkins it reminded me that your wife, Rose Burgunder Styron, was originally from Baltimore. In fact, for someone with your background, Rose was very different. She is of the Jewish faith and must have grown up in a very stratified society, too—because, to me, Baltimore is as socially stratified as Virginia. How did the two of you ever come together, and what were you both doing in Rome?

WS: I gave a talk at Johns Hopkins in a writing class after I wrote *Lie Down in Darkness.* I met Rose there but just to shake hands. About eight or nine months later I found myself in Rome on a fellowship to the American Academy. Rose had been in a class with Louis Rubin, a very distinguished teacher, and he urged her to get in touch with me when she went to Rome. She was in flight from her family, the Baltimore family, at that time. She is on very good terms with them now. So she took up Louis Rubin on his advice and dropped me a letter while she was in Rome.

BLDS: Why did he want the two of you to meet?

WS: I think he just thought that we would get along. He liked me and he liked my work.

BLDS: So the introduction wasn't for professional purposes.

WS: He thought that we might become friendly. And so I responded to the note and we met the same night. That night, three people got together in the bar of the Hotel Excelsior—people who didn't know each other before this encounter. The other person was Truman Capote.

BLDS: He was with the two of you?

WS: He had written me, too. He lived in Rome.

BLDS: So you figured you might as well get rid of the two of them at once!

WS: At once. We all had a wonderful time and saw a lot of each other all during that period in Rome. It was the fall of 1952. Rose and I were married in '53.

BLDS: In Rome? Were you still living there?

WS: Yes. I was at the Academy, but I decided to get out of it.

BLDS: What was Rose doing in Rome?

WS: She was just sort of lolling about. As I said, she was having a little pressure from her mother, and getting smothered by the Baltimore family, so she decided to take a year or two abroad.

BLDS: A *Wanderjahr*. It was particularly touching to me that when you were ill you told Rose to divorce you because you thought you might remain institutionalized. Of course, she refused to do that. Your marriage has lasted now for more than forty-three years, and obviously endured a great deal: not only a writer's life, but a lot of other stresses. What has held it together?

WS: I think we just get along very well. We are good companions. And she is the most tolerant person. She puts up a lot more with me than I put up with her. We have some sort of glue that keeps us together. We've had some famous rocky moments—who hasn't? But they have not been serious, and we've always gotten along. She is enormously patient. I attribute most of it to her.

BLDS: You have four children and none of them so far has taken to writing as a profession.

WS: Not the kind of writing I do. One daughter is doing screenplays and my youngest daughter, the ex-actress, is trying to do fiction. I think she is very gifted. I read several of her stories. I think she can make it.

BLDS: Does this please you?

WS: Not particularly, but you know you can't do anything about it.

BLDS: Why would it not be a great flattery, let alone bring pleasure to you?

WS: Well, I know, but it's such an incredibly difficult profession.

BLDS: As compared to what?

WS: Compared to anything I know.

BLDS: There are many who credit the stability of your personal life as being the fertile soil that has allowed you to work on the level you have for so many years. Would you agree with that appraisal?

WS: I would agree with that. It's almost a cliché but I want to quote the line from Flaubert that I made famous because I discovered it many years ago and put it up on my wall, where it still remains: "Be regular and orderly in your life like a bourgeois, so you may be violent and original in your work." It is from a letter that Flaubert wrote to Louise Colet. I have always believed in that.

BLDS: Singular events that you haven't yet focused on in your work are the Vietnam War and that watershed in American history, Watergate and the era of Richard Nixon. Have you ever considered writing about either of them?

WS: I was violently opposed to the Vietnam War. I was a vigorous activist for Eugene McCarthy and labored hard and mightily to get him nominated. I went out to Oregon and California, places like that, to campaign for him because I felt he was our hope to end the war. So I did have that involvement. I also might add that I wrote about the 1968 Chicago convention in the *New York Review of Books,* and later was a witness for the defense in the Chicago Seven trials, the Abbie Hoffman trial.

BLDS: In your work you have dealt with the most difficult subjects of the twentieth century. What do you foresee as the major crises of the early part of the twenty-first century? Will they be different from those of the past?

WS: No, they're going to be quite in line with the past. Again, I really think the evil lies in this drug and gun culture. Unless something is done about that there can be only limited hope for black people in America. I'm talking about the core. You cannot have a civilization that permits this to happen.

BLDS: Blacks are 12 percent of the population, Hispanics are a greater number, and we will have an even greater number of Asian minorities in the country. Do you foresee the same problems in those ethnic minorities?

WS: Not as much. Possibly with some of the Chinese gangs in New York, but I don't think so because the economics of the Asians are entirely different. The Koreans and the Chinese manage to jump right out of the lower income brackets. It is in the lower income brackets, in the ghettos, where this violence occurs. I don't mean to say that the Asians are not having problems, too, but not on the scale of blacks.

BLDS: What is the most difficult subject you have ever tried to put into words?

WS: Love, I guess. I've always bitten off more than I can chew. But I've felt that kind of necessity is a challenge. No one wants to hear another routine love story. You want a love story but you want it immersed in a broader panorama of life. For instance, *Sophie's Choice* is a love story, but it is a love story against the background of something that I regarded as the central event of the twentieth century, and one that had to be addressed. One that I had to address.

BLDS: In the end, are there any topics that you felt you could not address, that you had to shy away from?

WS: I felt absolutely no restraint about dealing with black people; however, that black person had to be a black man who lived 150 years before. I would never have thought to try and enter the soul and body of a kid in Watts or Harlem or in the ghettos, because I don't know that vernacular, I don't know that lifestyle. However, I felt that I knew the lifestyle of the slave as well as any black man, because I am removed in time to a degree in which I can know as much about a slave as a contemporary black person can. That allowed me to go into that territory. I would never go into the ghetto because I don't know that world.

BLDS: What do you believe that your novels tell us about you?

WS: I'm not really concerned that my novels tell people anything about me. I think that's putting the cart before the horse. I want my novels to have made significant statements about the human condition viewed through the prism of my own sensibilities. Plainly, in some of my work I have involved myself as a kind of autobiographical narrator, but that's different from asking the reader to understand anything about me personally.

> I want my novels to have made significant statements about the human condition viewed through the prism of my own sensibilities.

BLDS: In all your writing do you have any favorite sentences or passages?

WS: I think the one that sticks in my mind from *Sophie's Choice* is the line toward the end of the book in which I say (I'm paraphrasing myself), "Auschwitz remains incomprehensible." I then wrote: "The most telling thing about Auschwitz, the most powerful thing ever said about Auschwitz, was not a statement but the question that was also the answer to a question. And the first question was, 'Tell me, at Auschwitz where was God?' And the answer was, 'Where was man?'" Those words seem to sum it up as well as any I know.

TWYLA THARP

BLDS: You are a leading avant-garde artist of the twentieth century. If what I read is accurate, during your early years you spent several months of the year living with your grandparents—your Quaker grandparents—in a nineteenth-century way. How did you leap forward a century and a half, and so quickly?

TT: My family moved to Southern California.

BLDS: And that did it?

TT: That'll do it.

BLDS: And you moved from the Indiana farmlands to the edge of the California desert.

TT: Right.

BLDS: How old were you?

TT: Eight.

BLDS: Now that you've gone through the kind of exhaustive self-examination that writing an autobiography requires, what would you describe as the four or five most important elements of your childhood? How do they affect your life and your work?

TT: Well, head and shoulders above the rest is the education that my mother provided and the fact that she was persistent and wide-reaching in her search for excellent instructors—people who could teach stenography, as well as those who taught music composition.

BLDS: Your mother was a musician, a piano teacher, and at a very early age she exposed you in the most exacting, and exhausting, way to her interest in music. Can you describe that?

TT: Well, when I was a tiny, tiny, tiny kid, even before I was a year old, I was taken to all of her lessons. She was still studying formally herself. And I was always with her when she practiced.

BLDS: How frequently was that?

TT: Every day. She was still very serious about her own perfor-

> *I wasn't responsible for my own schedule, shall we say, until I was about three or four, but then I was.*

mance. I'm sure that the ways in which a performing artist works, how they take things apart, and hearing music at a very young age and in that way is very different from hearing it on recordings where it's played from beginning to end perfectly. You hear what's involved in making it work.

BLDS: Yes. the process. You had exposure to a true professional early on, and appear to have realized that performance requires a daily discipline.

TT: Yes. I wasn't responsible for my own schedule, shall we say, until I was about three or four, but then I was. I had to schedule my own rehearsal periods and practice sessions and keep track of them, and do a certain number of hours a week.

BLDS: When did you start to play the piano?

TT: When I was probably about three years old. Even before that my mother had done ear training. She did so with all of her kids.

BLDS: What does that mean?

TT: In much the same fashion that people who have a loved one in a coma will continue whispering to them, she believed that communication is possible even with infants. She held babies on her lap, she did it with all of us, and played harmonies, indoctrinating the scale and the tonal system in the ear before we had any vocabularies, any English vocabularies. My father was also a big influence. Both of my parents were very hardworking people. My father not only ran businesses, but he was a builder. He built both of the houses that I spent my childhood in. The house in the Midwest was in brick, and the other was a rambling, California-style house.

BLDS: Was he involved in the actual construction?

TT: He *did* the construction. He did the masonry, he did the plumbing, he did all of it: all aspects of the building and carpentry. So I grew up around two people who were very active, aggressively and very creatively so. Basically they felt that you could accomplish quite a lot. All you had to do was work very hard.

BLDS: Is there anything else that stands out in your memory?

TT: Probably my dancing teachers. There was a woman named Beatrice Collonette whom I studied with when I was about twelve. She had been a professional dancer with Pavlova and her sense of standards and excellence was something that was very important to me. I had as teachers two sisters from the Paris Opera when I was even younger than that, in Fontana. They both married dentists or something of the sort. Being around people who are acclimated to performing professionally is very different from having an education that often is afforded children by people who haven't really practiced themselves. And let's see, what else? I started working at the drive-in movie in California when I still just a kid.

BLDS: Did your father own the drive-in?

TT: My mother owned the drive-in. The drive-in was her project. It was a six-hundred-car theater, the biggest drive-in theater in Southern California, and it had a huge screen.

BLDS: Where was it located?

TT: In Rialto.

BLDS: Perfect setting for it.

TT: It was called the Foothill Drive-In Theater.

BLDS: Who selected the films?

TT: My mother. She did all the advertising, she did all the marketing, she ran the drive-in, that was her business. My father sold cars. He had several car agencies—Ford at first, then DeSoto-Plymouth.

BLDS: He moved from the construction business to the auto business, or did he do both?

TT: He did both. My parents worked very hard.

BLDS: Their involvement in the drive-in must have generated a lot of dinner-table conversation about what was playing, or what might be playing.

TT: We never had dinners. Even at Christmas we were always at the snack bar at the theater, putting up the hot dogs and doing the popcorn and running a business. As a kid I grew up seeing how businesses are run and accepting that as part of one's life.

BLDS: You have twin brothers and a younger sister.

TT: Right.

BLDS: Since they were exposed to the same environment, do they have the same work ethic that you do?

TT: You would have to discuss with them these issues.

BLDS: But from your perception?

TT: I'm not really in a position to judge that.

BLDS: What do they do?

TT: I don't see them that often. My sister is an architect. One of the twins is a commodities broker in Chicago, and the other one is in Seattle and does some kind of work with computers.

BLDS: One of the recurring themes as your life evolves, and you talk about it in *Push Comes to Shove*—the title of both your autobiography and one of your great dances—is the rage that you felt toward your mother. I suspect if one never has a dinner, or celebrates a holiday, it's just the beginning of feeling divested from the Hollywood-sponsored idea of home life.

TT: I held it against her for a very long time that I was basically alienated from society in order to develop the habits and the discipline and the ability to focus and concentrate that she demanded, and that I gradually absorbed. I cut off what is ordinarily called "the rest of your life" and had no capacity for relating to other people. I could do certain jobs extremely well but I had very little sense of how the world actually functioned, and that was perhaps too great an exchange rate. I have acquired some of these skills by conscious effort over the course of the last fifteen or twenty years. I no longer think the exchange rate was that bad.

BLDS: From your musical beginnings, how did you happen to come to define yourself as a dancer?

TT: I had started dancing when I was a teeny baby. Before I was five years old I was studying dance formally as well. One of my first memories is always of figures that move in relation to music. I've never not seen moving figures. It's not very far from seeing moving figures to skipping and hopping and running around, if you have a body that is physically adept, which mine was and, to

159

a lesser degree every day, still is. In any case, I started tap and ballet lessons with teachers in the garage when we were still in Indiana, on concrete floors. By the time we moved to Southern California my mother had started locating serious instructors.

BLDS: How do you explain the theatricality of some of her pursuits in the light of her Quaker, very restrained, and, as you describe it, unemotional background? It seems such extreme counterpoint.

TT: This is a very good question and one that, unfortunately, I didn't come up with early enough myself to ask her while she was still alive, because it's a very fair question. She had obviously an extremely flamboyant imagination. She was born, as was my father, on a farm and she had no exposure whatsoever to theater or to the arts. Her interest was a creation of her mind. The only thing she had was an uncle who paid for her piano lessons.

BLDS: Why did he choose to do that?

TT: I have no idea. For some reason he bought an upright piano for the parlor. Unfortunately, I have no idea why, as you say, she started having the notion that playing music could be a reality in a person's life.

BLDS: Let alone the notion that one could make a way of life that way. But then again, she had the courage to move from Indiana to California, so there must have been a great deal of determination and discipline in her character.

TT: That is absolutely true. It's determination, and it's also vision. At the time we saw it as complete villainy, but it's not true. It obviously takes a lot of courage. All the roots for everyone were there. It really was her prodding and insisting that it was going to be a new deal.

BLDS: Were your sister and brothers exposed to the same music?

TT: My mother tried. Let us only say that the three of them banded together. They were so close in age that essentially they had this little closed society, the three of them. And they managed to be more than she could manage. To be absolutely fair, the amount of time that she had begun giving me, and continued to invest in me, made me a full-time job. In all fairness they got slightly shorter shrift, but they didn't want to practice. I didn't want to practice either, but I learned how to do it, even when I didn't want to. And I think that's a very valuable lesson.

BLDS: Whatever gave you the discipline, the insight, the determination at an early age to know this was something you had to do if you wanted the desired results?

TT: It was because, whatever the reason, I liked the idea of being very, very good.

BLDS: And you knew what it took?

TT: And I was willing to do it. I didn't know what it took, I learned.

BLDS: Was this idea ever communicated to you orally, or was it mostly by demonstration?

TT: I think it was twofold. First of all, both of my parents insisted on excellence. I'm sure you've heard that if you're going to dig a ditch, that's fine, just make sure it's the best ditch that can be dug. Secondly, the component of religion that was in my life put forth the idea of absolute values and absolute concepts.

BLDS: You were members of the Society of Friends. Did you and your family participate in Quaker meetings?

TT: As a kid I did. When we moved to Southern California there weren't Quaker meetings in the neighborhood and my parents were frankly too busy. My mother was more concerned with the ways of the modern world than she was with preserving the ways of the community.

BLDS: I guess a lot of those values remain with you. Can you name some of the most important things that you learned?

TT: I was given a context that comes both from the presentation of the concept of God and from being in nature as a child, which the farms still were. There were pieces of wild land on the farms. And I think the combination of these powerful forces put one in one's place.

BLDS: You mentioned that when you were an adolescent, leisure produced only dread. For someone whose visible work is filled with an extraordinary sense of play, why was it so difficult for you to envision life as a game?

TT: I learned.

BLDS: What was the catalyst?

TT: I don't know. I suppose boredom in the studio. Boredom is the only thing that is ultimately really dreadful, and you'll try anything, even playing games, which I'm not that serious about and never really have been. There's not enough at stake somehow. The business of restlessness is something that

> I didn't want to practice either, but I learned how to do it, even when I didn't want to.

we all have to address, and the more deeply involved in discipline you are, the more fearful restlessness is. For people who are rather more casual in their styles of life, another couple of hours won't kill them, but for a person who says, "Oh my God, there are three minutes here. What am I going to do with them?" there is suddenly a vacuum to fill. Am I using this time in a worthwhile fashion? Will I be stricken by thunderbolts from the heavens for wasting time?

BLDS: Your childhood and adolescence sound like an intense, slightly terrifying period of training and education. You had music training by the age of a year and a half, performances and dance training before you were five, all accompanied by a ruthless insistence on excellence, not only in performance, but also in school. Your mother sounds like the orchestrator of all of this. Is there a truth to my impression? And what were your father's and your siblings' roles in your life? Your grandparents' roles?

TT: I think that your impression is accurate. My father's role was to reinforce my mother's definition of these things. Education was her job, not his, and he would support it. He would work very hard to pay for college educations and the rest of it, which is not a small accomplishment.

BLDS: What's the age difference between you and your siblings?

TT: My twin brothers are three years younger and my sister, Twanette, is four years younger. She was born three days before they were a year old, so they were essentially triplets. And the three of them were much more socially inclined than me.

BLDS: Well, they began with their own group.

TT: That's exactly right. And I was already very isolated.

BLDS: Did you feel that way all through your childhood?

TT: Totally. But I made advantages of it. I created my own memory. I made my own rituals. I had my practices to tend to.

BLDS: You described the move from Indiana to California as "villainy." Obviously, it was a very unsettling experience for you. In fact, I think you've said that it provided you with a sense of restlessness that you've never managed to escape. Has that subsided at all now?

TT: Well, let's say it's on the brink of subsiding. I'm beginning to perhaps accommodate the concept of a home. I haven't really locked into it yet, but I'm beginning to see it as possibly acceptable.

BLDS: Of the two girls in your family, one followed the interests of your mother and the other of your father, at least on a manifest level. Actually, you got some of both. You are an artist, a builder,

and a businesswoman. Wasn't your company the first, in 1975, to give dancers a fifty-two-week work year? That was unheard of before and since.

TT: That's right.

BLDS: I can understand now what gave you the fortitude to combine aesthetic and managerial innovations.

TT: Absolutely. I've never seen the contradiction between being an artist and earning a living, because my parents were in the capacity of shopkeepers. I grew up as a shopkeeper, and I considered it perfectly creative. It seemed to me just as creative to get 650 people into that theater as it was to make the movie that they were watching.

BLDS: What did you do at the drive-in?

TT: I car-hopped. A car-hopper is the person that sits in the booth behind the glass, with the gun down there for the robberies and the safe down there with the money, punches the tickets, walks over to the car, counts the number of heads in the car, analyzes how many people are under the back seat and if there is a possibility there are more in the trunk, takes down the plate number, brings their money back to the booth, gets the change, takes it back out to the car, and leaves the number there so that later the person who is car-hopping can check the fields, find the plate numbers, and recount heads, all while learning human nature. That's car-hopping. Then you work in the snack bar, preparing everything for the evening's intermission rush when everybody comes all at once.

BLDS: Was popcorn always a profit center?

TT: Hot dogs spoiled, but you could freeze them anyway. Ice cream was a problem because it melted and it wouldn't refreeze properly. Yeah, popcorn and Cokes, those were the big profit margins.

BLDS: And all of you kids worked at the drive-in?

TT: They played. They went to school events. I worked in the drive-in.

BLDS: You could have had a choice too, couldn't you?

TT: No, I was not given a choice. And I didn't realize that I could have had a choice. You're right, I could have been a rebellious teenager, but that never occurred to me.

BLDS: You just waited a while to rebel.

TT: Yes, I suppose I had a bigger revenge in mind.

BLDS: One of the chapter headings in your autobiography is "Art Is the Only Way to Run Away Without Leaving Home." What did you mean by that, and what did you mean by home?

> Part of being an artist is constantly reinventing, but you have to have something to start with.

TT: I meant that as an artist you have the best of all possible worlds, which is that you have an ongoing continuity in your life, but you also every day have the responsibility to take that continuity in a slightly different direction; otherwise, it freezes up and becomes stale. For example, as a dancer or any performing artist, you have to do the same series of exercises every day of your life, but you have to find a way of using those exercises that is fresh or you go bats. Part of being an artist is constantly reinventing, but you have to have something to start with. One of the things that ultimately and ironically is the biggest lesson in relationships, and something I did learn from my mother, is that you have to be capable of making a commitment and yet seeing the liberty within the boundaries of that commitment. It's seeing both sides simultaneously.

BLDS: There is an enormous physicality and sensuality to your work. You've described your childhood behavior, and we can conclude that it was thought best that most things—including your dance lessons—were best taken in total privacy. It sounds like a very repressive environment. There was little or no show of affection, either between your parents or directed toward their children.

TT: Well, this is probably the reason that I became more of a choreographer than a performer. It may have been different had I, as a child, been in a situation where I was learning through the participation of a watcher, as some kids are. For example, children in well-run schools have opportunities to perform every year in operas and ballets. I didn't have that opportunity. All of my lessons had to be dealt with in private. And that means that I became my own watcher. Performing artists don't understand about being their own watchers; they need to have an audience. I never really had that driving need for an audience.

BLDS: How do you explain that? You've said that you didn't want to be a star, you wanted to be a galaxy. To control and direct an entire company, I think, is much beyond being a dancer, even if one is assigned the best solo on stage—alone for a few minutes.

TT: There are ways of doing it. For example, Martha Graham controlled her galaxy but she did it from the inside. She didn't do it from the outside. She always sensed her work as generating from her own physical presence at the center of things. I much more have seen it from being back, and being at a distance. Probably it has to do with things like growing up in a drive-in theater where you're accustomed to being a watcher. I was both the audience and behind the scenes.

BLDS: You describe yourself now as a participant and a Hover-craft.

TT: Right. I've gotten a little better at shifting gears back and forth, because the two are very different things. If your mind is inclined in the director's division of labor you will see every possible place something can go wrong. If you also put yourself onstage with an awareness of everything that could possibly go wrong, it's a fearful place to be. But if, as a performer, you're onstage and you have no awareness of this—that's somebody else's job, not yours—then you can perform to an audience.

BLDS: You have often spoken of your creative and personal debt to Martha Graham. Do you think of yourself as the natural inheritor of her role?

TT: No, I don't think there is such a thing in the arts as a natural inheritor. As an artist you learn your lessons and go about blundering forward for the rest of your life. You don't inherit someone else's accomplishments, ever. It never really has made sense for me to go into an institution that someone else has built, because someone else has built that institution to service their own needs. My needs are very different. Our time is very different.

BLDS: What are they? Would you care to talk about them?

TT: Well, it's a difficult question. When Martha was making her work there was not the same intense cross-fertilization that the media have afforded us. Certainly she worked with the visual arts and was always very concerned about contemporary music. It's not that she didn't know about contemporary arts, but the aesthetic settlement was that one formulated one's own voice. Now one formulates one's own voice but with the impact of so many sources of information. For example, for a long, long time Martha would not allow anyone in her company to study ballet. People did sneak out and take ballet class, but if she heard anyone was doing it there was hell to pay.

BLDS: Because she feared the classical influence?

> All of my lessons had to be dealt with in private. And that means that I became my own watcher. . . . I never really had that driving need for an audience.

162

TT: Because she felt it would be a pollutant. And also because, frankly, it was somewhat disloyal. She expected you to be in her classes doing that technique, and it was a very different kind of thing. We have accessible to us many different vocabularies and techniques, and I've always felt it inefficient and uneconomical to disregard them. Part of this is probably the formal training. I've always felt that it would be wasteful not to utilize that which is still good and valuable, and then discard it.

BLDS: In 1993, on the centennial of Martha Graham's birth, you choreographed a dance in honor of the occasion. I wonder if you can compare her early female companies and your early female companies?

TT: Well, I'm not totally familiar with the time frames, and by the way, Martha lied about her age like mad.

BLDS: So how old was she?

TT: She was over a hundred, but no one knows exactly when she was born. One of the only documents that has any kind of dates on it was her marriage certificate with Eric Hawkins; however, she told a number of people she lied by fifteen years on that document, which I don't quite believe.

BLDS: How old did she claim to be?

TT: Forty on the document.

BLDS: So how old would she have been when she died?

TT: The papers said ninety-two or ninety-three, but she was over a hundred. She was 103, 104. What that really means to me is that *Clytemnestra* is a piece that she made when she was, by the books, sixty-two. That means she was really over seventy when she did *Clytemnestra*. Now, that is phenomenal.

BLDS: Not only is it phenomenal, it is a worthy role model for you.

TT: That's right. It shows you what the body can do. It is amazing. Of course, Merce Cunningham is still onstage, and Merce is seventy-eight, I think.

BLDS: What is the average professional life span of a dancer?

TT: It depends on the dancer and the kind of dancing. The shortest life span for a dancer is the classical male dancer. Ordinarily the jumping is gone by the time they reach their mid-thirties. That means that their career is very difficult after that.

BLDS: Is that because of physical limitations?

TT: It's just that the body no longer has the resiliency to get the depth, the plié, and the force needed to get real height. For a classical ballerina of first rank, mid-forties; if she has a reputation she can carry it until she is about forty-four, forty-five, forty-six. After that very few dancers continue. They either become choreographers or a few are celebrity dancers. Margot Fonteyn danced much longer, really, than even she wanted to, but it was a purely financial matter for her. And then there are simply people who are addicted. Nureyev, for example, was addicted to performing. He full well knew he shouldn't be onstage but he just couldn't get off, which is okay, too. I didn't see him for the last couple of years but I did see one late performance of his. There was a gut to his drive even then that I would have rather seen from him than from kids who could properly execute the pirouettes. There was still a passion about being on that stage. It was very moving.

BLDS: What happens to old dancers—dancers who might be only thirty-five years old. What do they do with their finely tuned machines? What does the body do with the rest of its professional life?

TT: Well, the first thing it must do is reconcile itself to the fact that it has had a very good life, and get over being bitter at the age of thirty-five and a half. The dancer must acknowledge the fact that it has been a privilege and an honor to be able to exist in the body. And then there's the opportunity for a whole other life. Dancers are not stupid. Very good dancers are very intelligent people. Just because they don't speak doesn't mean they're stupid. Quite to the contrary. And dancers also have wonderful work skills. They are extremely disciplined, very punctual, very pragmatic. These are talents, and if not talents, they are certainly skills and approaches that transfer very well to a number of other occupations. But the dancer has to be willing to leave the stage. That's the first thing.

BLDS: It's very tough. You've described dancing as a lifelong commitment to the body, a constant daily reminder.

TT: You have two choices. If you do it, it feels awful. If you don't do it, it feels worse. Those are the two choices.

BLDS: So you believe in serotonin and everything else that is pumped up during warm up and dancing?

TT: Oh, and so on. Yes, I do. Absolutely.

BLDS: Therefore, the absence of the habitual performance can have a limiting effect, so you've got to keep it up.

TT: Yes, it's true. The problem is it becomes more time-consuming. For me now to really feel as though the body is being worked, as though I know where everything is, takes between two and three hours. That's a big chunk out of the day.

BLDS: Can we take you back to your early lifetime? I left you in the drive-in theater; you were then counting heads and also involved in the enormous discipline of your own training. Can we talk about the evolution of your own professional training, from the drive-in theater to the Twyla Tharp Company? Just lead us through that evolution.

TT: I was in and out of private schools and public schools until I was graduated from high school, and then I went to junior colleges. In San Bernardino, California, there's a junior college called Valley College. Then I went three semesters to Pomona, transferred to Barnard, and was graduated from Barnard in '63 in art history.

BLDS: How did you make it from Pomona to Barnard and how did you get sanction from your family to make that change?

TT: Well, first of all, I managed to get thrown out of Pomona so I would have to transfer, and then I was able to talk my mother into Barnard since it was one of the Seven Sister colleges and she would find an Ivy League school acceptable, and I wanted to go to New York because of the dance training.

BLDS: You do recount in lively, and sometimes lurid, detail in your autobiography some of your escapades during that time.

TT: I did my best to make it raunchy. I'm afraid it doesn't really stand up too well.

BLDS: It is actually rather mild, especially by current standards.

TT: I did my damnedest.

BLDS: Why did you get thrown out of Pomona?

TT: My first husband—actually I did have to get married anytime I kissed anybody—and I were making out in a chapel during a rainstorm.

BLDS: You were apprehended and your parents found out about the incident?

TT: Right.

BLDS: And what did they do about it?

TT: They wouldn't take me out of school, so I had to transfer schools.

BLDS: But did they also insist that you marry?

TT: Yes, that happened down the line. That was the same guy.

BLDS: So you came to New York,

> New York City was still where the artistic bohemia was, it was still where the best dance and the best dancers were, and if one wanted to try oneself out, it's where you had to go.

where he was.

TT: Yes, he had already moved.

BLDS: So there were several motivations for your coming here.

TT: This was true. But I think in the back of my mind it did have to do with the arts. New York City was still where the artistic bohemia was, it was still where the best dance and the best dancers were, and if one wanted to try oneself out, it's where you had to go.

BLDS: Do you think that is still the case?

TT: I don't think it is still the case. It would take an enormous amount of imagination to really "make it" outside of New York, but I think that someone with a real training, and a background, and their own vision could do the same outside New York.

BLDS: There are exceptional cases, but for dancers in the main is it still New York where they have to come and train and perform?

TT: If dancers want to join one of the principal companies, which are still based in New York, usually that's the route that they go. I had not set my sights on joining a company. I think in a very vague way I just wanted to be an artist, and that can be done now outside of New York.

BLDS: What happened after you were graduated from Barnard?

TT: I spent one year with the Paul Taylor Company as a professional dancer.

BLDS: How did you come to meet Paul Taylor?

TT: I went to him. I saw him with Graham on Broadway and I thought he was really fabulous. It was his quality of movement. He was unique. I've never seen anyone else move with the kind of vibrancy that Paul had. So I just went there.

BLDS: And hung around?

TT: He was smart enough to know I was trouble from the beginning. He really didn't want to take me, and he was right. He shouldn't have.

BLDS: Why?

TT: Because I was trouble.

BLDS: How so?

TT: Because I thought my own thoughts, and I let everyone know that I was thinking my own thoughts, and I challenged him.

BLDS: Isn't that the creative spirit?

TT: No. You have enough challenges and demons of your own. You don't need somebody who's very short looking at you as if they know better than you do what you're doing. This you do not need!

BLDS: So why did he tolerate you?

TT: Because I amused him and I was a very good dancer. And if he could have won me over I could have been very useful to him.

BLDS: And how long did you stay there—a year?

TT: Not quite. Then I considered going to other companies—Merce's company, the Graham company—but ultimately I decided that I was just confronting other problems and that I should just bite the bullet and make my own dances. If my body wanted to dance it should figure out what it wanted to do instead of saying, Well, I don't like this or that about so-and-so's work. Fine, you've done that once, now go do what you do like.

BLDS: You were then twenty-three?

TT: Twenty-one. Maybe I was twenty-two.

BLDS: And you decided you'd just make dances. Where would you perform them?

TT: It didn't occur to me until I had one to perform. There are two ways of going about it. One is you can think about your career and start building your career and then worry: Oh, my goodness, I wonder what we're going to perform? Or you can do work and say: Gee, I wonder where we'll perform this. I always preferred doing the work, and then worrying about the showcase.

BLDS: How long did it take you to create the first dance?

TT: A lifetime, it seems like.

BLDS: What and where was its first public manifestation?

TT: It was a little concert. The entire evening was three minutes long, because I thought that maybe I could manage to do a good three minutes. I certainly didn't want to be in a group show. Therefore, it was going to be a very short evening. It occurred at Hunter College. It was done in a small auditorium that was attached to the art department. I designed my little three-minute spectacle and put it up and sent out the flyers and did all costumes.

BLDS: Did it all yourself?

TT: Put a show on. Did it all myself. I knew how to do all those things. I wasn't afraid of doing any of them. I knew how to get an audience. I didn't know how to suffer the reviews, but I learned very quickly.

BLDS: Your first show wasn't reviewed, was it?

TT: The first show wasn't reviewed, which was even worse.

BLDS: Did you expect it to be?

TT: Of course I did!

BLDS: And you searched the newspapers?

TT: Of course I did, yes. I was very disappointed. Ultimately, I don't know which is worse, no review or a terrible review.

BLDS: No review.

TT: Probably.

BLDS: How many performers were there in that first dance?

TT: There was myself and four nondancers who rushed across the performing area carrying banners.

BLDS: And what was that dance called?

TT: *Tank Dive.* I figured, okay, here you have a very high platform and here you have a teacup and these are your chances of success. Go ahead and jump, let's see.

BLDS: Did you ever explain that to the audience?

TT: No. At that time I wasn't concerned with explaining anything to the audience. In fact, it was part of the milieu of the time that the audience should not only not be explained to, preferably they wouldn't get it at all! You could feel very good then.

BLDS: And superior, too.

TT: Absolutely.

BLDS: Let's talk about your ascent from the time of that first three-minute dance. What happened next?

TT: Then I did two more three-minute dances, and so on and so forth. Then I did the next concert. I worked as quickly as I could.

BLDS: Where did you live, and where did you rehearse?

TT: I lived in a loft downtown on Franklin Street that I had taken when I graduated, which at the time cost a low seventy-five dollars a month. By the time I moved out almost twenty years later it cost about fifteen hundred dollars a month. I worked in one end of the loft. Also I snuck around in those early years. We worked in the Judson gym a lot, which was a free space for the community and was very important to us, and also in other gymnasiums where we could find them. Just any kind of public space that we could lock up for three or four or five hours a day. I was committed to doing as much as I could, as quickly as I could, and I didn't want to waste time. The next concert was with dancers. Then, in the next year, 1966, we had the first tour. Sarah Rudner was already with me by then. She danced with me for the next twenty years. And then we added on, one by one.

BLDS: Why do you think that the prominence and development of women in the various arts has been so very uneven? There are women writers, poets, choreographers, yes. But composers, theater directors, and conductors? Why are those fields so slow to accept them?

TT: I'm not quite sure.

BLDS: Is it true that women in the arts, not unlike those in the high levels of corporate life, have had their own glass ceiling?

TT: With the exception of writers. It certainly is true in music as well as in the visual arts and theatrical arts. I can only think it's financial. Do you have any theories as to why lady writers have managed to escape this?

BLDS: Perhaps because they write films about male subjects and subjects that are agreeable and acceptable to large numbers of people. Most often you don't see the writer; a book contains text, something bound between covers. Also, there's a historical tradition of women writers, which is probably the reason more than anything else. And it is a solitary activity, not dependent on others for its creation. But the opportunity for publication and distribution is another story. At the end of this century women are still handicapped by second-class status in many areas of life. However, in modern dance there is room for women as choreographers. If there wasn't, would you have chosen another discipline?

TT: Probably one of the reasons I chose modern dance is because I didn't feel that women in the field were so handicapped as artists; it is a discipline that women are very intimately connected with. In fact, there is an argument to be made that people like Loie Fuller, Ruth St. Denis, and Isadora Duncan founded the category of modern dance, that men are latecomers there, and that women have always been the more potent voice in modern dance.

BLDS: You were quoted in *The New Yorker* as saying, "I have the kind of dancers you have to have if you're going to get the primary truth of how something is made." What kinds of dancers are those, and can you describe that kind of truth, apart from dancing it?

TT: You probably can't describe it apart from dancing it, but you can discuss some of the components that make it possible to accomplish. In the case of those dancers, we went back to the very beginning conditions that prevailed, when the company was first all women. What compelled us to work at that time was community, and just simply working for the sake of working. It was not goal-oriented in any way.

BLDS: Let's talk about those endangered species—the NEA and the NEH. There is a true story about a creative grant application you made more than twenty years ago.

TT: It was indeed. It was more like thirty. It was 1969.

BLDS: You wrote a handwritten note, rather than an application, that said, "I make dances, not applications. Send the money. Love, Twyla."

TT: Right.

BLDS: And, believe it or not, you got the money. How much was it?

TT: I think it was probably ten thousand dollars. It was either five or ten, which were the amounts that they were doing at that time. Of course, to me it was a fortune.

BLDS: What did you do with the money? Did it help you in your career?

TT: Of course. What I did was what I always did when I got money in those early years, which was divide it three ways between Rose, Sarah, and myself. If anything came in we got paid, if nothing came in we didn't get paid. We worked, in any case. And it was always understood that if there were any fees or grants they would be divvied up in that way.

BLDS: How did you manage to exist?

TT: The sentimental stories are true, of Rose and Graziella and Sella living on the "alphabet avenues" in the East Village and eating yogurt. They froze it for variety. Literally, they were living on thirty, forty dollars a month.

BLDS: And you?

TT: I was living with my husband at the time, so my living expenses were minimal. I suppose Bob helped support me, but I didn't expect to get it from the dancing any more than the girls expected to make livelihoods from the dancing. We always managed to take temporary jobs. I was a Kelly Girl "temp" and also did some waitressing. And I baby-sat a lot. For one season I was on unemployment and tried to keep that unemployment alive as long as I possibly could. That was how we did it for the first three or four years. Then we started getting these small amounts of grant money or we'd get five hundred dollars for a performance, very infrequently.

BLDS: In 1993 you didn't apply for a grant, but you received one: the coveted MacArthur grant, which was then $310,000. What did that mean to you and your work? Did it buy the kind of time you needed to think and reflect and create?

TT: Well, I think it did give me breathing time. It did allow me to say, there is another way, and I don't just have to keep doing these works for hire, which is a very different way of working.

BLDS: Other than the MacArthur grant, have there been any grants or fellowships that have meant a great deal to you and your work?

TT: Yes. All of them. All of them have seemed to me to be an encouragement because of the recognition as much as the dollars. I felt blessed and was very fortunate with grants during the time that I had the company in the seventies and eighties. I'm grateful for it.

BLDS: Why did you disband the company?

TT: Partially because I saw this economic climate coming. It was becoming harder to find the dollars, it was becoming more difficult to fund the payroll, there was more competition for the same dollars, the granting agencies were unpredictable in terms of one's future, and it just became too much to try to run a business that some people could accept going into a deficit position. Most dance companies run a deficit, but I couldn't abide it. My parents never bought anything on time. I was taught debt is a very dangerous thing.

BLDS: We talked earlier about your involvement, at least in some measure, with Martha Graham. What is your inheritance from Balanchine?

TT: Propriety. I never knew Balanchine, I never studied at the school, and I didn't have close associations with him or the dancers, but when I saw performances as a paying member of the audience, as one coming in off the street, what I saw was propriety. Things properly done. And I have always found that as moving as anything in the arts.

BLDS: Are there other choreographers whose work impressed or influenced you?

TT: I'm sure that there were. At one time I went to see absolutely everything, and I remember components from them all.

BLDS: In an interview in the *New York Times*, you said that you've learned that education is entertainment. I think you were specifically referring to your City Center workshop performance several years ago; but did you mean education in the wider sense as well, beyond that specific experience?

TT: Oh, yes. The piece I've been working on will have a Rossini score and so I wanted to learn something about nineteenth-century behavior. Someone recommended that I read Balzac. I'm now on my fifth novel. And if anyone ever thought education is entertainment, Balzac did. I mean, he was an encyclopedia. His knowledge of the making of paper, of finance, of the nitty-gritty was vast. Here's how you mix the mortar, here's how you put the bricks into place. From how shoes are made to how people deceive one another. It all is very educational and enormously entertaining.

BLDS: Would you call the intensive, relentless regime of your childhood education entertainment?

TT: I've tried to. I don't get too far with that one.

BLDS: You've coined the phrase *crossover dance*. Do we need another new word to describe this second generation of modern dance?

TT: Well, you have *postmodern* and then you have *post-postmodern*.

BLDS: No, but a word that really covers this period more generically and one that people can comfortably, and not disingenuously, use to refer to themselves. Since you are a genuine wordsmith, it's one of my assignments to you.

TT: Okay, but as an artist I think it's traditional that labels are not looked on fondly.

BLDS: Except in your reference. I think it needs a more refined, evolved meaning.

TT: Well, I do actually have a phrase that I use.

BLDS: What is it?

TT: *The stompers.* It indicates a kind of energy, and a kind of earthboundness, that I think of as very diametrically opposed to the lightness in ballet.

BLDS: But you do use classically trained dancers. Tell us what you mean by crossover dancers, and, therefore, is there such a thing as a crossover dance?

TT: What is becoming sort of the granddaddy of crossover dance is *In the Upper Room,* because it has two camps of dancers in it, with a very clear line drawn between the two. On the one side you have what we call the stompers, which is half the cast, and on the other side you have the lighter, higher dancers, the women who work on pointe, and the men who are much more aerial. But there is a fallacy in my system. It comes from a sense of democracy. In other words, when I was a very technical dancer and obviously a much younger one I used to think, well, there's no reason why I should not be able to do the Cunningham training techniques or a Graham repertory. Of course, my pointe work was always terrible, so that didn't really count, but I always thought from the education that I had that a well-educated dancer would be capable across the board. She would be able to tap, she would be able to go the entire spectrum. This is not true. The great classical ballerinas are never going to be able to get their weight grounded like one of my dancers. It's like asking a broad jumper to win a swim meet. The idea of approaching that center ground, that common point, has been valuable in expanding both arenas, but it is a fallacy to say that you are going to have one dancer who can operate equally well in all of these disciplines simultaneously.

BLDS: How important is a sense of theatricality to your dancers?

TT: This is an interesting question. What do you mean by theatricality? I'm stalling.

BLDS: Well, you said before that you never felt discomfort in performing within a commercial setting, rather than pure "art" spaces. Nothing dirty or sinful about it, it's how you made your way. But it requires more "theatricality" to be in a commercial forum.

TT: This is where maybe the crossover performer makes more sense. I like to believe that it is possible for a dancer to be absolutely committed to the purity of their discipline and also be a great entertainer. One can be very theatrical, be very dramatically astute, and also be capable of going into morning class and focusing purely and simply on the nuts and bolts of dancing.

BLDS: While we're on the subject of class, it seems to me that ballet dancers, no matter how modest their origins, take on the values of the social aristocracy, as contrasted to the more egalitarian performers involved in modern dance. Is that why you chose a word that is essentially such a nonart word like *stompers*?

TT: I think that there's some truth to that. I think that it is changing, and the current arts climate is going to change that radically.

BLDS: How so, and why?

TT: As patronage becomes less and less the modus operandi and more a blessing, people are not going to be able to assume that they must be supported.

BLDS: Is that a blessing because one wouldn't need to cater to the whims, the preferences, the tastes, and the social values of the so-called benefactor? One could be liberated from that imposition?

TT: It is a double-edged sword. Is it going to be the audience or the individual patron who supports dance? Again, this is another issue to which Balzac applies himself a lot: the aristocracy as opposed to the middle class. You're caught between a rock and a hard place.

BLDS: And where would you rather end up?

TT: They are just very different beasts. I have often said that I would take the audience, that I would appeal to them in the blood-lust way that is the relationship between the performer onstage and the audience. In a way it's more predictable than the tastes of the individual patron, which can be very quixotic.

I like to believe that it is possible for a dancer to be absolutely committed to the purity of their discipline and also be a great entertainer.

BLDS: Is dance, particularly in New York, very much a cult activity, a really hip thing to be interested in, and involved in? If you look at the audiences in concert halls and in theaters, you realize that it is long past due that new audience development take place. If you go to a dance performance you see people of all ages, but by and large, a much younger, enthusiastic, responsive, and informed audience, even though the tickets are equally expensive.

TT: You think more so than at the opera or at theater? Well, I feel it's a problem again for all components of live performances and concerts, excepting some rock and roll concerts. Sure, audience enticement is a necessity and one of the pleasures. It's one of the things for which I have great regard that was done by Lincoln Kirstein and Balanchine at the New York City Ballet. They got a wonderful subscription audience that was really engaged and felt a part of the team. That's a wonderful thing to have.

BLDS: Well, since you understand it so well, it's clearly going to be one of the needs that your new company has to confront. What are you going to call it?

TT: Well, we'll see it first and then we'll name it. It'll be Twyla Tharp Dance, same as the old one was.

BLDS: Speaking of Twyla Tharp, obviously that was a name given to you with a marquee in mind. In fact, I always thought it was an invention until I read a story, which I still believe is apocryphal, about the person for whom you were named. And while you're at it, you might also talk about the names of your twin brothers and your sister. Who was Twyla?

TT: It's not apocryphal. In the archives there's a clipping of the pig princess Twyla at the county fair.

BLDS: Was this in Muncie, Indiana?

TT: It was in Indiana. The name spelled was with an *I*, and my mother changed the spelling to include a *Y*.

BLDS: What is a pig princess in Muncie, by the way? Is it anything like being cotton queen in Nashville?

TT: It was competitive, and she was the icon for the biggest hog.

BLDS: But was she also lovely?

TT: Primo. We would like to think so. Yes, my mother changed the spelling for the purposes of a marquee. My sister's name would have been Antoinette if my mother had not immediately docked

168

the first syllable so that it would be alliterative. Twanette Tharp. TT. Such things are very important, no matter what you're going to do. Got to be well equipped.

BLDS: Then come the twin brothers.

TT: Stan and Stan.

BLDS: You did say Stan and Stan, commonly referred to as the Stans?

TT: The Stans, and if they were going to be unidentifiable, they might as well be. You wouldn't misname them this way. My father couldn't tell them apart for a long, long time.

BLDS: And what were their given names?

TT: Stanley Wayne and Stanley Vaughan. Let's be fair—my mother did her best to give everybody their best shot. She tried to supply us with everything we could possibly need.

BLDS: What did she do for your father?

TT: I don't think that I am the right person to ask that question. I know that he was absolutely committed to her and they had what appeared to be a very good marriage.

BLDS: Do you find that your work is more appreciated by European audiences than by American ones?

TT: Differently appreciated. Audiences in different countries respond to different pieces in different ways. I think it's probably sentimental to say that the Europeans have a higher regard for our performances than American audiences do. What the European cultural situation has that we don't is a greater appreciation for the education of artists and for making that education almost an industrial matter and a possibility. In other words, it is accepted that the arts can also be an industry and that children can be prepared to go into a profession as a dancer. That's not the way here.

BLDS: If someone gave you as much money as you needed to begin another Twyla Tharp company and/or a Twyla Tharp school, what would you create? What would you teach? And how would you select your company and your students?

TT: What a nice pipe dream. How many minutes shall we allocate to this?

BLDS: For the winner of the MacArthur, you never know what comes over the transom.

TT: No, I'm afraid that the money doesn't go far when you're founding a dance school.

BLDS: No, but it still was a surprise in your life—and if not you, who?

TT: I don't know. The school would be essentially a scholarship-based school and a residential school. It would involve a very eclectic faculty. It would involve not only physical training, but also a curriculum of the other disciplines.

BLDS: Which disciplines?

TT: Composition and music, structure and painting, the ability to go into a museum and find your way around, the ability to pick up a novel, to pick up nonfiction, to look in a newspaper, to know something about politics.

BLDS: Does this imply that dancers are less well educated, less cultivated than others?

TT: It is unfortunately true that dancers don't have that much time and that their educations in this country have been so helter-skelter that they have had to pick up what they can without it being very well coordinated. It would be fair to say this about most folks, but in particular dancers; they could be a great deal more broad-minded and ultimately it would make much stronger performers of them. Certainly, for the dancer to have substantial dramatic work, to learn how to fight their way through a monologue, would be a very valuable thing. Practically no dancers onstage can do that. It makes a big difference in the emotional reservoir that a performer has. The school would probably be away from New York and its distractions, as would the company.

BLDS: Where should it be located?

TT: I don't know, but not here, probably. There's too much going on here. One must spend as much energy screening influences as drawing in the ones that one wants.

BLDS: What is your idea of a perfect day?

TT: The sun shines, no appointments, no meetings. The day is completely open-ended and my work is in the future, far enough away so that there are no deadlines or pressures at the moment.

ROBERT VENTURI AND DENISE SCOTT BROWN

BLDS: Let's start with the genesis and evolution of your careers. This interview was originally proposed to you, Robert, yet you were insistent that you and Denise be interviewed together. While I appreciate and encourage egalitarianism, and certainly keeping the peace at home, what motivated this condition? I know there is a history to this, and I think it would be a good time for you to set the record straight. What is the nature of your relationship and why do you refer to Venturi, Scott Brown and Associates as a "one team" firm?

RV: We came together naturally as fellow faculty members at the University of Pennsylvania many years ago. Denise was a very young faculty member; I was a less young one. And we found we agreed with each other a lot and stimulated each other. Then we did some projects together, some competitions while Denise was still in Philadelphia.

DSB: We also talked a lot.

BLDS: What were the initial projects that you did together?

RV: We did a competition for a fountain for Philadelphia's Benjamin Franklin Parkway, which we did not win. And I was a lecturer in a course on theory at Penn. At the time it was the only course on architectural theory in the United States, in any school. Now all schools have four or five courses in theory. The pendulum has swung. Out of that course came *Complexity and Contradiction in Architecture*. We taught together; Denise ran the seminars. Then she moved to California to teach at UC Berkeley and UCLA. She invited me to UCLA to be a visiting critic and took me on a trip to

Las Vegas. She introduced Las Vegas to me. Soon we married, Denise came back to Philadelphia, and we became formal rather than informal partners, in our thought and work.

DSB: Perhaps we should reverse the question. How come you didn't ask me? There are lots of reasons but they're mainly to do with the architectural journalists; you don't ask me because they don't. And the reasons they don't are complex. There's a strange psychodynamic between architect and critic. The critic's reward comes from crowning kings—finding and announcing the heroes of architecture. The architectural historian, Siegfried Gideon, was the great king maker of the modern movement in architecture. In his writings he emphasized some early moderns and ignored others. Many critics since then have seen crowning as their role, but their self-esteem would derive little benefit from anointing a woman, and perhaps even less, a pair. There's no psychic reward in crowning a mom and pop king.

BLDS: There have been significant opportunities that you, Robert, have turned down because the honor, the crown, was offered only to you. Would you comment on that?

RV: I've turned some

> Architecture is, more than the other arts, collaborative. I think it's probably right that Beethoven would not have had a partner. The same goes for a poet. But architecture is different.

down. The Pritzker Prize I accepted. I probably shouldn't have without Denise. Later, I was informally but explicitly approached for the gold medal of the American Institute of Architects but they would not award it to two people, for the reasons Denise has just mentioned. I think the romantic idea of the artist as sole genius still exists in architecture. Many architects seem to believe that, to be really good, you have to be original and you have to be alone—preferably in an ivory tower—which is significantly difficult for an architect, given the collaborative nature of our work.

BLDS: But isn't it widely acknowledged that architecture is a collaborative effort?

RV: Absolutely. That's the other irony. Architecture is, more than the other arts, collaborative. I think it's probably right that Beethoven would not have had a partner. The same goes for a poet. But architecture is different.

DSB: There are even some artists who paint together.

BLDS: You have been married and partners since 1967. Do you ever attempt to leave your work at the office, or is your life so seamless it just floats along with the two of you?

DSB: I see my career as everything I do. It's being a homemaker, being a mother, a teacher, plus the many different careers I have at the office.

BLDS: And what are they?

DSB: I'm a principal in the office. I'm an architect and a planner, so I work on projects in both fields. All of us share management. We don't have an office manager or managing partner. Running our kind of business is a way of life as well as a living. Keeping it all going is a challenging job—trying to make beautiful buildings yet at the same time ensuring we don't lose our shirts, and also wanting to help the people in our firm feel a sense of individual achievement—it needs creativity, too. Bob and I both work on management, but I tend to set up the systems. I work out the structure and sharing of management in the office. There are big and small things I have to do in public relations, office systems, and general troubleshooting. If I see a problem I will try to move in and help find a way to solve it, then move out and leave others to run it.

RV: Ironically, one of the prices we pay for having our own firm, and therefore control of what we do, is that we must do an awful lot of noncreative, business-oriented work. I enjoy saying an architect must be a lawyer, a psychiatrist, a business executive, a salesperson, an actor—all of these, and more than ever before. We try to share some of those roles. Here, too, the architect is not necessarily a sole genius. The concept of the architect or artist as a hero is another derived from the Romantic movement. Modern architecture took it up, formulating an image of the architect as revolutionary hero and encouraging the idea that to be good, you had to be original. But we take a stand that's pragmatic, not ideological, and not heroic. When I was young, Vincent Scully said, "You're an antihero." I loved that. This is a more difficult role to play than that of the unambiguous hero. It makes you more difficult to define and less interesting for journalists to write about. Le Corbusier essentially said tear down Paris (except for the Ile de la Cité) and begin all over again with high-rise slab buildings set in parks. Frank Lloyd Wright said essentially the same thing in promoting Broadacre City, which was to be completely controlled by himself. Wright ironically claimed to be within the traditions of Emersonian American individualism, even as he tried to design everything. If he could have, he would have designed the women's clothes, the automobiles, and the furniture, unifying everything within his own motival order. Our role has been more pragmatic. We accept and rely on convention; we don't start all over again as overt originators. We take the everyday and ordinary as our point of departure. Many great artists have done that. Pop artists adapted the conventional and ordinary. The realist painters painted bohemians in cafes rather than gods or aristocrats in arcadia. We work in the tradition of the bohemians in cafes. This modest approach makes our work unusual and hard to define and makes life difficult for us.

BLDS: In what way difficult? There is a widespread view that there is none other like Venturi and Scott Brown. Obviously, not everything that one has in mind, in life or in work, is achieved. Are your expectations realistic?

RV: Well, I think we are in a period of hype sensibility. Music is loud, paintings are big, women's clothes have big shoulders and short skirts (at least, they did last year). There's a sensibility that connects with nonsubtle things. I don't think this is necessarily bad. It relates to directions our work has taken, toward commercial and iconographic art—including its dissonance; but it does make for art that is not obviously new.

BLDS: Let's talk about your relationship for a moment. You have been working together and living together for thirty years now. What has changed or has not changed in that thirty years of Venturi, Scott Brown and Associates? And who has the last word in your collaborations?

DSB: Over the years we've changed. Some architects are doing today what we were doing thirty, twenty, and ten years ago. Through that process our work has gained acceptance, but our followers get more opportunity than we do because we're always at an edge, which many potential clients find unacceptable.

BLDS: That's probably true. The younger generation has taken advantage of your ideas and you have gone ahead.

DSB: Yes.

RV: The other day I found myself saying, If you're lucky you live long enough to see your good ideas become bad ideas —as they are misinterpreted or perverted.

DSB: Your followers sometimes get to do it first. Yet we've had amazing opportunities. In a sense, we've had several careers in one career because the nature of our projects has changed. Although we've seldom found work in markets we've targeted, ones we have not noticed have found us. We've worked mostly on academic buildings, and we fit well with academics; but lab design, an area that we now have great experience in, was not something we looked for. A marriage was made between a firm of lab specialists and ourselves by a client. In another market, museums, we did spot one particular case, the Sainsbury Wing. The other museums found us.

BLDS: It seems to me museums would be a natural expression of a range of your interests. Your expertise in art history is dazzling, as you know. You have the ability to invoke many periods, many references. Do you identify yourselves as artists, architects, or both? Denise, why don't you start?

The word *architect* refers to one who works within a certain kind of artistic medium. So we consider ourselves artists.

DSB: There's an artistic dimension to what we do, but there are many other aspects to our work as well, and we may be in trouble if a client thinks we're interested in aesthetics alone. Yet, the artistry is extremely important to us; it makes everything else worth doing. It is difficult to define where art lies in architecture. For us as architects, and as the kind of architects we are, there are many ways of being artists.

RV: I think a composer is an artist, and an architect is an artist. I think the word *architect* refers to one who works within a certain kind of artistic medium. So we consider ourselves artists. But it's true that there are different types of careers inherent in our profession. Nowadays you have multiple clients who very often are committees. Architects have always had to work with committees, but much more so now. There are also whole areas of technical and financial considerations. So it's extremely complex, and the complexities may tempt you to be less an artist and to compromise your art. There's such a thing as good compromise, which connects with reality and also requires tolerance, and there's bad compromise, which is the easy way out. But most difficult for us is, as Denise says, that we have always been a little ahead and are hard to take. Even now, our approach is not well accepted, though I believe it will be within a few years. What we're doing now is not totally different from what you've seen in our work for many, many years; we're just being more explicit about it now.

BLDS: What is it?

RV: Let's put it this way: One of the essential characteristics of modern art and architecture has been abstraction. Modern art discarded iconography and symbolism as horrible leftovers from the past, and modern architecture, in general, had little concern for graphics, even less for iconography and symbolism. In actuality, reference and symbolism were present in modern architecture because, in the early part of the century, European architects appropriated the vernacular industrial architecture of American factories. They felt these buildings were beautiful, and applied their industrial formal vocabulary to social housing and other buildings. Ironically, when it was brought back here with a European polish, this factory vocabulary suited the industrial overtones of corporate capitalist architecture. But architects pretended that the vocabulary and the form derived from function, not refer-

172

ence. Yet there is a long tradition of symbolism and iconography in architecture: Egyptian temples and pylons were covered with hieroglyphics; beautiful mosaics adorned the interiors of Early Christian basilicas. Mosaics were decoration applied to a generic form of architecture, but they weren't only decorative. If you were a Christian you could read them and understand why one saint was next to another. Baroque architecture, too, was highly scenograph-ic. Our idea is to return to scenography and iconography, but to use a truly up-to-date technology. Industrial technology is out now; we all know we are no longer in an industrial age. The beautiful old factories that line the rail tracks from Philadelphia to New York are in ruins. The technology of now is electronic. In Japan, especially Tokyo, you see the mosaics of today—great electronic screens used for commercial purposes. As modern architecture once learned from an industrial source, we can now learn from a commercial source, soon to be considered as no more debased than the industrial. We have learned much from the commercial vernacular. Its electronic technology will be understood as appropriate for architecture in a few years.

BLDS: Before we begin discussing specifically your distinguished careers, could you each describe what initially sparked your interest in architecture and urban design? When and where did it happen? Is it the same thing that drives you today?

DSB: When I was about four years old, I wanted to be an architect. My mother had studied architecture for two years at the University of the Witwatersrand, in South Africa. She had been part of the early modern movement there.

BLDS: I know just where "Wits" is. Did you have a view of the Lutyens museum building from where you lived? I was thinking that splendid building obviously influenced you more than I realized.

DSB: I knew the building. In fact, we lived quite near Lutyens's war memorial in Johannesburg. My mother's classmates included the greats of early modern architecture in South Africa. In his *Oeuvres complètes,* I think the 1936 volume, Le Corbusier writes to a certain Rex Martienssen, a young modern architect in South Africa. If I remember, he says, "Can you find a Creosus who could

give us all a job and I would come out and work with you?" It never happened, but my mother's school friends were part of that group. My parents built a house in what we now call the International Style. I was perhaps three years old and I can remember seeing the blueprints; they were the traditional blueprints with white lines. As a child, I knew my mother had studied architecture and I thought it was women's work. When I got to architecture school I said, What are all these men doing here?

BLDS: It may end up being women's work.

DSB: It could be, eventually. In grade school I wanted to be a teacher like my teacher. A normal pattern. Then I began to love books and words and wanted to write.

BLDS: Was your father an architect, as well?

DSB: No, a businessman. About the time I went to architecture school, a few years after World War II, he started to be a developer; so he was building buildings while I was studying how to design them. I also wanted to study languages when I was young. As a child I didn't know city planning existed, so I didn't dream of being a planner. A few years ago, reexamining my childhood ambitions, I realized that I have, in fact, done most of them, though it's all been through architecture—if you take a broad view of what constitutes architecture. This relates to our problem of being difficult to define. I say I'm an architect of particularly broad scope who likes to be profound, and Bob is an architect with a particularly focused stance who likes to be broad. Bob and I share the core of our profession, though we take different approaches to it, related to other dimensions in our lives. Although each of us understands and sympathizes with the other's outlook, we offer different areas of thought derived from particular personal interests. We think this makes our collaboration richer. With clients in particular, I can watch the reaction to an explanation Bob has given and, if needed, find a second explanation to reinforce the first. He can do the same for me. A client once said, "If you have Bob Venturi and Denise Scott Brown together you have double your

> I'm an architect of particularly broad scope who likes to be profound, and Bob is an architect with a particularly focused stance who likes to be broad.

173

problem."

BLDS: You double your—

DSB: Richness.

BLDS: Denise, did you ever consider the possibility that you are penalized for the clarity and forcefulness of your thought?

RV: Yes.

DSB: It could very well be. Another client said, "Whenever this committee asks you a question you give wonderful reasons for what you do, and all the reasons are utterly convincing. Then we look back at the building and we still don't like it."

RV: We have a difficult role and it's probably because we are mannerist architects; we tend to do things in ways that are hard at first to understand. I'd love to tell you how I became an architect.

BLDS: I'd like to hear that.

RV: It's a corny story, but it's actually true. I cannot ever remember not wanting to be an architect. I had favorite buildings I looked out for on the way to grade school. My dad was an immigrant from Abruzzi, Italy, and his family brought him here when he was nine. He always wanted to be an architect, but he couldn't be. Anyhow, I learned a few years ago something I'd never known, from an architectural historian in Philadelphia, who referred to the plans for a fruit store for Robert Venturi in 1909, by the architect Phineas Paiste. Phineas Paiste was a well-known architect in Philadelphia. My father was twenty-eight in 1909 and he was poor. He hadn't finished high school, he had to work in the family business; yet he got one of the best architects, the architect of the Bellevue-Stratford Hotel built about five years earlier, to design his fruit store.

BLDS: Did he build it?

RV: It was never built. It was just a project. But in 1922 another locally well-known architect, Edwin Brumbaugh, built the Venturi, Inc. warehouse. Phineas Paiste had gone to Florida and designed most of the architecture in Coral Gables. When I was a small boy he returned on a visit and came to dinner at our house. He was an old man, but he got on the floor on his knees and built a beautiful building for me out of blocks. I loved to play with blocks. The story goes that, when the building was finished, I swept it aside and said, "Now let me show you how to do it." Phineas Paiste took it very well. I was completely influenced by my father, and my mother was also interested in art. That's why I became an architect.

BLDS: I have a question that I'd like to ask you, Denise. Do you think most people don't realize you are an architect, as well?

DSB: Yes, although I've had years of architectural education, earned several qualifying degrees, and have taught architecture. I don't know what more I can do.

BLDS: Perhaps you could describe the evolution of your own educational life, the path that took you from Johannesburg to London, to Pennsylvania, to California, and back to Philadelphia; and if you would, for my own interest, I'd love to know how influential Sir Edwin Lutyens was on your life while you were growing up.

DSB: I finished high school and entered university when I was sixteen, in 1948. I took a first year of liberal arts because everyone said I was too young to start architecture. That same year I started working in an architect's office and did so every summer while I was in South Africa. South African architecture students were required to spend their fourth year in an architect's office, at home or elsewhere. I decided to work in England. I fully intended to return to South Africa. I was an African xenophobe. As a child, I reacted against the tendency in South Africa during the 1940s to be dominated culturally by England. I believed that what I saw around me—the city, and a particular city, Johannesburg—was beautiful. I questioned why our Christmas cards should illustrate rural English snow scenes when we had Christmas in midsummer in South Africa.

BLDS: Had you been to England before that?

DSB: As a small child.

BLDS: From where was your family?

DSB: Lithuania and Latvia, at the turn of the century. My mother was born and grew up in Southern Rhodesia, an English colony. Her mother returned to Europe in the 1930s and we joined her in England when I was five. This trip left an indelible impression on my mind.

BLDS: There was a big migration from Lithuania and Latvia to southern Africa in that period. If I recall, Nadine Gordimer's family moved there then, as well.

DSB: Yes. Most South African Jews' origins were Lithuanian. Ours was part Latvian. The distance between the two was small, but it seems to have made a difference to my family. My grandmother went to the wilds of Africa as a mail-order bride. Have you seen the film *The Flame Trees of Thika*? I laughed when I saw it because it was so close to my grandparents' experience—the piano coming across the river on an oxcart, for example, or taking tea poured from a silver teapot in a mud house. My mother has her mother's teapot in Geneva, where she now lives. It was made in Birmingham. Rhodesia of the 1900s and 1910s was perhaps like the American West in the 1840s.

BLDS: Have you been back to South Africa?

DSB: Not since 1970. Although the South Africa I grew up in was dependent artistically on England, as a child I had an art teacher who said, "You can't be really creative unless you paint what you see around you." Now I think she was only half right, but she had a strong influence on my life at that stage. And that's the view I took to Las Vegas: Understand the landscape you see around you and use it artistically.

BLDS: How would you amend that thought now?

DSB: By noting that the language she and I spoke was English and that there was, in fact, in South Africa an oscillation among several metropolitan cultures, several colonial cultures, and numerous exuberant indigenous cultures. All were important. However, it seems to me that Africans and Americans alike remained colonials of the mind long after achieving political independence. We see it even now as we try to practice an American art. Those who come from overseas with European accents and portfolios have more cachet here than the second-generation "ethnics."

BLDS: But didn't that "outsider value" work for you at one point?

DSB: It doesn't seem to have helped us professionally, perhaps because I've been here a long time or because I'm assigned my husband's identity. But on one occasion being an outsider did help. Some members of the London National Gallery client group, in the early stages of our project, saw me, I think, as a cross-continental translator who could help them understand American practice.

BLDS: Can you continue the account of your intellectual journey from South Africa to America?

DSB: I had left to work my fourth year in England in an architect's office. I found a job with Frederick Gibberd in London. At the same time, I took the entrance exam to the Architectural Association school of architecture. I had read about it and it seemed fun, but I thought it wasn't a serious place and that, anyway, I wouldn't get in. When I was accepted I entered the Final School at the AA with some sorrow because I'd left behind a love in South Africa who was finishing architecture school: Robert Scott Brown. But I felt fate was pushing me. At the AA I was drawn to the thinking of the Brutalists, a group of young architects who were part of

the English *Look Back in Anger* generation. The AA was a tinderbox of architectural excitement. It was also rife with postwar social abrasion. The brightest students there had won major scholarships from their local communities. They found themselves at odds with the public school, i.e., private school, students. In our group were the brightest scholarship people and some rebels from public schools. They say the English are tolerant of the manners of colonials and gardeners. As a colonial and a woman I was not part of the schisms that split the school, and could move between groups.

BLDS: During which years were you there?

DSB: 1952 through 1955.

BLDS: And from the mid-fifties to the mid-sixties where were you?

DSB: In 1954, as soon as he had graduated, Robert Scott Brown joined me in London. We took a course in tropical architecture together at the AA, then found jobs and got married. We worked in architectural firms in London for about six months, then set off for Europe in the spring of 1956. Altogether I had been in England just over four years. For about nine months we traveled through Europe in a Morgan three-wheeler sports car, usually camping in fields at night. In Venice we attended a summer school for young architects and then we wintered in Rome, working for an architect and learning Italian. We returned to South Africa to visit and work for a year. In 1958 we left for the U.S. and the University of Pennsylvania. We chose Penn because Peter Smithson, the Brutalist guru, said the only place to continue studying was America and the only place to study in America was the University of Pennsylvania, because Louis Kahn taught at Penn's Graduate School of Fine Arts. In England and Europe, at that time, if you were a good architect you were interested in city planning. Our model was Le Corbusier, who, as a young architect, built a small house for his mother while developing his ideas for the Ville Radieuse. Another important influence in England at the time was John Summerson. I attended his lectures on English classical architecture at the AA. That's when I became interested in Lutyens. Lutyens's work tied in with the Brutalists' evolving sense of perversity. Summerson described Lutyens as a mannerist, one who deftly broke the rules of architecture. When Robert Scott Brown and I returned to South Africa, we took with us a perverse enjoyment in breaking the rules, a knowledge and experience of Italian Mannerist architecture, a love of the early modern movement and what Peter Smithson called a "whiff of the powder" of its revolutionary ardor, and a keen social conscience, particularly when it came to Africa and its problems. Social housing and urbanism in developing areas had been important components of our education in England. We applied to Penn's department of city planning because we believed good architects, socially concerned ones, should work at an urban scale. But in America it was different. We found Louis Kahn did not teach in the planning department. We tried to change to Lou's class but our advisor said, "With your interests, an American planning background could be useful for your careers. Stay in planning and I'll help you get the best out of Kahn as well."

BLDS: Were you planning to return to South Africa?

DSB: Yes. We were very idealistic. Robert Scott Brown was a brilliant and talented architect and a true South African patriot. We had intended to work together somewhere in Africa, probably in housing, but when he was killed at the end of our first year, I returned to Penn and finished, then stayed at Penn and taught. As the AA had been in the early fifties, Penn's city planning department was a hotbed of interesting social and economic thought in the early sixties. Herbert Gans and Paul Davidoff were there. I feel the New Left started there. Relating the social and the physical in architecture and urbanism has always been important to me, first as a South African with a conscience and harking back to my art teacher; then in England where the Brutalists said, "Look at the life of the streets and build for it"; and then forward to Herbert Gans. By the time Bob Venturi and I met, I had a series of interests that paralleled his. As a fellow at the American Academy in Rome, he had come to love Roman Renaissance and particularly Mannerist architecture. He was, I felt, the only architecture colleague who understood the tension between the social and the physical that I was experiencing in the planning department. His mother had been a socialist and a pacifist. He had marched on Washington. Our collegiality covered the artistic and the social. Both aesthetic and social issues spurred our development. When I first visited Las Vegas in 1965 it was because the social planners admonished, "If people are voting for Las Vegas with their feet by going there, why are you architects scornful?" They suggested we try to learn why people liked it. Also, my father had been there and loved it. So I went and I adored it, but felt, as well, a shiver—was it hate or love? That's the aesthetic question. I both hated and loved it and asked myself, What is this place? Why does it so intrigue me? I felt I must learn more about it.

BLDS: Did you have the same reaction, Robert?

RV: Yes, I had the reaction of love/hate and absolute fascination.

We enjoyed saying in the late sixties that we had gone from Rome to Las Vegas.

BLDS: Could you also comment on your mother being a socialist and a pacifist? How was that obvious as you were growing up?

RV: It steered me in the direction of being interested in liberal causes and made me somewhat comfortable as an outsider.

BLDS: What did she do?

RV: I never went to a public school. I went to private schools because in Pennsylvania public schools you had to pledge allegiance to the flag.

BLDS: Is that how you became a Quaker?

RV: She became a member of the Society of Friends largely because of the Quaker position on pacifism. I went to Quaker meetings on Sundays, and to Episcopal chapel at my school during the week. I also licked stamps for the Pennsylvania Women's Committee for Total Disarmament. It disbanded around 1940. In 1954 through 1956 I became a temporary expatriate in Rome at the American Academy. There I was very involved in Mannerism, as Denise said, and in Baroque architecture, in the architecture of urban spaces, and in Michelangelo. I also became interested in looking at America from the perspective of Europe. There was a tradition of expatriate American writers, Henry James being the first. Not to be pretentious, but I think this was why I could, after Rome, look at Main Street and go to Las Vegas. I could see America from a more objective viewpoint and become intrigued by what was everyday American because I was steeped in the beauties of Italian historical architecture. In one way, in taking to the ordinary, I paralleled the Pop artists. To this day we are interested in the everyday landscape, the ordinary scene, the gridiron pattern of streets, and the genius of the American city. We're happier than if we hated everything we saw around us. I remember reading Vincent Scully's book on what he called the Shingle Style, an architecture that was not much appreciated when he wrote about it. That started me looking at the everyday. Recently I went back to Columbus, Indiana. They're making a movie about it and wanted to interview me in front of a firehouse that we did there in the late sixties, which had a sign on it and a false facade with an ornamental pattern. That was unheard-of. It did not look heroic and original; it looked simple and ordinary. As a matter of fact, driving up from Cincinnati, we approached the town via the very street the building is on, and we missed it. We went beyond it. It's so ordinary that I missed it!

BLDS: Do you consider that a testimonial to your work?

RV: I think it was, yes.

DSB: The city has built up around the building. It was surrounded by empty space at the beginning.

BLDS: Both of you acknowledged the influence of your families in shaping your sensibilities, and I wonder if you would now acknowledge your own role in reshaping not only the contemporary house, but the skyline, and ushering in what is most often referred to as postmodern architecture.

RV: I worry about being called postmodern. Denise and I look askance at architects or artists who name their own style. There are moments when you do that. I'm sure the Futurists who wrote manifestos in the early part of the century had reason to do so; now it's trite. So we don't call ourselves postmodernists. We sometimes pretentiously say, "Marx didn't consider himself a Marxist and Freud wasn't a Freudian."

BLDS: How do you identify yourself?

RV: I think we're pragmatists.

DSB: We're modernists.

RV: We are modernists. That phrase I mentioned earlier: if you're lucky enough to live long enough, you see how your good ideas become bad; it applies to us. I think much of what we have said has been misinterpreted and misused. In the book *Complexity and Contradiction,* reference to history involved analogy. It was a method of analysis: We can learn from aspects of historical buildings or from historical trends. But it was taken literally, as an invitation to ad-lib with historical architecture. We feel unhappy with what we believe is the misdirection that resulted from some of the directions we took. Perhaps many who have been influential feel the good they suggested has gone bad.

DSB: Also, postmodernism took selectively from our ideas.

BLDS: For example?

DSB: The social basis for what we did, which was strongly defined in *Learning from Las Vegas,* was not noticed by the postmodernists. They missed our claim that a new aesthetic derives from changed sensibilities, which in turn derive from a way of life that has changed, probably in relation to social movements. I feel our new perceptions emerged from the churning up of this country by the civil rights movement in the 1960s. That was when we put these ideas together and made some kind of a whole for ourselves. That whole was eroded and trivialized, not augmented, by the postmodernists.

> Denise and I look askance at architects or artists who name their own style.

> . . . if you're lucky you live long enough to see your good ideas become bad ideas . . .

BLDS: Denise said the postmodernists were selective, but you had an even harsher indictment; you said superficial. What do you mean by that?

RV: They use the form without understanding its substance and meaning. The term *context* is used a lot today. I used it in the title of my master's thesis at Princeton, presented in 1950.

BLDS: And the title of your thesis?

RV: *Context in Architectural Composition.* Now context has become cliché. In those days, virtually no architect considered the setting of a building as relevant. Generally architects designed, as they said, from the inside out. But I thought architects should design from the outside in as well as the inside out, that a building must inevitably connect with its context, and I referred to Gestalt psychology and its theories of meaning and perception. Today design review boards and historical commissions have gone too far the other way. They decree all buildings must be designed historically and symbolically to match the neighborhood or the building next door. They have made a good idea a bad idea by taking it to an extreme. In some contexts buildings may be very different from each other and yet embrace contextual harmony. In the Piazza San Marco, for example, you have a Byzantine cathedral, a Gothic palazzo, and a Renaissance library. The current use of contextualism is a misunderstanding. It narrows and oversimplifies the possibilities of context and its results are awful in our eyes.

BLDS: You have often said that, unlike Frank Lloyd Wright, you don't think that a building should be built from the inside out, meaning that the first intended uses of its interior spaces should determine a building's form. You also said that a building should be designed from the inside out *and* the outside in. How does the building's program contribute to your idea of design? What other elements contribute?

RV: Well, I think you look for a balance. Very often a tension results from acknowledging clients' demands on the inside and clients' and others' demands on the outside. Outside demands are especially important in the city. But that doesn't mean you should make the outside of your building analogous to the outside of the building next door. There may be a need for revolutionary change in the context of a given place. Putting a Renaissance building beside a Byzantine cathedral in San Marco produced harmony—the kind that comes from contrast. American cities are full of that. Our gridiron streets are absolutely rigid and consistent, then all hell breaks loose within the grid. The buildings may sit perfectly correctly along the street and form the space of the street, but each may be very different from the next. All sorts of American individuality happens. It's a complex thing.

DSB: There's another way of considering inside-out and outside-in. The program usually defines the usable spaces of a building, but to move between those spaces requires circulation space, which usually isn't defined in the program. The circulation element is particularly important in the design of institutional buildings. It can become the foreground, the positive element, rather than the background, of the building. In both our National Gallery extension and the Seattle Art Museum the circulation system of each must accommodate hundreds of people. It's like a processional street that runs through the building, and it's designed and detailed to feel like an outside street. It sets the tone and character of the building. The interplay between public and private in the city interests us enormously. Streets are the largest part of the urban public sector. Public buildings and open spaces sit within the web of public streets and sidewalks. Public and private meet at the building facade. Immediately behind the facade are the building's most public spaces, through which most people pass as they enter. Even in a private house the public rooms—the parlor or living room—are near the entrance, and in a public building private spaces are kept away from the public circulation. These distinctions are also part of the outside-inside relationship.

BLDS: You have said that in order to perceive the ideal you must acknowledge the real. Is that form follows function, or is it a contradiction of what you said earlier?

DSB: No, I don't think so. We like to see a building as a system that approximates an ideal form, but gets distorted to face reality. The plans of classical buildings are often distorted in this way to fit irregular sites. Walls may be canted, bays uneven; what seems like a set of organized axes may, in fact, lead you along an irregular path; your experience is not as rectilinear as you think. That has fascinated us. We think setting up a system then breaking it to deal with reality makes architecture human—and much more interesting.

BLDS: How would you describe the current period in architecture; and, as we approach the millennium, what do you envision that we have in store for us?

DSB: Mal de siècle: the naming of architectural flurries and eddies as schools of thought to gain attention. Architects labeling their own school before they've ever designed a building. That's got to be a late-twentieth-century malaise.

BLDS: And what did the Brutalists do?

DSB: There's a mythology on the origins of that name. The Festival of Britain architects called themselves the New Humanists, and Peter and Alison Smithson, casting around for a definition of their work, said something like, "We're against this humanist thing. We're not the New Humanists, we're the New Brutalists." It was a self-mocking term. The Brutalists were steeped in the 1920s. They named themselves as the Futurists, Vorticists, or Constructivists had done. It wasn't for (or was hardly for) promotional reasons, as happens now. They were revolutionaries.

RV: I very much agree with Denise that one of the main problems today is overtheorizing. Now we have *archconcepture*, not architecture. To oversimplify, there's an overemphasis first on the technical aspects of building, then on concept. There's too much theorizing, too much paper architecture. We are in the last decadent throes of modernism—Deconstructionism. It reflects the overemphasis on theory. The contortions of Decon architecture involve using architectural elements that were originally functional or structural as decoration. There's an overemphasis on abstraction and a cynical misuse of functional and structural elements for purposes of ornament in sentimental adaptations of an earlier industrial vocabulary. Applying exposed steel-frame trusses to the facade of your building is no less historical than applying Renaissance pilasters. There's also an overemphasis on signature architecture in contrast to a generic architecture, whose rooms and interiors are generalized and not original in form and provide a system that accommodates rather than follows function. In a generic architecture, aesthetic effect may derive from the appliqué of symbolism, the honest appliqué of iconography on the building. Much iconography now will be for night architecture and will connect with new electronic technologies for lighting. The aesthetic sparkle will come from the LED systems the Japanese have promoted.

BLDS: Did you say night architecture?

RV: Yes, night.

BLDS: Would you like to expand on that?

RV: We've designed a building in Philadelphia for the so-called Avenue of the Arts, that is, Broad Street refurbished to be a nighttime boulevard for the performing arts.

BLDS: Did you conceptualize this, or did they come to you with this idea?

DSB: The idea has been around Philadelphia for over thirty years.

RV: Now it is being explicitly promoted. Most concert halls, even the very latest ones, are like the Parthenon, in that their form is designed to be lit by and perceived by daylight, by sunlight. How you see them at night is incidental. In our design the building is made to be a lantern. Its essential aesthetic quality comes from being used and seen at night. The effect at night will be at least as important as the effect by day. The building will give information at eye level using various information media, the way theaters do today.

DSB: Through posters and a marquee.

RV: But we're making the marquee and the posterboards electronic. They'll be constantly moving and they'll have the sparkling quality of mosaics.

BLDS: You have reinforced today something that you've said and written often: A lot of art has to do with finding the ordinary extraordinary. Surely you did that and found merit in the commercial sprawl of Las Vegas. Now that Las Vegas is among the leading family vacation spots, changing its image and its look, is there anything else we should be learning from it? I consider the transformation a miracle of marketing.

RV: Denise once said Las Vegas gives people a chance to pretend they're wicked for a while; now they pretend they're wholesome. A couple of years ago the BBC invited us to visit Las Vegas with a film crew to comment on the changes since we wrote *Learning from Las Vegas* in the early 1970s. Essentially, the city has been Disneyfied. Its neon-sign imagery has been replaced by Disney-like scenography.

BLDS: It is a theme park. And electronics drive it. Douglas Trumbull has done remarkable special effects, and the technology is there everywhere.

RV: That's right.

DSB: It is.

RV: Neon is now old-fashioned.

BLDS: There is an almost Teatro Olympico vision of things in Las Vegas. It's quite extraordinary, but there's no content that backs up the remarkable ability to do or make things. So we need people like you to be collaborating with people like them.

DSB: We talk so much about iconography that our clients have learned to use the word. But they often say, "Please take it off."

BLDS: So you need a new word. With your interest in the ordinary, there was certainly nothing ordinary about one of your early works, a seminal work of modern architecture, and that, of course, is the house you designed for your mother, the Vanna Venturi house.

DSB: It went back to an old tradition.

RV: The house was an example of complexity and contradiction. It involved layering, redundancy, explicitly appliquéd ornament, and complexity and contradiction in the plan. There was also, incidentally, some historical reference. It was the first house after modernism that had a gabled front. In those days you either did a flat roof or you did what's called a shed roof, but never a roof with a gable. The house had a symbolic dimension. It *looked* like a house, with a chimney, a front door, and windows—somewhat like a house drawn by a child, an elemental house. We are very interested in the idea of architecture as shelter, in the shelter aspect of, for example, Japanese traditional architecture. The neo-modern, post-postmodernism of today is essentially architecture as sculpture. Sculpture left out in the rain. People forget that, hey, architecture is essentially shelter. It is a place with a roof to protect us from rain, cold, and heat.

BLDS: Left out in the rain—does that also imply "shrunk" in terms of purposefulness?

RV: I think it was Frank Lloyd Wright who said, "Philip Johnson designs his buildings and then leaves them out in the rain."

BLDS: And do you recall how he got back at him?

RV: I can imagine.

DSB: What did he say?

BLDS: He said that Frank Lloyd Wright was the most distinguished architect of the nineteenth century.

DSB: It's true.

RV: That's right.

BLDS: We've talked about Robert's first major project, the house for his mother. What was yours, Denise?

DSB: My career began differently. At Penn I was a full-time teacher while Bob was a part-time one. When he was designing his first major project I was walking into my department chair's office and saying, "I may not be ready for this, but I have to teach my own studio." I was evolving a form of teaching that I have used ever since. It was, in a way, like setting up and heading a small planning agency, with all the interdisciplinary faculty that go with it and the need for hand-holding that goes with that. This was later the basis for our Las Vegas studio. I'd worked on architectural projects in various stages in offices in England, Europe, and South Africa. When I joined Venturi and Rauch, as the firm was then known, my projects became their projects. My first project in the firm was planning for South Street in 1968. It was an advocacy project. We worked as volunteers with a series of mainly low-income communities to help stop an expressway on South Street in Philadelphia.

RV: And succeeded in stopping the project.

DSB: Yes. I've since conducted over twenty planning and programming projects but you don't hear about them because for the most part they're unpublished. One was for the historic district of Jim Thorpe in Pennsylvania and another was for Washington Avenue in Miami Beach. We were the people who named the Deco District, in 1973, when we started agitating to save it. I've done a plan for downtown Memphis and several for Philadelphia.

RV: A lot of this stuff doesn't materialize, unfortunately.

DSB: Yes. I've also planned five blocks of property owned by the Houston Museum of Fine Arts and made a district plan and urban design for the Denver Civic Center cultural complex.

BLDS: Would it be fair, then, to say that you each have special areas of interest: that you, Denise, are more involved in urban planning than in other issues, and that perhaps you, Robert, are more the theorist?

RV: Well, I'm more the building architect and she's more the planner—we're both theorists and urban designers.

DSB: I am principal in charge of urban and campus planning and programming projects in the office. Bob is principal in charge of architectural projects. We're both responsible for urban design. I am a lot more involved with our architectural projects than Bob is with our planning projects. As planner or urban designer I may help determine the basic layout of important buildings in an urban or campus plan. These may then be presided over by Bob as architecture projects in our office. Where planning ends and architecture begins in these projects is not clear, and on many I continue my collaboration into the details. I love to work in the office on both my professions, and also to go down to the millimeter with Bob on some of our decorative-arts projects.

BLDS: Why don't we go through a typical project, if there is such a thing. Why don't we try to walk through it from the client contact to the negotiations, the design, the rework, the presentation, the construction. Also, add all those planning boards that you imply have more to do with designing and shaping a building than you prefer to think they have a right to.

RV: There is no typical plan. There are all kinds of clients, and it depends on the client. First of all, you have to get the job; that involves being a salesman and an actor. For many jobs you have to be a good politician. Once you get the job, you work on a contract. Contracts were once fairly easy. We'd use the standard AIA forms, modify a few paragraphs, and that would be it. Now lawyers get in on both sides and contract negotiations go on and on. Then, if you are working for an institution, a trustee might say, "I know an architect who works for four percent." Luckily, that isn't always the case. Most of our clients are universities that are experienced in building.

BLDS: In the main, are they universities?

RV: Yes. Currently we're working on projects at Penn, Harvard, Yale, Princeton, Dartmouth, UCLA, and the Universities of Delaware and Cincinnati. Another trend is for institutions that don't build regularly to retain project managers to represent them. Then you tend to lose the direct relationship between architect and client. The middleman can make it difficult for the architect. The worse the architect looks to the client, the better the middleman looks.

BLDS: When do clients ever give you free rein? Is that just a fantasy or does that ever happen?

DSB: It's a fantasy. If you had totally free rein, you couldn't develop your ideas from the reality of the client's problem and you wouldn't be challenged. But there's the other end of the spectrum.

We have clients who say, "Let's not micromanage the project, but make this yellow, make that red, turn this around, and I want to see it again on Tuesday." On just a few projects we're micromanaged beyond belief, much of it around questions of aesthetics. That's when you're tempted to fantasize that the client will butt out.

RV: Louis Kahn said good architecture requires a good client as well as a good architect. That's where ideally it's collaborative, with the chance of give-and-take. We have often said we get our best ideas from our clients. Of course, it doesn't always work that way; but when it does, it's a beautiful relationship that we love.

BLDS: What or who is the ideal client?

RV: Princeton was a wonderful client. When the university president is interested things usually go well.

BLDS: I assume that works the same way with a corporate client.

RV: Yes.

BLDS: Are major museums akin to corporate clients?

RV: Museums are hard to generalize about. We have had all kinds of museum clients. They can be difficult to work for.

BLDS: I assume their projects would especially challenge you.

RV: Donors may want to place their mark on the building design. This may not help to keep the project rational.

DSB: Sophisticated donors will tell the institution, "This is your baby. You do it the way you want."

BLDS: Does the result and the final product, if you will, ever surprise you upon completion?

RV: Always. I think an honest artist will have to admit there's a lot of surprise, because there's such a jump from the drawings and the models to the reality. It was different in the old days when architects worked with the workmen. Now the whole design has to be perfect and the last screw put down in the contract before construction starts. So, inevitably you're in for some surprises. The details are the hardest part to predict. If you're honest you often say, "Oh, my God, I can't believe. . . ."

BLDS: You've been criticized for that "Oh my God." You've walked through buildings and said all you ever see are the errors and the things that you would do otherwise.

RV: I'm either honest or stupid.

BLDS: Don't you think that's a disarming technique as well?

RV: Pretty awful. I say I'm an exhibitionist—I go around exposing my doubts. But 90 percent of the things I criticize I think other people don't see.

BLDS: How do you respond to criticism?

RV: I usually don't agree with critics on what they criticize. They generally bore or infuriate me.

BLDS: And more frequently?

RV: It depends on the nature of the criticism. The British make me laugh because their criticism tends to be absurd or naive.

BLDS: How about royal criticism?

RV: We didn't get it. The queen and the prince liked the Sainsbury Wing.

DSB: But the British architectural critics didn't. They panned us for not meeting some ideological demands of modern architecture that date from the 1930s and forties. The critical debate that occurred in London in mid-1991 during the Sainsbury Wing opening was named the Second Battle of Trafalgar. On opening night, my African xenophobia tempted me to describe the newspaper brouhaha as "The natives are restless."

BLDS: You had to wait a lifetime to say that!

DSB: That's right.

BLDS: Is there a dream project out there somewhere that's just waiting for you? And do you envision any of these dreams being translated into realities?

RV: We've never been asked to design a high-rise building. I'd love to, but developers don't ask us. Yet the buildings we design are mostly more complex than a high-rise office building.

BLDS: Well, what's so dreamy about a high-rise building? Other than its size, what would be so challenging?

RV: What we would do would probably, in a way, look like what other people have done. I'd love to do a church or a synagogue.

DSB: People who have designed many high-rise buildings tell us, "You would be so bored." We say we'd like the chance to be bored, maybe ten times. It would also help our business survive, because fifty-story buildings with a great deal of repetition, even if the fee is relatively low, earn their architects money and help support their institutional work.

BLDS: So part of this aspiration is pragmatic. It would be, so to speak, the bread and butter of the office, but it certainly would not be the same aesthetic challenge as your other work.

DSB: Not true. Aesthetic interest would come first and pragmatic considerations second. The aesthetic challenge would be on several levels. There's the problem of the ground floor, which must welcome people into a lobby that is public but not civic. It must not have the scale of a city hall, but must be both sturdy and elegant. Its materials must be durable and feel good everywhere people can touch. The attention to detail required in almost all areas of an art-museum building will be given only to the lobby of an office building. That's developer economics. If it's a big building, its main facade must often be different from its sides. The roof must be visible and look good on the city skyline. The facades must be composed of individual elements that are relatively small in scale and not too expensive, yet they must look good and, like a Pointillist painting, add up to a greater whole from a distance. The office floors must offer flexibility and, at the same time, require a degree of standardization. Upper-floor lobbies must be welcoming and public, yet appropriately scaled to their tenants. Also, people must be helped to find their way through the maze of activity of an office-system design. These quasi-urban problems of high-rise buildings we would love to face. However, we noticed during the last recession that the architects who suffered most were those who had seventy-five people in their firm working on two high-rise buildings and both were shelved. They could, perhaps, downsize quickly to five people, but they still had to pay rent on an empty office. Architects can't afford to rely on only one market, particularly if it's in real estate. From that point of view, designing high-rise buildings could hurt, not help.

> Much architecture will now derive light and sparkle from changing iconographic patterns on surfaces, especially on civic buildings, where in the past there were inscribed statements . . .

BLDS: In your latest manifesto, Robert, *Sweet and Sour,* you discussed virtual architecture. Have technology and engineering kept up to speed with your design schemes, or exceeded them?

RV: I don't know because I am not quite literate electronically. Perhaps it's a generational thing. Someone my age really can't understand the details of the tech-

nology of today. We architects still have an obsession with the earlier technology of the industrial revolution. However, I think I can be visionary about the effect of electronic technology on architecture. Much architecture will now derive light and sparkle from changing iconographic patterns on surfaces, especially on civic buildings, where in the past there were inscribed statements, such as the motto on New York's Eighth Avenue post office, or the inscriptions on the facade of the Pantheon, or the statues in the pediment of the Parthenon. In each case there's an iconographic message separate from the form and space of the architecture. I think we are about to come back to appliqués of information on buildings. Ours won't be for eternity, but will change. The informational elements will derive from electronic technology and LED systems. The pixels of today can be the equivalent of the tesserae of the mosaics of yesterday.

BLDS: Is this theory the influence of your trips to Japan?

RV: To some extent, but also the influence of American commercial signs and buildings, too. It's something we've been considering for years.

BLDS: Instead of a hand-painted sign there is an electronic image that keeps moving.

RV: Yes. Ours will move, too. There are dangers with iconography. Hitler and Mussolini used iconographics with fascist wording.

BLDS: Colors, too.

RV: Right. But one advantage we have is that we can erase our iconography.

DSB: We don't believe in being technologically advanced just for the sake of it; on the other hand, we wouldn't mind tweaking today's technology a little, giving it a push in directions we think could be good for a building. But that's at another level.

BLDS: To your mind, did architecture ever make that great leap beyond shelter and/or symbolism?

DSB: You mean to this new technology?

RV: It will make the leap. It will get back to symbolism. Generic architecture is the shelter; it's the practical, underneath part. You're not original, you're just sensible. Then you apply the art to it. In this we can learn so much from our everyday landscape. A hundred years from now people are going to be bidding in antique auction sales on today's billboards as great examples of American craft art.

DSB: And McDonald's signs.

RV: And McDonald's signs.

BLDS: They are already ready for museumization. One of the difficulties with these large signs is storage.

RV: Storage and maintenance, too. Forty percent of the cost of a building today goes into mechanical equipment to heat and cool it. That's why our buildings can't be clad in the nice materials that were specified before. Also, there are enormous maintenance costs. It's true that this new iconography probably won't last 2,000 years like the Parthenon figures, but that's the way we are.

BLDS: In addition to technology, what did you learn from Tokyo?

RV: That's a huge subject. Essentially we learned about the validity of chaos, or apparent chaos, and that Tokyo rather than New York is the city of now—for its enormously dissonant juxtapositions of little and big, of varying symbol systems, and for its complex and contradictory, even deconstructive, order. Here deconstruction makes sense. Tokyo is also important for its city planning, modern buildings, and historical lessons about the value of shelter. That's putting it very, very quickly.

BLDS: Forgive my presumption, but I think that Tokyo is not the city of now. I think its moment in many ways has passed. Hong Kong is the city of now. And potentially Singapore or, way down the road, Kuala Lumpur, in Malaysia. As you watch the deconstruction of Japanese society you realize that it is not the front edge of now. That place, I believe, is really Hong Kong, and I think it has been for nearly a decade.

DSB: Hong Kong must be fascinating.

BLDS: The Pritzker bronze medal has three words inscribed on it: Firmness, Commodity, and Delight. This is part of Sir Henry Wotton's seventeenth-century treatise on the elements of architecture. Those were the three conditions of architecture. Is there anything that you would add to that? You said earlier that perhaps you shouldn't have accepted the prize. Would you comment on that?

RV: "Firmness, Commodity, and Delight" is still an absolutely valid formulation, eternally valid to the extent you can think such a thing. I think the modernists' mistake was that they said, "Commodity and Firmness *make* Delight," rather than "Architecture *is* Firmness, Commodity, and Delight." They believed delight would derive from dealing effectively with function and technique.

DSB: Structure.

RV: Function and structure: Modernists said combine good func-

tion and structure and automatically you get delight. Wotton said one plus one plus the other, not one plus one equals the other. Wotton's version suggests that the aesthetic part of architecture can be considered separately from its function and structure and does not necessarily have to evolve directly from them. You can apply beauty to structure. It isn't necessarily that structure is beauty.

BLDS: What is it about Philadelphia that has caused you to keep your office and your home there?

DSB: First, Bob was born there. His family fruit-and-produce business supported the architectural business for some years. He ran both.

BLDS: For how long was that?

RV: The business lasted until 1973, I think.

DSB: We had a manager but we both tried to help run it. In the end, the architecture was supporting the fruit-and-produce business, so Bob liquidated it. I thought it was romantic—old men in there sorting tomatoes and calling Bob, Bobby. Another reason to stay was that the fruit-and-produce business was intended to support his mother. We had finally to face the fact that it wasn't going to, and we had some worrying times. Also, there's a depressed housing market in Philadelphia. We could afford the house we bought there. When we married, we were invited to go to Los Angeles to teach at UCLA, where I'd been teaching, and to help set up the Office of Architectural Innovations there. We said no. We felt we had few connections on the East Coast but even fewer on the West Coast. So we stayed in Philadelphia, where there are good schools and good health care, and where we can live in a way that we could not in New York.

BLDS: Can you share with us a little bit about how you do live? What kind of house do you live in?

DSB: We live in a large old mansion, you'd have to say. It's on a property that was subdivided, so along our shared driveway are five suburban ranch-style houses. We bought the almost three acres at the back. The guy who sold us the house considered it a white elephant, but it's an Art Nouveau house built in 1909. It had really only one owner before us. It has a beautiful yard. The location is six minutes from our office, twenty from downtown, and thirty from the airport. It's pretty ideal from that point of view. West Mount Airy, our community, is integrated racially, though not economically. Upper-middle-class African-American people live around us. The key to keeping a stable, integrated neighborhood is good schools. Ours has excellent schools. Also, it's

quiet in Philadelphia. Few people visit, you don't get disturbed much, you can do your work.

BLDS: What have been the least favorite aspects of your careers?

RV: I'm not a good salesman. I'm not good at making connections and being political.

BLDS: What do you think you are good at?

RV: I think I'm just good at being an architect. But in order to have a chance to do your work you have to have some of the other qualities and I haven't been too good at that. But that's okay. In the end we haven't compromised ourselves. We've limited ourselves because of what I've just said, but we haven't compromised ourselves.

DSB: Our work is a journey of discovery for us and we've made it a way of life. That's what we wanted. At times the going has been hard, on our staff and us. A few years ago everyone was on a four-day week and Bob and I took no salary. When things improved we tried to make it up to everyone. But we had to change the complexion of our office and say good-bye to some people who had been with us for twelve years or more because the fee structure of architecture had changed and clients wouldn't pay their salaries. These are the hard things. But considering the overall range of our opportunities, we can't complain. Had I gone on my own, would I have been better or worse off professionally? There's no easy answer. During the years I've practiced the profession has not been open to women being high-profile designers or large-scale practitioners. Only rarely have women been principals in big firms. Many have become academics rather than practitioners because that gave them greater opportunities for personal advancement.

BLDS: They became academics but often not by choice.

DSB: That's where the opportunities were. I have integrated one of the world's great offices and, in so doing, I've seen the outline of my own professional contribution blurred to the public—though not in the office or to my clients. However, at the time I was starting my career almost no women ran their own offices. As part of Venturi, Scott Brown and Associates I've had opportunities I probably wouldn't have had on my own.

BLDS: Which moments in your career have brought you the most satisfaction, fulfillment, pleasure?

DSB: The times when Bob and I are working together and our ideas cap each other in developing a design or a theory. It's very exciting working together when something begins to grow.

RV: You could say the thrill of working together is really the best part. It is when we're walking or traveling and constantly saying, "Look at that! Look at that! Wow, look at that!"

BLDS: You never say, "Avert your gaze?"

RV: No.

DSB: Yes, on some recent architecture! It's also enormously exciting to travel to a foreign country and almost immediately be on whispering terms with people who are your clients. You're not a tourist, you're flung into reality.

BLDS: If you had it to do over again, what would you do otherwise?

RV: I would go to business school and I would study drama. Try to be a good actor.

BLDS: And you think that's a very necessary component? But maybe your style is so disarming that you've learned to use the truth as a fiction.

RV: I'm very shy, and these days you have to sell yourself. You have to go in front of committees, and you watch the guy come out who was in before you, and you come out and there's someone else waiting to go in. And I don't want to sell myself. I can't do it. It bores me. I'm not good at it. That's the part that's hateful.

BLDS: That seems to me both complex and contradictory. Architecture is such an act of servitude, how can a reticent person commit this inescapable act?

DSB: Bob is reticent *and* strong. He's a set of opposites that let him do that.

RV: Weak and strong—how's that?

DSB: I'm not sure that's so unusual for an artist.

BLDS: Is *vulnerable* a better word than *weak*?

DSB: You need to be

> You could say the thrill of working together is really the best part.

vulnerable—to bravely let your vulnerability lead you where your creativity should go.

BLDS: Are these the best years of your life?

DSB: They've all been pretty good. It's like the question, "What is your ideal home?" I make every home my ideal home. The question is too general for us. It's not enough distorted by reality.

BLDS: Can I distort it somewhat for you, Bob?

RV: I agree with Denise. I think all along there have been—and there continue to be—ghastly moments and happy moments. Back and forth. That's the kind of life we lead. Up and down every day. It really is amazing.

DSB: He'll say, "I can't believe this is happening to me! How can they be doing this?" And yet, look at the things we've been able to do. In the end we're very, very privileged.

ELIE WIESEL

BLDS: It must be hard for you to believe that your childhood was on this planet, let alone in this century. Can you describe the world of your childhood and what you once thought your future in it would be?

EW: My town started in Romania; then it became part of Hungary.

BLDS: And now it is in Romania again.

EW: It used to be part of the Austro-Hungarian Empire. My childhood was not exemplary. I was just like many other Jewish children. I went to the same schools, followed the same customs, and had the same worries as they did.

BLDS: What was the name of your town?

EW: Sighet. At that time the Jewish population numbered twelve thousand in a city of twenty-five thousand inhabitants. Now there are some eighty-two Jewish people—old people, mainly, which means by the time we finish this interview there will be eighty-one, eighty—and fifty thousand inhabitants. Otherwise, the city has not changed much. I was brought up in an extremely religious family, but then the entire community was religious. Even those who claimed they were not, were. In my own case, my mother was brought up as a Hasidic woman. Her father was a fervent follower of the Wizsnitzer Rebbe.

BLDS: Is this grandfather Dodye Feig, whom you have said was one of the greatest influences on your life? How so? Was he a rabbi? A Hasidic scholar?

EW: My father's father was killed in the war in 1918. My maternal grandfather was a scholar and a Hasid. He lived about seven or eight kilometers away from Sighet, in a small village called Bitshkev. He had a farm with a few goats and a cow. I would visit him twice a year during Passover and the High Holidays. He was always on the edge of ecstasy when he prayed. I felt close to him. You know, grandfathers and grandchildren always get along, even in America. Whenever I had complaints I confided in him. He was loving. So was I. I observe how children behave today, how they speak to their elders. I never dared to say something without first asking my father's permission, not because I was afraid, but because I was in awe.

BLDS: Does your son respond in that way?

EW: Today's children are different. I want my son to speak up. I don't want him to be what I was, I want him to be what he is. My grandfather had a great influence on me. He would speak to me about the rebbe, whom I admired. He was a legend in the Hasidic movement of Wizsnitz. He was better known among them than I am today. I evoke him a lot in my tales.

BLDS: What did you then think your future would hold?

EW: I knew I wanted to be a *rosh yeshiva*, a head of a Talmudic school, and an author. I wanted to write commentaries on the Bible and the Talmud, which I did at the the age of twelve and thirteen. After the war, I found most of the pages I had written as a child; they were not good, to put it mildly.

BLDS: Where did you find the documents? I know you went back to your house and found it almost unchanged.

EW: I found my manuscript in a synagogue. All the Jewish books were removed from Jewish homes by our neighbors and were stored there. We used to write notes in the margins. I wanted to be a writer and a teacher.

BLDS: And you wanted to study the Talmud. From what I understand you now read the Talmud every day.

> I'm a protester, but not an atheist. A Jew can be a Jew with God or against God, but not without God.

EW: Every single day. I study. And I teach.

BLDS: So, in spite of external forces, you have managed in some extraordinary way to fulfill some of your earliest ambitions.

EW: Not the same ones. I would have preferred to stay home over there, be the head of a very small Talmudic school, and write very obscure books. But, who can go back? Actually, I did return to Sighet a few years later, just for a few hours.

BLDS: It is difficult to believe that it was unchanged.

EW: That's what made it so weird. The first time I went back it was especially weird. Had the town changed I wouldn't have recognized it. But it hadn't changed—only the Jews were not there. Otherwise, everything was the same.

BLDS: You called your grandfather a Hasidic scholar. I know that Hasidim is the strand of Judaism to which you belong, but I really don't exactly understand what it means when one refers to someone as Hasidic. Perhaps you could explain for me and others who don't understand the meaning.

EW: Hasidim has gone through many phases. It began in the eighteenth century with a man called Rebbe Israel Baal Shem Tov, the master of the good name. He brought beauty, joy, and simplicity to Jewish life. This meant that the soul was as important as the mind. Before his time, a Jew had to use every means at his or her disposal to be rational and nothing else. Rigid laws produced aridity. In the seventeenth and eighteenth centuries the Jewish people suffered from a variety of persecutions. Many Jewish communities were decimated; had it not been for Baal Shem, Jewish life might have ceased altogether. He went from marketplace to marketplace, spreading his beliefs and his stories. People came to hear him, mainly women because the husbands were working. He explained to people that they didn't have to be terribly learned or pious to be Jewish. He gave them the conviction that God is not absent from the universe; He is not a stranger in His own creation. God is here. You see, Jews were afraid that God may have deserted them. If so, why should they remain Jewish? So the Hasidic movement began with stories, with songs, with ideas of brotherhood and friendship. I have studied the history of many religions and have not found another religious tradition that emphasizes more urgently and more intensely the elements of friendship and camaraderie than the Hasidic movement.

BLDS: And what did your father call his faith?

EW: My father was more of a rationalist. He was also very religious, of course, but he did not belong to one group alone. He was interested on an intellectual level to experience all of them. They all knew him. He was a kind of intercessor, a contact man, for the community. I remember during the war, about 1940 or '41, refugees came to Sighet from occupied Poland. Sighet was a border town—Czechoslovakia was on one side and Poland was on the other—and Jews managed to sneak through the border illegally. My father would take care of them.

BLDS: What was his occupation?

EW: We owned a grocery store, but he was rarely there. He would go to the Hasidic masters to watch them, to observe them. Did he believe in their mystical powers? I doubt it.

BLDS: And where do you place yourself on that spectrum of belief?

EW: Like my mother, I was a Hasid.

BLDS: And you continue to be?

EW: Well, let's say today, in America, I live in-between, but remain a Hasid.

BLDS: The movement has had many opponents. To what do they object?

EW: They objected to the Hasidic way of life, I suppose. They didn't want the Jews to spend too much time praying and rejoicing. Learning, only learning, is serious, they said.

BLDS: Is that the origin of the expression, Ask a Hasid a question, and you get a story?

EW: Hasidic men and women love stories. Some consider them holy.

BLDS: Isn't their oral tradition part of what permitted the survival of Jewish faith?

EW: All our traditions secured our collective survival. In the beginning the Talmud—whose legends nourish me to this day—had not been allowed to be written down. It had to remain oral.

BLDS: The word that you have used to describe yourself and your life's work is *witness.*

EW: I have also said that I remained a student. I am still a student. At the same time, we are all witnesses.

BLDS: I read that you referred to atheism as the most current form of protest against God.

EW: Yes, but I never believed it. I have advocated rebellion, not heresy. Some people are atheists, and it's none of my business to judge them, but I was never one of them. I'm a protester, but not an atheist. A Jew can be a Jew with God or against God, but not without God. At times, I protest against God.

BLDS: How do you describe your faith?

EW: My faith is mutilated.

BLDS: How do you describe your own commerce with God?

EW: Ask God. He may tell you. I still feel anger about the Holocaust. When I think of what happened to His creation and His people—but then all people are His. I am compelled to ask, why? But I understand human beings, human beings can be cruel and inhuman—but what about God? In a play I wrote there is a character who keeps on repeating, "And God in all this? And God in all this?" It's a seventeenth-century story based on the Khmelnitsky massacres. But I too ask, Where was God when more than a million children were killed? You cannot conceive of that tragedy without God, yet it is inconceivable with God. Between these two impossibilities you try to find a way of reconciling them. I haven't found it yet.

BLDS: All of the work in your life seems to draw from time-honored traditions and to glorify centuries of Jewish culture. Speaking from two perspectives of your life, on the one hand the teacher/scholar and on the other the witness, do you see your scholastic work falling within the Jewish scholastic tradition or within the Western cultural tradition?

EW: I would say a synthesis of the two. I have not sought to innovate, I simply try to recapture the child walking in the darkness. I have a passion for study and a passion for teaching, which is the same passion. I am committed to memory and its secrets. I love stories. They remind you of how yesterday's events, discoveries, ideas, and experiences can affect men and women today, at the end of this century. So if there was a dialogue two thousand years ago, between an emperor and a scholar in Rome, somehow its echo reaches us to this day. Nothing is isolated; everything is linked. Not only because of history, but because of what we would call genetic connections.

BLDS: At the end of this millennium, is the world more divided than it has ever been?

EW: More divided, and less, at the same time. Why? Because never before have all human beings on the planet responded to the same fears. Never have they felt closer to one another because of the abundance of information, and yet people are more alone. Dangers that threaten society are not only here, they are there. Now there is no geographic distance; *there* is *here*. Should there be a nuclear attack, the whole world would perish, which means that when people commit crimes they are not alone to be punished. People who live in other cities, in other lands, in deserts, have nothing to do with what we are doing here, and yet one crazy guy, for reasons that escape us, could press a button and the planet would go up in fire. Hence, we are united in fear. The question is, can we be united in hope? Hope, after all, is a motivating force. Not as profound and as intense as fear, but everybody knows how much it can influence general behavior. We are not isolated.

BLDS: For more than ten years after you left Auschwitz, you didn't write, or couldn't write, about your experiences.

EW: Yes. I still can't. I didn't want to then. I kept a self-imposed silence. I wanted to be sure that I found the right words. I didn't want my writing to be a catharsis. I didn't want it to be therapeutic. I don't like easy remedies. I want to remember more, not less. I was afraid that once I remembered, once I wrote, I would forget. For ten years I did not speak or write about my experiences. The real shock is that people don't understand it even today. They think that it's possible to grasp the full horror of the event. It's a tragic truth that the enemy pushed his crimes to their limit and beyond, thus depriving those who were his victims of the possibility to tell about it. We do not possess a language. Whenever I read or see pictures of the ghettos and death camps I say to myself, look well but you will not understand. Anyone who was not there will never understand.

BLDS: I don't understand how those who were there could comprehend.

EW: They can't.

BLDS: And that is the final victory, in many ways.

EW: We try. At least it's easier to talk about a killer than a victim. Why, I don't know.

BLDS: Please tell me about your famous conversation with

> It's a tragic truth that the enemy pushed his crimes to their limit and beyond, thus depriving those who were his victims of the possibility to tell about it. We do not possess a language.

François Mauriac, who challenged you and told you it was your duty to be a "witness" and tell the world your story. Can you in any way describe these philosophical and personal exchanges, in which such a transition was possible for you?

EW: I met him in 1954 and I began to write in 1955.

BLDS: Were you then a journalist in Paris?

EW: Yes, I became a journalist in about 1948–49. I had learned new words, but I was afraid of writing. On the other hand, I was a good student. I have studied history, a lot of literature, and psychology; I read everything about the tragedy. My writing didn't come as a change; it was here in my mind and in my heart. I thought, okay, ten years have passed, it is time to start. And I did. So I wrote a lot and cut, and cut, and cut. It became a small book. Eight hundred sixty-five pages were reduced to a slim volume.

BLDS: What happened to the rest of the material?

EW: A collector in Paris and scholars here said they wanted me to publish the rest for the archives. A Brown University professor retranslated several pages from the Yiddish version.

BLDS: And then you came to New York in the middle of 1956.

EW: Yes, I came here as a journalist for an Israeli evening paper called *Yedioth Ahronth,* whose correspondent I had been in France. In both places I was rather poor. My initial monthly salary in New York was $160, out of which I paid for the hotel, buses, and other expenses. Then I took a position with the *Jewish Daily Forward.* The two salaries together weren't enough.

BLDS: How did you survive that period?

EW: I was hungry, but it was not so bad. Nobody knew about it. Then I was hit by a taxi.

BLDS: And you were devastatingly injured.

EW: I spent a whole year going in and out of hospitals. It happened in Times Square, of all places. The taxi hit me on 45th Street and the ambulance picked me up at 44th. I flew a whole block in the air.

BLDS: Among other things, the accident provided you with a year to reflect, to think about things.

EW: After a few months I began working again.

BLDS: What did you write about while you were recuperating? Weren't you confined to a wheelchair?

EW: I wrote for the paper about the 1956 presidential campaign and the U.N. debates on the uprising in Hungary.

BLDS: After the war, why did you decide to go to France rather than Israel? I know that was a difficult decision for you.

EW: It was not my decision. In 1945, I had no choice. I was one of four hundred adolescents who survived the camps. We couldn't go home, because there was no home. The American army, which liberated us in Buchenwald, asked us, where do you want to go? I said Palestine. Everybody said Palestine.

BLDS: You were then sixteen years old.

EW: I was sixteen. The British refused to give us certificates. It was de Gaulle who brought us to an orphanage in France. The place was Ecouis, near Normandy. Fifty years later, its high school wanted to bear my name. It was sweet. For three years I was in children's homes. In 1948, of course, I could have emigrated to Israel, but I wasn't ready. I went there in '49 as a foreign correspondent.

BLDS: Where were you educated?

EW: At the Sorbonne.

BLDS: And how did you manage to do that?

EW: It was cheap. At that time for twenty dollars you could complete all your studies. I gave private lessons to Bible students. I had financial problems until 1964. Strange—in 1987 I received an honorary degree from the Sorbonne. The rector said nice things about me. All of a sudden I remembered my student years when every morning I had to choose between taking the bus and giving up a sandwich for lunch, or walking and having enough money to buy a sandwich. Poor economist that I was, I walked, and ruined my shoes. In Paris, I was always in a panic during the last week of the month. I was afraid because I had no money for the landlady.

BLDS: So why did you eventually come to New York rather than go to Israel?

EW: I went to Israel in 1949 as a French journalist, not that they paid me so much, but at that time with a press card you could go anywhere. I stayed a few months and returned as a correspondent for *Yedioth Ahronth*. The executive editor persuaded me in 1956 to move to the United States for a year and then return to Paris. The accident changed everything.

BLDS: Who took care of you after the accident?

EW: I had a sister in Montreal and a few friends also helped me, but I was a stateless person. The French consulate wanted me to go back to Paris to validate my travel document, but I was in a wheelchair. A kind and compassionate immigration official took pity on me and said, "Why don't you become an American?" At that time to be a citizen would have really given me more joy than the highest honor. That protection.

BLDS: Who was this person?

EW: A simple official in the department of immigration and naturalization. Therefore I still have a soft spot for American bureaucracy. Five years later I became an American.

BLDS: Was that in 1963? What does it mean to you to be an American citizen? In some ways you are a citizen of the world.

EW: It was 1963. No, I'm really not a world citizen. I feel very grateful to this country, so much so that when François Mitterrand became president of France and one of his ministers encouraged me to become a French citizen, I immediately answered, "When I needed a passport, I got it from America. I'll keep it."

BLDS: How do you, or how does anyone, balance the very strong tribal loyalty such as yours to the Jewish people, and particularly to the nation of Israel, with an awareness of responsibilities to all mankind?

EW: I feel that the more Jewish I am the more universal is my work. Once upon a time, when Jews decided to help others, they had to relinquish their Jewishness. It's like saying, we must forget our children in order to take care of other people's children. It's not human, not natural. If a person works for his or her people, that person is ultimately open to other people's concerns as well. I never felt I had to fight for other people's human rights at the expense of my people, the Jewish people, or of Israel. Why would I live a lie? Many left-wing spokesmen are terribly angry, claiming that I helped everybody except the Palestinians. There is some truth in it. The Palestinians were victims, too, but there were many

terrorists among them. Naturally, there are people you cannot help, but you try. But always, as a Jew, I try to help the Jews first. Then come the others. When journalists asked me at the Cambodian border in 1979, "Why did you come here?" My response was, "When I needed people to help me, nobody came. Therefore I must try to help those who need help right now."

BLDS: Your life as a witness involves not only your experience, but the entire human condition as you have just described it. It is an almost relentlessly public role that you fill.

EW: Which I don't like.

BLDS: Being a public figure always has its burdens, but in your instance it is even more personal. In a world that is so media-addicted, these burdens must be very substantial ones for you. How do you cope with being a human symbol?

EW: I'm not, really.

BLDS: But you are—so how do you deal with it?

EW: I avoid it in every way I can. I am very good at saying no to television. I don't like it. My view is to work with my students and continue my studies. I only go on TV when I must, but I don't like that role. It is not for me.

BLDS: You have said that all you need is your students. You don't even take sabbaticals.

EW: I feel close to my students.

BLDS: Are they so nourishing to you?

EW: They give me their future, I give them my past. That exchange deepens the mysterious relationship between student and teacher. My students need me and I need them even more.

BLDS: Have your international distinction, your fame, and the media attention given to even your quasi-public statements inhibited your ability to explore your questioning?

EW: No, oh no.

BLDS: Are you free to lead your life and make your pronouncements in private? Everything you say seems to have reverberations.

EW: It is true that I must be more careful. Not only because I am afraid of saying something silly, but because the media may distort it.

BLDS: It has been more than a decade since you won the Nobel Prize in 1986. How has it changed your life?

EW: My schedule has become heavier. Too many pressures. Many

> I feel that the more Jewish I am the more universal is my work.

invitations to answer. Everybody feels that they own me. And then the lectures—I'm too weak in these matters. I say no, but when they call back ten times, it's easier to say yes. It is less time-consuming.

BLDS: Have you ever, or have you frequently, asked yourself, Why did I survive?

EW: Naturally. I do not know the answer.

BLDS: It is rare that a writer can be said to possess a word, but certainly the word *witness*, and sadly the word *Holocaust*, are two words that you do possess. *Witness* has many applications, but you have sharply criticized the trivialization of *Holocaust* to describe any large misfortune. Do you feel that the word only should be used to describe the atrocities of World War II?

EW: Absolutely. If we allow the term to be diluted then we will lose much of our memory. Even that word is not good, because there are no words to describe what happened to the Jews in World War II. I heard once a sportscaster saying, "It was a defeat for that team, it was a holocaust." "A fire, seven people—holocaust." Shouldn't this word be preserved for something that was unique, that never happened before, and must never happen again? I read in the paper: "Auschwitz, in Bosnia!" It was bad enough, it was cruel enough, it was tragic enough, but it wasn't Auschwitz.

BLDS: What word would you use to describe what happened in Bosnia?

EW: *Atrocities* is a strong word. *Massacre* is a strong word. *Mass murder* is terribly strong. I try to find such exaggerations but I lose all my fights.

BLDS: How do you respond to the criticism of other writers, such as William Styron, who challenge your view that they are not appropriate interpreters of the Holocaust?

EW: I have not read his views on this subject.

BLDS: What battles have you lost that you feel are the important ones?

EW: Racism, anti-Semitism, even memory. I teach—very few, but some people—how to preserve the purity of the transmission of testimony. And if I lose, it's my loss. I never thought that I would have to fight anti-Semitism, murder of children, hunger, disease, indifference. The only successful battle in which I was involved was for the freedom of Russian Jews.

BLDS: Do they agree with you in Israel that it's a good idea?

EW: Israel absorbed half a million Russian Jews. More will always be welcome.

BLDS: What motivates you to continue to fight your battles?

EW: The children deserve better. The children have always been the reason for my despair and, at the same time, the motive for my hope. Each time I get involved in a human-rights cause, it's because of children. We can make them invincible and also terribly vulnerable. If a child cries, I cry. If a child smiles, I'm happy.

BLDS: Is one of your central contentions that listening to a witness makes the listener a witness?

EW: I like to be a teacher. It's much simpler than that. In America, unfortunately, teachers are not respected enough.

BLDS: One day in Saigon, I saw women, of all ages but especially the young, wearing long pale silk tunics over pants, gliding along the street on their bicycles, and in the baskets of their bicycles were small bouquets of flowers. There were so many of them that I knew it could not be coincidental. So, I asked a knowledgeable person if there was some special meaning to the day. He said, "Yes. Today is the day that you honor your teacher." Each person was bringing a bouquet, an homage, to a teacher who had a special meaning or influence in his or her life.

EW: That's beautiful. Here, too, those kinds of things happen. Children ought to respect their teachers. And the other way around.

BLDS: Does society venerate its teachers? You talked before about how difficult it is for a second generation to interpret the experience of the first. In my limited experience I have found the least effective interpreters are often the second genera-

I heard once a sportscaster saying, "It was a defeat for that team, it was a holocaust." . . . Shouldn't this word be preserved for something that was unique, that never happened before, and must never happen again?

Each time I get involved in a human-rights cause, it's because of children. We can make them invincible and also terribly vulnerable. If a child cries, I cry. If a child smiles, I'm happy.

191

tion, in part because of the inexplicable nature of what their families have lived through, and in part because of their rage at being victims of a world that they did not create.

EW: Children want to know what their parents went through but are also afraid of knowing what their parents know. It wasn't easy for children to grow up with parents who came from the other side of life. One student asked me, "Can one believe in God now?" And I said, one cannot, but one must. The same thing: Can one believe in humanity? We can't, but we must.

BLDS: Do you believe that evil is stronger than good?

EW: Both are mysteries. We know the question, but we don't know the answer. The problem with the human condition is somehow more centered. The racist knows who to hate—the Jew, the black, the Hispanic, the white, whoever is different from him. We must fight racial hate, prejudice, and fanaticism. But where do you start? There are so many challenges, so many directions. On the street, there are able-bodied men who want our alms. Many people go by and don't even look. I confess, I am weak. I cannot help but give something, although I know very often it is used for alcohol or something else.

BLDS: I rarely pass by without giving something. It is inhumane to see human beings in such a condition, although I know that my small response is not a solution.

EW: That's my feeling.

BLDS: You said France was a haven and a new beginning, an opportunity to start expressing yourself in a new language, and, in fact, a defiance. I was listening to your French conversation earlier, and I see you surrounded by French books in your library. What do you think of as your first language now?

EW: It's French, but it used to be Yiddish. Now, I teach in English.

BLDS: Do you apply your different languages to different purposes? For example, is French your language of defiance?

EW: French is the language that is my connection to all the other alien languages, so to speak. In 1944–45, I didn't know a word of French. After the war I spoke French, mainly French. Now, of course, I converse in English.

BLDS: You said that Yiddish is great for laughter or for tears.

EW: And melancholy. It's also a melancholy language.

BLDS: To whom do you speak Yiddish now?

EW: Oh, only to friend—old friends.

BLDS: But there are very few people who speak Yiddish.

EW: Yes and no. I have a friend in Brooklyn, a fellow inmate in the camps. He comes from a city not far from mine; he is now a rebbe.

BLDS: A rebbe—what inner resources does one have to possess to be able to believe on that level after his experiences?

EW: He is a great scholar and writer.

BLDS: What does your friend write about?

EW: He writes important books on decisions regarding ancient problems his students face in a modern world.

BLDS: And he speaks Yiddish.

EW: He speaks Yiddish, yes, a learned rabbinic Yiddish.

BLDS: Do you write in Yiddish now?

EW: Occasionally I write articles for a weekly journal called *Der Algemeiner*. I want to pay my sentimental dues to Yiddish.

BLDS: By the way, why are the camps still referred to as concentration—rather than extermination—camps?

EW: There were many concentration camps and fewer extermination camps. Buchenwald was one of them. The most notorious were Auschwitz, Majdanek, Belzec, Treblinka, Sobibor, and Chelmno.

BLDS: You used the opportunity and the funds from the Nobel Prize to establish the Elie Wiesel Foundation for Humanity. Is that correct? When did you do that?

EW: Almost immediately. It really wasn't that much money; it was $270,000. So we decided to create a foundation.

BLDS: Is your wife, Marion, a survivor of the Holocaust?

EW: Marion was born in Vienna and went through the war in French internment camps.

BLDS: What does that mean?

EW: They were tough camps. Marion and her parents managed to escape to Switzerland. She was very young. Her father, sister, and mother—they all escaped.

BLDS: She is your true collaborator.

EW: Yes. We are allies. We decided together to start the foundation. It wasn't announced publicly, but some people knew that I received a letter from Milton Petrie asking me to come and see him. He had heard what I planned to do. He said, "You have no right to do what you are doing. You have a family, you have a young son. Don't give away your money. I will give you a hundred thousand dollars to start your project." I was moved by the way he did it, with such grace, such elegance. We established the foundation and held annual conferences on "The Anatomy of Hate."

BLDS: What did you learn that you didn't know?

EW: One concrete lesson was that children begin to hate at age three.

BLDS: What defining moment occurs?

EW: The children begin their long road of learning. They learn how to hate, but it also means they can learn how not to hate.

BLDS: You convene groups of individuals, from students to academics to Nobel Prize winners, to discuss the issues of peace and hate and discrimination. I see that as another way that you have chosen to make your testimony active. It does combine your own interests as a teacher and a listener with your privilege and influence as a public figure.

EW: No, I am not a public figure.

BLDS: Which of the meetings that you have convened did you find the most satisfying?

EW: The most unexpected was the one I had with François Mitterrand in 1986. All he wanted to know was what I intended to do with the Nobel money. I told him of one idea: to create a foundation and organize meetings. I suggested to him that he help conceive a symposium of only Nobel laureates. It turned out to be a great event: seventy-nine participants, closed doors, no press, nothing. The title was "On the Threshold of the Twenty-First Century."

BLDS: On the threshold of the twenty-first century, what are the threats and the promises that face us?

EW: The threats? Hate, racial prejudice, nuclear proliferation, terrorism, senseless, useless bloodshed. The politics of hate. What about the violent fanatics here and abroad? Think of the assassination of Rabin, the bombing of the World Trade Center. And the promise? I think the young people and children are getting to know their responsibilities, facing a world they are called up to conquer in order to share it.

BLDS: How should Jews and the larger population react to today's resurgence of anti-Semitism?

EW: Unmask it. Denounce it. Fight it.

BLDS: Did the most recent meeting of the Foundation for Humanity take place in Japan?

EW: Yes. It was called "The Future of Hope."

BLDS: And where was it held?

EW: In Tokyo and Hiroshima.

BLDS: I would like to return to our discussion of generations. Now you have the responsibility of inspiring a third generation, your son's generation, in fact. Is informing your goal?

EW: Instructing.

BLDS: Instructing. But how does the testimony of the firsthand witness need to be translated for those more and more removed by place and by time? How do we eliminate the inevitable dulling of the transmission?

EW: You leave behind images. We have built museums. Nevertheless, I believe words are stronger than images. Somehow I think history has preserved its values, its treasures, its meaning through words, not images. So, in a strange way, I am optimistic. Hasn't the Holocaust become popular?

BLDS: You pointed out in your writing, too, that the documents exist. What do you say to people who say the Holocaust is an event that never occurred?

EW: I would never dignify them with a debate or an answer. They are morally deranged. The documents exist in the millions. I am not so concerned with the obvious danger of forgetting. I am much more concerned with the question of how one can communicate this experience without diluting it.

BLDS: What memories are the strongest weapons?

EW: Memory itself. Nothing is stronger. Without it we are lost. Without it our past itself is reduced to nothing.

BLDS: When I realized how short your Nobel acceptance speech was—and I've read it a number of times—it reminded me of the

Declaration of Independence, in which one says so much in so few words. The main point for me was when you evoked the image of yourself as a child confronting your adult persona. You said something like, "Tell me what have you done with my future? And what have you done with your life?" Those are haunting questions.

EW: They're still haunting.

BLDS: How do you answer those questions?

EW: Well, I don't really. I say wait. A child is asking me questions all the time.

BLDS: And how does the adult reply?

EW: Wait.

BLDS: Is the real story, which you have said you have yet to write, contained in your memoirs?

EW: The story itself. I have more in the memoirs than in any of my projects.

BLDS: What motivated you to finally publicize your memoirs?

EW: I've kept a diary since 1945.

BLDS: You still do?

EW: Every day.

BLDS: But you still remain so personal, so secretive about your grief and your experience.

EW: I speak when other people suffer.

BLDS: Does suffering have any meaning, if the suffering is done in silence?

EW: I am still looking for the meaning of suffering.

BLDS: Do you share some of that in your book?

EW: Some, not all.

BLDS: Do you do that in part for your son?

EW: Whatever I do is for my son.

BLDS: What experiences in your career have brought you the most pleasure and the most fulfillment?

EW: My career and my life are linked to my twenty-four-year-old son.

BLDS: Where is he?

EW: He graduated from Yale last year and is working with Goldman Sachs for two years.

BLDS: I often ask people a certain question, and asking you that same question takes on a whole other meaning. The question is really a very simple and a slightly provocative one. It is, if you had your life to live over again, what would you do otherwise?

EW: I wouldn't have chosen the place or the time. Once the work is done you cannot undo it, but on the other hand, for us to have this conversation here is against the law of chance. Only one in six billion or something.

BLDS: Why?

EW: Think of what had to happen for you and me to be here. We both came from far away.

BLDS: Are these the best years of your life?

EW: For me, "good" is sufficient.

JAMES WOLFENSOHN

BLDS: You were born in Sydney, Australia, and went both to university and to law school there. Did you always have career goals that were outside of your native country?

JW: I did not. I thought I would be a lawyer in Sydney. My move came accidentally rather than by design.

BLDS: When did your career path become clear to you?

JW: It was during an antitrust action for which evidence was being taken in Australia in connection with the RCA vs. Zenith triple-damages suit. During the course of the proceedings it became clear that I couldn't read a balance sheet. The American lawyer for RCA suggested to me that it might be a good idea if I went to the Harvard Business School. I was so embarrassed by what I did not know that I decided to apply immediately.

BLDS: Just like that?

JW: Yes. I wrote that night to Harvard. I had previously thought I would study at Oxford and come back as a lawyer in Australia, but going to Harvard changed all that. I became far more involved in finance and particularly international finance. I returned to Australia after Harvard, but the natural progression for international investment banking was to go back to New York or London, which is what I did.

BLDS: Much has been written about your father's influence on your life. What was his legacy to you?

JW: In the first instance it was a desire to get academic qualifications, which he never got because of World War I. He felt frustrated that he never returned to complete either medical school or law school, and so he wanted me to do that. He was a pivotal influence.

BLDS: What did he do? What was his occupation?

> I hitchhiked on a Royal Australian Air Force plane to Harvard through London.

JW: He was a business adviser in Australia. He spent a great deal of my youth helping refugees from the Nazis relocate themselves in Australia, as did my mother. He worked on the humanitarian side of the effort and also on the business end of it. His wish for me was that I should get my basic qualifications in both law and business administration. What he hoped was that I would return to Australia and practice commercial law.

BLDS: In your previous career did you ever describe yourself as a business adviser?

JW: No, although I think I was probably influenced by the quality and care that my father took with his clients, and maybe I learned something from that.

BLDS: Who were his clients, and in what way did he advise them?

JW: He dealt with mainly small- to medium-sized businesses in a lot of fields. He advised them on business management and strategy.

BLDS: While he did a great deal for humanitarian efforts, as I recall, he never was a burgeoning financial success.

JW: No, he was not.

BLDS: Then how did you manage to be trained at the best university in Australia and go off to Harvard in 1957?

JW: In Sydney, university fees were not very great and during law school I was able to pay for myself because I worked as an articles law clerk, which helped financially. Harvard was a different story. I hitchhiked on a Royal Australian Air Force plane to Harvard through London.

BLDS: How do you get to hitchhike on an official plane?

JW: It was approved by a benevolent air minister. I was in the reserves at the time. I went to him and said, "I'm going to Harvard Business School and it would be a very good thing for the Australian Air Force to have someone who had been to the Harvard Business School." He thought it was so outrageous that he agreed. And so I went with the chief of air staff of the New Zealand Air Force to London, where a benevolent uncle gave me a passage to the United States on the *Queen Elizabeth*. I arrived at Harvard with three hundred dollars. They had told me to come with four thousand dollars and they would match it with a loan. I went to the aid bureau and spoke to a woman named Florence Glynn. I told her that I didn't have the requisite amount of money and I hoped that I could work my way through. She said I was "a very naughty boy." We agreed that if I did reasonably well in the first term she would advance all the money they were going to lend me the first year. In the second year I ran the laundry service. I never had much money, but there was a lot to do. I didn't have a car, but I had a secondhand bicycle. Everything worked out.

BLDS: Wasn't there a wealthy Australian who selected worthy and promising young men like yourself and helped them?

JW: If there was I don't know who it was. However, a lot of people influenced my life. Up until then I was working in the leading law firm in Australia: Allen, Allen and Hemsley. I was fortunate enough to work with Sir Norman Cowper, Gabriel Reichenbach, and Bob Stevenson.

BLDS: Did you do so well in law school that you were placed at the ranking law firm?

JW: I was regarded as having a certain amount of *nouse*, which is an Australian expression that means a certain amount of capacity and diversity in one's life. My grades had been all over the place, from failing to passing, but at law school I presented a composite of someone who was a student leader and a would-be Olympian, as well as a reasonable lawyer. So it was the mix in my background, rather than my genius as a lawyer, combined with the support of the leading law professor, Julius Stone.

BLDS: What of your mother's influence in your life?

JW: It was very strong. She had a great interest in music and was a won-derful musician herself. She played piano and sang professionally for a while in Australia. She had a radio program on which she sang lieder. She spoke seven languages.

BLDS: Were your parents immigrants to Australia?

JW: They came from England. My father was born in England; my mother lived all her life in England but had been born in Belgium.

BLDS: And what caused them to emigrate from England?

JW: My father had been in Palestine during World War I and his training and career in London were disrupted. In the thirties they decided that they would try and have a new start, so off they went to Australia. It was right at the beginning of the Depression, which was not the most optimum time to go, and whatever resources he had were lost. It was a pretty tough time for them. My sister Betty, born in London, is ten years older than me. I think they all loved Australia. Australia is a very open place, much like America, and built on immigrants. They were well received and, although they didn't have much money, they made a full life for themselves in the Jewish community. My mother ran the National Council of Jewish Women and my father was on the executive committee of the board of deputies, which was sort of the umbrella organization for the Jewish community. They gave a lot of time and what little money they had. In fact, that aspect of generosity from my mother and my father obviously had a very important influence on the way I have lived my life.

BLDS: You mentioned that you were a student leader and a would-be Olympian. Weren't you a member of the Australian fencing team? How did that team fare in the 1956 Olympics?

JW: We didn't do very well, but we managed to march around the arena and I won a few unlikely matches against the world-champion Italian team. More importantly, I represented my country, which was quite a thing, and in the spirit of the Olympic Games I competed and did my best.

BLDS: I assume you will be representing the world, for the World Bank, at the 2000 Olympics in Sydney.

JW: One of my friends who was in the '56 games is actually organizing the 2000 games. It is his intention that we might all march at the opening ceremonies, which would be quite a kick. I would need to have a new blazer made since I can't fit into the old one. It would be great fun. I only hope I will still be able to walk at that time.

BLDS: Having once been a fencing counselor at summer camp, I

> I was regarded as having a certain amount of *nouse*, which is an Australian expression that means a certain amount of capacity and diversity in one's life.

196

have always been interested in other people who fence. Was there anything, any strategy, that you have learned from fencing that you have applied to the rest of your life?

JW: Fencing is a very strategic sport. It is, of course, an individual sport. It's a bit like playing chess and doing exercise at the same time. It's also a sport that has very honorable rules, provided you play by the rules, which both you and your opponent need to do in order to be safe. It's at once a wonderful exercise and a wonderful intellectual challenge. Stretching it a bit farther, the sense of integrity and honor that you have in fencing carries through to business. It so happens that's the way I've lived my business life. It happens to be the same.

BLDS: What did you learn at Harvard Business School that you consider most useful as your life unfolded?

JW: Well, the first thing I learned was what it was like to live outside of Australia. Every other foreign student will tell you the same, I'm sure. The single most important thing about studying in this country is getting to know America. The second thing was the people I met. It was a fantastic group of American and international colleagues.

BLDS: Some of whom, I assume, you still work with.

JW: Yes. After I had spent a year at the Harvard-related Institute IMEDE. in Switzerland I started a little company called Catena Investments, which was composed entirely of guys I had met at Harvard.

BLDS: What did Catena represent?

JW: *Catena* means "link" in Greek. The idea was to have a chain of people around the world who could give information and advice on international business. We all put in something like a thousand pounds or two thousand dollars—that was the figure that I could manage as an equal partner, which is why we all didn't put in more. I started this small business in Australia; it was composed of two Englishmen, a Swiss, a Hong Kong Chinese, an American, and myself. We started what amounted to the framework of an international business, with each of my partners working part time in their own countries. It lasted about a year before it was clear that we were undercapitalized. So I folded it into my work with an Australian brokerage firm and then an investment bank in which I became a founder. That was in 1961.

BLDS: Which bank was that?

JW: It was called Darling and Company; it is now Schroder Darling. Schroder's, the British investment-banking group, had an interest in Darling and Company, which led six years later to my going to London as a partner. But getting back to Harvard, what was most important was that the professors threw a lot of material at you. You were forced to master a brief quickly, to synthesize it, to get the essentials. That's what I learned. When I became an assistant professor at the University of New South Wales in Sydney, where I started the finance course, the ability to conceptualize a problem and then explain and teach it was very valuable. My experience at Harvard was fundamental in everything I have done since.

BLDS: So after Harvard you returned to Australia and worked at what is now Schroder Darling, which led you to England and work at the investment bank Schroder's. What was your life like at Schroder's?

JW: It doesn't sound like a huge leap now, but in the mid-sixties to move from Australia to become a director in a London merchant bank was a huge jump. Today it's much more normal for people to change around. Thirty years ago it was a mammoth step. That was at the beginning of the Eurodollar market, when Sigmund Warburg was dominating the international banking scene. Sigmund was a great friend and patron and an enormous influence on my life. My duties then were all international. It was clear that my British colleagues did not want me in England, so I traveled a lot, about a hundred to two hundred thousand miles a year.

BLDS: A pace you have kept up ever since.

JW: In a sense I was one of the founding fathers of the Eurodollar market and international markets. I can say that now because we are all older and there are only a few of us left. At the time it was a small group of twenty or thirty people and we all knew each other. Some of the other people involved were Jacob Rothschild, Stanislas Yassukovich, Minos Zombanakis. We all knew each other, and we were all inventing as we went along, because there were no precedents for Eurobonds, nor was there Euro commercial paper. There were none of these international instruments, all of which we helped create and develop. It was a unique time to be in business. My friendship with Jacob culminated many years later when we formed a bank together in London.

BLDS: In the early nineties?

JW: Yes. But the 1960s was a remarkable time. I came to the States at least a half-dozen times a year. In the early seventies Lord Richardson, then Gordon Richardson, the chairman of Schroder's, invited me to become president of Schroder Banking Corporation in New York, which was quite a remarkable thing for him to do, given that I had never run a commercial bank. It was then a medium-sized bank, with six hundred million dollars in assets, and one of the most renowned international banks in New York.

BLDS: You said it was clear that your colleagues didn't want you in Britain so you traveled a great deal. What was the cause of their response?

JW: When I say they didn't want me in Britain, what I mean is they didn't want me to be in the domestic U.K. business, because that was their field. To be honest with you, they were right, because I didn't know anything about it. My added value was not in learning how to do English business; rather, it was to develop an even more international projection of the firm. Subsequently I became chairman of Schroder's international company and then ultimately the chief executive.

BLDS: You have been proud to say that Sigmund Warburg was one of your really important mentors. A distinguished businessman once told me a story that in a conversation he asked Sigmund Warburg if he had ever made a mistake. Warburg said, "I can admit to one, and that was not keeping James Wolfensohn close to my side and my company."

JW: I am very proud to hear that he said that. Sigmund and I were friends and he invited me many times to join him at Warburg's, but I had already built my career at Schroder's. In an interview in the *Institutional Investor* he was asked who were the successors that he had in mind. He named two: one was David Scholey, who became chairman, and the other was me. In fact, he wanted David and me to work together. I thought that was silly, and I'm sure David did too, because David and I were very close friends. The two of us being together at Warburg's would not have been a good idea. I kept in very close contact with Sigmund right until he died. In fact, in my office you will see a picture of him still today.

BLDS: Why did you leave Schroder's?

JW: Part of it was pique. I had gone back to England as an executive deputy chairman when Gordon Richardson became governor of the Bank of England. I had essentially been the group chief executive under the chairmanship of Michael Verey and had understood that when Michael retired I would become chairman. There was a difference of opinion in the board, in which the family, and broadly the foreign directors, including people like Paul Nitze and Harold Brown and others, were very much on my side and some

of the English directors, but by no means all, were against me. They were anxious that there should be an English chairman, with me remaining in the lesser public role. I was young enough and foolish enough to think that it was not a good idea, so I left. In fact, I left before the terminal meeting when the board was likely to decide. I came back to New York and put the kids in school in the summer before the September meeting of the board, and then I announced to the board that I was necessary to New York. It was really failed expectations on my part. I thought that at that stage I should be made chairman and they—the British—wanted to have a chairman and chief executive separate. It was, in fact, a tremendously good thing for both of us, because I think Schroder's has done wonderfully well ever since. Then I ended up at Salomon Brothers, and worked there for five years. When I went there, I said to Billy Salomon and John Gutfreund that I would love to head up Salomon International and the corporate finance department, and that I would either stay forever or for five years. I explained that I had a hankering for setting up my own little business in a brownstone, with a piano upstairs, and for the complete financial freedom to do all my nonbusiness and cultural activities at the same time. I had always wanted to do that and I told them right at the beginning. Five years later I opted to do so, after a wonderful and very rich experience at Salomon Brothers.

BLDS: Just about that time, in the pre–Rupert Murdoch conversion days, you chose to become an American citizen. What motivated you to do that?

JW: I became an American citizen because in 1980 Bob McNamara asked me if I would consider becoming president of the World Bank if he nominated me.

BLDS: And that post traditionally went to an American?

JW: Yes. Then I was told by the White House that I was on the short list.

BLDS: Who was the then president?

JW: The president was still Jimmy Carter, just as he lost to Ronald Reagan. Within a week I got my American citizenship, arranged through the White House by Sarah Weddington, who was then an assistant to the president.

BLDS: And who then went on to work for you.

JW: She did, indeed. I think that was the first time I met Sarah. A few weeks later my wife, Elaine, woke me one morning to say Tom Clausen had just been made president of the World Bank—which, again, was remarkably fortunate, in retrospect.

BLDS: Was he from Bank of America?

JW: Yes, he was then chairman of Bank of America and obviously a much better choice than I was anyway. That caused me to think about what I then would do, and so I followed through to create my own business.

BLDS: Was the idea of the World Bank still someplace in your mind?

JW: No, actually it was not. A lot of nonsense has been written about that. I was deeply and totally committed to my own business. I had completely put out of my mind the idea of the World Bank. It really came up again only a year or so ago when there was a story in the *Financial Times* that claimed I was competing with Larry Summers to become president of the World Bank. At that time I didn't even know that Lew Preston was sick or that the job was offered. It even said that I was coming in with a plan to cut 30 percent of the staff. The whole thing was a total and absolute fabrication. I've subsequently learned that it is likely that the rumors started here at the World Bank. Once the rumors started then I started to think about it again. I guess it had always been in the back of my mind. The possibility of public service has never been away from my mind; neither have the international field, the environment, poverty, women's issues, and all those things that I have always been interested in.

BLDS: Knowing what you know now through your experiences in the intervening sixteen years, it seems fortuitous that you did not achieve that role in 1980.

JW: I am much better qualified and experienced to be president now. I hope I would have done a decent job then, but I can do it now in a totally different frame of mind. I have made a lot of mistakes in my own business that I won't make here. I come with more maturity, more security, and far more breadth than I had then. Now I'm realizing just how narrow I was.

BLDS: In your own business you created a very successful financial consulting firm, one which has been consistently remarked upon for its ability to provide objective and disinterested advice on its clients' activities by maintaining a rather rigid arm's-length distance from any investments in those activities. That's a fairly unusual arrangement in American business consulting, especially in the last decade. How did this business style develop? Was it deliberate, and what inspired you to design it that way?

JW: Consulting is probably not the right description because we did a very substantial number of transactions every year, which is a distinction between consulting and investment banking. I could guess when I left we were doing something like fifty to sixty billion dollars of transactions a year, which is not an insubstantial amount. What led me to this concept was the belief that the large investment-banking firms gave an opening to smaller firms that could conduct themselves without conflicts of interest with large numbers of clients or conflicts caused by investing in competition with clients. The trend that I identified fifteen years ago has gotten to the point now where most of the leading investment banks make as much, or more, on their investment activities as they make on their advisory and deal-making activities. I predicted that this idea for independent nonconflicted service would be a salable product and I discussed it with Sigmund. I thought, if I had a low-overhead firm with only ten clients I could give them good independent advice; I could also play my cello, continue in my Carnegie Hall Foundation and my other charitable work, and have a good life. I wouldn't be the richest man in town, but I would have a good living. That was the strategy. In fact, Sigmund sent me my first client.

BLDS: And who was that?

JW: Daimler-Benz, which is the largest company in Germany. The then chairman, Dr. Gerhard Prinz, came to see me a few weeks after I had started the business and we had lunch in my office on a cardboard packing case. I offered him a Coca-Cola and a sandwich. He seemed to think that the occasion was so unusual that he engaged me. Wolfensohn & Company has been adviser to Daimler-Benz ever since.

BLDS: Your community of business and professional relationships is legendary. I think someone once referred to your Rolodex as the Holy Grail.

JW: I think David Rockefeller's is the Holy Grail. Mine compares as just another Rolodex.

BLDS: It's clear that your skills are successfully transferable across a very wide spectrum of activities. Which do you think are your most valuable skills and traits?

JW: I hope the first is integrity. I don't lie, which has the merit of being helpful. The second thing is that I care about people a lot. If I didn't, I wouldn't be in this job. The personal part of business has always meant a lot to me. The third thing, I suppose, is that I try very hard to understand the technical and substantive aspects of issues. I master the brief. I work very hard. What success I have had is not the result of the golden Rolodex and being social. That is manifestly ridiculous. My success is a result of the type of business I have been in, the hard work I have done, and the good fortune of having some great associates and clients. And nowhere is that more evident than at the World Bank today, where there are quite specific and varied issues that I deal with fifty times a day. I couldn't do this job if I hadn't had my own business previously. It's a combination of integrity, mastering the brief, and caring about people. Within that context, caring about people translates to maintaining a very wide set of relationships with people, which has not only been built on business, but also through my activities outside of business.

> What success I have had is not the result of the golden Rolodex and being social. . . . My success is a result of the type of business I have been in, the hard work I have done, and the good fortune of having some great associates and clients.

BLDS: You mentioned earlier your notion of what a good life would be, and it included playing music. When did you first begin to play the cello?

JW: When I was forty-two years old.

BLDS: What gave you the idea?

JW: Jacqueline du Pré, who was then certainly the greatest woman cellist in the world and the wife of Daniel Barenboim, who was then, and still is, one of my closest friends. Jackie contracted multiple sclerosis. On the night in London that she was finally diagnosed, she and Daniel and I had dinner together at their house. And she said, "I don't know what I'll do." I told her she should teach. Jackie said nobody would study with her because she didn't really have formal training until much later in her career. She was truly a genius and her talent was God's gift to her. So I said I would study with her. That was on a Sunday. The next morning after my partners' meeting at Schroder's, I got a call from Jackie, asking me if I meant what I said about studying with her. And I said yes. She said she found me a cello. We made a date for Sunday at three. That was the total conversation. For two years I went to Jackie's every Sunday—I came back early from the country—and I studied the cello. She was a wonderful and a very unusual teacher. At the first lesson she asked me what I would like to play. I said, "Jackie, I don't know how to hold the cello." And she said, "Well, you've got to start with some music." I said, "What about the Bach *G Major Suite?*" For two years I drove my family, and myself, and no doubt Jackie absolutely mad with my principal work being the Bach *G Major Suite*, which we did bar by bar. She made me promise that on my fiftieth birthday I would play a concert.

BLDS: And indeed you did.

JW: That's what led to the concerts on my fiftieth and sixtieth birthdays. Daniel called me when I was forty-nine and said, "What about the concert?" I said, great. He asked me where it was going to be. I said at the house. "No, no, no," he said. "That's not a concert. You have to do it at Carnegie Hall." That's what led to the wholly preposterous idea of these two concerts I gave.

BLDS: Had you studied any other music?

JW: I played piano as a kid.

BLDS: With any facility, in spite of your mother's gifts?

JW: I think I'm very musical. And my kids are. My son is a composer; my oldest daughter is a concert pianist.

BLDS: Musical ability is said to be one of the things that is genetically transmitted.

JW: Yes, I think it is. I think I could have been a decent pianist, but I reacted against the wishes of my mother and father, as a lot of kids do. I had a teacher who always used to rap my knuckles when I got a note wrong, and that turned me off completely.

BLDS: One of the things that you have said about yourself is that the only thing you know is what sells and what doesn't sell.

JW: I don't remember having said that, but I hope it's not the only thing that I know. Certainly, judging what people will buy and how far you can go are the essential elements of negotiation and of counseling. Judgment is a very important element in advisory work, in fund-raising, and in doing what I am doing at this moment. You have to balance the possibilities. Perhaps the skill is seeing how far you can determine what will sell. I don't remember the remark, but I think it has some element of truth to it.

BLDS: You were instrumental—that's a bad pun, isn't it?—in saving Carnegie Hall and you have had a very significant role as chairman of the board of the Kennedy Center. Are there similarities, as you just pointed out, between marketing cultural performances and marketing countries at your current World Bank post?

JW: Yes. I think there are some similarities. First, you have to be passionate about what you're doing. In the case of Carnegie Hall, of which I was chairman for a long time, the decision to rebuild the hall was perceived to be somewhat unrealistic because we had to raise sixty million dollars. Until then Carnegie Hall had never raised more than half a million a year.

BLDS: What originally led to your involvement in Carnegie Hall, and your agreement to take on what seemed like an impossible assignment?

JW: I said I would do it. It was my idea to do it. The hall was falling down. It was a decision that Isaac Stern and I made jointly. If we didn't do something, we would have nothing. It would have been a public danger. Brooke Astor gave us a million dollars to put together the plans and to try and see if something could be done. It came up that it was going to cost us sixty million dollars. The decision to pursue raising the sixty million dollars was my decision. Isaac was involved in the spiritual and artistic aspects of it; I was then the chairman and had come in being the financial guy. We had a real partnership then and a lifelong friendship. I decided that the best way to do it was to jump into the water. With the assistance of a lot of other people, including Sandy Weill, who became cochair of the campaign and, I am happy to say, is now chairman of the board, we got it done.

BLDS: When you mention your lifelong friendships I realize that this relatively young life of yours has been spent on three continents, in each of which you feel very much at home. Is there something about being born and raised in Australia that permits one to dare? Is there a sense of the frontier, is it the valedictory ego—or not knowing about that larger world until you have been immersed in it?

JW: First of all, Australia is a wonderful country. I think it breeds innovation. It is a place where you feel that everything is possible and where you grow up without a lot of constraints. You don't have the constraints of a real class structure or of a very long-standing structure based on family wealth. It's much more of an egalitarian society than the U.K. That is one thing that gives you the capacity to move into other places. It gives you a sense of yourself because you grow up doing lots of things for yourself. It's a much more basic life and a smaller environment. That's why people from small towns become presidents of the United States, because they can encompass the framework. The second important factor in this regard is being Jewish, which I am very proud of. I think Jews generally have a certain world citizenship. They have the capacity to move from country to country; historically, they have either chosen to do so, or have been forced to do so. Having that sense of both religion and world community, combined with an Australian bravado and background, are what probably helped form my character. Of course, you don't have to be Jewish. Just look at Rupert Murdoch. Rupert is the prime example of somebody who has taken the sense of being able to do anything, and done it.

BLDS: In June 1995 you were appointed the president of the World Bank. How many hours a week do you work on average?

JW: Quite a lot. I'm always working, that's the first thing. I'm here in the office most nights quite late. It amounts to seventy, eighty hours a week. Everything I do relates to the bank. I think the more significant thing is that I am basically giving up nearly everything in terms of a private life and a cultural life. I'm hanging on to bits of it, but when you have four billion clients, 1.2 billion people living under a dollar a day, and seventy-eight countries in the International Development Agency that have populations living under two dollars and fifty cents a day; when you are involved in Bosnia and Serbia, Gaza, and Angola; when you're running the world's largest environmental facility; when you are concerned with economic development and social issues for women, there isn't much time for anything else. There are many issues that are involved in assisting governments. Our activities are not just eco-

> Australia is a wonderful country. I think it breeds innovation. It is a place where you feel that everything is possible and where you grow up without a lot of constraints.

nomic, but also social and humanitarian, not to mention the usual infrastructure building and other projects we are engaged in. We are dealing constantly with not only crises, but world development issues, which can't be solved overnight. It will be impossible to say whether I will succeed or fail in this job because there will be just as many problems when I leave as when I came, but I think what I can do is to make the World Bank machine more effective. It's the most interesting job I can imagine having.

BLDS: When the fiftieth anniversary of the World Bank took place in 1995, there were critics who suggested that the bank should mark its fiftieth anniversary by going out of business.

JW: Right. Fifty years is enough, they all said. And I read all that literature. When I accepted the job I thought there were many observations written about the bank that were accurate, in terms of things that could be improved and mistakes that had been made in the past; however, the positive case for the bank overwhelmingly outweighed the negative case. You only have to look at the history of the bank, starting with post–World War II reconstruction and its aid to Japan and other countries. It helped France, which was the bank's first client after the war.

BLDS: Did the World Bank become established as a result of the Bretton Woods Conference?

JW: Yes, it was a Bretton Woods institution concerned with post-war reconstruction, and then it mutated and became an institution that had a far broader view on development.

BLDS: Was that its most important evolution in the five decades of its existence?

JW: It underwent a gradual evolution concerning different places at different times. High points include the creation under Eisenhower of IDA, the International Development Association, to deal with very poor countries; then the IFC, which deals particularly with the private sector; and the MIGA, the insurance of private-sector investments in developing countries. Those things led me to think, when I assessed the question of whether or not the bank should go out of business, that the critics were being unfair.

So I came in here with the view of listening and expanding our relationships with them. I have opened the door to all of the critics. In every one of my field offices in Africa and Latin America we now have a permanent member of the staff who deals only with the nongovernmental organizations. What started as a new initiative has now brought an absolute flood of ideas and achievement that is already visible. I am now seeking to engage civil society as a partner. And I think together we can do a lot. Frankly, I think nongovernmental organizations need us to achieve their objectives as much as we need them.

BLDS: A part of your mission that almost seems impossible is to reverse the cycle of poverty in so many parts of the world. The World Bank is seen as the savior of third-world countries. How do you plan to go about this?

JW: First of all, I don't think it is impossible at all. I think it's a necessity, not just for the third world but also for those of us that live in the developed world. Forty percent of American exports today go to the developing world. Seventy-five percent of growth in the next ten years will come from the developing world. Fifty percent of the total growth of the world in the next ten years will come from Asia alone. This is not a time when we can sit in New York or Washington and think about the rest of the world as though it is some irrelevancy. Four billion people live in the developing world. One billion live in the developed world. Although you and I grew up thinking of London, Paris, Zurich, and Frankfurt, our kids are already thinking of Djakarta, Beijing, Cairo, São Paolo, and Lagos. There is a role for the bank that is real and has enormous potential for growth and for poverty alleviation. Development may not be measured in the same way that we measure the aspirations of an American in Milwaukee, but to a villager in Mali the value of having water, knowing how to plant crops while stopping environmental degradation, giving small loans to women, and teaching women how they can be central business and financial figures in their villages are absolutely clear and fundamental issues. Women are the essential element of development in Africa. We are putting nine hundred million dollars a year worldwide into education of girls in

. . . when you have four billion clients . . . when you are involved in Bosnia and Serbia, Gaza, and Angola; when you're running the world's largest environmental facility; when you are concerned with economic development and social issues for women, there isn't much time for anything else.

primary schools. It is one thing to spend money getting young girls into school. What is much more important is to make it a part of the system to allow these girls to find jobs. In villages we are doing two extra things. We are going in with grass-roots business management for women, many of whom are illiterate. Therefore, we are not only doing work in literacy, but also we are teaching people how to do bookkeeping. We are doing this in India, too. We now have a huge institute there. It's a remarkable thing because once you prepare the women then you can make small loans to them. It's the women who do all the work anyway. If you've been to Africa you know that. They are absolutely the unrecognized, unrewarded backbone of society. I was in Beijing to close the women's conference with Mrs. Bruntland and P. M. Fujimori. The World Bank has not had a particularly good record as perceived by women's organizations, but I am making a major effort to reverse it. Four of my first five appointments to vice-presidential levels at the bank were women. In fact, the new director of personnel is a Japanese-American woman. So I am really trying to demonstrate in the bank that women have an equivalent role to play. In Africa and in the developing countries I think candidly that they have more than an equivalent role to play because you will not get development without opportunities for women. That's a very, very important component. It's also interesting to see the societal shift that you need in many of these places. There are 120 million kids in the world who don't go to school; 70 percent are girls. By the year 2005 we plan to have every one of those kids in school. We hope that ten million women in the next fifteen years will have the chance to have enough money to run little businesses. You can change the world. It is not hopeless. The people in Africa and in Uzbekistan have a pride and a sense of themselves that is at least as visible and as real as it is in Manhattan. I have come away from this experience with a great sense of reality, with a belief in the people of the developing world, and with a great sense of idealism. I think it can be done.

BLDS: If I recall, the lending practices of the World Bank were always criticized before you came. How have you reconstituted them?

JW: I have not done everything at the bank, nor have I invented all the new ideas for change. Many things were being done already to the enduring benefit of the world. It's a question of refocusing

. . . you will not get development without opportunities for women.

our efforts on programs with visible results, for example, on the capacity to provide small loans to small enterprises and to implement agricultural programs within the context of integrated rural and village development. Seventy percent of our clients in Africa are in rural communities. If you can keep them in rural communities and give them a decent standard of living within a traditional tribal structure, isn't that much better than coming in with large-scale farming that pushes them off the land and into the cities? Then you create an urban problem. These are the things we are thinking about. What is crucial and what makes me feel that I did not know the world at all until I started this job are the images of these people within their own context. I went to Uzbekistan with my wife, Elaine, who has been my partner in all of this and who is doing the most fantastic job, particularly on education and women's issues. We visited a town near the Aral Sea. The sea has lost 150 square kilometers of area. The Russians decided to grow cotton in Uzbekistan, Turkmenistan, and Tajikistan, so they flooded the fields there by creating uncontrolled irrigation, instead of using the water properly. The result was that no water flowed into the sea and this huge area dried up, causing poisonous salt to blow all over the country. We went to a little village of about four hundred people, twenty kilometers from the sea. All they have ever known how to do is to dry fish. We saw boats up on sand dunes, but there was no sea in miles. They are growing fish in some wetland areas, but very modest quantities. The people are extremely poor. We met up with forty kids in the village field. Their teacher happened to speak English. All you see is poverty and yet they are proud people. As we were ready to leave one of the kids, who couldn't have been more than six or seven, rushed up to me and thrust into my hand a five-sum note, which is worth about five cents, and rushed off. To them, this is a lot of money. I asked the teacher what it was for and he said that in their culture one gives visitors money to help them on their journey. Of course, tears came to my eyes. The significance of this is that these people have not lost their roots, their culture, or their strength. They are as strong and as proud as you or me. We came away from Uzbekistan not thinking about the salt and the degradation of the villages, but rather that if the people are that strong you have a resource beyond money. I could repeat that sort of story to you in many countries—in fact, in almost every country. There is a human dimension to the development field. If you can tap it and provide the appropriate resources, it is my personal belief that the job of reversing the cycle of poverty is doable.

BLDS: When you first took office, why did you choose to spend the first several months traveling to see many of your projects?

JW: The only way you find out what is going on is to talk to your customers. That's true in banking; it's true in advertising; it's true in development. I wanted to find out what the bank was doing in the field, because that was the only place where I could determine if our efforts were successful or not. It has been a remarkable experience. I visited twenty-six countries in 1995, most of them with Elaine, and I'll see another twenty-nine in 1996.

BLDS: More than one hundred countries are the recipients of World Bank involvement. Are there any countries that are excluded?

JW: Yes. Those that have a gross national product of above eight or nine thousand dollars a year per person, maybe even less than that.

BLDS: Are any countries excluded because of political reasons?

JW: We try not to take political views, but economics very often follows politics. If you have a closed society with a leader who won't follow economic plans that we think make sense, then you can't win. However, our analysis is not started on the basis of politics.

BLDS: You have managed to deputize successfully and reliably in your investment banking firm. Do you have any association with that firm any longer?

JW: No. When I left the firm I left it completely, and my former partners now own the business. I have no shares in trusts, nothing. I didn't want anyone ever to think that I was in a conflict-of-interest situation. It just seemed to me that if I was going into the public sector I was probably better off to be out of the commercial field. It was a very expensive decision, but I think it was a very proper one, both for me and my former partners.

BLDS: When you have completed whatever you had in mind for a role, you seem to have the ability to literally walk away from the situation.

JW: I'm not different from anybody else. I have nostalgia. When I

> The only way you find out what is going on is to talk to your customers. That's true in banking; it's true in advertising; it's true in development.

left Carnegie Hall I had pangs, but I was glad that it was in good hands. Now I get tremendous pleasure from being in Carnegie Hall. I'm sure that in the first months after leaving the Kennedy Center I will be looking over my shoulder. It was no less true when I left my firm because I created my firm. I was in tears in front of all my staff when I announced I was going to leave. I feel very emotional about it. But it was a phase in my life—a very important phase—and it was over. It is apparent that what I established now lives on. The firm is doing very well. I am privileged that Paul Volcker was chairman and very proud of my partners and all the professional and support staff. The real test for me, as someone who has always been interested in public service on a part-time basis, was to give up making money to work for a public institution. I can tell you honestly that I have not given two minutes' thought to that choice since I got into this job. It is a real privilege to serve the World Bank.

BLDS: It was only after some hesitation that you were willing to give up your Kennedy Center commitment after the World Bank assignment was given to you. Has the assignment been even larger than you originally thought it was going to be?

JW: Yes, it's been much larger. I had hoped to stay on as nonexecutive chairman of the Kennedy Center, but I have come up with a very good solution, which is that I chair the artistic quality committee, freeing me of all the obligations of administration. From that point of view I have exactly what I want, which is to keep a hand in on the artistic and educational qualities. The center has a wonderful new chairman in Jim Johnson. I don't care about missing the receptions and I am relieved at not having to raise money. I care that the quality of the institution will not drop. I have kept two other things: one is the chairmanship of the finance committee of the Howard Hughes Medical Institute, and the other is the chairmanship of the Institute of Advanced Study in Princeton. However, I am finding it very difficult to keep up.

BLDS: Your appointment to the World Bank dovetails with the bank's rapidly growing interest in and leaning toward the encouragement of private investment. Maybe some people are expecting you to accomplish personally what the bank has been unable to accomplish institutionally.

JW: Well, there are some constraints on what the bank can do because it is limited to lending to governments. That's in its charter. The IFC is free to lend and to invest in projects in the private sector, and MIGA insures the private sector for various political and expropriation risks. I have appointed a managing directorship to coordinate the private-sector activities group, with a view to bringing together all the things that we can do for the private sector: the need to educate private investors, to market to them, and to bring to them the benefit of over fifty years of experience. There are many initiatives we have in mind. We will be setting up an interchange program of outside executives with members of our team. I hope to have fifty executives from companies around the world who will be coming for one to two years to the bank. Each year I will be sending fifty executives at the middle and top management levels to courses at Harvard. I will be revamping the training programs at the bank. A new learning center will be established jointly with the Harvard Business School, Stamford, and European and Japanese institutions. I will be inviting advisory committees from the private sector to assist us in each of our specialties. Those are some examples of what we are doing and plan to do.

BLDS: This gives us some idea of how you plan to train and retrain your principal professional staff. What concepts and theories do you want to train them to act upon?

JW: Very simply, to move away from the culture of the approval of projects, which has been deeply imbedded at the bank, toward the culture of the effectiveness of our projects. We need accountability of people for results. Sometimes results are outside the control of the bank because we have to bring along governments, but the principal change is to give individual responsibility—and to have accountability. That is a profound change in a bureaucratic institution.

BLDS: Does your staff consider your changes promising, threatening, or both?

JW: Both. There is a measure of both enthusiasm and skepticism. But you must understand that many people want these changes. The bank group has a remarkable and experienced staff dedicated to development. I have not invented all these ideas. I am merely trying to implement them.

BLDS: How do you describe your management style and your strategy in assuming leadership of such a complex institution, one that has not only an established tradition but also an entrenched bureaucracy worldwide?

JW: Well, I think you have to establish an understandable dream and a heart in the institution. You've got to have something that turns you on in the morning, which is not just your salary. It has to be a vision; it has to be something that moves you. I am deeply interested in making sure that people go back to the human issues and the human visions of the institution at all levels of the organization. I think if you give an organization that sense of heart then you've got a chance. The second thing you have to do as a leader is to know the details of the jobs that people do in such a way that they treat you as a total professional in their field. That's where my background is helpful: in terms of analysis and of mastering a brief reasonably quickly and comprehensively.

BLDS: What is your dream?

JW: My dream is to make the world a better place. It is not to judge the institution by financial results but to judge a project by the smile on a child's face. I view the success of development efforts by the impact on the human condition. Behind that, of course, is a lot of professionalism. There's a lot of infrastructure being financed by the bank; there's a lot of technical work that has to be done. People don't live in an anonymous environment. They are not just economic statistics. And I don't lead in an anonymous way. So I may be mercurial, passionate, and artistic, but I think I'm consistent. You can be artistic and mercurial and still play the music very well. I'm trying to keep the tune.

BLDS: What are the most difficult and the most challenging aspects of your current role?

JW: First of all, the world. The bank didn't make the world as it is, we inherited it. There are many wars, there are too many poor people, there is a lot of inequity, and there is a history of racial and tribal conflict. It's a very tough world. I think you can do something about it, but you can never complete the job; that much I know. The second challenge is to take advantage of the remarkable people in the organization. We have a fantastic team and we have many achievers.

BLDS: Are there ten thousand employees worldwide?

JW: A little more, ten thousand five hundred. We are together

> My dream is to make the world a better place. It is not to judge the institution by financial results but to judge a project by the smile on a child's face.

seeking a new sense of commitment to vision and to the new organization. You don't do that overnight.

BLDS: What, if any, are your handicaps in dealing with this world?

JW: Time. Maybe capacity. I'm not God. I wish I had had five more years of actual development experience. I'd be better if I knew that the United States was in better shape with regard to support for overseas development. I don't know the bureaucratic process very well. I've never run eleven thousand people before. I can give you lots of reasons why I'll fail.

BLDS: Give me some why you'll succeed.

JW: Commitment. Hard work. A dream for the institution. And I hope that I have a capacity to excite people and to make them believe.

BLDS: What are the specific moments or events in your life and your career that you consider to be the turning points, the catalysts that helped direct your life?

JW: Well, first there was the American lawyer in Australia who told me I couldn't read a balance sheet and suggested I go to business school. Second was finding and marrying Elaine, because she brought tremendous stability and integrity into my life. Third was the kids. Fourth was Lord Richardson inviting me to London and then appointing me president of the bank in New York, which gave me visible administrative responsibility. Fifth was Billy Salomon and John Gutfreund suggesting I run corporate finance. Sixth was starting my own firm. Seventh was President Clinton asking me to head the World Bank.

BLDS: You didn't mention Carnegie Hall or the Kennedy Center.

JW: I'm about to do that—I was on a run on the professional side. I would like to jump back and say the first influence was my parents and their sense of charity without having a lot of money. The second thing was this great good fortune to be able to match a really full life in the arts and in the civil and social sectors with my business life. Very few people have had serious parallel careers. Some of my best friends, for example, don't have a clue what I do in business. I have to say one last thing, which is that my faith is a very important part of my life. I am not suggesting that only the Jewish religion can give you stability, but having a set of values and the sort of framework that religion gives is a very important element in attaining it. That has been a very big help to me.

BLDS: If you had your life to live over again, what would you do otherwise?

JW: I would spend more time with the family, although I have kept, I am happy to say, a very close relationship with them. For better or worse, I have done everything else that I wanted to do.

> . . . my faith is a very important part of my life.

DATE DUE

HIGHSMITH #45231